725

THE CONDUCT OF INQUIRY

Methodology for Behavioral Science

Chandler Publications in

ANTHROPOLOGY AND SOCIOLOGY

Leonard Broom, *Editor*

THE CONDUCT OF INQUIRY

Methodology for Behavioral Science

By ABRAHAM KAPLAN

University of Michigan

CHANDLER PUBLISHING COMPANY

An Intext Publisher • Scranton, Pennsylvania 18515

International Standard Book No. 0-8102-0144-5

Copyright © 1964 by Chandler Publishing Company

Library of Congress Catalog Card No. 64-13470

Printed in the United States of America

K–N–RC

To

I. J. K.

My Women of Valor

CONTENTS

II. CONCEPTS

III. LAWS

IV. EXPERIMENT

V. MEASUREMENT

VI. STATISTICS

VII. MODELS

VIII. THEORIES

IX. EXPLANATION

X. VALUES

PREFACE

IN THIS BOOK I have emphasized what unites the several behavioral sciences more than what distinguishes them from one another. The special problems of the various disciplines are dealt with only so far as may be helpful in clarifying the general method of inquiry.

With regard to the widely differing and often mutually hostile schools and approaches in behavioral science my position can be regarded, I suppose, as neutralist, and will therefore be condemned, no doubt, by both sides—not rigorous enough for one, and too demanding for the other. My aim has not been compromise, however, nor my ideal a golden mean. What seems to me important is yielding, not to demands externally imposed, but rather to those intrinsic to our own aspirations.

In methodology itself I have a corresponding range of sympathies— with logical construction and linguistic analysis, as well as with the more substantive concerns of the older methodologists, of whom I think more highly than is now fashionable. In particular, those who are acquainted with pragmatism will be aware of how much greater my indebtedness is to Peirce, James, and Dewey than is made explicit by citations. But I have sought the comfort of like-mindedness wherever I could find it, without regard to broader philosophical commitments. References are to whatever editions and printings among those at hand I judged to be most readily accessible to the reader.

The leisure to read and write—and what is more, the stimulus to think about both activities—was afforded me by the Center for Advanced Study in Behavioral Science at Palo Alto, and by the Center for Advanced

Studies at Wesleyan University, in Middletown, Connecticut; to both I am deeply grateful. I want also to thank Alexander Sesonske and Clyde Coombs for reading portions of the manuscript.

Abraham Kaplan

Ann Arbor, Michigan
1963

FOREWORD

IN THIS BOOK for the first time a philosopher makes a systematic, rounded, and wide-ranging inquiry into behavioral science. In doing so he has been guided by the experience of sciences with longer histories, but he has been bound neither to their problems nor to their solutions. Instead, he has addressed himself to the methodology of behavioral science in the broad sense of both science and methodology. The tasks, achievements, limitations, and dilemmas of the newer disciplines are the focus of his attention. The work is not a formal exercise in the philosophy of science but rather a critical and constructive assessment of the developing standards and strategies of contemporary social inquiry. Professor Kaplan is familiar with the fields he discusses; he is not a visiting philosopher recounting a sightseeing trip.

Philosophers of science usually choose to write about the most fully developed sciences because the problems are clearer there. But the result is ordinarily of little benefit to the behavioral scientist. His most difficult task is the clarification of method where the precedents and analogies of physical science are inappropriate or obscure. What he needs most is a direct confrontation of methodological problems immediately relevant to his own discipline. He needs to read from the strengths of his own understanding, insights, expertness, and subject matter and not from the insecurity of a limited familiarity with a remote discipline. *The Conduct of Inquiry* goes a long way toward filling those needs because it is appropriate to the present state of the art and to the stages just ahead.

Professor Kaplan draws upon the whole scientific enterprise but always with a purpose—to guide the behavioral scientist, to post warnings on pitfalls that may lie in his path, to remind him from time to time that he is not a nuclear physicist, to remind him that he is nevertheless a scientist in the somber and in the exciting significance of the term, and to place behavioral science in the context of an ongoing endeavor, particular as well as general.

This most useful philosopher is always lucid but he has not always made things easy. He is a hard taskmaster who holds high aspirations and high standards for behavioral science. He has no philosopher's stone that will turn empirical dross into theoretical gold or even empirical mud into theoretical pots. He does make it easier to distinguish the dross from the gold and the mud from the clay. It is clear that Professor Kaplan thinks behavioral science both feasible and worth the effort—worth his effort as a commentator and worth ours as practitioners.

The book, being an orientation in methodology for behavioral scientists, is indispensable for behavioral scientists and for aspiring ones irrespective of their orthodoxy or heterodoxy, but perhaps it will prove more palatable to the heterodox. It will be durable in its usefulness, and it will be useful to a wide range of readers many of whom will discover unsuspected strengths and weaknesses in their disciplines. The book proves by the fact of its existence that there is a community of scholarship between the humanities and behavioral science and that the validity of one does not depend upon alienation from the other.

There is a consistent emphasis on the common concerns of all the social sciences rather than on their parochial problems and their perhaps temporary points of isolation, an emphasis on major issues rather than side arguments, a concern with problems that are intrinsically important and recurrent rather than with transitory considerations or matters of technique. The author's intellectual tolerance does not extend to fads and fashions whose claims for attention rest on currency alone.

Professor Kaplan departs from the stylistic presumptions that anything interesting must look as if it is being said for the first time, that anything important must be said sententiously, that anything difficult must be made to appear more difficult—and therefore more important—and that anything that bears upon error must begin with a destructive attack on someone—as if human fallibility needed to be proved all over again. In the pages that follow, the simple is said simply and the difficult is said clearly. A genuine erudition is opened to the student and the advanced scholar. The book fills a gap and does it with admirable clarity and often with engaging wit. It lacks pomposity, pedantry, and pretension, and it is bound to make an impact on the teaching of and, with luck, on research in the behavioral sciences.

LEONARD BROOM

Austin, Texas
1963

THE CONDUCT OF INQUIRY

Methodology for Behavioral Science

Chapter I

METHODOLOGY

§*1   Logic-in-Use and Reconstructed Logic*
§*2   Logic and Psychology*
§*3   The Task of Methodology*
§*4   "Scientific Method" in Behavioral Science*

§1. Logic-in-Use and Reconstructed Logic

It is one of the themes of this book that the various sciences, taken together, are not colonies subject to the governance of logic, methodology, philosophy of science, or any other discipline whatever, but are, and of right ought to be, free and independent. Following John Dewey, I shall refer to this declaration of scientific independence as the principle of *autonomy of inquiry*. It is the principle that the pursuit of truth is accountable to nothing and to no one not a part of that pursuit itself.

SCIENTIFIC AUTONOMY

Note that the declaration applies not to the several sciences but only to all of them taken together. There is no doctrine of states' rights, as it were, in accord with which the sovereignty of a particular discipline can be interposed between a parochial creed and the stern judgment of the scientific community as a whole. It will not do to say, "You people simply don't understand our problems!" or, "We have our own logic, our own sources and standards of truth." There are indeed differences among the

3

various disciplines, and these differences are important to the conduct of inquiry in each case. But they do not serve to cut the sciences off from one another.

For the domain of truth has no fixed boundaries within it. In the one world of ideas there are no barriers to trade or to travel. Each discipline may take from others techniques, concepts, laws, data, models, theories, or explanations—in short, whatever it finds useful in its own inquiries. And it is a measure of its success in these inquiries that it is asked in turn to give of its riches to other disciplines. Even more, it may find itself unexpectedly in an area conventionally identified as "belonging to" another science. Some of the most exciting encounters in the history of science are those between workers in what appear to be quite distinct fields who are suddenly brought face to face as a result of their independent investigations. The autonomy of inquiry is in no way incompatible with the mature dependency of the several sciences on one another.

Nor does this autonomy imply that the individual scientist is accountable only to himself. Every discipline develops standards of professional competence to which its workers are subject. There are certain acceptable ways of interpreting a projective test, of carrying out a dig, of surveying public opinion. Case studies, experiments, hypotheses, theories—all must meet certain conditions if they are to be taken seriously by the profession. These conditions are seldom made wholly explicit, and they differ for different disciplines and at different times; but in any case, their demands are likely to be firm and unyielding.

Every scientific community is a society in the small, so to speak, with its own agencies of social control. Officers of the professional associations, honored elders, editors of journals, reviewers, faculties, committees on grants, fellowships, and prizes—all exert a steady pressure for conformity to professional standards, as their counterparts in the larger society provide sanctions for the more general norms. In certain respects scientific training functions to produce not only competence but also a kind of respectability, essential to membership in the professional community. Doctoral examinations, most candidates agree, have much in common with the tortures of initiation rites—and with the added tribulation of fear of failure: no one has ever had to repeat his Bar Mitzvah.

The innate conservatism, or at least inertia, of professional standards has from time to time stood in the way of scientific progress. The martyrs of science have sometimes been victims of the faithful rather than of the infidels. Ignaz Semmelweis and Georg Cantor (to go back no more than a scant century) were hounded by their respectable colleagues for their revolutionary ideas about puerperal fever and transfinite arithmetic. More recent, if less dramatic examples, are not hard to find. Yet for every resisted scientific genius there are numberless crackpots, for every martyr to the truth there are countless victims only of their own paranoid delusions. Standards of scientific excellence, though they may occasionally be self-defeating, on the whole and in the long run make for success. Adherence to the Law is the surest, and perhaps the only, safeguard against being misled by false Prophets.

The principle of autonomy does not deny authority to norms of scientific practice but rather derives their authority from the sovereignty of science itself. Standards governing the conduct of inquiry in any of its phases emerge from inquiry and are themselves subject to further inquiry. Both historically and on the present scene, the chief importance of an insistence on the principle of autonomy lies in its defense of the integrity of science against encroachment by other social enterprises.

Theology, politics, morals, and metaphysics have all exerted a dubious and often repressive authority. The history of the warfare between science and theology (a more accurate expression here than "science and religion") has often been documented. Though the physical and biological sciences have largely won their independence, behavioral science in many parts of the world—including our own—is still subject to the influence, if not the authority, of theological doctrine. (Consider, for example, inquiry into such problems as the population explosion, capital punishment, drug addiction, and deterrents to war.) Political pressures on science are best known to us from the Nazi and Stalinist eras, with their dogmas not only in history, political science, and economics, but also in such fields as anthropology, genetics, linguistics, and mathematics. (In a public debate, Sidney Hook led off with a brilliantly effective question put to the professor of chemistry who had accepted the chancellorship of the East German University of Berlin: "What do you think of Stalin as a chemist?") But in our own country, too, the autonomy of science must recurrently be reaffirmed: psychoanalytic psychiatry is as suspect among the Radical Right as it is in the land of Pavlov. And legal restrictions affect not only atomic research, but also some inquiries into the workings of, say, the jury system, as an American sociologist found when his study was denounced on the floor of Congress. Considerations of a moral kind (in the root sense as relating to the mores) make themselves felt equally in studies of the relations between the sexes and the races.

The part played by the influence and authority of metaphysics over science is more equivocal. The values of its contributions to scientific progress have been traced by E. A. Burtt, Philipp Frank, Karl Popper, and many others. Yet there is no doubt that it has also had a pernicious effect. Hegel was not unwilling to supply an *ipse dixit* on a variety of scientific questions, and many other metaphysicians since his day have sought to shape a priori the course of scientific inquiry.

It is no part of my purpose to argue that the scientific enterprise either is or ought to be dissociated from the larger world of men and affairs; quite the contrary (§§43 and 45). What I am insisting on is that the standards of scientific practice derive from science itself, even though the science of any period is intimately involved with every other human concern. My position is not that enterprises outside science have no authority over science; it is rather that, where such an enterprise does govern, it has the right to govern only by the consent of the governed.

AUTONOMY AND LOGIC

So far, scientists and philosophers of science are likely to agree, among themselves and with one another. But there *is* an issue concerning the normative force of logic in relation to science. Is not logic, and its practical elaboration as "methodology", the ultimate source and ground of the norms of scientific inquiry? Even God cannot violate the laws of logic; can the scientist? Of course, every scientist is "logical" or aspires to be so; the issue is whether logic is to be conceived as validating the process of scientific inquiry, or as ultimately validated by that process.

Some years ago a deservedly famous textbook was published with the title *An Introduction to Logic and Scientific Method*. To the word "and" in this title John Dewey took exception, for logic, in his view, is nothing other than the theory of inquiry. It is as though literary criticism were to be "applied" to literature: without such application it is nothing. In perspective it might be said that Dewey did not sufficiently appreciate the self-contained richness and vigor of the mathematical logic being developed in his time. Yet this logic is purely formal, and in a strict sense of the term, empty. Even where it deals with induction, as in Carnap's recent work, it remains in fact deductive, a logic of consistency rather than of truth. An inductive principle like "Use all the evidence available" is extralogical, not a tautology validated by the rules for the calculus in whose use it plays a part. The truths of formal logic are indeed ineluctable, as are the truths of pure mathematics, from which, in the current view, they are ultimately indistinguishable. But it would beg the question to conclude, on the basis of a formal analysis, that this formal logic *is* the logic of science. "Prove to me," Epictetus was challenged, "that I should study logic." "How will you know that it is a good proof?" was the reply.

A great deal hinges on whether science is viewed as a body of propositions or as the enterprise in which they are generated, as product or as process. An account of the norms bearing on the finished report of an investigation might well be expected to differ from one concerned with the conduct of the investigation itself. (The former is sometimes called "logic" and the latter "methodology", but this is not a happy usage.) In recent times the emphasis characteristically put on the process of science by pragmatists like Dewey and his great predecessor Charles Peirce has come to be more widely shared by philosophers than it was a few decades ago. I shall return shortly to the question whether there is such a thing as a "logic of discovery".

There is, then, something not quite so old-fashioned as we used to feel about John Stuart Mill's definition of logic: "the science [sic] which treats of the operations of the human understanding in the pursuit of truth." We might say, not only the pursuit of "truth", but perhaps also the pursuit of explanation, prediction, or control. In short, logic treats of "the operations of the human understanding" (it *does* have an old-fashioned ring after all!) in solving problems; we need not commit ourselves beforehand to any single characterization of what constitutes "solutions".

It is important to point out that logic treats these operations evaluatively. What is central is not the fact that they are performed by certain people under certain circumstances, but whether or not under those circumstances they succeed in producing the solutions to which they are directed. There is a nonevaluative sense of the term "logic", which occurs in phrases like "the logic of the Unconscious" or "the logic of the Radical Right". I prefer in these cases to speak of the *cognitive style;* we can then say of a cognitive style that it is logical or illogical, in varying degrees, or in one respect or another. (There is also a transposed sense of the term "logic" in expressions like "the logic of events", which refers rather to what logic would disclose about the events—their necessary connections or outcomes, their explanation.) Logic, in short, deals with what scientists do when they are doing well as scientists.

Now the word "logic" is one of those, like "physiology" and "history", which is used both for a certain discipline and for its subject-matter. We all have physiologies and histories, and some of us also think and write about these things. Similarly, scientists and philosophers use a logic—they have a cognitive style which is more or less logical—and some of them also formulate it explicitly. I call the former the *logic-in-use,* and the latter the *reconstructed logic.* We can no more take them to be identical or even assume an exact correspondence between them, than we can in the case of the decline of Rome and Gibbon's account of it, a patient's fever and his physician's explanation of it.

Though I have said that a field of inquiry—say, psychoanalysis or parapsychology—cannot claim to have its "own logic" as a defense against scientific criticism, it is true that there are many logics-in-use. What is objectionable is only the claim to proprietorship, the implication that criticism is inadmissible unless the soundness of the criticized method is first granted. The policy is objectionable, equally in science and in politics, that what's mine is mine and what's yours is negotiable. The logic-in-use in any inquiry must prove itself; such proof consists in the success of the inquiry and is discernible to any other sound logic-in-use. (The condition that the other must be "sound" generates a circle, but it is not a vicious one.) That the world of ideas has no barriers, within or without, does not call for one true "Logic" to govern it. The conviction that there is such a logic—as it happens, ours—is a parochialism like those of which comparative ethnology made us painfully aware in the course of the last century. The myth of a "natural logic", defining a universal rationality, has been penetratingly analyzed by Benjamin Lee Whorf and his successors among linguists and anthropologists. Not only language and culture affect the logic-in-use, but also the state of knowledge, the stage of inquiry, and the special conditions of the particular problem. There is more than one way to skin a cat, and the family *Felidae* has some remarkable specimens.

Whatever our position regarding logics-in-use, there can be no doubt that there are many reconstructed logics. John Locke, in discussing the syllogism, remarked that "God has not been so sparing to men to make them barely two-legged creatures and left it to Aristotle to make them rational." There were logics-in-use, that is to say, before Aristotle's reconstruction. And other reconstructions came after him. Augustus De Morgan pioneered the modern movement in logic with the observation that Aristotle's logic (that is, his reconstruction) could not prove that, because a horse is an animal, the head of a horse is the head of an animal; this proof waited for the development of a logic of relations. In the present century, Russell, Quine, and others have created reconstructions incomparably richer than Aristotle's, of which Kant had the misfortune to proclaim, just as its reign was ending, that it left no room for any further advances.

Locke and De Morgan between them remind us that a logic-in-use may precede and be superior to its own reconstruction. This reminder is true not only of the logic-in-use in everyday life but of the logic-in-use in science as well. Newton and his followers made excellent use of the calculus in physics, despite the astute criticisms of its foundations made by Bishop Berkeley, criticisms which were not satisfactorily met till the reconstruction by Weierstrass some two hundred years later. Conversely, a reconstruction may become, or at any rate influence, the logic-in-use. Aristotle's logic certainly played a part in the biology of fixed species, as well as in the logic-in-use in a wide variety of other disciplines. Russell's reconstruction of logic, together with those of other contemporary logicians, significantly affected the logic-in-use in mathematics and related sciences.

What Carnap and Reichenbach have called the "rational reconstruction" of science is the application to the scientific product, not of "Logical" analysis, but of the contemporary reconstructed logic. For some time, the most widely accepted reconstruction of science has been in terms of the so-called "hypothetico-deductive method", especially in a postulational form. According to this reconstruction, the scientist, by a combination of careful observation, shrewd guesses, and scientific intuition arrives at a set of postulates governing the phenomena in which he is interested; from these he deduces observable consequences; he then tests these consequences by experiment, and so confirms or disconfirms the postulates, replacing them, where necessary, by others, and so continuing.

This reconstruction has been serviceable for some time, chiefly in application to the more advanced parts of physics, though in a few instances also to biological and behavioral science. But a reconstructed logic is itself, in effect, a hypothesis. As with other hypotheses, as time goes on it may become more and more awkward to "fit" the hypothesis to the facts—here, the facts constituted by the logic-in-use. It is not a question of whether the facts *can* be so construed, but rather whether it is still worthwhile to do so, whether the reconstruction in question continues to throw light on the sound operations actually being used. The "hypothetico-deductive" reconstruction fails to do justice to some of the logic-in-use, and conversely, some of the reconstructed logic has no counterpart in what is actually in use. The formation of hypotheses is treated as though it were largely an extralogical matter. On the other hand, formal deductions in postulational systems are so seldom found in science that the logician is called upon to construct such systems himself, so as to provide his reconstructions with a subject-matter.

To be sure, a reconstructed logic is not meant to be merely a description of what is actually being done by scientists, and for two reasons.

First, because logic is concerned with evaluations, it may be less interested in what is being done than in what is being left undone. But the formation of hypotheses in science and their replacement by more satisfactory ones is, on the whole, a matter of sound operations, and not something illogical or even extralogical. The criticism I am making is that in the "hypothetico-deductive" reconstruction the most important incidents in the drama of science are enacted somewhere behind the scenes. The growth of knowledge is surely basic to the scientific enterprise, even from a logical point of view. The conventional reconstruction presents the denouement, but we remain ignorant of the plot.

Second, a reconstructed logic is not a description but rather an idealization of scientific practice. Not even the greatest of scientists has a cognitive style which is wholly and perfectly logical, and the most brilliant piece of research still betrays its all-too-human divagations. The logic-in-use is embedded in a matrix of an *a*logic-in-use, even an *il*logic-in-use.

The reconstruction idealizes the logic of science only in showing us what it *would* be if it were extracted and refined to utmost purity.

This defense is important and, I think, sound—but only up to a point. The idealization may be carried so far that it is useful only for the further development of logic itself, and not for the understanding and evaluation of scientific practice. Reconstructions have been so idealized that, as Max Weber (*135*:114) wryly observed, "it is often difficult for the specialized disciplines to recognize themselves with the naked eye." At worst, the logician becomes so absorbed with enhancing the power and beauty of his instrument that he loses sight of the material with which it must work. At best, he commits himself to a questionable Platonism: that the proper way to analyze and understand something is to refer it to its most ideal form, that is, its form abstracted from any concrete embodiment. This is *a* way but it is not the only way; and I am far from convinced that it is always the best way.

The great danger in confusing the logic-in-use with a particular reconstructed logic, and especially a highly idealized one, is that thereby the autonomy of science is subtly subverted. The normative force of the logic has the effect, not necessarily of improving the logic-in-use, but only of bringing it into closer conformity with the imposed reconstruction. It is often said that behavioral science should stop trying to imitate physics. I believe that this recommendation is a mistake: the presumption is certainly in favor of those operations of the understanding which have already shown themselves to be so preeminently successful in the pursuit of truth. What *is* important, I believe, is that behavioral science should stop trying to imitate only what a particular reconstruction claims physics to be.

When the reconstruction is mathematically elegant, precise, and powerful—as is true of the "hypothetico-deductive" logic—its attractions are nearly irresistible. But the crucial question concerns, not the intrinsic virtues of the reconstructed logic taken in itself, but rather its usefulness in illuminating the logic-in-use. There is a story of a drunkard searching under a street lamp for his house key, which he had dropped some distance away. Asked why he didn't look where he had dropped it, he replied, "It's lighter here!" Much effort, not only in the logic of behavioral science, but also in behavioral science itself, is vitiated, in my opinion, by the principle of *the drunkard's search*.

§2. *Logic and Psychology*

A rational reconstruction, after all, may have something in common with rationalization in the psychological sense. (It is not to be forgotten that a proposition serving as a rationalization may nevertheless be true.) The new version satisfies standards of rationality which the old one may have been indifferent to or even violated. What is at work in rational reconstruction is rather like what psychoanalysts call the "secondary elaboration" of the primary dream process. The dream we report is not what we dreamt but something more sensible, more intelligible on the face of it. In the case of dreams, such "elaboration" does not wholly conceal the latent content, and may even facilitate a sound interpretation. The patient who says, "I fool my analyst: I don't really tell him my dreams, I just make them up!" is fooling only himself. The analyst of science is less fortunately situated.

JUSTIFICATION

The difficulty is that often in conventional logic much of what actually goes on in science is dismissed as belonging to psychology or sociology, until it has been transformed to suit an antecedently chosen reconstruction. Note that it is not just matters of cognitive style that are in question here. The mere fact that something is or is not done by a scientist is indeed irrelevant to the logic of science; not so the fact that the thing done has or does not have a certain outcome for inquiry. Logicians have properly dreaded "psychologism" if this term means a confusion between how we do think and how we ought to think. But the question of how we ought to think surely depends on what happens when we *do* think in a certain way, or what *would* happen if we did. Logic is normative in contrast to psychology as descriptive, but the norms are grounded in what is or can be described. The avoidance of psychologism does not commit us to a reconstructed logic in which a disembodied intellect moves in a realm of pure ideas. Such a reconstruction cannot yield an adequate account even of what goes on in pure mathematics or in logic itself, to say nothing of what goes on in the empirical sciences.

It has been urged that to admit into logic the actualities of scientific practice is to court the danger of succumbing to the genetic fallacy. This is the fallacy of judging the truth of an assertion on the basis of its source rather than by the evidence or argument available for it. The position is that to say that a certain operation of the understanding is logical because scientists perform it would be comparable to accepting a proposition because it is put forward by a "pure Aryan" or by a "good Communist" I believe, however, that the cases are not comparable. What is fundamental is not the mere fact that the scientist uses the operation but the further fact that it shows itself to be useful in his work. Not the origin of the proposition but its outcome is decisive. Genetic considerations are no longer fallacious when they can be reconstructed as inductive inferences based on past successes. (Some problems concerning criteria of success will be considered in §36.)

In this perspective the study of the history of science becomes of central importance. I believe that the timeless truths of an abstract logic contribute toward an understanding of scientific method just to the degree that what they have been abstracted from is the historical reality. Fortunately, there is a growing recognition—even among philosophers—of the importance for methodology of a study of the history of science, as well as a study of the timeless structure of an idealized "language of science". To be sure, logical norms grounded in scientific practice can no longer lay claim to the certainty and universality which for Plato were the only marks of genuine knowledge as distinguished from mere "opinion". But the surrender of certainty is a price which I believe that logic must be prepared to pay. Science itself manages quite well even though its own most basic principles are something less than necessarily and unconditionally true. That there is a sharp and absolute difference between logical and empirical truths has come to be questioned by many distinguished contemporary logicians. The heresy of what C. I. Lewis a generation ago called the "pragmatic a priori" is today well on the way to becoming an orthodoxy. It is at least a reconstruction of logic-in-use which deserves careful consideration.

DISCOVERY

Now what in fact goes on in scientific inquiry is usually marked off as belonging to the "context of discovery", while logic, it is held, deals only with the "context of justification". On this view, logic is indifferent to how the scientist arrives at his conclusions, but asks only whether he is justified in reaching them. The distinction between discovery and justification, and between their respective contexts, is valid and important. I suggest, however, that the limitation of logic to the context of justification stems from confusing *this* distinction with the one I have drawn above between logic-in-use and reconstructed logic. Because our reconstructions have occupied themselves with justifications, we have concluded that there is no logic-in-use in making discoveries. If logic is what we methodologists do, not what the scientist does, then it is indeed limited to the context of justification, for this context marks the limit of *our* involvement with the pursuit of truth.

That imagination, inspiration, and the like are of enormous importance in science is recognized by everyone. It can be granted that they belong to the context of discovery (including, of course, the discovery of justifications). But does it follow that they are therefore extraneous to logic, that they are a proper subject-matter only for the psychology of science? Let me follow the popular though loose usage and refer to all such faculties as "intuition". Then the point I am making is that intuition also has its logic-in-use, and so must find a place in any adequate reconstructed logic. There is surely a basic difference between intuition and guesswork —between the intuition of the great creative genius or even of the ordinary experienced scientific worker, and the complete novice's blind, blundering guesswork or mechanical trial and error.

The difference seems to me to lie in this: What we call "intuition" is any logic-in-use which is (1) preconscious, and (2) outside the inference schema for which we have readily available reconstructions. We speak of intuition, in short, when neither we nor the discoverer himself knows quite how he arrives at his discoveries, while the frequency or pattern of their occurrence makes us reluctant to ascribe them merely to chance. Countless scientists, like the mathematician Henri Poincaré, have aspired to some self-awareness of their intuitive skills. From a purely psychological standpoint, psychoanalysis has begun to throw some light on the matter. But study of such processes by no means need be limited to a psychological orientation. We can interest ourselves also in the effectiveness of the seeker's operations in achieving their end, and it is this effectiveness that is the concern of logic. From this point of view, for instance, G. Polya has examined the context of mathematical discovery. Similarly, Herbert Simon and Alan Newell have studied the programming of a computer to solve problems in the propositional calculus, not by a mechanically determinate procedure, but in a way that simulates the efforts of the logician himself to discover a proof. Intuition has "a logic of its own" only if we let it be "its own", have no interest in making that logic ours.

The logic of intuition does not in the least minimize the importance to science of serendipity, the chance discovery. But in science—and usually elsewhere, too—luck has to be deserved, as Lagrange once said of Newton. The lucky find must be appreciated to be a "find" at all: noticed, explored, and interpreted. Six months after Roentgen's chance discovery of X-rays the following interview with him was published (quoted from *113*:77): " . . . I had been passing a current through the tube, and I noticed a peculiar black line across the paper." "What of that?" "The effect was one which could only be produced, in ordinary parlance, by the passage of light. No light could come from the tube because the shield which covered it was impervious to any light known, even that of the electric arc." "And what did you think?" "I did not think: I investigated. . . ."

There is a traditional question whether there is a "logic of discovery" as well as a "logic of proof." What is it that is being asked? Clearly, we cannot have reason to predict today what the substance of tomorrow's discoveries will be, for in that case, we would be making the discoveries today. On the other hand, we may well have reason to predict in a general way what discoveries will be made, and even how, in a general way, they will come about. We cannot in 1964 say what our moon rockets will disclose in 1965 or 1970 concerning the volcanic or meteoric origin of the lunar craters, but we might be willing to predict that they will resolve the issue in favor of one alternative or the other. The question then might be, Can we formulate logical norms operative beforehand in making such inquiries, or will the norms only tell us afterwards whether a particular inquiry was successful? Can logic tell us how to do science, or only certify that we have in fact done it?

To ask for a systematic procedure which guarantees the making of discoveries as a corresponding procedure guarantees the validity of a proof is surely expecting too much. "Invention," says Mill, "though it can be cultivated, cannot be reduced to rule; there is no science which

will enable a man to bethink himself of that which will suit his purpose."
The point is, however, that "invention" *can* be cultivated. Though the
scientific enterprise has a significant element of luck in it, it is not wholly
a game of chance, and scientific training surely enhances in some degree
the skill of the players. The "logic of discovery" is, so to say, the
strategy of playing the game.

Here, I do not mean "strategy" in the strict sense of the contemporary
theory of games: a determination of exactly what move will be made for
every possible eventuality that may arise in the play of the game. Such
a determination would correspond to a complete set of rules for making
discoveries (unless, to be sure, the game is one that we are bound to lose
even with optimal play). I mean, rather, strategy in the sense in which
it is known to a good chess player. Norms like "Seize the open file!"
and "Rook behind the pawn!" cannot be demonstrated to produce a win,
but the novice is well advised to follow them.

The question we have been considering can then be phrased, Do such
strategies of doing science have only psychological interest, or do they
also have import for the logic of science? So put, the question answers
itself, it seems to me. Of course they also have import for the logic—
provided we do not restrict logic to what is available to us at any given
time in our reconstructions.

The play of chess illustrates nicely the bearing of the distinction between logic-in-use and reconstructed logic on the matter of "psychologism". Available reconstructions are far from adequate to the subtleties
of actual play, and masters like Tarrasch and Nimzowitch who excelled
in the formulation of principles nevertheless failed to achieve world
championship. But there is no need to invoke a mystique of "positional
sense." Intuition in chess, as elsewhere, is a logic-in-use different from
available reconstructions but *not* therefore incapable of being more and
more closely approximated by better reconstructions. It is entirely possible that before long computers will be programmed so as to play chess
with superhuman success. Such a program is essentially a reconstructed
logic of the game, and the more successful it is as compared with chess
masters the better reconstruction of their logics-in-use it is likely to be.

Now what is crucial is that the considerations that make for good play
lend themselves to logical as well as psychological analysis. The great
Lasker was famous for "playing his opponent" rather than "the board":

making objectively inferior moves, even known by him to be such, in order to exploit temperamental and other weaknesses in his adversary's personality. But what makes such play extraordinary is precisely that we *can* conceive of a move as being "good" without regard to psychological considerations. No doubt Lasker's style is a reflection of his own temperament, and his approach to the game embodies, as he himself tells us, his "philosophy of struggle". Every *use* of a logic is a matter of psychological fact, and being so, is subject to the factors that determine all such facts. But the logic-in-use itself is occupied, not with *those* factors, but with the factors of the problem at hand. Thinking, whether logical or illogical, is always a psychological process; but when it is logical, it reaches out to the larger world where the problem that occasioned thought has its locus. The question how we ought to think and not merely how we do think does not make psychology irrelevant but instead gives relevance to a good deal else besides.

That logic can and should concern itself with the process of scientific discovery, with the process of reaching conclusions as well as with the proof of the conclusions reached, is a position taken by many philosophers, from Aristotle to Peirce and Popper. Recently it has been suggested (N. Hanson in *41*) that the "logic of discovery" can be construed as a study of the reasons for entertaining a hypothesis, in contrast with the logic of proof, which deals with the reasons for accepting a hypothesis. To some extent, unquestionably, these reasons coincide. We entertain hypotheses with high antecedent probability, and this antecedent probability enters into the assessment of its confirmation by the evidence. The maxim "Look for the woman!" guides the detective, and the hypothesized motive it provides is an important element in the case against the suspect. But not all reasons for entertaining a hypothesis are of a kind which necessarily play a corresponding part in its acceptance.

The drunkard's search is relevant here; the pattern of search, we feel, should be closely related to the probability of the thing sought being in the place where the seeker is looking. But the joke may be on us. It may be sensible to look first in an unlikely place just *because* "it's light there". We might reasonably entertain one hypothesis rather than another because it is easier to refute if false, or because it will eliminate a greater number of possibilities, or because it will show us more clearly what steps to take next. We may conduct the search of an area by going up one side and down the other, or by moving outward from the center in a spiral, or in a variety of other ways, according to circumstances. The optimal pattern of search does not simply mirror the pattern of probability density of what we seek. We accept the hypothesis that a thing sought is in a certain place because we remember having seen it there, or because it is usually in places of that kind, or for like reasons. But we entertain the hypothesis, that is, we look in a certain place, for additional reasons: we happen to be in the place already, others are looking elsewhere, and so on. I do not see that the difference between these kinds of reasons is one only of "refinement, degree, and intensity".

It might be said that these other sorts of reasons are to be distinguished from purely logical considerations as being of a merely practical kind. I agree to the adjective, but not to the adverb; there is nothing "mere" about it. If logic relates to scientific practice, it is inescapably concerned with what is "practical"—that is, with what works in science. I believe that the tendency to exclude such concerns from the domain of our reconstructed logics stems from the demand, of which I spoke earlier, for universality and necessity. What is practical in one set of circumstances may not be so in another, and in any case, we cannot establish that it *must* work. To be sure, logic is interested in the greatest possible range of application of its norms, and in the firmest possible grounding of their claims. But may it not stop short of the ultimate in both respects? Must logicality be, like the Stoic conception of virtue, a perfection which does not admit of degrees? What a scientist does in a particular case may be more or less reasonable, sensible, intelligent. What makes it such is not something in his psychology nor in ours who are appraising what he does, but something in his problem and in the appropriateness to it of the operations of his understanding. This latter something is the subject-matter of what I am calling logic.

§3. The Task of Methodology

The word "methodology", like the words "physiology", "history", and "logic" mentioned earlier, is also one which is used both for a certain discipline and for its subject-matter. I mean by *methodology* the study—the description, the explanation, and the justification—of methods, and not the methods themselves. Often when we speak of the "methodology" of, say, economics, we refer to the method or methods used by economists (more likely, some particular school of economists). Though the ordinary usage is ambiguous in this respect, it does not, I think, lend itself to any serious equivocations. The uncertainty in the meaning of the term lies elsewhere. I distinguish four usages.

TECHNIQUES

Let me call "techniques" the specific procedures used in a given science, or in particular contexts of inquiry in that science. For example, there are certain techniques associated with the use of the Rorschach test, or with a mass opinion survey; there are statistical techniques, like those involved in factor analysis; techniques for conducting an interview or for running a rat through a maze; techniques of carbon dating and of deciphering unknown inscriptions; and so on endlessly. There is a right way and a wrong way to do everything, in science as in any other work; or at any rate, there are better and worse ways of doing it. The techniques of a science are the ways of doing the work of that science which are regarded, for more or less compelling reasons, as being acceptable. Scientific training is to a significant extent the mastery of techniques.

Now, what is often called "methodology" is a concern with techniques in this sense (if only the word "technology" did not already have another meaning!). In particular, "methodological studies", so-called, are usually inquiries into the potentialities and limitations of some technique or other, or explorations of some of its variants. Sometimes, no doubt, the concern with the technique is spurious, and the presumed "methodological" interest is in fact a retreat to a previously prepared line of defense against criticisms of the substantive outcome of the inquiry. Yet genuine "methodology" in this sense has a secure place in scientific literature, and indeed, again and again, has been connected with important scientific advances, as in the case of Freud's technique of free association and Pavlov's technique of conditioning.

HONORIFICS

There are other cases in which the term "methodology" is used as though it concerned, not the particularities of specific techniques, but rather what is thought of as "the" scientific method. In this usage,

a "methodological" prologue is something of a ritual, an invocation to
the presiding deities of scientific method, serving to ensure an appropriately "scientific" status for what follows, and avowing the proper concern with meeting standards of scientific acceptability. This honorific use
of "methodology" expresses that concern without any clear indication of
how the concern was embodied in the inquiry itself. It is my impression
that the honorific usage was more frequent two or three decades ago than
it is today; it may well have been a response to the truly spectacular developments in logic in that period. Logic today, being more familiar, is
perhaps not quite so awesome as it once was. The principle of autonomy
does not imply, be it noted, that there are no norms of scientific inquiry
but only that they are not derived from something outside science.

EPISTEMOLOGY

As used by philosophers, "methodology" is often indistinguishable
from epistemology (theory of knowledge) or philosophy of science. In
this sense, the subject-matter of methodology consists—very roughly
speaking—of the most basic questions that can be raised concerning the
pursuit of truth. Characteristically, this "methodology" deals with what
can be said about science, or particular sciences, "in principle" or "in the
last analysis". Its problems arise either from its own reconstructed logic
or from various philosophical positions, rather than from recurrent difficulties encountered in the course of scientific inquiry itself.

For instance, the problem of the justification of induction, as it is
known, has been of enormous importance in philosophy since Hume.
The proposition that the patterns we have so far experienced will persist
in what is yet to come, Hume pointed out is neither a tautology nor can
it be grounded in experience without begging the question. How we can
know that the future will resemble the past, and whether, indeed, some
principle of "uniformity of nature" is even presupposed by science—such
questions have exercised many philosophers of science. Yet scientists
themselves—and surely behavioral scientists—would be quite content to
have only as much justification for their predictions as we have for expecting the sun to rise tomorrow.

Again, determinism-indeterminism is an issue widely debated, with
reference not only to quantum mechanics but also to human behavior and

so-called "free will". Yet dialectical demonstrations that everything *is* "causally necessitated" do not assist inquiries into any particular causes, nor do demonstrations of an "ultimate indeterminacy" prevent us from trying to learn more than we now know about such determinants as there are. And as for the "free will" which is philosophically affirmed or denied, it appears to be quite remote from the freedom which is the concern, say, of the political scientist, economist, or child psychologist.

A less clear-cut example is provided by the problem of the so-called "counterfactual conditional" ("If X *had* happened, then Y *would* have followed"). In the last decade or so a voluminous literature on this problem has accumulated. The problem is that if the antecedent of a hypothetical (if—then) proposition is false, the proposition as a whole is true regardless of what the consequent is; yet we feel that it is reasonable to complete it with some consequents and not with others. The difficulty appears to be generated by a particular reconstruction of implication, the logic-in-use with "if—then". Here, however, the more narrowly philosophical problems shade over into other problems with direct bearing on scientific inquiry: the analysis of counterfactual conditionals seems intimately involved with the structure and function of scientific laws (§11).

There is no doubt that broad philosophical perspectives, and even specific metaphysical doctrines, have played a significant part in the history of science, exercising a considerable though indirect influence on the direction of inquiry and on the formation and acceptance of scientific hypotheses. The works of the mind are all of a piece; what happens in one science is affected, not only by what is going on in the others, but also by the thought of the period on matters of religion, politics, art and whatever.

Descartes' metaphysics, to select a simple illustration, was important in the history of medicine, for it encouraged viewing even the human body as a material thing. The anatomists who came after Descartes had fewer difficulties in getting cadavers for dissection than had afflicted Vesalius before him; and the concepts of physics and chemistry that were developed during the next two centuries found readier application to human biology. But the example illustrates also that the influence of a metaphysics on science can be a pernicious one. Cartesian dualism slowed the progress of psychosomatic medicine, and may still be operative in what Norman Reider has called the "demonology" of modern psychiatry.

In a similar vein it has been suggested that the failure of any Greek historian to attempt excavations at the site of Troy was due in some measure to the Greek metaphysics of time as the moving image of eternity. For the Greeks, the past was not, as for Schliemann and the nineteenth-century evolutionists, still present in its residues; it was the vanished shadow cast on matter by timeless ideas.

On the contemporary scene, the effect of philosophical methodology on the actual conduct of scientific inquiry is not easy to assess. Among behavioral scientists, psychologists have been most anxiously aware of developments in philosophy, yet a panel of psychologists recently concluded that "philosophy of science has little or nothing to do with how research gets done in psychology" (quoted in 42:473). This conclusion may respond to the fact that the interests of philosophy of science are primarily philosophical rather than scientific.

Consider, for instance, the logical positivist thesis of physicalism. Suppose that a psychologist agrees to the following early formulation of the positivist view (37:378): "All psychological statements which are meaningful, that is to say, which are in principle verifiable, are translatable into propositions which do not involve psychological concepts, but only the concepts of physics. The propositions of psychology are consequently physicalistic propositions. Psychology is an integral part of physics." Agreement with this position does not commit the psychologist to any explanation whatsoever of any psychological phenomena. The proposition does not make the theories, laws, or data of physics any more readily applicable to the problems of psychology. Nor does the proposition give any logical basis for turning psychological inquiry in the direction of a search for specific physical structures or processes. For on the thesis stated, whatever the psychologist was doing all the time, provided only it is subject to empirical test, is *already* translatable into propositions involving only concepts of physics. As the author of this formulation points out (37:381), physicalism "does not demand, as does behaviorism, that psychological research restrict itself methodologically to the study of the responses made by organisms to certain stimuli. . . . It seeks to show that if in psychology only physicalistic statements are made, this is not a limitation because it is logically impossible to do otherwise." In short, the physicalist thesis does not bear on choices to be made by the psychologist, but only on choices to be made by the philosopher. It does not run counter to gestalt psychology, say, or to psychoanalysis, but only to a metaphysics, like the so-called "rational psychology" of neo-Thomism. And this detachment is generally characteristic of philosophical methodology. It affects science only very indirectly.

METHODS IN METHODOLOGY

Now the contrast I have drawn between "methodology" as concerned with very special scientific techniques and "methodology" as concerned with very general philosophical principles (the honorific usage stands apart from both of these) is a matter only of degree. Techniques differ from one another in the scope of their application, some being appropriate only to very narrowly defined contexts, others playing a part in a wide variety of inquiries. Similarly, philosophical issues differ in the breadth of their import; some, like the problem of the justification of induction, bear on the whole of human knowledge, while others, like the problem of determinism, relate more especially to some particular science or part of it. In what follows I shall mean by *methodology* a concern with mid-range techniques and principles, which I shall correspondingly designate *methods*. Methods are techniques sufficiently general to be common to all sciences, or to a significant part of them. Alternatively, they are logical or philosophical principles sufficiently specific to relate especially to science as distinguished from other human enterprises and interests. Thus, methods include such procedures as forming concepts and hypotheses, making observations and measurements, performing experiments, building models and theories, providing explanations, and making predictions.

The aim of methodology, then, is to describe and analyze these methods, throwing light on their limitations and resources, clarifying their presuppositions and consequences, relating their potentialities to the twilight zone at the frontiers of knowledge. It is to venture generalizations from the success of particular techniques, suggesting new applications, and to unfold the specific bearings of logical and metaphysical principles on concrete problems, suggesting new formulations. It is to invite speculation from science and practicality from philosophy. In sum, the aim of methodology is to help us to *understand*, in the broadest possible terms, not the products of scientific inquiry but the process itself.

Flatly stated, this aim is more than a little presumptuous, for it implies that we others rather than the scientist himself best understand what he is about. Indeed, some methodological awareness is likely to be present in every successful inquiry, and a division of labor which assigns such awareness only to onlookers is indubitably inaccurate for the past and of dubious wisdom for the future. Yet the aim of methodology can be viewed more modestly: not to do the work which, for better or worse, science must do for itself, but to make the scientist's task easier. Camp followers do not fight battles, but they can contribute mightily to the morale of the troops.

What is to be resisted is the notion that the cultivation of methodology is either necessary or sufficient for successful scientific endeavor.

It is surely not necessary. Methodology, Weber (*135*:115) rightly says, "can only bring us reflective understanding of the means which have demonstrated their value in practice by raising them to the level of explicit consciousness; it is no more the precondition of fruitful intellectual work than the knowledge of anatomy is the precondition for correct walking." This is to say that methodology provides a reconstructed logic, from which the logic-in-use may be quite independent. Yet explicit consciousness *can* improve what is being done without full awareness. Esthetics does not produce art; but it may free both artist and audience from constraints that stand in the way of its creation and appreciation. I believe that the most important contribution methodology can make to science is, in Peirce's phrase, to help unblock the roads of inquiry.

THE MYTH OF METHODOLOGY

And methodology is very far from being a sufficient condition for scientific achievement. There was widespread not many years ago—especially among behavioral scientists—what I might call a *myth of methodology*, the notion that the most serious difficulties which confront behavioral science are "methodological," and that if only we hit upon the right methodology, progress will be rapid and sure. The logicians and the philosophers of science at the time, in the vigor of their attack against "pseudo science", may unintentionally have given some support to this myth. Or possibly, a more pervasive trait of American culture is manifested in the overemphasis on what methodology can achieve. Riesman has called attention to "the excessive preoccupation with technique which often sets in when Americans realise that they are not able to do certain things—raise children, make love, make friends—'naturally'." Whether or not we show this tendency with regard to other activities, we certainly seem to have manifested it in behavioral science. And as Riesman concludes, this methodological preoccupation is "congenitally self-defeating". An anxious concern for the condition of the body is not likely to make for a healthy life.

Nothing that I have said about the relation of methodology to science is intended to undermine the normative force and function of methodology. The charge has been made that when methodology takes actual scientific practice as its starting point, and is considered reasonable only when it "mirrors" such practice, it "propagates the acceptance of unsatisfactory hypotheses on the ground that this is what everybody is doing. It is conformism covered with high-sounding language. . . . Against such conformism it is of paramount importance to insist upon the normative character of scientific method" (41:60–62). To be sure; but the issue is not whether there are norms, but how the norms are grounded. I do not see that the insistence that the norms of scientific practice are validated by that practice implies that they are not norms at all, or that whatever is, is right. For the criterion being put forward is decidedly *not* the question whether everybody's doing it, but the very different question whether anything gets done by it. What I am protesting is the conception of the methodologist as baseball commissioner, writing the rules; or at any rate as umpire, with power to thumb an offending player out of the game. He is at best only a coach, and the merit of his recommendations rests entirely on what the play of the game shows to be effective.

Even sound norms can be unwisely urged. Excessive effort can be diverted from substantive to methodological problems, so that we are forever perfecting how to do something without ever getting around to doing it even imperfectly. Not a little behavioral science has a markedly *programmatic* character, traceable to its methodological sophistication; and while the program, deriving from what must be true "in principle," may have much philosophical interest, it is likely to be deficient in exploiting the real possibilities of the scientific situation. By pressing methodological norms too far we may inhibit bold and imaginative adventures of ideas. The irony is that methodology itself may make for conformism—conformity to its own favored reconstructions—and a con-

formity even less productive than one at least imitating scientific colleagues. And the push toward logical completeness may well make for
"premature closure" of scientific conceptions (§§8 and 32). The situation
in science is not unlike that in the arts: the critic with his standards dis-
courages daubers, but he also becomes the mainstay of the Academy, and
art eventually passes him by.

I believe that actual scientific practice is and must remain at the focus
of the methodologist's attention, and that the principle of autonomy of
inquiry must not be compromised. A reconstruction of the actuality is
always to some extent an idealization, as I have noted earlier. But from
this truistic premise the remarkable conclusion has been drawn that, in
so far as the methodologist's model and scientific practice differ, so much
the worse for science! There are certain philosophers who bravely set
out to do battle for Truth, when it is they themselves, like Don Quixote,
who stand in need of succour. There have been many, from Kant on-
wards, who determined to "save science" from Humean skepticism; it
occurred to few that it was the skeptical philosophy that needed the
saving.

Norman Campbell (*13*:47) has sharply criticized the assumption that
if any branches of learning do really arrive at truth, "it can only be because they conform to logical order and can be expressed by logical formulas. The assumption is quite unjustifiable. Science is true, whatever
anyone may say; it has for certain minds, if not for all, the intellectual
value which is the ultimate test of truth. If a study can have this value
and yet violate the rules of logic, the conclusion to be drawn is that those
rules, and not science, are deficient." This was written, with remarkable
prescience, almost a half-century ago. Today behavioral science especially may be as much in need of self-acceptance as of methodological
approval.

A corresponding moral is to be drawn by the methodologist. Reconstructed logics have been developed having remarkable subtlety and
power, but it is their very virtues that may constitute also their most
serious shortcomings. They are too good to be true to their ultimate
subject-matter. Methodology must remain alert, Michael Scriven
(*42*:93n) recently warned, to "the logician's perennial temptation—make
the portrait neat and perhaps the sitter will become neat. Usually there is
more to be learnt from a study of the disarray than is gained by inten-

tionally disregarding it." It may even be that what we see as a disarray is to more perceptive eyes a style of dress both useful and elegant.

§4. *"Scientific Method" in Behavioral Science*

This book will contain no definition of "scientific method", whether for the study of man or for any other science. My reason, in part, is that I believe that there are other and often better ways of making meanings clear than by giving definitions (§9). But I also forgo a definition because I believe there is no one thing to be defined. To revert to an earlier metaphor, one could as well speak of "the method" for baseball. There are ways of pitching, hitting, and running bases; ways of fielding; managerial strategies for pinch hitters and relief pitchers; ways of signaling, coaching, and maintaining team spirit. All of these, and more besides, enter into playing the game well, and each of them has an indefinite number of variants. We could say, of course, that there is only one way to play: to score runs if you are batting, and to prevent them if you are not. And this statement would be about as helpful as any general and abstract definition of "scientific method". The questions important to the players arise at a more specific and concrete level. A reconstructed logic is helpful in making clear the unity underlying a multiplicity of particular techniques; it can show, for instance, that a very large class of inferences can be construed as governed by a very few simple rules of deduction. But the simplicity of any one reconstruction of any one method is not meant to deaden awareness of the complexity of the process of inquiry taken as a whole. If we are to do justice to this complexity, I think it is hard to improve on P. W. Bridgman's remark that "the scientist has no other method than doing his damnedest."

My uneasiness with the unitary conception of "scientific method" has, it seems to me, a pragmatic justification quite different from the captious insistence that our logical analyses are never able to take everything fully into account. It is that if a definition of "scientific method" is specific enough to be of some use in methodology, it is not sufficiently general to embrace all the procedures that scientists may eventually come to find useful. The emphasis by historians and philosophers of science that there is no such thing as *the* scientific method, Conant has said (22:35), is a public service. It may well be, at any rate, a service to those scientists who are struggling with ways of working for which their colleagues—to say nothing of methodologists—have little understanding and less sympathy. For the most part, these struggles may come to nothing; but the few which do succeed contribute markedly to the expansion of the frontiers of science. It is less important to draw a fine line between what is "scientific" and what is not than to cherish every opportunity for scientific growth. There is no need for behavioral science to tighten its immigration laws against subversive aliens. Scientific institutions are not so easily overthrown.

TECHNIQUES

The more realistic danger is that some preferred set of techniques will come to be identified with scientific method as such. The pressures of fad and fashion are as great in science, for all its logic, as in other areas of culture. In his classic work on the design of experiments, R. A. Fisher (43:184) pointed out that "any brilliant achievement, on which attention is temporarily focussed, may give a prestige to the method employed, or to some part of it, even in applications to which it has no special appropriateness." This observation can be fully documented in the subsequent history of behavioral science.

In addition to the social pressures from the scientific community there is also at work a very human trait of individual scientists. I call it *the law of the instrument*, and it may be formulated as follows: Give a small boy a hammer, and he will find that everything he encounters needs pounding. It comes as no particular surprise to discover that a scientist formulates problems in a way which requires for their solution just those techniques in which he himself is especially skilled. To select candidates for training as pilots, one psychologist will conduct depth interviews, another will employ projective tests, a third will apply statistical techniques to questionnaire data, while a fourth will regard the problem as a "practical" one beyond the capacity of a science which cannot yet fully predict the performance of a rat in a maze. And standing apart from them all may be yet another psychologist laboring in remote majesty—as the rest see him—on a mathematical model of human learning.

The law of the instrument, however, is by no means wholly pernicious in its working. What else is a man to do when he has an idea, Peirce asks, but ride it as hard as he can, and leave it to others to hold it back within proper limits? What is objectionable is not that some techniques are pushed to the utmost, but that others, in consequence, are denied the name of science. The price of training is always a certain "trained incapacity": the more we know how to do something, the harder it is to learn to do it differently (children learn to speak a foreign language with less of an accent than adults do only because they did not know their own language so well to start with). I believe it is important that training in behavioral science encourage appreciation of the greatest possible range of techniques.

It sometimes even happens that a conspicuously successful technique in some area of behavioral science is not only identified with "scientific method," but comes to be so mechanically applied that it undermines the very spirit of scientific inquiry. Electronic computers, game-theoretic models, and statistical formulas are but instruments after all; it is not *they* that produce scientific results but the investigator who uses them scientifically. Paul Meehl (*40*:498) pointedly asks (in a paper with the question as title), when shall we use our heads instead of the formula? The question is one that behavioral science must continue to face. For having so long been a poor relation of the well-established sciences, it must continuously resist the impulse to see in every new development the promise at last of quick and easy riches.

SCHOOLS

I am pleading, in short, for a certain catholicity of outlook in behavioral science. Catholicity does not imply that every approach is as good as any other, and certainly not that in a particular inquiry we must use them all. An artist may see the beauty in the products of other styles without therefore sacrificing his own; esthetic judgment may be all-embracing even though personal taste remains limited. And coworkers in science surely have at least as much to learn from one another as do those in the arts. The fragmentation of a science into "schools" is by no means unknown even in as rigorous a discipline as mathematics; what is striking in behavioral science is how unsympathetic and even how hostile to one another such schools often are. Their internecine struggles bring into play the tactics of *defensive incorporation* and *exclusion:* "everybody ought to work on ——" and "nobody ought to ——". In the end, each goes his own way, and goes alone.

These tactics lend themselves to rationalization by their identifying some particular phase or other of the complex process of inquiry as the core of "scientific method." For the experimentalist science progresses only in the laboratory; the theoretician views experiments rather as guides and tests for his models and theories; others see as the most important task making counts and measures, or arriving at predictions, or formulating explanations; the field worker and clinician have still other viewpoints. All of them are right; what is wrong is only what they deny, not what they affirm. A full elaboration of any of the phases of inquiry, as I hope to clarify in what follows, involves all of the rest. The story can be told with any one of the characters in the leading role.

DILEMMAS

In the conduct of inquiry we are continuously subjected to pulls in opposite directions: to search for data or to formulate hypotheses, to construct theories or to perform experiments, to focus on general laws or on individual cases, to conduct molar studies or molecular ones, to engage in synthesis or in analysis. It is seldom of much help, in the concrete, to be told that we must do both. In the constraints of specific problematic situations these are genuine dilemmas. But they are a species of what have come to be known as *existential dilemmas:* not characteristic of some special historical situation but intrinsic to the pursuit of truth. We do not make a choice of the lesser of two evils and abide by the unhappy outcome. The problems which the existential dilemmas pose cannot be solved at all, but only coped with; which is to say, we learn to live with them. "We need hard workers and empiricism, not inspiration", it is urged with good reason (*61*:103). But equally good reason can also be given for the converse. The fact is, we need all we can get.

THE GENERALITY OF SCIENCE

This state of affairs is in no way peculiar to behavioral science. Its methodology, as I see it, is no different from that of any other science whatever. If this identity is contemplated in speaking of "*the* scientific method", I warmly approve of the usage. The phases of inquiry into a subject-matter that involves human beings do not lack counterparts in any other inquiry, for these phases are determined by the form of inquiry and not by its content. To emphasize likeness is not to deny, however, that there are unlimited differences in the techniques that are called for. Kenneth Colby tells the fable of an object that arrives from outer space and that resists all efforts by the physicists and astronomers to determine its composition, structure, or function, till at last a psychologist has the happy thought of asking, "What's your name?" and the object replies, "Ralph"! The circumstance that behavior includes speech allows to the behavioral scientist precious techniques denied to other scientists. But for that matter, each science—and indeed, each inquiry—finds some techniques appropriate and others inappropriate and even impossible. The microscope is of very limited use to astronomy (for the present, at least), while the biologist cannot learn much about extra-terrestrial life with the telescope. But to note this difference is not to say that these two sciences have different "methods".

The division of labor in the economy of science is, after all, a historical product and not the reflection of a logical necessity. As science progresses, old partnerships (like natural philosophy or political economy) are dissolved, and new ones (like physical chemistry or social psychology) come into being. Nor are the barriers between physical, biological, and behavioral science fixed and impermeable, a fact illustrated by the recent growth of such disciplines as biophysics, cybernetics, and space medicine. If the classification of the sciences is intended as something more than a device to facilitate storage and retrieval of information, it can be based only on the relationship to one another of problems and also of the respective resources available for their treatment. Interdisciplinary approaches have become widespread, and although such techniques sometimes have glamor in greater measure than homely virtues—perhaps just because of this fact—they can be seen as expressions of deeply felt needs. The unity of science is more than an abstract philosophical thesis; it marks the ever-present potentiality of fruitful unions. It is in this sense that all the sciences, whatever their subject-matter, are methodologically of one species: they can interbreed.

THE SPECIALITY OF BEHAVIORAL SCIENCE

What is distinctive of behavioral science, therefore, is basically its subject-matter; the techniques that the subject-matter permits or demands are only derivative. If some single discriminant of this subject-matter is called for, I believe the most generally applicable one is that suggested by C. W. Morris: the use of "signs". Behavioral science deals with those processes in which symbols, or at any rate meanings, play an essential part. Just how broadly "meaning" is to be construed, and how much of animal behavior it comprises even in its broadest construction, are questions which need not trouble us here. There is no doubt that behavioral science spills over into biology however we choose to circumscribe its limits. But this difficulty is more administrative (for foundations, librarians, and deans) than methodological.

What is significant here is that the data for behavioral science are not sheer movements but actions—that is, acts performed in a perspective which gives them meaning or purpose. Plainly, it is of crucial importance that we distinguish between the meaning of the act to the actor (or to other people, including ourselves, reacting with him) and its meaning to us as scientists, taking the action as subject-matter. I call these, respectively, *act meaning* and *action meaning*. I shall return to this distinction later (§42); for the present, we may note that behavioral science is involved in a double process of interpretation, and it is this which is responsible for such of its techniques as are distinctive. The behavioral scientist must first arrive at an act meaning, that is, construe what conduct a particular piece of behavior represents; and then he must search for the meaning of the interpreted action, its interconnections with other actions or circumstances. He must first see the act of marking a ballot or operating a machine as the action of casting a vote, and then pursue his study of voting behavior.

Now although interpretation for act meanings usually involves special techniques, these are subject to the same methodological norms that govern interpretation for action meanings (and thereby other sciences as well). We interpret speech-acts (in our own language) without any special effort—indeed, usually without any awareness at all of the acts as acts (we do not hear the words, but what is said). Yet every such interpretation is a hypothesis, every reply an experiment—we may, after all, have misunderstood. When it comes to interpreting foreign languages, and in general to interpreting the patterns of another culture, the situation becomes clearer, though it is essentially no different. Some implications of this state of affairs will be explored in connection with the role of "verstehen" in behavioral science (§16). The point I am making here is that the behavioral scientist seeks to understand behavior in just the same sense that the physicist, say, seeks to understand nuclear processes. The difference is not that there are two kinds of understanding, but that the behavioral scientist has two different things to understand: for instance, a psychiatrist needs to understand why a patient makes certain noises (to tell his therapist how much he hates him), and why he says the things he does (because he has not yet worked through the transference). Admittedly, we have special ways of understanding noises, because we are ourselves human; but for the same reason, we also have special ways of interpreting light waves, but need quite other techniques for radio waves. The point is that even what we see is not always to be believed. Every technique is subject to validation, and the same norms apply to all of them.

CONCEPTS

§5. *The Empirical Basis*

If science is to tell us anything about the world, if it is to be of any use in our dealings with the world, it must somewhere contain empirical elements (or, like mathematics, be used in conjunction with such elements). For it is by experience alone that information about the world is received. We can continue to process the information when the channels are closed, but we must have something to work on. Perception is fundamental to all science. Just what the channels are need not, and indeed, cannot be prejudged. Whether there are extrasensory perceptions, or whether yogic states and the like have any cognitive worth, are questions which can be answered only on an empirical basis. The limits of possible experience cannot be drawn, for as Wittgenstein pointed out, we would have to stand outside experience to see on both sides of such limits; we can point to them only from within.

It is in the empirical component that science is differentiated from fantasy. An inner coherence, even strict self-consistency, may mark a delusional system as well as a scientific one. Paraphrasing Archimedes we may each of us declare, "Give me a premise to stand on and I will deduce a world!" But it will be a fantasy world except in so far as the premise gives it a measure of reality. And it is experience alone that gives us realistic premises. "Some fool has put the head of this nail on the wrong end." "You idiot, it's for the opposite wall!" To be sure, if the space of physical objects allowed motions of translation only, and not also rotations. That space has such a geometry is a fantasy; experience shows otherwise. It is only experience that makes this complaint and the rejoinder a dialogue of madmen.

What knowledge requires of experience, and what experience provides, is an independence of our mere think-so. The pleasure principle governing the life of the infant gives way to the reality principle as wishes encounter obstacles to their fulfillment. The word "object", it has been said, can be understood as referring to that which objects. That is objective which insists on its own rights regardless of *our* wishes, and only experience can transmit its claims to us. Experience is ultimate because it confronts us with a continuous ultimatum. For a man to by-pass experience in the pursuit of truth is to make himself God, for only He can say, "Let there be!" and there is. The subjectivist lives in a fool's paradise; in truth, he is damned.

Now a fool's paradise is good—but only while it lasts. Inevitably our wishes urge us on from subjective fantasies to the objective world which is the locus of their fulfillment. A hungry man may dream of food but he wakes to the reality that he cannot feed on dreams. However selfless the love of truth for its own sake may be, the self, to satisfy its needs, needs knowledge of what to do. And appropriate action on things depends on experience of them: only empirical knowledge provides a basis for successful action.

Moreover, human beings interact, and act jointly; the locus of social action is a shared world which each individual must make his own in order to play his part effectively. Now it is experience through which private perspectives open out onto public objects. Subjectivity is held in check with the question, "Do *you* see what *I* see?" Many philosophers, to be sure, have conceived of experience as ineluctably private and of an "external world" as problematic. But the solipsism to which such an epistemology is inevitably impelled is, for methodology at any rate, a reduction to an absurdity. Science itself is a social enterprise, in which data are shared, ideas exchanged, and experiments replicated. It is precisely the cumulation of empirical evidence which shapes a welter of diverse opinions into scientific knowledge common to many minds.

SEMANTIC AND EPISTEMIC EMPIRICISM

What has been stated so far is an *epistemic empiricism:* we cannot know without depending somewhere on experience. This is the position taken by epistemologists from Locke through Kant. In the last hundred years or so a further doctrine has emerged: that not only knowledge but even meaning is dependent on experience. We may call this *semantic empiricism*. It is the view that to be meaningful at all a proposition must be capable of being brought into relation with experience as a test of its truth. Its meaning, indeed, can be construed only in terms of just such experiences as provide a test. That semantic empiricism entails the epistemic is clear, but not the converse. For semantic empiricism asserts that what cannot be known by experience cannot be said either, or more accurately, that there *is* nothing more to be said. Epistemic empiricism, as in Kant, may allow for truths which cannot be known because they transcend experience, but which may somehow be acknowledged by faith. But semantic empiricism does not deny these truths; rather, it denies meaning to the statements that allege them.

Three main variants of semantic empiricism have been influential on the contemporary scene: logical positivism, operationism, and pragmatism.

LOGICAL POSITIVISM

The logical positivist position is embodied in what has come to be called "the verifiability theory of meaning." As its proponents have often pointed out, it is better construed, not as a theory, but as a rule or methodological norm. Loosely, it prescribes that a statement is to be taken as meaningful only if it is capable of empirical verification, and its meaning *is* the mode of its verification. The problems encountered in the search for a strict and generally acceptable formulation have been traced by Hempel (57) and others. A few problems may be noted here.

To start with, falsification rather than verification is also sufficient for meaningfullness. Of course, a proposition which is manifestly false is often colloquially dismissed as "nonsense". But such a proposition is only the negation of a truism (we should call it a "falsism"); and if a proposition is meaningful, so also is its negation. Popper, indeed, has urged that falsification is the basic process. The important scientific propositions have the form of universals, and a universal can be falsified by a single counterinstance, while no number of supporting instances correspondingly establishes it. Scientific laws may always be taken as denying the existence of something: the second law of thermodynamics states in effect that there are no perpetual-motion machines, and Michels' "iron law of oligarchy" states that there are no persistently democratic organizations. Experience is of particulars only. We might some time be in a position to say, "No, *here* is a black swan!" but never can we say "Quite right, all swans *are* white!"

But in both cases the possibility of being mistaken still remains. The supposed counterinstance may only look like one. On the other hand, we may have very good reason indeed to believe that there really are none, if we have looked carefully where they would be found if there were any. ("Not known to be subversive" means one thing in a smear sheet and quite another in the report of an intensive security clearance.) Verification and falsification, in short, must be replaced by some process admitting of gradations. Carnap speaks here of "degree of confirmation", and Reichenbach of the "weight" which can be assigned to a proposition. A proposition is meaningful if experience can give it some weight or other, whether low or high.

But what does it mean to say that we "can" assign a weight to a proposition? It is a matter of whether it is possible to carry out a process of confirmation, and several kinds of possibility are involved. Reichenbach distinguishes three: "technical", "physical", and "logical" possibility. It is technically possible if as a matter of fact, given the circumstances and the state of technology, we are able to do it. It is physically possible if no laws of nature would be violated by the process of confirmation called for, and logically possible if the laws of logic at any rate would not be violated. (Note that the possibility applies to the process of confirmation, not to the fact alleged in the proposition being confirmed.) We can confirm statements about the behavior of Siamese twins by ob-

serving them. A confirmation that calls for joining the nervous systems of
two distinct organisms is only physically and not technically possible.
On the other hand, a wholly disembodied mind is not even a physical possibility, though (we may suppose) it involves no logical contradictions.

Each of these kinds of possibility determines a corresponding domain
of meaning. Science needs all three. We must be able to entertain a
hypothesis before we have a way of checking it, even before we know
whether the laws of nature would permit a way, for it is sometimes by
such inquiry that we determine what the laws of nature are (the theory
of relativity is usually cited in this connection). Our conception of what
is possible, even of what is logically possible, grows with the growth of
knowledge. As a result, the situation is not that we first establish what
propositions are meaningful, then determine which of them are true.
Truth and meaning move forward hand in hand.

Historically, the verifiability theory of meaning was employed primarily as a "criterion of demarcation", to use Popper's phrase. Its significance lay in the distinction it proposed to draw between scientific and
unscientific statements, not on the basis that the latter were false, but on
the basis that they said nothing at all. In the main, however, attention was
focused on philosophical issues, and only derivatively on the scientific
ones. The criterion was a needle with which to prick metaphysical pretensions in science, or, in a more robust metaphor, a cathartic for purg-
ing science of metaphysical wastes like vitalism and holism in biology
or like dualism and epiphenomenalism in psychology.

The scientist himself, however, cannot do much with a criterion for
demarcating the scientific from the unscientific. For him the problem is
not so much to set aside metaphysical nonsense as it is to identify and
clarify scientific meaning. How are we to understand and use concepts
like "unconscious motivation", "social structure", and "the utility of
money"? These are not characteristically metaphysical notions, but what
meaning have they?

The verifiability theory of meaning in fact has two parts, of which only
the first is a criterion of demarcation, defining the class of meaningful
propositions, while the second proposes a procedure for specifying *what*
the meaning is.

Consider Reichenbach's formulation of this second one. Roughly, two
propositions have the same meaning if they are given the same weight

by all observations, and the meaning they have is nothing other than the class of all the propositions which have the same meaning they do. The appearance of circularity in this definition is only an appearance; it is formally unobjectionable, and is known as "definition by abstraction". Compare the following sort of definition of mass: Two objects have the same mass if they balance one another (on a suitably constructed scale); their mass is specified by the set of all equally massive objects, for to assign to something a mass of, say, one thousand grams, is to say that it balances *this* object (the standard kilogram) and any other object like it in mass.

Some difficulties remain, however. Whether two propositions *are* equisignificant (apart from trivial verbal equivalences) is not always easy to determine. How shall we find out just how much weight a particular observation gives to each of them, and not knowing how much, can we nevertheless know that it must be the same weight for both? In practice, the confirmation of any particular proposition is likely to involve the whole theory of which it is a part, so that connecting two concepts at work in different theories is a subtle and complex task. In any case, the relationship between the concept and the observations is seldom simple and direct, and even straightforwardly descriptive terms have a penumbra of vagueness. I shall return to the problems of theoretical terms and openness of meaning in §§7 and 8.

OPERATIONISM

The form of semantic empiricism that has been most influential on behavioral science is operationism. A few decades ago the cry for "operational definitions", especially in psychology, rose almost to a clamor. It was felt that here at last was the way to give our concepts of human behavior a solid scientific basis. By now those early extravagant claims and hopes (for which, it must be said, Bridgman himself was not responsible) have been considerably moderated or even abandoned altogether, in a way that parallels the history of the verifiability theory of meaning.

The basic idea of operationism was attractively simple. The application of concepts to the materials of experience calls for the performance of physical operations on the objects of experience. Quantitative concepts like "length" and "mass" depend on appropriate measurements; and even qualitative concepts depend for their application on laboratory manipulations (like those of the chemist), or at least, on operations on the instruments of observation (as in astronomy) with which we make the appropriate discriminations. To each concept there corresponds a set of operations involved in its scientific use. To know these operations is to understand the concept as fully as science requires; without knowing them, we do not know what the scientific meaning of the concept is, nor even whether it has a scientific meaning. Thus operationism provides, not just a criterion of meaningfulness, but a way of discovering or declaring *what* meaning a particular concept has: we need only specify the operations that determine its application. Intelligence, in the famous dictum, is what is measured by intelligence tests.

Difficulties begin to arise almost at once. One common line of objection to operationism is, I think, misdirected, and may be set aside. It is expressed in the question why one set of operations is selected rather than another, why *that* particular concept is given an operational definition. If intelligence is defined only by the tests, how shall we explain why the tests were constructed in just that way, or even why they were constructed at all? The question is indeed an important one, but that operationism itself provides no answer is no shortcoming of operationism. For the same question can be directed to *any* principle of specifying meanings. The task of such a principle is only to show how concepts can be analyzed and understood. Why they are selected for service in the scientific enterprise is a matter, not of their meaning (provided only it be clear), but of their validity or truth. We need not suppose that intelligence tests are designed to measure something whose meaning is already known. The meaning is defined by certain operations, and the intelligence test constructed as it is, in the expectation that the decision to select *those* operations will be useful for the formulation of psychological laws and theories. Operationism displays no fault in not making clear the logical ground for such an expectation. Its task is only to make clear what the expectation is about.

Other difficulties, however, cannot be sidestepped. We speak of "the" operations for applying a particular concept; but specifically what constitutes the identity of an operation? There is a proverb that when two say the same, it is not the same; how is it when two do the same? What justifies the assumption that the operation I perform is the same as the one you carry out? The operationist principle is that different operations define different concepts. Without the assumption, therefore, no two scientists could ever understand any scientific idea in the same way, and mutual criticism or corroboration would become impossible. The difficulty arises even for a single scientist: each performance of the operations is different in some respects from any other. Unless these differences are dismissed as irrelevant, it is impossible to replicate even one's own experiments. As Gustav Bergmann has pointed out (46:53) an extreme operationist would presumably refuse "to 'generalize' from one instance of an experiment to the next if the apparatus had in the meantime been moved to another corner of the room. Yet there is no a priori rule to distinguish relevant from irrelevant variables." Constancy of meaning would depend on empirical constancies which cannot always be anticipated.

It will not do to reply, "We simply stipulate which variables are to be taken as irrelevant, and finding we have not made a wise choice does not imply that we have not clearly specified the meaning of the concept, but only that the concept is not as useful as we had hoped." The reason why this reply will not do is that science must allow for the possibility of the same concept being measured or applied on the basis of totally different operations, that is, operations differing precisely in the relevant variables. Present estimates of what is misleadingly called "the age of the universe" are of the order of six billion years or so; what makes this figure of scientific interest is that about a dozen different lines of inference from correspondingly different observational data lead to substantially the same magnitude. Operationally we should have to say that twelve different "ages" are in question. Even though in these terms it would remain of scientific interest that they all have approximately the same numerical value, the significance of this fact would be obscured. We should like to be able to say that it is because they all measure the same thing, and this statement is precisely what operationism must deny. But the objection is far from conclusive (§21).

There is also a difficulty of quite another sort. Most scientific concepts, especially the theoretical ones, relate to experience only indirectly. Their empirical meaning depends on their relations to other concepts as fixed by their place in the theory, and it is only these others that have a sufficiently direct application to experience to allow for specifying operations. We do not measure how high is the morale of a group or how deep is the repression of a memory by the manipulation of physical objects in any way at all comparable to the manipulation involved in measuring the temperature of a gas or the hardness of a mineral (both of which are also "intensive" magnitudes like the first two). Operations are used, but the interpretation of their outcome depends on the meanings of an open set of other terms. The attempt has been made to meet this difficulty by speaking of "symbolic operations" as those involved in tracing the connections among theoretical terms, or between these and more directly observational ones. But criteria for the scientific usefulness or even admissibility of such operations are virtually impossible to formulate. Once "symbolic operations" are included, the operationist principle is so watered down that it no longer provides methodological nourishment. To find what a scientific concept means, examine how you apply it, or how you apply other concepts related to it. But what else has any one ever done? Indeed, what else *is* there to do?

PRAGMATISM

Both logical positivism and operationism ask essentially the same question about any statement whose meaning is in doubt: Is it possible to establish the truth of the statement, and if so, how do we go about doing it? The pragmatist version of semantic empiricism takes another tack. It asks instead, what difference would it make to us if the statement were true? The meaning of the statement lies in these implications, and, as William James put it, a difference which makes no difference is no difference. The test of meaningfulness, the criterion of demarcation, is simply whether we can make something of a statement, whether it could conceivably matter to us, in a word, whether it signifies. And a statement's meaning lies in the difference it makes. Classic epistemic empiricism was retrospective: it traced the origin of ideas in sensation, then analyzed meaning in terms of the experiences from which the idea emerged. The pragmatic approach is prospective; what counts is not origins but outcomes, not the connections with experience antecedently given but those which are yet to be instituted.

The positivist and operationist are quite right to insist that meaning is inseparable from the capacity for truth, even more, for truth which can be known. But knowledge is not a reflection of its object, not the contemplation of reality reflected in the mirror of the mind. Knowing is not one thing that we do among others, but a quality of any of our doings: its logical grammar is that of the adverb, not the verb. To say that we know is to say that we do rightly in the light of our purposes, and that our purposes are thereby fulfilled is not merely the sign of knowledge, but its very substance. Meaning is purpose abstracted and generalized so as to fit any occasion. Every meaningful statement, Peirce suggested, may be regarded as determining a correlation between desire and action. The statement that such-and-such is the case means that if we want *a* we are to do *x*, if we want *b* we are to do *y*, if we want *c* we are to do something else again, and so on. We understand a statement only in so far as we know clearly what we would do, if we believed it, in any conceivable circumstance. The meaning is nothing other than this plan of action.

In spite of the fact that this pragmatic approach is the oldest of the three versions of semantic empiricism I am considering (Peirce first formulated the pragmatic maxim in 1878), it is in some ways the most modern in spirit. It invites reformulation in the contemporary idiom of the theory of games, of rational decision making, and the like. A statement is meaningful if it can enter into the making of a decision, and its meaning is analyzable in terms of the difference it makes to the decision taken. To get at the meaning of a statement the logical positivist asks, "What would the world be like if it were true?" The operationist asks, "What would we have had to do to come to believe it?" For the pragmatist the question is, "What would we do if we *did* believe it?" To believe a proposition is not to lay hold of an abstract entity called "truth" with a correspondingly abstract "mind"; it is to make a choice among alternative sets of strategies of action.

Pragmatists have been persistently and widely misunderstood (they themselves may be partly responsible) by reason of the impossibly narrow sense given to the key word "action". There is a vulgar pragmatism in which "action" is opposed to "contemplation", "practice" to "theory", and "expediency" to "principle". It goes without saying (that is, I am afraid I must say it and apologize for doing so) that this vulgar doctrine is almost the direct antithesis of pragmatism, which aims precisely at dissolving all such dualities. The "action" that is relevant to the pragmatic analysis of meaning must be construed in the broadest possible sense, so as to comprise not only the deeds that make up the great world of affairs, but also those that constitute the scientific enterprise, whether it be as "practical" as performing an experiment or as "contemplative" as formulating a theory. The "usefulness" that pragmatism associates with truth is as much at home in the laboratory and study as in the shop and factory, if not more so. If we are to continue to speak with William James of the "cash value" of an idea, we must be careful to have in mind a universally negotiable currency, and especially one that circulates freely in the world of science itself.

There is another difficulty, however, that cannot so readily be dismissed as merely a misunderstanding. We are concerned, not with what difference believing a proposition would make in fact, but with the difference it *should* make, that is, the difference it would make if the believer were affected only by the logical content of the proposition. For first, our actions are often affected by differences in the mere form of a statement even if these do not correspond to differences in content. Bavelas has shown, for instance, that groups in identical communication nets perform differently if they are given geometrically different but topologically equivalent representations of the net. Second, we react to extralogical contents (so-called "connotations" and the like) even if these are not part of what is strictly meant: a map in which the oceans were pink and the continents blue would be disturbing. And third, meaning depends on the action that would be taken under any "conceivable" circumstance, but what a man can conceive depends as much on him as on the proposition he is entertaining. In short, pragmatism faces the problem of marking out the core of logical meaning within a psychological matrix.

Though the difficulty is a genuine one, I believe that it is unduly magnified by the reconstructed logic which draws too sharp a distinction between so-called "cognitive meaning" and "emotive meaning." Often what passes for "emotive" has a cognitive content, in the sense that it could enter into cognitions if the context were such as to make them appropriate. The same is true of "mere" differences of form. The difference in meaning between "A is larger than B" and "B is smaller than A" is a real one, and could very well be important: the first puts A at the focus of attention and the second B. Though identity is symmetrical, nevertheless, if I were Caesar I would be a Roman, whereas if Caesar were I, he would be an American. And as for "mere" connotations, William Empson and an increasing number of other students of poetic discourse are directing attention to the referential basis of the "emotive" quality of language. A girl with "raven tresses" does not just have long black hair, but some of the other attributes of a character in a romantic ballad or something worse. What appears to be a merely psychological effect of a statement may well be a part of its logical content when it is properly analyzed. Nevertheless I believe that the pragmatic approach encounters problems here just as do those of logical positivism and operationism.

The distinctive contribution to methodology of the pragmatic version of semantic empiricism lies, it seems to me, in this: If meanings are to be analyzed in terms of action, they must make reference sooner or later to the ordinary objects and situations which provide the locus for action. Some empiricists have held that all scientific propositions can be interpreted, "in the last analysis", as being "about" sensations—subscribing to the phenomenalism of the older positivists like Ernst Mach and Karl Pearson. Others take the physicalist position that every statement "ultimately" says something about electrons or the like, since this is all there is for the statement to be about. Now both the phenomenalist and the physicalist reconstructions may well be possible, though both have encountered enormous difficulties ın detail. But for methodology, neither of them begins to compare in usefulness with the pragmatist reference to the sorts of discriminations on which everyday action depends. Eddington's famous pointer-readings are neither merely patches of black on white nor merely the eye and hand movements of a strict operationism; they are the results obtained by a properly trained observer from scientific instruments of determinate character and calibration. Otherwise put: Every scientific language, however technical, is learned and used by way of the common language of everyday life; it is that everyday language to which we inevitably turn for the clarification of scientific meanings.

For some decades English-speaking philosophers, especially under the influence of the British schools, have been emphasizing the basic role of "ordinary language". Though the label, I suppose, would be anathema to many, the position taken is in my opinion essentially that of pragmatism. What is insisted on is that language is an instrument, and that to use

language is to perform an action. The analysis of meanings must therefore focus on the particular contexts in which the action is performed,
and on the purposes which the action as a whole is meant [*sic*] to achieve.
This prescription incorporates, I believe, the methodological import of
semantic empiricism. What more that doctrine implies in one or another
more exact formulation is primarily a matter of philosophic rather than
scientific interest.

§6. *Functions of Concepts*

The position just sketched, especially with reference to Dewey's elaboration of it, has come to be known as *instrumentalism*. It identifies the
procedures of analyzing concepts by an attempt to get at the use that is
made of them. The instrumentalist looks at the problems the concept is
used to deal with, and at the ways in which it contributes to the solution
of those problems. We may say that he analyzes the structure of the
language of science (or some part of it) in terms of its function. This
reference to function is by no means a commitment to the primacy of
functionalist explanations throughout behavioral science (see §42). A
condition is met here which by no means holds generally, namely, that
what is being analyzed is unquestionably purposive. A scientific concept
has meaning only because scientists mean something by it. The meaning
is scientifically valid only if what they intend by it becomes actual:
problems are solved and intentions are fulfilled as inquiry continues.

Since Kant, we have come to recognize every concept as a rule of
judging or acting, a prescription for organizing the materials of experience so as to be able to go on about our business. Everything depends, of
course, on what our business is. A "man", for example, is not just a rational animal or a featherless biped, but many different things, different
as conceived not only by the soldier, statesman, and scientist, but different even among scientists—different for the economist and the anthropologist, different even for the physical and the cultural anthropologist,
and perhaps different according to whether a prehistoric or a contemporary culture is in question, and so endlessly. A concept as a rule of
judging or acting is plainly subject to determination by the context in
which the judgment is to be made or the action taken.

Within the context, there is also a range of possibilities as to the specific function the concept is to perform—for instance, relating directly to the perceptual cues that call forth a certain response, or serving to select which among several subordinate rules of action is to be brought to bear (the "descriptive" concepts, "explanatory" ones, and others to be discussed shortly). Differences in these various contexts and roles are by no means always marked by differences in the words used for the corresponding concepts. I shall speak in this connection of *functional ambiguity*, as of the term "man" in the example of the preceding paragraph. It is functional ambiguity that is responsible for the absurdity that an incapacity to work is due to "laziness" (a descriptive term is being used as though it were explanatory), or the confused idea that an incapacity to love is the product of an oral fixation (a theoretical term is being used as though it identified a causal agency).

A specification of purpose, however, does not of itself constitute an adequate account of any instrument. What must also enter into the account is that the instrument has certain properties by which it can fulfill the purpose. We may be free to choose the purpose, but we are not free to determine that the purpose shall be fulfilled as we ourselves choose. If following a certain rule of action, employing a certain concept, is useful for us, or even just "convenient", the reason is that something in the real world answers to our purposes. (Naively, we construe the term as though it labeled that "something".) The notion of a "useful fiction" is strictly speaking self-contradictory: just in so far as it is useful it is not fictitious. It determines a rule of action that works out in the appropriate contexts, but functional ambiguity may lead us to apply it inappropriately, and thus unsuccessfully. A corporation *is* quite like a person *in the relevant respects* (for instance, it makes decisions affecting other persons). The legal concept for which the word "person" is used is sufficiently like the conventional one to account for the sameness of the word, but this very fact may also gloss over the differences.

TERMS

What we are confronted with, however, is always only the word rather than the concept; how do we move from the one to the other?

In the concrete, language consists of acts of speech (or writing). Let us call any such act, performed by a particular person at a particular

time, an *utterance*. As a segment of purposive behavior the utterance has a
use, the specific function it performs in the context of its occurrence.
Now, a number of utterances may be very like one another, and, by and
large, similar utterances have similar uses. Accordingly, a set of utterances is grouped together and identified as a *term* (the word "word"
sometimes refers to an utterance, as in telegraph rates, and sometimes to
a term, as in size of vocabulary). In a corresponding way, the set of uses
may be said to constitute a *usage* for the term. The construction, as it
were, of a term from utterances and of a usage from uses is not a matter
simply of sheer frequencies: some occurrences count for more than
others. Different constructions will be made according to our interest in
various dialects or modes of discourse. Once established, the usage serves
as a norm, and a particular utterance may be identified as a *misuse* of the
term.

In the nature of the case, every usage involves an element of generality,
since it comprises an open set of distinct uses. Subsets are sometimes
distinguished as marking off various *senses* of the term. Philosophical
analysts have sometimes tended to regard every different application of
a term as its occurrence in a different sense, as Quine has pointed out
(*116*:131 ff.). In the extreme, such atomization would deny usage altogether, for a term would have a different meaning every time it is
used. Nevertheless, some differentiations must be made, but just how
they are to be made is problematic. Wittgenstein provides us with the
illuminating metaphor of a "family of meanings": family resemblance is
not a matter of some definite features common to all the members of the
family, but the sharing of some features or other, enough to show the
resemblance, by any two members of the family. The meaning of a term
is a family affair among its various senses.

CONCEPTIONS

How this meaning is taken in a particular use may be spoken of as the
conception. A conception "belongs to" a particular person (though, of
course, others may have very similar conceptions), and it will differ, in
general, from time to time. My conception of an atom is different from a
nuclear physicist's, largely because of ignorance, and different again from
what it was before I was aware of nuclear reactions. Associated with

the *usage* of a term is a *concept*, which may be said correspondingly to be a family of conceptions.

We may, if we choose, regard a concept as impersonal and timeless, in contrast to its conceptions, since it is an abstract construction from the latter (the term "concept" itself is a construct, or a theoretical term; see §7). But this abstract quality must not obscure the fact that as the conceptions change which enter into the construction, so also will the concept. The situation is *not* that conceptions are psychological events and concepts logical entities. Both may be viewed either in terms of what is in fact at work in the process of conceptualization, or else in terms of what ought to be at work to fulfill the purposes of that process; the latter is the logical viewpoint. To be sure, every concept, like the corresponding usage, serves as a norm. But this normative role is a fact, a psychological fact, if you will. We can raise the question whether the norm is a good one, and in answering this question we are making a logical assessment.

Now the importance of a scientific term does not always depend in any direct way on the concept embodied in its usage. It may play its part as a shorthand for a more cumbersome locution by which the concept is expressed. I shall speak of such terms as *notational* and the others as *substantive;* there are in addition *auxiliary* terms, ranging from those that play a minor part in the notation to those required by the grammar of the language in which the scientific discourse is embedded. Substantive terms cannot be eliminated without loss of conceptual content, but notational terms are fundamentally abbreviations, and could be replaced.

But notations not only follow the process of conceptualization; they may also precede and help direct that process. Calling the thematic apperception test the "TAT" is of no scientific significance; but the notations for chemical compounds, especially the notations of stereochemistry, are rich and powerful. A good notation spares us the painful necessity of thinking, as Whitehead has said about mathematics in general. Yet the complexity of a notation does not of itself endow the notation with scientific importance. Behavioral science has suffered often from the illusion that a commonplace formulated in an uncommon notation becomes profound—rich with scientific promise. The theory of functions, topology, vector analysis, symbolic logic, and other formalisms have all been pressed into service. It is true that a notation may itself generate ideas, and has repeatedly done so in the history of mathematics and other disciplines. But it cannot bear the whole conceptual burden. Nothing is easier than to say "Let $y=f(x)$", but nothing is gained if we do not have the faintest idea of how to solve the equation, or even how to characterize the function sufficiently so as to allow for the further use of the notation in taking derivatives or whatever. Substantive terms remain fundamental.

CLASSIFICATIONS

By and large, then, the important terms of any science are significant because of their semantics, not their syntax: they are not notational, but reach out to the world which gives the science its subject-matter. The meaning of such terms results from a process of conceptualization of the subject-matter. In this process the things studied are *classified* and *analyzed:* several things are grouped together and particular things assigned to the several groups to which they belong. (Groups in turn may be grouped together, and analyzed in terms of such "higher-level" groupings.) The concept of "paranoid," for example, puts into a single class a certain set of persons, and is itself analyzed into such patterns as delusions of persecution, auditory hallucinations, impairment of ego-functions, or the like. Each of these patterns in turn is a classification, grouping together a set of actions, verbal or otherwise as the case may be, and without regard to the actors performing them. (Not everyone who hears voices is paranoid, but "hearing voices" determines a class of people, just as "paranoid" does.)

What makes a concept significant is that the classification it institutes is one into which things fall, as it were, of themselves. It carves at the joints, Plato said. Less metaphorically, a significant concept so groups or divides its subject-matter that it can enter into many and important true propositions about the subject-matter other than those which state the classification itself. Traditionally, such a concept was said to identify a "natural" class rather than an "artificial" one. Its naturalness consists in this, that the attributes it chooses as the basis of classification are significantly related to the attributes conceptualized elsewhere in our thinking. Things are grouped together because they resemble one another. A natural grouping is one which allows the discovery of many more, and more important, resemblances than those originally recognized. Every classification serves some purpose or other (the class-term has a use): it is artificial when we cannot do more with it than we first intended. The purpose of scientific classification is to facilitate the fulfillment of any purpose whatever, to disclose the relationships that must be taken into account no matter what.

Plainly, the significance of a concept in this sense is a matter of degree. Even an artificial classification is not wholly arbitrary if it really serves its own limited purposes. A classification of books by size and weight is not as "natural", we feel, as one based on their content. But the printer and the freight agent have claims as legitimate as the librarian's. The point is that the former stand nearly alone in their interests; the librarian is joined by every reader, and by everyone else who is concerned about his reading. Whether a concept is useful depends on the use we want to put it to; but there is always the additional question whether things so conceptualized will lend themselves to that use. And this is the scientific question.

A century ago Mill stated as the requirement of a scientifically valid concept that it should identify properties which are causes or "sure marks" of many other properties. Nowadays this requirement is formulated as calling for statistical relationships rather than strict causal connections. We conceptualize a subject-matter in ways which we anticipate (or hope) will yield significant intercorrelations. Lazarsfeld's "latent structure analysis" may be viewed in this perspective as a technique of conceptualization, a way of finding a set of attributes which will maximize the correlations among the types initially identified. The statistical approach in general has the merit of providing warrant for a conceptualization which may have heuristic value even though it does not wholly solve the scientific problem to which it is addressed. It may be, to pursue an earlier example, that not all paranoids exhibit repressed homosexuality; but the facts that the supposed persecutor is so often of the same sex as the "victim" and that sexual problems are so frequently associated with other functional disorders, these correlations, I say, add something to the validity of the concept of "paranoia" itself.

Yet low intercorrelations do not necessarily invalidate a concept. As Clyde Coombs has pointed out (33:26n), it may even be that various procedures presumed to measure the same trait are only moderately correlated; yet this low correlation would not invalidate the concept of such a trait, but only the notion that it is unidimensional. Many different things go to make up, say, the morale of a group; the finding that no group scores high in all the indices of morale, or low in all of them, or that changes in morale are not reflected by corresponding changes in any one of the indices, would not of itself make "morale" a scientifically useless concept, but only a more complicated one than we might have supposed. On the other hand, psychiatrists have found "epilepsy" almost a useless concept; it long resisted understanding because it labeled several different diseases, of distinct etiology; the concept was an artificial one because patients were found to resemble one another in little more than the seizures which were the basis of the diagnostic classification.

Concepts, then, mark out the paths by which we may move most freely in logical space. They identify nodes or junctions in the network of relationships, termini at which we can halt while preserving the maximum range of choice as to where to go next. If all roads lead to Rome, then, by the same token, once in Rome we can go anywhere. When we are told the color of a substance we have learned little, but when we are told its chemical composition we have learned a very great deal—all the known reactions that depend on that composition. There is a chemistry, as it were, for all things, and our scientific conceptualizations aim at identifying the elements and compounds of this chemistry. In Dewey's reconstructed logic, general propositions are of two sorts. Universal propositions group existents into kinds sharing distinctive characters; generic propositions define categories sharing characteristics or traits. The latter are not existential in import but abstract, implying significant interconnections among kinds. It is these that formulate the appropriate chemistry. The function of scientific concepts is to mark the categories which will tell us more about our subject matter than any other categorial sets.

CONCEPTS AND THEORIES

It follows that concept formation and theory formation in science go hand in hand—another great insight owed to Kant. In modern times Hempel especially has emphasized the interdependence of concepts and theories. The characteristics that make up scientific categories are likely to be "dispositional", that is, they identify the characters that *would* be exhibited *if* certain conditions were fulfilled (hostility is the disposition to exhibit anger under a wide range of appropriate circumstances, anxiety the disposition to exhibit fear, and so on). Any proposition containing such a dispositional term is thus a generalization, making a claim about what would happen *whenever* situations of the proper kind might obtain. Every conceptualization involves us in an inductive risk. The concepts in terms of which we pose our scientific questions limit the range of admissible answers. We are forever asking of our subject whether he has stopped beating his wife.

The Bacon-Mill reconstructed logic makes it seem as though the task of science is to discover what connections obtain among phenomena *given* as manifesting certain preestablished characters, and therefore as grouped in a certain way. "There is nothing more deceptive," Dewey has said, "than the seeming simplicity of scientific procedure as it is reported in logical treatises. This specious simplicity is at its height when letters of the alphabet are used", to represent the articulation of the subject-matter. One occurrence of the phenomenon manifests ABCD, another BCFG, a third CDEH, and so on; plainly, it is C that is responsible for the occurrence. But this alphabetical notation in our reconstruction is "an effective device for obscuring the fact that the materials in question are already highly *standardized*, thus concealing from view that the whole burden of inductive-deductive inquiry is actually borne by the operations through which materials are standardized." The appropriate conceptualization of the problem already prefigures its solution. Ask someone to arrange six matches into four equilateral triangles; he will find it impossible, until he realizes that they need not all be in the same plane, whereupon the tetrahedron becomes obvious. But he must first be able to free his conception of geometric figures from the restriction to the plane. Such freedom is as hard to come by—and to live with—as any other.

In consequence, we are caught up in a paradox, one which might be called *the paradox of conceptualization*. The proper concepts are needed to formulate a good theory, but we need a good theory to arrive at the proper concepts. Long before the scientific revolutions of the twentieth century, Jevons (64:691) remarked that "almost every classification which is proposed in the early stages of a science will be found to break down as the deeper similarities of the objects come to be detected." Every taxonomy is a provisional and implicit theory (or family of theories). As knowledge of a particular subject-matter grows, our conception of that subject-matter changes; as our concepts become more fitting, we learn more and more. Like all existential dilemmas in science, of which this is an instance, the paradox is resolved by a process of approximation: the better our concepts, the better the theory we can formulate with them, and in turn, the better the concepts available for the next, improved theory. V. F. Lenzen (*81*:19) has spoken explicitly of "successive definition". It is only through such successions that the scientist can hope ultimately to achieve success.

§7. *Theoretical Terms*

The terms of any science differ markedly from one another in the way in which they relate to the experiences that they conceptualize. Setting aside the notational and purely auxiliary terms, there are still important differences among substantive terms themselves. These differences can be expressed in any of the three empiricist idioms discussed earlier: positivist, operationist, or pragmatist. I shall formulate them first with reference to the mode of verification of the terms (that is, of the propositions predicating the terms of some subject), or with reference to the operations by which they are applied or defined; later I shall consider corresponding differences in their functions in the scientific enterprise.

REFERENCE TO DIRECT OBSERVATIONS

Observational terms are those whose application rests on relatively simple and direct observations: "dream report", "marked ballot", "stone artifact", and the like. Terms of this kind are also variously known as "concreta", "empirical terms", or "phenotypes"; on the basis of their usual function they are sometimes called "descriptive terms", "experimental variables", and the like. Usage here, as for the other differentiations about to be made, is varied and uncertain. What all the labels point to are terms which lend themselves to easy and confident verifications. To be sure, there may well be cases where in point of fact it is not easy to tell whether the term applies, either because we cannot make the observations, or because, having made them, we are still unsure whether the concept is meant to comprise something of just that kind. Yet on the whole we have no doubts. The psychoanalyst cannot observe his patient's dreams, but he has no particular difficulty in recognizing when the patient is reporting one: the patient says so. A ballot may have been faked, or smudged rather than marked, and a stone artifact may actually be of bone, or be insufficiently worked to be really an "artifact"; yet on the whole, if someone were to ask (without skeptical intent), "How did you know it was a such-and-such?" we might well reply, "I saw it myself" or, "I could tell just by looking at it."

REFERENCE TO INDIRECT OBSERVATIONS

Indirect observables are terms whose application calls for relatively more subtle, complex, or indirect observations, in which inferences play an acknowledged part. Such inferences concern presumed connections, usually causal, between what is directly observed and what the term signifies. The dream, for instance, as contrasted with the dream report, is remembered, or else reconstructed from the report or perhaps from observations made on the sleeper. We all see an eclipse of the sun, but the dark companion of a spectroscopic binary is inferred from periodic variations of light intensity, which are all that is "seen". Molecules make their motions manifest in the Brownian movement; but do we see genes when we look into a pair of blue eyes? In all these cases, the substantive terms designate something which *might* be a matter of "I saw it myself", but the seeing is of rather an extraordinary kind; it probably involves special instruments, and even in the usual cases leaves much room for the objection, "But after all, all you actually *saw* was . . . " Such terms have also been called "illata" and "genotypes", and even, in some usages, "hypothetical constructs". Hypothetical they are, but there is nothing constructed about their referents. We infer their existence, but if the inference is justified, they are as much a part of the furniture of the world as are the trappings named by observable terms.

REFERENCE TO OBSERVABLES

Constructs are terms which, though not observational either directly or indirectly, may be applied and even defined on the basis of the observables. Clearcut examples are provided by what Nagel has called "limiting concepts", like "instantaneous velocity" and "frictionless engine". Velocities can be directly observed, if they are neither too fast nor too slow, or else inferred from observations of positions in space and time; but we neither observe nor inductively infer the velocity at an instant— we calculate it. It is the limit of velocity through an interval (which *is* directly or indirectly observable) as the interval progressively contracts;

but an interval of zero length is a notational device, a manner of speaking—and a very useful one, too. Constructs, indeed, might be regarded as notational terms of sufficient importance and familiarity to acquire substantive import. It is for this reason that they are sometimes called "auxiliary symbols" or "intervening variables".

Other examples do not lend themselves so well to exact analysis. It may not be perfectly clear *which* direct or indirect observables determine the meaning, while there is no doubt that the meaning is determined in *some* such way. Consider such terms as "government", "money", and "taboo." We do not observe the government in action, but only the President, or members of Congress, or the Justices of the Supreme Court, and so on. Yet the actions of these men do not provide a basis for *inferring* that the government is doing something or other, as the Brownian particles allow us to infer the molecular motions of the liquid. Somehow, what the officials do *is* the government in action. But an exact specification of just how the abstraction "government" is defined by the concrete actions of these various men would be a hopelessly demanding exercise in constitutional law. Reichenbach uses the label "abstracta" for what I am calling constructs. They are definable at least in principle by observables, though in practice we may give them only partial and perhaps shifting anchorage in concreta.

REFERENCE TO THEORY

For *theoretical terms* a full definition by observables is even in principle impossible. Carnap speaks of "rules of correspondence" or "correspondence postulates" which give what he calls a "partial interpretation" to theoretical terms. As I shall point out below, what is important is not so much that the interpretation is incomplete as that the observations do not give meaning to the theoretical term but rather mark the occasions for its application. Its meaning derives from the part that it plays in the whole theory in which it is embedded, and from the role of the theory itself. Hence these terms are sometimes called "explanatory terms" (as contrasted with the "descriptive" ones), or "hypothetical constructs" in recognition of the ideational (as contrasted with the empirical) component in all theory formation.

Consider such terms as "castration complex", "marginal utility", or "Protestant ethic". Such terms are not even constructs, let alone observables. We may speak of government in a variety of political theories, and perhaps without explicitly theorizing about it at all. But "castration complex" is meaningless if dissociated from psychoanalytic theory. Even to make the relevant observations already involves the theory: we do not see the superego at work as we do the Supreme Court in the case of the construct "government", nor is the ego a session of Congress, and so on for the more tempting developments of the metaphor. A theoretical term has *systemic meaning:* to discover what it is up to we must be prepared to send not a single spy but whole battalions. This systemic quality is what makes the analysis of theoretical terms so difficult: what begins as the effort to fix the content of a single concept ends as the task of assessing the truth of a whole theory. The meaning of a theoretical term is fixed by horizontal as well as vertical members of the conceptual structure, and only the structure as a whole, at best, rests firmly on empirical ground.

THE EMPIRICAL-THEORETICAL CONTINUUM

These four types of terms are usually treated as two, the first two being combined as "observational" and the last two as "symbolic"; or else, the first three are lumped together as "empirical" or "descriptive" and contrasted with the "theoretical". However the lines are drawn, it is important to recognize that drawing them is to a significant degree arbitrary. The distinctions are vague, and in any case a matter of degree.

Consider first the difference between observational terms and indirect observables. The distinction between naked and instrumented observation is surely not an easy one to draw—especially for someone who, like myself, wears glasses! Variations in perceptual skills, whether native or trained, allow one person to observe directly what for another must be inferential (for example, the tachistoscopic identification of aircraft, or the length and direction of meteor trails). The number of elements in a group may be directly observed if they are few; but larger numbers must be counted, or grouped into recognizable subgroups. Are these observations indirect? Some inferences are involved in all observations (at least in the reconstructed logic of the process); what we call direct observations are those in which the inferences are so common and so sure that they are made without awareness and remain unproblematic. Do we ever really see anything on television? (I am raising a logical question, not an esthetic one.) And what we see has a different status as evidence in a court of law from what we hear, though often the latter is more veridical: we infer events not only from sounds, but sights also are inferential data. Molecules and genes are fundamentally no less observational than are tsetse flies and brain tumors. We could see them for ourselves if only we knew just where and how to look, and were capable of doing it.

The distinction between constructs and theoretical terms is similarly uncertain and at most a matter of more or less. Constructs are definable on the basis of observations, but alas, they are usually thus observable only "in principle", as I pointed out in the case of "government". The concept of "money" is similarly analyzable in terms of observable transactions with pieces of paper, metal, or other substances. But also involved are certain expectations, habits, attitudes, beliefs, and very likely, mythologies. Just which such elements enter into the concept, and in what way, may already be a matter of economic theory. Constructs, in other words, have systemic as well as observational meaning, and in practice may have their meaning specified by horizontal rather than vertical connections. Strictly speaking, the difference between constructs and theoretical terms can be localized in the nature of the vertical connections alone: for constructs the relation to observations is definitional, while for theoretical terms it is a matter of empirical fact. Unfortunately, this distinction itself is by no means unequivocally clear and certain; it is increasingly doubtful whether it can be taken in an absolute sense (see §12).

The basic point is that no observation is purely empirical—that is, free of any ideational element—as no theory (in science, at any rate) is purely ideational. The classical positivists attempted a reconstruction of knowledge on a phenomenological basis, whose first premises were "protocol sentences" describing here-and-now sensations. But the terms of even the barest description carry us beyond the here-and-now, if only because they must be capable of more than one utterance to have a usage. When I say, "This object is red", I am inescapably relating the present occasion to others in which "red" is properly used. And this relation is in some way inferential: it is always possible that I am mistaken. All inferences implicate theories, in the broadest sense of the term. Error is of our own making; it has no part in God's world.

The same point might be put in this way, that the human being is himself an instrument of observation and requires, like other instruments, a theory for its proper use. What is involved is more than a matter of dealing with the errors of the "human equation" (as will be discussed in §§15 and 16). It is by way of the norm as well as by way of the idiosyncratic that theory enters into observation. When we see that someone is pleased or angry, we are relying on a whole framework of ideas about cultural patterns in the expression of emotion, just as we understand what is said not just on the basis of what we hear but also in terms of a whole grammar somehow brought to the hearing. Such theories are tacit, loose, and above all, perfectly familiar, like the geometrical optics with which we make out what we see at a distance. Its very familiarity may hide it from us, but it is at work for all that. I once heard a distinguished experimental physicist seriously deny that theory plays any part in his observations of nuclear reactions—on photographic plates in cloud chambers and the like! Does the chess master "see" what is happening in the game or does he "understand" it? Both "see" and "understand" are manners of speaking.

In short, the line between the observational and the theoretical is differently drawn according to the purposes and contexts of our reconstruction of the logic-in-use. As inquiry proceeds, the invention of new instruments, the growth of knowledge of empirical connections, the incorporation of well-established theory into the conceptual frame of emerging problems—all affect the placing of this line (41:13–15). Norwood Hanson (42:80–81) speaks of theoretical terms as sliding up and down on a "semantical zipper": " 'neutrino' began as an algorithmic invention [construct]; now it names what can be 'seen'. 'Electron' began as something 'seen', but for most contemporary theoretical physicists it seems now to designate a most disembodied abstraction [theoretical term]." For such reasons it might be best, as P. Feyerabend has suggested (42:82–83), to speak of "quickly decidable" terms rather than "observational" ones, so as to avoid the implied contrast with the "theoretical".

The upshot of this discussion is not that there really are no differences among the various sorts of terms discriminated. It is rather that the differences are not to be construed ontologically, as though observational terms name other kinds of things than theoretical terms do. There are not these several sorts of entities, but rather several ways in which terms serve the purposes of inquiry ("lunch" and "dinner" do not identify dishes, but the circumstances of the eating). Dewey (*28*:147) traces the whole notion of sensory "qualities" as constituents of what is observed to the tendency to mistake a constancy of evidential function for a continuity of some existent. Because apples are ripe when red we tend to think of the redness as somehow a constituent of the apple, after the manner of skin and seeds, or malic acid and fructose. Then this constituent is said to be observed, while the others are said to be inferred or constructed. But apples do not consist of visible and invisible parts, and there is no mind's eye which parallels that of the body. Perception and memory, thought and imagination, do not parcel out the acts of knowing but act all together in every cognition; but they do not all do the same thing.

THE FUNCTIONS OF TERMS

Roughly speaking, observational terms localize problems and marshal the data; constructs and theoretical terms propound solutions and lead on to the next problematic encounter. But this distinction is very rough indeed. The drama of science is not a commedia dell'arte with stock characters improvising lines to fit a preassigned plot: the whole play is an improvisation, and character is defined only as the action proceeds. What status to assign to a term depends on the use being made of it in a specific context of inquiry.

For a time it was fashionable, especially among positivists, to regard theories as essentially instruments for establishing linkages among observational terms. In this perspective, these were usually called "descriptive" terms, being the only ones that tell us what the world is like, and the others "auxiliary" terms, as though they were essentially notational. Now this may be a perfectly good account of the ways in which these various sorts of terms sometimes function—but only sometimes, not always. The so-called "descriptive" terms may only be instrumental to the formation of a satisfactory theory, and it is *this* achievement at which a particular inquiry (or phase of inquiry) may aim. For that matter, the substantive terms—observational and theoretical both—may in a given case be significant only as materials and guides for the construction of a more effective notation. A theory may generate observational concepts just as the latter may give rise to a theory. Freudian slips are observational, but the eponym reminds us of its origin in theory, just as "conspicuous consumption", while belonging to Veblen's theory of the leisure class, makes reference precisely to something that can easily be seen by others.

The point is that we cannot restrict beforehand the ways in which a concept may make itself useful, and we cannot define a priori even what all the possible uses are. What is important is that these various functions not be confused with one another, and this is the primary purpose that is served by distinguishing the various sorts of terms. MacQuorcodale and Meehl made their famous distinction between "hypothetical constructs" and "intervening variables" so that, if a term is introduced as an intervening variable it is not treated, in that same context of inquiry, as though it were something capable of having causal efficacy. The "superego" cannot inhibit us from doing anything if it has been introduced as a way of speaking about our inhibitions. Reification is more than a metaphysical sin, it is a logical one. It is the mistake of treating a notational device as though it were a substantive term, what I have called a construct as though it were observational, a theoretical term as though it were a construct or indirect observable.

Recent developments in reconstructed logic pose the question whether theoretical terms perform any substantive function at all, for they are apparently expendable. Carnap has explored the method of the so-called "Ramsey sentence", which dispenses with theoretical terms by speaking instead of the existence of whatever it is that satisfies the observational conditions by which the theoretical terms were given an empirical application. Much interest attaches in this connection to the work of William Craig, who was able to show ("Craig's theorem") that the empirical content of a system is contained in its observational terms, not by translating theoretical statements into purely observational ones, but by showing how to construct another system, without theoretical terms, empirically equivalent to the first one. Craig himself, however, calls attention to the care with which the implications of his results must be assessed.

First of all, the distinction between theoretical and other terms (Craig calls them "auxiliary" and "non-auxiliary") is, as I have urged above, "hard to make or else artificial" (26:40). In the second place, the procedure calls for a highly formalized treatment, and "few subject-matters can be systematized" as required. "Even in a fairly rigorous subject such as physics the speed with which the subject changes and the coexistence of competing theories, among other factors, seem to make systematization practically impossible" (26:41). Moreover, the axioms which must be introduced "fail to simplify or to provide genuine insight" (26:49); they may well be infinite in number and too complex to serve as premises for actual deductions. Finally, Craig points out, our main concern is not with whether theoretical terms can in principle be replaced, but with how in fact their meaning can be clarified; and the method he has devised "fails to provide any such clarification" (26:52). To all this Nagel (103:134–137) also adds the compelling consideration that the method shows how we can dispense with theoretical terms only when we already have a good theory, but not before. We must wait with the reconstruction till "every possible inquiry into the subject-matter has been completed." In a similar vein Braithwaite has pointed out that in this treatment we could not incorporate a theory into a more general theory with a wider range of application.

In short, the reconstructed logic is in this respect far from the logic-in-use. Theoretical terms, however their meaning is to be analyzed and brought into connection with the empirical basis of all knowledge, are indispensable to the actual pursuit of scientific inquiry.

§8. Openness of Meaning

The devices by which theoretical terms are brought into relation with observations have been variously called "meaning postulates", "correspondence rules", "coordinating definitions", and the like. Carnap has elaborated the way in which such devices provide "partial interpretations" of the theoretical terms, partial because the range of application of a theory, as well as the way it is to be applied in particular cases, cannot be fully specified beforehand. This situation was familiar from disposition terms, which refer to what would happen if certain conditions were realized. The classical example is "soluble": to say that a substance is soluble is to say that, if it is placed in water, then it will dissolve. But how if it is not placed in water? When the conditions are satisfied, we can say that the substance is soluble if and only if it dissolves; but when they are not satisfied, we do not know what to say. Of course, we can make inferences about what would happen *if*, but the point is that the specification in the example is only a partial one. Quite other tests of solubility might be developed, and incorporated into the very meaning of the term. The rule given leaves other possibilities open. This state of affairs has come to be called, by Hempel and others, *openness of meaning*. I shall use this expression in a general way for any respect in which the specification of meaning of a term leaves its usage uncertain.

In the case of theoretical terms, Sellars (42:59) has pointed out that the correspondence rules are not translations at all, even partial ones. It is not that they provide observational equivalents for the theoretical terms but only under certain special conditions. The situation is rather that the rules constitute a "verbal bridge" between theory and observation without pre-supposing or establishing any identity of meaning. There are many ways in which the gap can be bridged, and many places at which it can be done. To pursue the metaphor, what is characteristic of a theory is that we do not cross these bridges, or even construct them, till we come to them. It is required only that we be able to do it as the need arises. As the theory is used—for scientific as well as for "practical" purposes—its meaning is progressively more fixed; but some degree of openness always remains.

I shall distinguish four types of openness which I believe to be of particular importance for the terms of behavioral science.

SYSTEMIC OPENNESS

There are many terms whose meaning can be specified only as they are used together with other terms, or in full sentences. The medievals called them "syncategorematic", and in modern times, Russell has made extensive analyses of them as "incomplete symbols". They do not name constituents of the propositions which they help formulate, yet they contribute to the meaning of the sentences in which they occur. Russell's famous example is the definite description, any phrase of the form "the such-and-such". The sentence "The present king of France is bald" may be said to be about baldness but not about the present king of France, for there is no such person. But the statement as a whole has a determinate meaning, which Russell formulated as: "There is a present king of France, there is only one, and that one is bald." The definite description is an incomplete symbol; we can explain what is meant by "bald" taken by itself, but not what is meant by "the" alone. We may say that terms like "bald" have *word meaning*, while terms like "the" have *sentential meaning*. It may be that a fuller analysis would give primacy in every case to sentential meaning; but so much the better for the point I wish to make here.

That point is that there are terms which require for a specification of their meaning not one sentential context but the context of the whole set of sentences in which they appear. Such meaning I have previously called "systemic meaning." Each sentential occurrence is a partial determination of the meaning, but only as we encounter the term in more and more contexts of varying sorts do we come to understand it more fully. (This description is as true of what we ourselves mean as of what is being said by another.) What Marx meant by "class" or by "capitalism" is made manifest only in the whole corpus of his writing, as is Freud's meaning of "libido", or Durkheim's of "anomie". Notice that a term may have systemic meaning even though it is apparently explicitly defined somewhere. There is a certain kind of *pseudo definition* in which a meaning is set down although the term is not in fact thereafter always used in accord with the "definition". The chances are, indeed, that a key term of this kind is "defined" several times and in several different ways. This diversity does not necessarily mark a lapse either of logic or of memory, but the occurrence, rather, of systemic meaning.

All theoretical terms have systemic meaning. The theory as a whole is needed to give meaning to its terms, even those parts of the theory in which the terms in question do not explicitly appear. Logicians sometimes speak of "implicit definition" as provided by a set of postulates in which an undefined term appears; it is the postulates of geometry which in this sense define "point", and not expressions like "a position without extent". Scientific theories are not ordinarily couched in postulational form; all the propositions of the theory serve as the implicit definition of its key terms. The occurrence of systemic meanings in behavioral science therefore, is not of itself a symptom of scientific immaturity. They play an important part in even the most advanced sciences. A "white dwarf" in astronomy, for example, is not just a small star of a certain color; the concept is intimately bound up with theories of the formation of stars and of stellar evolution, and its meaning cannot be specified outside the context of such theories. The term might be construed observationally (as an indirect observable), and then indeed it may no longer have systemic meaning, but by the same token it would no longer be of theoretical import. And even so, systemic meaning might well be involved on a secondary level, by way of the theories invoked for the interpretation of the data yielded by the astronomer's instruments of observation.

Systemic meaning is always open, for the set of propositions making up a theory is never complete. The value of a theory lies not only in the explanations it was constructed to provide but also in its unanticipated consequences, and these in turn enrich meanings in unforeseen ways. No single specification of meaning suffices for a theoretical term, precisely because no single context of application exhausts its significance for the scientist using it. We are tempted to think that new applications only add to our knowledge of truth but leave meaning unchanged. But this view is doubtful even for strict observational terms; for theoretical terms it is surely false. As evidence accumulates in support of a theory, we simultaneously come to a better understanding both of the world and of our own ideas about the world.

VAGUENESS

Even taken by themselves, terms have an openness of meaning because of the ever-present possibility of the occurrence of borderline cases. Experience is a succession of continuities, and everything discriminated in the continuum has fuzzy edges: the ravel'd sleave is never quite knit up. "Pure" elements are mixtures of isotopes, "empty" space contains swarms of particles, "absolute" temperature is measured from an approximate zero, "ideal" gases and "perfect" engines are nowhere to be found. I do not say that it is the indefiniteness of fact which of itself makes for an uncertainty of meaning. Whatever we can discriminate in the facts we can distinguish in our meanings; we can always call the fuzzy edge a definite fringe. The point is that facts are *indefinitely* indefinite: however fine a mesh we use, finer differences slip through the conceptual net. And the more discriminations we make, the more opportunities we create for borderline cases to arise. We must leave off our discriminations somewhere, but the facts never quit. They are never content to leave well enough alone; sub specie aeternitatis nothing human ever is enough.

This fact about facts does not imply, however, that our thinking should be fuzzy so as to correspond to a fuzzy world—God forbid! Such talk is self-defeating, for what it calls for is, indeed, a more exact correspondence. (One might even say, that is *precisely* what it calls for.) The law of excluded middle is not being thrown overboard, but only the easy identification of a reconstructed logic with a logic-in-use, and even worse, the projection onto the world of the traits of our own logic. Everything surely is just what it is, and just as surely either does or does not belong to any class we may define. The trouble comes in deciding which alternative is true. Things themselves know very well where they belong, but every signal they transmit to tell us where comes over to us on a background of noise.

The vagueness of our terms does not consist in the fact that we are continually confronted with the problem of "where to draw the line", but in the fact that we cannot solve this problem beforehand and once for all. The point is that lines are drawn and not given; that they are drawn always for a purpose, with reference to which the problem is solved in each particular case; that our purpose is never perfectly served by any decision; and above all, that no decision can anticipate the needs of all future purposes. Every term directs a beam of light onto the screen of experience, but whatever it is we wish to illuminate, something else must be left in shadow. Vagueness has never been better characterized than as the penumbra of meaning.

That all terms are to some degree vague, that they *must* be vague, is apparent just from the way in which we learn to use language (*116*:125–126). To do that we must perceive similarities and make inductions. Now similarity is always a matter of degree, and induction is always short of being conclusive. The result is that for every term the situation can arise, and sooner or later does arise, in which we do not know whether it properly applies—not because we are unsure of the facts but because the meaning is uncertain. One by one we can pluck the hair from an Ainu till at last he is unquestionably bald; but just when he was transmogrified is always open to question. It is not enough to say that it is only our grasp of the meaning which is uncertain. The concept is constructed from conceptions which are all uncertain in just this way. I have never known an empirical term, even from the most exact sciences, in which I could not, when pressed, bring to light a shadow of vagueness.

But though vagueness is necessary, it is not necessarily an evil. For first, precision is not always so devoutly to be wished: there can be too much of this good thing as of any other, and there are circumstances in which it is not particularly good to begin with (§23). Second, vague terms can be so conjoined as to yield quite a precise meaning. I. A. Richards (quoted by Quine, *116*:27) makes the point that "a painter with a limited palette can achieve more precise representations by thinning and combining his colors than a mosaic worker can achieve with his limited variety of tiles, and the skillful superimposing of vaguenesses has similar advantages over the fitting together of precise technical terms." It is no part of my intention to encourage deliberate vagueness, or even apathy towards its occurrence. But we are victims of our reconstructed logic if we think it can be defined away. We cannot learn to control it, and to live with it, so long as we suffer from that illusion. To say simply that a scientific term is vague is not thereby to diagnose a failing but at most only to report a symptom.

INTERNAL VAGUENESS

Meanings are open not only at the edges, so to speak, but internally as well. If uncertainty of meaning is to be described always as a matter of borderline cases, then the border reaches all the way into the interior. For not all the things to which a term can properly be applied are equally deserving of the application. To borrow from Orwell, if they are all equal, then some are more equal than others. Of any species whatever there are good and bad specimens. In talk about the species, what is meant is best understood with reference to the good specimens, or at least, to those which are not too bad. There is, after all, something to be said for Plato's semantics: the ideal case is an embodiment of meaning as well as of worth. We say of it, "Now *that's* what I call a such-and-such!"

Ordinary vagueness is external—that is, it concerns the difficulty of deciding whether or not something belongs to the designated class. Here we say that belonging is in any case a matter of degree, as it were. Meanings are open not only with respect to what is comprised under the term but also with respect to what should be taken as a typical, standard, or ideal instance. The external vagueness of the concept of the "living", for example, lies in the uncertainty concerning viruses and such like; the internal vagueness results from the fact that every organism begins to die from the moment of its birth. We are driven to idioms like being "wholly", "fully", "*truly* alive". The visitor to the famous cemetery, impressed by the luxurious grounds and monuments, exclaims, "*That's* living!" Internal vagueness has turned a meaning inside out.

Classical logic requires that the meaning of a term be fixed by laying down a set of necessary and sufficient conditions for its application. These conditions must all be met, and each of them met completely. "A class must be defined by the invariable presence of certain common properties. If we include an individual in which one of these properties does not appear, we either fall into a logical contradiction, or else we form a new class with a new definition. Even a single exception constitutes a new class by itself" (*64*:723). But as against all the defining conditions being met, generally speaking we are confronted instead with family resemblances. No one property (or fixed set of properties) runs through the whole class. We could, of course, construct one by a disjunction: every member of the class shares the property of being either P or Q or . . . ; but the very point is that the whole range of alternatives cannot be exactly specified beforehand. And as against any condition being fully met there are always only partial fulfillments. Biological species are distinct when crossings are sterile; but hybrid sterility, like fertility within the species, turns out to be a statistical affair rather than all-or-none.

Internal vagueness, therefore, stratifies denotations, according to whether they are central or marginal cases or something between. A variety of reconstructions of the situation are possible. New terms, for instance, can be introduced for each of these sorts of cases, yielding more homogeneous subclasses. Absolute terms may be replaced by comparatives, which call for a specification of degree, as "democracy" may be replaced by "(more or less) democratic". (See the discussion of Weber's "ideal types" in §10.) And defining conditions may be explicitly treated as an open set of indicators (§9), so that in each case a term may be expected to apply in one respect and not in another. In short, internal vagueness, while always present (to some degree!), can itself be made an instrument for conceptual clarification.

DYNAMIC OPENNESS

The noun "meaning" derives basically from the verb "to mean"—so far as logic is concerned, if not philology. Meaning is a process, a succession of acts of speech in which utterances are used to fulfill purposes. As time goes on these purposes inevitably change, as do correspondingly the acts by which we seek to fulfill them. With the growth of knowledge our conceptions of things are modified, sometimes quite radically, and so therefore are our concepts. Changes in meaning may very well be more marked than increments of truth. We may not know very much more about psychosis than the medievals did, but we certainly think differently about it. The progress of science does not consist simply in making additions to a store of truths. Dialogues in limbo evoke not only "Well, what do you know!", but much more frequently, I am sure, "What in the world do you mean?"

Now the logic of science is not properly restricted to an analysis of instantaneous states of knowledge (see §2). We are interested not only in the timeless relations of entailment among abstract propositions but also in the processes by which in time one concrete scientific assertion gives way to another, and usually an assertion making use of new, or at least modified, concepts. Boltzmann (27:250) views it as "a genuine defect of the deductive method" that it does not make visible to us the path by which a new scientific "picture" is arrived at. A reconstructed logic which tacitly assumes fixity of meaning is a consequence only of our own fixation on the state of science at a given moment. "Any form of meaning invariance," P. Feyerabend has pointed out (41:31) "is bound to lead to difficulties when the task arises [of giving] a proper account of the growth of knowledge, and of discoveries contributing to this growth."

Dynamic openness is, so to speak, the leading edge of scientific terms, their permanent possibility of change in meaning. That dispositional terms have such openness is easily recognized, for as time goes on we add "reduction sentences" to give them meaning in an ever-increasing range of circumstances. But even when the conditions are exhaustive and the meaning therefore complete, dynamic openness remains. The whole concept may give way to another, subtly or radically different. Consider the growth of the concept of "acid" in chemistry, from something with a sour taste (still reflected in the German "Säuere"), corroding metals, and turning litmus red, to something yielding a certain concentration of hydrogen ions in solution. To speak of chemistry in the abstract—that is, abstracted from contexts of inquiry into chemical reactions—is to risk overlooking the important fact that its concepts change with its theories. "Introducing a new theory involves changes of outlook both with respect to the unobservable features of the world, and corresponding changes in the meanings of even the most 'fundamental' terms of the language employed" (*41*:29). The operationist is sound in his insistence that even new instruments and experiments, to say nothing of new theories, must be taken as specifying new meanings.

The point is that we cannot accommodate these facts about the norms of scientific usage without providing for openness of meaning. If meanings are taken to be always wholly fixed, logically speaking, relations between an old concept and new ones can be described only as overlap, inclusion, or complete replacement. The details of the process of change, its intermediate steps, its locus and justification—all remain unspoken. If the question of motivation arises, it must be treated as "a matter of psychology or sociology"; a logical motivation becomes a contradiction in terms. When openness of meaning is openly acknowledged, the situation is altogether different. The anatomy of science is supplemented and enriched by a study of its physiology. Like all life, the life of the mind is continuous change, both growth and decay. The fixed form in which it is embodied at any moment is only the outer shell, beautiful in its symmetries but already dead; the life within is a form in the making.

That meanings are open does not imply that they are altogether unspecified: as with minds, "open" is not the same as "empty". Initial contexts of application must provide enough closure to contain a usable empirical meaning, and most subsequent applications are sufficiently like the initial ones so that borderline cases seldom arise. But as contexts are extended, the situation may change. Openness of meaning is fundamentally a consequence of the fact that there are no terminal contexts of inquiry. New problems always arise, confronting us with unforeseen issues of both meaning and truth. The penumbra of vagueness is not a "surplus meaning," scientifically expendable. Because meanings are open, our conceptualizations can reach out for a firmer grip on reality.

PREMATURE CLOSURE

The demand for exactness of meaning and for precise definition of terms can easily have a pernicious effect, as I believe it often has had in behavioral science. It results in what has been aptly named the *premature closure* of our ideas. That the progress of science is marked by successive closures can be stipulated; but it is just the function of inquiry to instruct us how and where closure can best be achieved. "When sentences whose truth values hinge on the penumbra of a vague word do gain importance," Quine observes (*116*:128), "they cause pressure for a new verbal convention or changed trend of usage that resolves the vagueness in its relevant portion. We may prudently let vagueness persist until such pressure arises, since meanwhile we are in an inferior position for judging which reforms might make for the most useful conceptual scheme." There is a certain kind of behavioral scientist who, at the least threat of an exposed ambiguity, scurries for cover like a hermit crab into the nearest abandoned logical shell. But there is no ground for panic. That a cognitive situation is not as well structured as we would like does not imply that no inquiry made in that situation is really scientific. On the contrary, it is the dogmatisms outside science that proliferate closed systems of meaning; the scientist is in no hurry for closure. Tolerance of ambiguity is as important for creativity in science as it is anywhere else.

§9. Specification of Meaning

Comparable to the myth of methodology (§3), that the major obstacle to the progress of behavioral science is methodological, is another myth concerning specification of meaning. We might call it the *semantic myth*, the notion that the trouble is chiefly linguistic: if only the behavioral scientist were to eliminate vagueness and ambiguity, define his terms, use definitions of the right kind (operational or whatever), all would be well with him. The fact is that for the most part the behavioral scientist, like everyone else, manages his semantics very well without extreme and self-conscious exertions. The human mind—even the mind of a behavioral scientist—is quite remarkable for its capacity to understand and to make itself understood. Children, everyone agrees, learn more, and more quickly, than they have any right to; adults are no longer geniuses, but they are not therefore fools. In the scientific community, communication is also a matter of goodwill, the wish to understand. Scientists engage not only in mutual criticism but also in mutual support. I think that one of the roots of the semantic myth is that among behavioral scientists today critical attitudes are so much more widespread than supportive ones. In my experience, semantics usually comes into question when we already feel that what is being said is trivial or false: what is ill-advised presents itself to us as being ill-conceived. Like Alice, we are often in that state of mind in which we want to disagree with something, even if we don't know what.

Yet a man is not always being disagreeable when he wants to know how a term is being used. There are circumstances in which an explicit specification of meaning is indeed called for. There are a number of ways in which the demand can be met.

The most basic device is *ostension*, pointing to or directly presenting the denotation. It is basic from the standpoint of semantic empiricism, for which observational terms, which lend themselves to ostension, are fundamental. It is also basic from the standpoint of scientific training. Apprenticeship begins with ostensions in the laboratory, the clinic, and out in the field, as the student is introduced (in several senses of that term) to his instruments and subject-matter.

A second procedure for specifying meaning is *description*, which serves for indirect observables as well as for observational terms. Calling the Rorschach the "ink-blot" test may be quite enough to identify it; of course this does not tell us what it tests or how, but we are concerned here only with specifying the meaning of the name. Similarly, when the term "shaman" is given the meaning of "medicine man", we have some understanding of it, and our understanding grows as descriptions are added of just what he does, with which "medicines", and to what end. Other ways of explaining what is meant by a term describe possible ostensions, giving examples of what it denotes or instances of its use.

DEFINITION

By far the most frequently mentioned device, though not the most frequently used, is *definition*. This term itself has a loose sense in which it applies to any procedure for specifying meaning. More strictly, a definition provides a set of terms synonymous, as a set, with the term defined, so that they are mutually replaceable. The definition formulates the conditions which are both necessary and sufficient for the applicability of the term defined. For this reason it is most suitable for specifying the meaning of a notation, which is essentially an abbreviation. Definitions are also appropriate to constructs, provided that these are sufficiently "definite", that is, provided that the materials and manner of their construction are relatively clear and simple. On the other hand, theoretical terms—and in practice, most constructs—are not capable of definition in the strict sense. More accurately, such definitions at best provide synonyms, but do not in themselves perform the function of specifying meaning. Thus an anthropologist, for example, can define a notation like "cephalic index" and can define constructs like the various kinship relations; but he cannot define a construct like the "joking relation", or a theoretical term like "culture". I must emphasize that I am not saying that such terms cannot or do not have their meanings specified; I am saying only that, because of the openness of their meaning, the specification is not by way of definition in the strict sense.

The procedures that *are* used are often called "definitions" of various kinds: "implicit", "conditional", "probabilistic definitions," and the like. But they are not procedures which allow free replacement of the term whose meaning is being specified. Most generally, they specify the meaning of a term by formulating statements whose truth would provide evidence for, or receive warrant from, the truth of statements containing the term in question. They tell us what would verify or be verified by such statements, without claiming that the former are translations of the latter, equivalent in meaning It is for this reason that they are partial specifications, only conditional, probabilistic, and the rest. We learn what is meant by "culture" in a certain theory as we see what the theory says about culture, what inferences it draws from these assertions, what evidence it adduces on their behalf. We are provided, not with a dictionary of the terms, but with a guidebook to their subject-matter. It is this kind of meaning that is specified by "implicit definition".

INDICATION AND REDUCTION

I shall refer to these procedures, broadly considered, as the process of *indication*, as contrasted with the *reduction* of meaning provided by strict definition. (Carnap's "reduction sentences" are indications in the present sense; I wish to avoid the nothing-but connotation of the term "reduction", for this connotation is appropriate only to definitions.) I shall speak also of *vertical* or *horizontal* indication, according to the primacy of observational or theoretical terms in the specification. These two types of indication are not sharply distinguishable from one another; and both types are likely to be present in any given case.

What is involved in the process of indication may be sketched as follows (see *66*, *72*, and *127*). We begin with a set of discriminations imposed on the relevant field of inquiry. (Of course, it is the reconstruction that begins here, not necessarily the logic-in-use). This set fixes an *articulation* of the field, having two components. One is the *conceptual structure* (or "framework"), basic to horizontal indication. It consists of the whole set of independent terms, that is, the terms not strictly defined by the others, used in the theory presupposed in and emerging from the inquiry. The other component is the *attribute space*, basic to vertical indication. It consists of the set of categories with reference to which the elements of the field are more or less observationally characterized. Each category comprises a set of discriminable qualities, sometimes ordered, sometimes even quantitatively specified (when each is usually known as an "index"). Every individual can then be assigned a *profile*, consisting of the quality by which it is characterized for each of the categories in the attribute space. For example, family-budget studies might include in the conceptual structure concepts like "income elasticity of demand", "liquidity preference", and "external economies of consumption"; and in the attribute space categories like family size, amount of savings, and standard of living. Each family would then have a profile consisting of a specific size, dollar savings, and standard of living, and like attributes. It is on the basis of this articulation that the meaning of the terms used are specified.

For vertical indication, each profile is a potential *indicator* of meaning. A weight, not necessarily numerical, is associated with each profile with respect to any given term, according to the significance of its indication for the applicability of that term. The meaning of the term is specified by the whole set of these weights. The term does not designate a well-defined set, in the sense that for each element, given its profile, we can say definitely whether the term does or does not apply to it. We have only an *open class*, whose members justify the application of the term only to some degree or other, according to the weight associated with their respective profiles. The open class corresponds in ontology to the semantic openness of meaning. It is the familial resemblance among profiles that makes for a family of meanings. Terms designating open classes are sometimes called "polytypic terms", "cluster concepts", or "terms of controlled vagueness".

Note that the weight assigned to a particular profile (for a given term) is not necessarily complementary to the weight of the complementary profile. That is, the presence of a profile may have a high weight for the applicability of the term even though the absence of the profile does not have a correspondingly low weight. A good positive test is by no means equally good always as a negative test.

Instead of considering the degree to which a particular profile justifies the application of a given term, we may ask the converse question: Given that the term applies, how likely is it that an individual subsumed under that term has a particular profile? From this standpoint each profile may be regarded as a *reference* of the term to some degree, according to its respective reference weight. Reference and indicator weights are not, in general, identical: a reliable diagnostic indicator is not necessarily inferrable (or meant) when an individual is assigned to the corresponding (open) diagnostic class. If 90% of the A's are B's, while only 5% of the B's are A's, A is a good indicator for B but a poor reference of B.

With respect to some attribute space, then, a concept has been vertically specified when a set of indicator and reference weights has been provided for the term symbolizing it. If these have been arrived at in a wholly arbitrary manner, the concept is an artificial one, rather than natural (§6), and the specification of meaning is said to be "nominal" rather than "real" (traditionally, these adjectives characterize definitions). A real specification has a cognitive content; if we do not speak of it as being strictly "true", we assign some other mark of cognitive worth, like "valid" or "sound", or at least, "useful". (A specification of meaning may be true in a sense irrelevant here, namely, if it is truly descriptive of a given usage.) The methodologically interesting question is not whether it is true that a term has a certain specification, but whether the specification itself is a true one, in the appropriate sense. Suppose the specification were simply stipulated; what would be its worth?

Hempel speaks of the "justificatory sentence" for a definition as a previously established statement which justifies the introduction of the definition into some theoretical system. For example, the definition of the melting point of a substance presupposes the truth of the statement that all samples of that substance melt at the same temperature. The cognitive content of a specification of meaning which is in question here refers to more than the satisfaction of such presupposed conditions. The justification of a specification is, in general, something *to be* established: the usefulness of the concept so determined for the performance of the functions in inquiry intended for it. The specification is justified in so far as it has marked out a natural concept. This is to say that its indicators exhibit a considerable *congruence:* overlap or correlation (the term "correlation concept" has been used in this connection). Every concept actually introduced in inquiry claims that such congruence exists, to a significant degree. Its scientific worth is, in this respect, a matter of whether or not the claim is justified.

While a specification of meaning, therefore, can be regarded as the outcome of a decision, the decision in turn may be said to be empirically grounded. "Conventional" is by no means the same as "arbitrary": experience may show that one convention is far preferable to another. A specification of meaning is usually taken as recording, or laying down, a logical equivalence. It is correctly so taken for definitions, in which the defined term is indeed synonymous with the set defining it; but it is not thus correct for the process of indication. Indicator and reference weights are in general less than absolute (let us say, neither 0 nor 1), so that no profile *entails* the applicability of the term, and none is entailed by it. What weights the profiles have can be viewed either as a semantic assignment or as an empirical determination. The weight is an assignment expressing a belief in an empirical fact of congruence, or alternatively, an empirical finding expressed in a suitably specified meaning.

PRECISION AND RELIABILITY

I am saying that what is regarded as "a matter of definition" in one context may well be empirical in another. "In theoretical science," Quine has said (*116*:57), "unless as recast by semantics enthusiasts [that is, in a certain reconstructed logic], distinctions between synonymies and 'factual' equivalences are seldom sensed or claimed." As inquiry proceeds, meanings change just as do hypotheses and theories. A man's conceptions grow as his knowledge does, and when the conception is sufficiently different we identify it as marking a different concept. With the progress of science, different conceptual structures come into play, different attribute spaces, and at least, differences in the indicator weights or in the reference weights. Concepts are *sharpened:* the weights come closer to extreme values (0 or 1) as more subtle discriminations are made, and made in ways that increase congruence.

In so far as the sharpening is thought of as conventional, we speak of an increase in the precision of the term; and in so far as it is taken to be empirical, we speak of an increase in the reliability of the indicators. It is easy to sharpen concepts as much as we like; what is hard is to determine whether this sharpness is worth achieving in a particular way. If the sharpening is wholly conventional, the resulting congruence may be so low that even though the term has been made quite precise it may be virtually without any predictive power. Tariff laws may define "work of art" well enough to allow any customs officer to decide what duty to impose on a particular import; but it is unlikely that anything can be inferred from the decision other than that the object satisfies the specifications stated in the law. The concept does not enter into a "law" in the scientific sense.

In short, the process of specifying meaning is a part of the process of inquiry itself. In every context of inquiry we begin with terms that are undefined—not indefinables, but terms for which *that* context does not provide a specification. As we proceed, empirical findings are taken up into our conceptual structure by way of new specifications of meaning, and former indications and references in turn become matters of empirical fact. Lenzen's method of "successive definition" is to be found in behavioral science as well as in physics (*81*:19): "Initially, physical quantities are defined in terms of special operations and provide the basis for the empirical discovery of general laws, which may then be transformed into implicit definitions of the physical quantities involved in them. But it then becomes an experimental fact that the measure of a quantity which is obtained by special operations approximately satisfies the definition of the quantity in terms of the general laws."

THE PROGRESS OF SPECIFICATION

What I have tried to sketch here is how such a process of "successive definition" can be understood so as to take account of the openness of meaning of scientific terms. For the closure that strict definition consists in is not a precondition of scientific inquiry but its culmination. To start with we do not know just what we mean by our terms, much as we do not know just what to think about our subject-matter. We can, indeed, begin with precise meanings, as we choose; but so long as we are in ignorance, we cannot choose wisely. It is this ignorance that makes the closure premature. I do not think that Freud was merely rationalizing

the shortcomings of his own semantic patterns in making explicit this
methodological precept (*48*:278 and *20*:65): "We have often heard it
maintained that sciences should be built up on clear and sharply defined
basic concepts. In actual fact no science, not even the most exact, begins
with such definitions. The true beginning of scientific activity consists
rather in describing phenomena and then in proceeding to group, classify
and correlate them. . . . It is only after more searching investigation of
the field in question that we are able to formulate with increased clarity
the scientific concepts underlying it, and progressively so to modify these
concepts that they become widely applicable and at the same time consistent logically. Then, indeed, it may be time to immure them in definitions. The progress of science, however, demands a certain elasticity
even in these definitions." The questions the scientist puts to nature and
the answers she gives have the form of a Platonic dialogue, not an Aristotelian treatise; we do not know just what has been said till we have
done—and then new questions crowd in upon us.

§10. Concepts in Behavioral Science

Among the methodological problems concerning behavioral-science
concepts in general, three have aroused widespread interest: the locus
problem, or what behavioral science is "really" about; the nature of
collective or holistic terms; and the role of "ideal types".

THE LOCUS PROBLEM

The locus problem may be described as that of selecting the ultimate
subject-matter for inquiry in behavioral science, the attribute space for
its description, and the conceptual structure within which hypotheses
about it are to be formulated (Edel, *53*:172–173). Quite a number of
alternatives present themselves, and have been selected in various inquiries: states of consciousness, acts, actions (segments of meaningful
behavior), roles, persons, personalities, interpersonal relations, groups,
classes, institutions, social traits or patterns, societies, and cultures.
With respect to each of these there is the associated problem of the *unit*,
that is, of what constitutes the identity of the element selected. Are legal
institutions, for example, quite distinct from the institution of the state
or part of it, and if so, in what sense of "part"? Are Dr. Jekyll and Mr.

Hyde one person or two? Does the Mason-Dixon line divide two societies or only localize certain social patterns?

Semantic empiricism implies that whatever elements be chosen, the terms by which we refer to them must have their meanings specifiable on the basis of observables. These observables are the same whatever the locus of inquiry. Whether we talk about mental states or muscular movements, about individual human beings or whole cultures, what we say is established by what we can see. This statement is as true for the most "mentalistic" psychology as for the most "materialistic" physics; indeed, the mentalism and materialism belong to the philosophical reconstructions and not to the sciences themselves. The unity of science does not imply that the study of man must ultimately be couched only in terms of molecular motions, and in the meantime in terms of biochemical processes and structures. What unites behavioral science to physical and biological science is not that the "behavior" it studies is physical and biological, but that the study itself is, like the other sciences, an empirical one. And experience is all of a piece, a seamless whole.

I am saying that the locus problem can be solved only within inquiry, and not on the basis of some philosophical premise or other. To the principle of autonomy of inquiry we may add the corollary principle of *autonomy of the conceptual base*. A scientist *may* use whatever concepts he *can* use, whatever ones he finds useful in fact. The restriction to which he is subject is only that what he says be capable of being checked by experience, or alternatively, capable of providing some guidance to action. To be sure, the choice of one conceptual base rather than another may make more readily available the findings of other sciences. A psychiatry with an organic approach is obviously in a more favorable position to exploit the laws and data of neurology and biochemistry than is a psychoanalytic psychiatry. Such unions are always promising, but they can also be premature. For fruitfulness a certain maturity is demanded of both partners: child brides do not found dynasties while they are still children. The choice of locus is subject to the demand of empirical anchorage, but not necessarily to that of physicalistic reduction. The "behavior" in "behavioral science" does not serve to limit the science's choice of conceptual base but only to emphasize its ultimate empiricism.

A special problem as to subject-matter is posed by the view that the study of man is fundamentally a study of "human nature"; can such a concept be made methodologically respectable? To be sure it can, if it is taken as positing an order or regularity in human behavior. As such, it affirms only the possibility of a behavioral science, without prejudging what that science may uncover. "Human nature" implies only a constancy, not a fixity, of behavior, a regularity of pattern which may embrace a great range and plasticity of responses. The trouble is, as A. Edel has pointed out, that the label does not in itself distinguish between "a search for regularities, a search for constructs to systematize such regularities, a search for causal relations, and a formulation of standards for evaluating whatever regularities may be found." The term "human nature", in other words, is functionally ambiguous.

Even more serious is the fact that the term "human nature" is "normatively ambiguous" (§43), being used both for statements of fact and for judgments of value. In particular, the range and plasticity of human responses may be prejudged to be limited in just the ways required to defend and rationalize a status quo. Locke's liberal political philosophy and Hobbes' absolutism both were derived from what they each conceived to be the "nature" of man. In quite the same way the Marxist conception of "classes" is made an instrument of social doctrine rather than of social science. But the fact that a concept is used badly in one way does not of itself imply that the concept cannot be put to good use in another way. That the human being has a nature is no more and no less true than it is of everything else *in* nature.

COLLECTIVE TERMS

More vexing problems concern the status of collective terms, those embodying what have been called "group concepts", "institutional concepts", and the like. These have been of enormous importance in ideological contexts as well as in scientific ones. A variety of philosophies of history, with their associated political doctrines, have been holistic, taking as the locus of historical meaning the fate of classes, races, or nations. Methodological individualism, of course, must be clearly distinguished from the individualism which is counterposed to the collectivist doctrines. Methodology's concern is with the role in science of collective terms, not with the place in society of collectivist institutions or practices. The two may well have a bearing on one another, in ways that Karl Popper has elaborated, but this relation is far from being a matter of strict logic.

From a methodological point of view, the most serious shortcoming of collective terms is the continuous temptation they hold out to commit the sin of reification. Though they are constructs or theoretical terms, they invite treatment as indirect observables, as if they designated individuals of a larger and more elusive kind than those ordinarily encountered in experience. This notion is reinforced by a mystique of "wholes", according to which these are "more than the sum of their parts", the parts being individuals and the whole the entity presumed to be labeled by the collective term. In his penetrating criticism of such views Nagel has listed a number of very different sorts of wholes and parts: an object or event and its spatiotemporal parts; a class and its members; a class and its subclasses; a resultant and its components (as with mechanical forces, or different sources of illumination); a series and its stages (like a melody and its constituent notes or phrases); a process and its phases; an object and its properties; a system and its dynamic dependents. The point is that any of these, and others besides, can well be involved in the relation between a construct and the materials for the logical construction, or between a theoretical term and its observational indications or references. For each of them the term "sum" takes on a distinctive meaning; whether the sum does nor does not measure up to the whole is a matter of how its meaning has been specified. A resultant force *is* the (vector) sum of its components, and a class *is* the (logical) sum of its subclasses. On the other hand, there is nothing remarkable in the fact that a whole may have properties that its parts do not even partly exhibit: the sum of two odd numbers is even, but it would be odd indeed to say that each of the numbers making up the sum is half-way even.

I believe the root confusion is that between indication and reduction. If methodological individualism requires that collective terms be strictly definable by reference only to individuals, the requirement is false as a matter of fact, and at best, highly questionable as a matter of principle. What is true is that individuals and their properties and relations are the indications and references for collective terms; there is no other way by which meanings can be empirically specified. But if the collective term is a theoretical one, or even a construct with open meaning, it cannot be strictly defined. It is in this sense, fundamentally, that the "whole" is not reducible to "the sum of its parts". But this nonequivalence does not imply that there is any other way to understand or to verify statements about "wholes" than by observations on "parts".

Even this conclusion, however, must be qualified. Once we recognize that essentially collective terms (that is, those not definable by individuals) are not necessarily without scientific status or function, we can see also that in any given context their meanings might be specifiable with the help of other collective terms. A statement about a political party, for example, does not necessarily have to be interpreted as a reference to the individual members of the party; it might well be understood and verified in terms of cliques and coalitions, power structures, ideologies, and such like. Methodological individualism is defensible only as the insistence that sooner or later we are committed to observations on individuals if we are to give our statements empirical anchorage. Beyond that, it does not set limits on admissible modes of conceptualization.

We introduce collective terms when we find it useful to deal with dispositional properties of whole sets of individuals (*51*:97–98). A group is organized, for example, when its members act jointly to some end (they cooperate), and when shared expectations of one another and mutual identifications give them solidarity as a group. If we are interested in the formation and dissolution of groups, we might well concern ourselves with the individual members. But we might also wish to study group behavior, and make the organization itself the locus of inquiry. It may be conceptualized in a construct, as just sketched above, or introduced as a theoretical term, as in Michels' classic study of political parties. In either case, observations on individuals must ultimately be made; the actual conduct of inquiry, however, concerns itself, not with ultimates, but with the next steps to be taken.

IDEAL TYPES

This same instrumentalist approach throws light, I believe, on the status of other special sorts of concepts, and in particular, Weber's *ideal type* or what Merton calls a "paradigm". An ideal type does not function as an observational term or even an indirect observable; the fact, therefore, that there is nothing in the world corresponding to it does not of itself rob such a concept of scientific usefulness. (The dangers involved in idealizations will be discussed in §32.) "If one perceives," says Weber (*135*:106), "that concepts are primarily analytical instruments for the intellectual mastery of empirical data and can be only that, the fact that [certain] concepts are necessarily ideal types will not cause him to desist from constructing them." Whatever their mode of empirical anchorage, concepts do not simply mirror reality, but perform a service in our dealings with it. And some of these services (those connected with the role of theories) are best performed by those concepts that are most tenuously and indirectly connected with experience.

An ideal type may be a construct like the limiting concepts mentioned earlier. It specifies something "with which the real situation or action is compared and surveyed for the explication of certain of its significant components" (135:93). As such, it is a particularly useful device for dealing with internal vagueness. No state in history has been wholly, fully, "truly" a democracy, just as no male has exhibited all the traits of masculinity in superlative degree—Athens did not extend suffrage to slaves, and even Achilles was given to tears. But we can conceptualize perfect specimens of any species. They are those whose profile has a weight of 1 as indicator and as reference for the term whose meaning in being specified. It is *really* a such-and-such though it has no place in reality. Other reconstructions are also possible. Hempel, for example, has proposed one in terms of the logic of relations. Instead of setting up a typology of classes we might order our elements; an ideal type is a terminus of such an ordering.

The most important function of an ideal type, however, as Hempel also points out, is as a theoretical term. Weber makes the mistake, I believe, of concluding that, because an ideal type refers to an individual, albeit a fictitious one, it serves only in the study of individuals rather than of the generic kinds with which theory is concerned. While recognizing that the ideal type "offers guidance to the construction of hypotheses" (135:90), he states that "the goal of ideal-typical concept-construction is always to make clearly explicit not the class or average character but rather the unique individual character of cultural phenomena" (135:101). The question of whether and how behavioral science is concerned with the unique individual must be postponed (§14). But no concept, ideal or otherwise, is lacking in general significance. Generality is a trait of all meaning. The individual case is but a resting place for the movement of thought; meaning is the trace in verbal behavior left by the movement itself.

Chapter III

_____

LAWS

§11   Functions of Laws
§12   The Content of Laws
§13   Types of Laws
§14   Laws in Behavioral Science

§11. Functions of Laws

   Generalizations of a number of different kinds play a part in the process of science, and perform a number of correspondingly different functions. The outcome of every successful inquiry is usually thought of as being either particular or general; if particular, it is said to have established a "fact", and if general, a "law". Whatever other generalizations are formulated in the course of inquiry are thought of as being only laws in the making. A hypothesis, for instance, is conceived to differ from a law only in not yet having been sufficiently well established. This view of laws is rather like the one of children a generation or two ago: that they are only small adults, pre-matures as it were. Such a view, it has been found, fails to do justice to children, not only as objects of love but also as objects of investigation. The psychology of maturation and learning suffers because the processes have been telescoped into obscurity, and as a result the adult is also poorly understood. Correspondingly, an appreciation of the nature and significance of scientific laws requires some attention to the research settings out of which they emerge and to the manner of their emergence.

84

From an instrumentalist standpoint, various kinds of generalizations can be distinguished according to the work they do in inquiry.

IDENTIFICATIONS

The most basic of all generalizations—omnipresent in inquiry and indispensable to it—are *identifications*, the marking of enduring or recurrent constituents in the flow of experience. Knowledge begins with discrimination of differences, but every difference presupposes an identity. A differential response becomes a cognition—as Aristotle, Kant, and Peirce all emphasized—in so far as a habit of response is engendered, which confers on the stimulus a meaning, embodied at last in a symbol. There is no cognition without recognition, that is, without a constancy of some kind by which what is being known is recognized for what it is. "Recognition is the source of all our natural knowledge," Whitehead has said. "The whole scientific theory is nothing else than an attempt to systematize our knowledge of the circumstances in which such recognitions will occur." This is to say that science is a search for constancies, for invariants. It is the enterprise of making those identifications in experience which prove to be most significant for the control or appreciation of the experience yet to come. The basic scientific question is, "What the devil is going on around here?"

Every answer to this question is inescapably a generalization, in which the particularity of the goings-on is subsumed under a universalized "what", universal because it is not necessarily restricted in application to this particular, or to any fixed set of particulars. It is this act of predication which underlies the logic of the copula. Every such act rests on an identification, recognizing a sameness beneath differences in space, time, or appearance—a One in the Many. It is for just this reason, indeed, that what is given for knowledge is called an "appearance", for in itself it is as real as ever was. The reality we seek is so called only as the terminus of the cognitive process. Appearance is what is to be known; reality, what it is known as. Identification is the seed from which knowledge grows, its embryonic form; to conceive something is indeed to be impregnated with knowledge—if all goes well. Every scientist is first of all a poet, giving to airy nothing a local habitation and a name.

The role of identifications undercuts the supposed difference between "idiographic" and "nomothetic" sciences: those which aim at knowledge of the individual and those which aim at knowledge of general laws (§14). For what is taken to be individual is already a product of generalization. Identifications link particulars given here and now with what has been or might yet be given, in accord with general laws. Such laws play a part in the grouping of a variety of givens in such a way that they are all appearances "of" one and the same individual, and in providing the boundaries that set different individuals off from one another. Individuals do not present themselves already labeled as such in the flow of experience: the stream of consciousness lacks punctuation. Individuals are constructed; in perceiving them we are making them out. Conception informs the perceptual process from the beginning. Even bare spatio-temporal identifications ("Italy in the fifteenth century", or "the person 'inside' that skin") are heavily committed to implicit theories; and these become explicitly involved as our conception of the individual becomes either material or instrument of inquiry. *That* place and time belongs to "the Renaissance", *that* body is the locus of roles that span continents. What we identify as an individual must be believed to be seen.

SUPPOSITIONS AND PRESUPPOSITIONS

A second function of generalization in inquiry is as *presuppositions*. Not everything is or can be problematic all at once. Descartes' "methodological skepticism" is a reconstruction of knowledge hopelessly at variance with logic-in-use. Nowhere in science do we start from scratch. There is only one place from which we ever can start, Peirce said, and that is from where we are. This proposition is not a matter of "mere" psychological fact; it is essential to the logic of inquiry. Every inquiry is into a problematic situation set over against what Mead called "the world that is there". Where all is problematic, nothing is left with which a problem can even be formulated, let alone be solved. Science is no miraculous creation out of nothing, no spontaneous generation of knowledge from ignorance. When presuppositions are denied logical status, we remain mired in skepticism: epistemic bootstraps give no more leverage than any other. The task is not to move from wholesale ignorance to knowledge, but from less knowledge to more, from knowledge of some things to knowledge of others, from the vague and uncertain to what is clear and warranted. We presuppose, in every inquiry, not only a set of data but also a set of generalizations, both about our materials and about the instruments by which they are to be transformed in the cognitive enterprise. We draw our presuppositions from earlier inquiries, from other sciences, from everyday knowledge, from the experiences of conflict and frustration which motivated our inquiry, from habit and tradition, from who knows where. Methodology does not rob us of our footing; it enjoins us, rather, to look to it.

Presuppositions are brought to the problematic situation. There are, besides, beliefs arising in and pertaining to the situation, as inquiry gets under way. We may call them *suppositions*. They are the beliefs that make the situation problematic, either because we cannot clearly articulate them in the conceptual frame already available, or because they are in conflict with one another, or because they contradict some of our presuppositions. It is the suppositions that are likely to be modified as a problem is carried to its solution. Changes in presuppositions are much rarer, and usually mark what we call a "scientific revolution". When Freud became interested in the interpretation of dreams, he presupposed certain generalizations about the nature of sleep, consciousness, and related phenomena. In addition, he made suppositions about dreams themselves, what they are about and when they occur. In the outcome, some presuppositions were rejected so as to allow for unconscious meanings and purposes, and some suppositions were refined so as to differentiate between "manifest" and "latent" dream contents.

RESOURCES

The work of solving a problem requires *resources*, what Dewey has called "material means" and "procedural means". The resources include what are loosely called the "data" of the problem—loosely, in that they comprise knowledge not only of particular matters of fact but also of the general patterns of interaction and change among the particulars. Whatever we know about processes of rational choice, for example, may be among the resources for the solution of a problem in economics. Resources include also techniques of inquiry, the state of the art of dealing with problems of the kind in question. Mathematical theorems, laws of the workings of instruments of observation or of measurement, principles governing the processing of information of the relevant sort—all are in-

cluded among the resources. Note that what works in one context as a
resource may in another context be among the presuppositions or suppositions. The difference here as elsewhere depends on what is being
done with "what works", not on some distinguishing mark to be found
within it. Science grows by what it feeds on, but its food is of no substance different from its own.

ASSUMPTIONS AND HYPOTHESES

To carry forward an inquiry we may formulate *working hypotheses*.
These serve to guide and organize the investigation, providing us something to go on with. The working hypothesis is not a guess at the riddle,
a hunch as to what the answer might be. It is an idea, not about the outcome of inquiry but about the next steps that may be worth taking.
The working hypothesis formulates a belief pertaining to the course
of inquiry but not necessarily pertaining to its ultimate destination.
We may also make certain *assumptions*, propositions not put forward as
assertions at all, whether about the solution or about the problematic
situation itself. Instead, an assumption is affirmed only so as to test its
consequences (when conjoined with certain suppositions and resources).
(For the difference between an assertion and an affirmation, see 67.)
Often what are called "models" consist largely of assumptions in this
sense (§§30 and 31). When the Famous Detective undertakes to check
the alibis of everyone who was at the fateful dinner party, even though
he knows that the murderer may very well not have been among the
guests, he is being guided by a working hypothesis. And in checking an
alibi he may assume that the murderer had a helicopter waiting, not because the Famous Detective thinks it in the least likely or even possible,
but in order to establish a minimum for the time needed to get to the
scene of the crime.

After the inquiry is well under way a conjecture or surmise may
emerge as to the solution to the problem. We call it the *test hypothesis*.
This is what we think may very well be the truth of the matter, and we
then organize the inquiry so as to facilitate the decision on whether the
conjecture is correct. Colloquially, a test hypothesis is often called a
"theory" about what is going on (the Famous Detective, as well as the
reader, knows at once that "the theory of the police" is a mistaken one).
Like "theory", the word "hypothesis" is used in a variety of ways—

for a working hypothesis, an assumption, or a supposition, as well as in the sense given it here. When the test hypothesis has been established, it is said to constitute a *fact* or a *law*, according to whether it is particular or general in content. We quite literally reach a conclusion: the inquiry, and the process of deliberation as to its outcome, have been concluded.

FACTS AND LAWS

What I have been getting at is that laws do not enter into inquiry only as conclusions. They are involved throughout the whole process, in all the various ways just distinguished, and in others as well. They may serve as starting points for inquiry just as well as they may mark its termination. Scriven has called attention to the use of laws, not as rules under which particular matters of fact are to be subsumed, but as standpoints from which to survey events for the nonconformists, the precious exceptions (41:313). Laws are not generalizations at which we arrive after we have established the facts: they play a part in the process of determining what the facts are. Indeed, we may without a vicious circularity accept some datum as a fact because it conforms to the very law for which it counts as another confirming instance, and reject an allegation of fact because it is already excluded by law.

Too often when we say of a hypothesis that it is "heuristic" we do so with the intent of bestowing a kind of consolation prize. The attribution does not specify just what function in inquiry the hypothesis has, but states only that it has one; and it fails to appreciate how intimately involved this function is with our concluding that the hypothesis is true. Some philosophers, on the other hand, have been so impressed with the functional import of general statements as to hold that this exhausts their significance, and that they lack the reference to matters of fact that particular or singular propositions have. This view was that of Wittgenstein and Schlick, for instance, who held that general statements do not formulate propositions but rather lay down rules for the construction of propositions. The current view is that laws *can* be so reconstructed, but that, conversely, a reconstructed logic in which laws appear as rules "can always be replaced by one which includes them instead as scientific statements" (Hempel, in 41:112). Ryle has spoken of generalizations as "inference-tickets", and Toulmin in the same vein calls attention to derivations in science made *in accord with* a generalization, rather than *from* a generalization as premise. There is no doubt, it seems to me, that generalizations do sometimes function in this way as rules—when they are among our presuppositions and resources, for instance. But it seems to me equally clear that they sometimes function precisely as premises— as assumptions, for instance, or as test hypotheses. I believe that the concept of scientific law cannot be understood save functionally, but by the same token I believe that no one function can suffice.

The classical positivist view was that laws are formulated basically only to facilitate the memory and anticipation of particular matters of fact, which are the only realities. Thus Mach (in *140*:446–451) calls laws "compendious rules", and speaks of the "economical office" of science, which he regards as consisting of "the completest possible presentment of facts with the least possible expenditure of thought". In the same way, Karl Pearson (*106*:73–77) regards scientific law as existing "only when formulated by man", because it is nothing other than "a resume in mental shorthand, which replaces for us a lengthy description of the sequences among our sense-impressions". This view has the merit of directing attention to the ways in which laws are used in science, rather than assuming out of hand that they mirror universal patterns in just the way in which particular propositions correspond to specific matters of fact. But there are several shortcomings in the positivist position.

For one thing, reference to mental shorthand and economy of thought does not distinguish the role of laws from that of a notation (§6). It is true that a notation may presuppose laws which justify and explain its usefulness, as the law of definite proportions and the law of conservation of matter underlying the usual notation for chemical equations. But the notation is not to be confused with its own presuppositions. Laws do make for economy of thought, but they do other things as well, which notations, however compendious, cannot do. And the characterization of law as a description, whether economical or not, overlooks the point made by both Braithwaite (*9*:348) and Nagel (*103*:119), that in a strict sense the law may not be describing anything at all. For a law is by no means restricted in its formulation to observational terms; it "describes" the future as well as the past and present, if we can use the term in this way; and because it is conditional in form it "describes" something that may even never take place.

What then distinguishes laws from other scientific statements? In recent years the attempt to answer this question has focused on the difference between so-called *nomic* (or "nomological") generalizations and those which are said to formulate only "accidental" universals. This distinction emerged out of a consideration of counterfactual conditionals: statements about what would be the case if something else were true, though as a matter of fact it is false. "If wishes were horses . . . " tells us that beggars would ride if they could, and reminds us that in fact they can't. But if we begin by assuming that we already know to be false, what keeps us from arriving at any conclusion we choose? When the "if—then" is reconstructed in the usual way (by what is called "material implication"), "If p then q" is equivalent to "Either p is not true, or else q is true"; and when we know p to be false, we can safely make the assertion using any q whatever. If wishes *were* horses, beggars might well be content to stay where they are. Reichenbach has attempted a quite different reconstruction of the "if—then", defining what he calls a "connective operation" which does not depend merely on the falsity of p or the truth of q. Many philosophers, like Nelson Goodman, regard counterfactuals as justified when they are supported by nomic universals. A proposition like "If this match, which I have just broken, had been scratched, it would have lit" is true, not because its condition is false, but because scratched matches do light. And that generalization does not merely happen to be true; it expresses a law.

Not every true universal statement is a nomic generalization. The following requirements have been proposed by Nagel, Hempel, and others.

First, the generalization must be truly universal, unrestricted as to space and time. It must formulate what is always and everywhere the case, provided only that the appropriate conditions are satisfied. That the Japanese regard the back of the neck as an erogenous zone may be a matter of fact, but it is not a law; that the neck will be so regarded in any culture in which the infant is carried on its mother's back, and facing it, might be one—so far as this requirement is concerned.

Second, the generalization must not be vacuously true, that is, true only because nothing satisfies the conditions stated—unless the generalization in question is derivable from other laws. The statement "every female president of the United States balances the budget" is true: there are no contrary instances. But it would be a law of political economy only if it could be deduced from other laws concerning the budgetary behavior of women in a democracy.

Third, the evidence for the generalization must not coincide with the range of its application: this range must not be known to be closed. In the 1920–1960 presidential elections, the big-party candidate with the longest name was elected; but we cannot say that this statement in any way reflects a law so long as our reasons for asserting it are limited to our knowledge of the particular matters of fact to which it refers. We would need other evidence concerning the effect of names on an electorate. This example violates the first condition as well; but consider the generalization that every planet in the solar system has a diameter of either less than ten thousand or more than twenty thousand miles. Here there is no restriction to a particular place or time, at least not explicitly. But the generalization only happens to be true, so far as concerns the usual grounds for asserting it, to wit, a knowledge of the diameter of each of the planets. It may, however, reflect a law, according to certain theories, as yet not established, of the origin of the solar system.

Fourth, a nomic generalization must be derivable from other laws, that is, must play a part in a scientific theory. Otherwise we obtain what might be called an "empirical generalization" rather than a law (§13). Generalizations about seasonal or geographical variations in the color of animal skins, or about the difference between the ventral and dorsal shading of fish, remain "merely empirical" in this sense, until we can relate them to the role of protective coloration in natural selection.

Finally, to be a law a nomic generalization must, of course, be true. Statements satisfying all conditions but this one have been called by Goodman "lawlike". A law is a true lawlike statement.

The usual treatment of the problem is occupied with the form of scientific statements, and with their content as it is reflected in their form, by way of the occurrence of certain operators (like "all" and "some"), proper names, predicates of various types, and so on. Most notably, Hempel and Oppenheim have attacked the problem as referred to a formalized language rather than to the discourse of actual inquiry. None of these sorts of efforts has as yet met with general acceptance. Whatever be true in the arts of design, I believe that in the scientific enterprise form follows function, and that the distinction between laws and other statements is to be understood primarily in terms of the distinctive role that they perform in inquiry. Derivatively, we might then identify forms which are likely to mark the statements called upon to perform those roles, as the villain in a Western is recognizable by his unshaven jowls, though it is not the heavy growth that makes him the villain.

In this perspective, what I take to be most significant is the derivation of laws from a theory, or from other laws, and their capacity, in turn, to explain other laws. The term "lawlike", Braithwaite has said (9:302), "may be thought of as an honorific epithet which is employed as a mark of origin . . . [to] indicate that there are other reasons for believing it than evidence of its instances alone." A similar view has also been expressed by Scriven (in 42:100), a view which "absolutely precludes the possibility of a purely syntactic analysis of law which would distinguish it from accidental universals. The difference lies in the quality of evidence behind them . . . " And note that "quality" of evidence is by no means to be identified with its amount or weight. I would add, however, that what can be done with the law in further inquiry is as significant as what has been done in past inquiry to arrive at it. But we know what *can* be done only retrospectively, after we have in fact done it successfully, and so we are tempted to think of its functions by way of its origins. Whether our approach is functional or genetic does not matter so much. What *is* important, in my opinion, is that we view laws against the background of the process of inquiry, rather than see in them the ligaments which bind together an otherwise disjointed world.

The temptation is to suppose that what differentiates laws from other statements is what they affirm, as though laws are statements that truly declare the existence of a nomic connection, or causal relation. But the unchanging pattern of events that a law brings before us is nothing other than the "constancy of evidential function", to use Dewey's phrase. Such a constancy is easily confused with an "existential recurrence", and we imagine that a law tells us that identically the same thing appears over and over again, reaching across gaps of time and space to hold events together in an intelligible order. But if we are indeed talking about events, it is tautological that they cannot recur; and if we are talking about generalized conjunctions of abstract characters, it makes no sense to speak of them as occurring in sequences, regular or not. "Laws, while they are necessary means of determining sequences in given singular cases, are not of sequential contents, and the singular events determined by them are not recurrent" (28:454).

Generalizations are of two sorts: generic propositions, with existential

reference, ascribing traits to discriminated kinds; and universal propositions, of an abstract if—then form, specifying the characters or operations which can be relied upon in making the discriminations. The former
record what we happen to have found true; the latter formulate our convictions as to what must be true, what can be counted on to lead us to
the truth. It is these that we call laws, and not merely statements of
known constant conjunction or succession. The mistake lies in "taking
the function of the universal proposition as if it were part of the structural content of the existential propositions" (*28*:444). A law is a statement that successfully plays the part of a law in the scientific enterprise:
handsome is as handsome does.

§12. The Content of Laws

The usual form in which laws are reconstructed for methodological
discussion is: "For all x's, if x has the property f then it has the property
g," or more colloquially, "All f's are g's." Often the law concerns not
a single x at a time but a double or even an n-tuple x, and correspondingly
the f or g may stand for a relation, or for a whole conjunction of properties and relations. Thus, the law of gravitation states that, for all bodies
x_1 and x_2, if x_1 has a mass of m_1 and x_2 has a mass of m_2 and x_1 and x_2
are separated by a distance d, then they will be acted on by a force of
constant proportionality to $m_1 m_2 / d^2$.

FIELD, RANGE, SCOPE, AND CONTENT

Now the content of a law depends first of all on the set of x's to be
regarded as relevant, the elements whose names may appropriately
replace the variable x. We may call this set the *field* of the law, or, as it
is often known, the "universe of discourse". The determination of the
field presupposes (or constitutes) a solution to what was called in §10
the locus problem. The laws are said to be "about" people or actions or
institutions or whatever, according to the field providing the proper interpretation for the universal variable. The property f (or set of properties) specifies in another sense what the law is "about": the law concerns all the x's only formally, while in fact it says something only about
those x's which are f's. We may say that f specifies the *range* of the law;
it presupposes (or constitutes) a determination of the attribute space in

which the elements of the field are located. The *g*, or the set of all those properties or relations which may meaningfully occur in its place, we may say defines the *scope* of the law. This scope may coincide with the attribute space, as is likely to be the case for empirical generalizations; or it may embrace all or part of the conceptual frame, as will be true for theoretical laws. To explicate the content of a law we must make clear its field, range, and scope—all three.

In the course of doing so, consideration of the context of occurrence of the law is inescapable: *content depends on context*. Reconstructed logic, to fulfill its own aims, attempts to make everything fully explicit, but the openness of scientific concepts foredooms this attempt to failure. The logic-in-use depends on context to provide sufficient closure for the particular use of the law then and there to be made. In reconstructed logic a formulation becomes fully specified only when we insert an "other things being equal" clause to complete the closure. In that case, however, we are impelled to interpret the result, not as the formulation of a law, but rather as a "schema" for constructing laws, a directive for filling in the "other things" that must be "equal" in order for us to obtain a true proposition. I should prefer to say, however, that all laws are themselves nothing other than such schemata or directives, so long as they are considered in abstraction from their context. The uncertainty in the qualifying clause is the price we pay for the formal closure achieved by making the abstraction.

It is especially for the proper interpretation of the range of the law that context is important, though context enters into the determination of the field and scope as well. The range must include all the conditions that are necessary to the truth of the law, but never are all of them made fully explicit. We speak of a law in a given context as "universally" true when it holds under the conditions which obtain in that sort of context. An expert is someone who knows what sort of context it is. There was once a proof sketched in the *Journal of Symbolic Logic*, in which the author acknowledged certain gaps, adding that those who were aware of the gaps would know how to fill them in. Whatever the propriety of this tactic in the formal disciplines, in empirical science it is wholly proper, and indeed, inescapable. When the student first learning the gas laws asks why a gas doesn't completely disappear at a sufficiently low temperature, thus violating the law of conservation of mass, it is misleading to inform him only that "we can't get to absolute zero". It is more appropriate to make clear to him that the gas laws no longer apply, to the same degree of approximation, in the neighborhood of absolute zero. For that matter, the law of conservation of mass itself is inapplicable in the context of nuclear reactions, or if the velocity of expansion of the gas approaches that of light. Subatomic or astronomical contexts call for new interpretations of old laws that have a macroscopic range, or perhaps for new laws altogether. We may say that every law has associated with it a set of "boundary conditions", as they are often called (*87*:50–55), which restrict its range, and perhaps also its field or scope.

EXCEPTIONS AND QUASI LAWS

Even under the appropriate conditions, so far as these are known at any given time, every law will almost surely have some exceptions. These may be merely apparent, either because not all the necessary conditions were in fact fulfilled (such as a vacuum for the law governing falling bodies), or because of errors of observation (the moon really does fall towards the earth, though it seems to rise). But when the exceptions are genuine, the classical view is that in that case the so-called "law" is a spurious one: "A single absolute conflict between fact and hypothesis is fatal to the hypothesis" (*64*:516). We might say instead, however, that a scientific law does not have the form of a strict universal, that this is only an idealized reconstruction. A universal proposition, such as might occur in pure mathematics, is indeed falsified by even one contrary instance. But in empirical science laws are enunciated and used even though contrary instances are known to be possible, or indeed, when some contrary instances are even known to occur. "The most interesting fact about laws of nature is that they are virtually all known to be in error," Scriven has remarked, in a paper with the informative title, "The Key Property of Physical Laws—Inaccuracy" (*42*:91).

Some methodologists apply a special label—for instance, "quasi laws"—to generalizations known to have exceptions. These generalizations function as laws when the exceptions are regarded as subject to being explained away: special though as yet unknown conditions obtain, or the law is fulfilled but its effect is masked by the simultaneous working of other laws. Here, "the exception proves the rule" but only in the sense that it tests the rule. The exception raises a presumption *against* the generalization, but we may continue to think of the latter as a law, and use it as such, in the expectation that, if only we knew more about what was going on, we could account for the exception without abandoning the generalization. In behavioral science our knowledge is virtually all in the form of quasi laws, at best. But if we cannot, in the present state of our knowledge, explain the exceptions, it surely does not follow that we know nothing at all, or even that what we know is nothing like a law but no more than a collection of facts about many individual cases.

TREND, TENDENCY, AND APPROXIMATION

When, having in mind some traits in which we are interested, we examine a set of cases, we find that the traits appear in certain proportions of the cases: we have acquired knowledge of a *distribution*. If we regard the cases examined as a sample from a larger or indefinite population, we may wish to attribute the same distribution to the population as a whole, and so speak of it as a *trend*. The trend statement does not provide any explanation of the distribution, but only affirms its continuation; it is a "descriptive generalization" (§13). The trends spoken of by commentators on election night are, be it noted, trends in tabulation not in voting. They are explained by voting trends (the up-state Republican majorities which come in late, for example), but the voting pattern itself is not explained by the trend—it is only restated.

We may, however, speak of "tendencies" rather than trends; generalizations of this kind have been called *tendency laws*. To say that something tends to happen is very different from saying that it usually happens, or that it happens in some other definite proportion of cases. It is, rather, to affirm that, when the cases are appropriately selected, but only then, it will invariably happen, or at least almost always. A "tendency" is the label for the implied explanation of a trend. That rural voters "tend" to vote Republican does not imply that in fact they all do so, or even that a majority of them do, but that they *would* do so were it not for the effect of other (unspecified) determinants of voting behavior. Bodies tend to fall in a way given by the equation $s = \frac{1}{2}gt^2$; but near the surface of the earth they never *do* fall in this way, because of the resistance of the air. We may say that the equation is part of a tendency law if the full formulation of the law makes no mention of air resistance. A tendency law is one put forward as a candidate for a law in the strictest sense, to be achieved when the countervailing forces have been identified and taken into account.

It follows that the scientific value of a tendency law depends on how effectively it serves to stimulate and guide the search for these other determinants or forces. In itself, it is only a promissory note, circulating freely in the world of science only so long as public confidence can be maintained that it will eventually be redeemed for something like its face value. The clause "other things being equal" is not the redemption but another phrasing of the promise (*51*:141–144). Whether in this form or in a form making explicit reference to a tendency, a tendency law alone tells us even less than a trend statement does, for we cannot infer from such a law what distribution actually to expect, as the trend statement allows us to do. Too often behavioral science has sought to enrich itself by printing its own currency, and has suffered from the resulting inflation. A plethora of laws are promulgated, but they are somehow inapplicable to concrete instances of human behavior: it seems that people seldom do what we are told they have a tendency to do.

Yet, increasing the flow of money may contribute to economic growth. Tendency laws may be important if they are viewed as working hypotheses rather than as conclusions already established. The value of such a law is heightened, as Braithwaite (*9*:365–366) has pointed out, when it is one of a "system of tendency statements all subject to the same, though unknown, condition. Observations which are *prima facie* contrary to the lowest-level tendency statements in such a system can then be used to give information about the unknown condition to which the whole system is subject." In their joint application the tendency statements are able to make explicit what for each of them singly remained wholly implicit. That slips of the tongue are intentional, that we dream about things which we wish were true, or that children have very strong attachments to the parent of the opposite sex are, in themselves, tendency statements with innumerable quite apparent exceptions. But in the whole system of propositions that constitutes psychoanalytic theory these isolated statements are given a much fuller meaning—in terms of such conditions as are involved in the concepts of latent content, repression, unconscious wish, and the like—which add enormously to determining the range of application of the statements. The monetary metaphor still applies: the richer and more productive the economy, the more confidence attaches to its currency. But this statement itself is only a tendency statement.

Yet I believe that it expresses an important truth, not only for behavioral science but for other sciences as well. The content of a scientific law depends not only on the context of its use but also on the whole system of laws used together with it. Some time ago Pierre Duhem elaborated the view that a law's "application to concrete reality requires that a whole group of laws be known and accepted" (in 27:185). In other words, laws have systemic meaning just as do concepts; just as concepts implicate laws, so do laws implicate theories. From the standpoint of a purely philosophical theory of knowledge, this view may be traced to Kant, with his insistence on the interplay in every act of cognition of the faculties of intuition, understanding, and reason. From the standpoint of methodology, it is a matter of how laws are brought to a closer approximation to reality or, some might prefer to say, it is a matter of how general statements are brought closer to the status of laws.

This bringing-close may be done in either of two ways. One, the *epistemic approximation*, directly affects the truth of the statement, what is now affirmed being more nearly true than previously. For instance, a law attributing a numerical value to some magnitude assigns one closer to the "true value"; or a qualitative statement ascribes a property closer (on some implicit scale) to the actual one, as when it more correctly states that something is pink rather than red. The other may be called a *semantic approximation*, affecting directly the meaning of the statement, and only thereby its truth. Of course, epistemic approximations also replace one meaning by another: "2.3" means something different from "2", as "pink" means something different from "red". But what I am calling semantic approximation is not so much replacing one meaning by another as it is bringing the "same" meaning towards closure. What was implicit and even to some degree indeterminate becomes explicitly specified. For instance, expressions like "normally", "other things being equal", "under usual conditions"—and their tacit equivalents—are replaced by specifications of just what is to be included in the antecedent of the law. The growth of knowledge is marked by the semantic approximation as much as by the epistemic. The situation is not just that as knowledge grows what we say is more nearly true, or that there is a larger proportion of truths among our assertions; it is also that what we are asserting becomes clearer, more definite. For any given law, this change is brought about by the growth of the contexts of its application, and more especially by the bearings on the one law of all the other laws to which it can be related by some theory.

MEANING

Every law, if it is to play any part in the scientific enterprise, must have a meaning sufficiently closed to subject the law to some sort of empirical control. This is not to say that it must be capable of being directly established or refuted by observations, but only that the decision to accept it or not, to make use of it or not in subsequent inquiry, must be capable of being affected by empirical findings. On this methodological point it is even easier to err than in making the substantive decision itself. A tautological statement, one might suppose, has a completely open meaning; it tells us nothing whatever about the world for it remains true no matter what is the case in the world. But more strictly, its meaning is closed just in so far as the statement quite clearly *is* a tautology, so that good use can be made of it in that capacity. The trouble is that whether it is a tautology is often far from clear.

The psychoanalytic doctrine of reaction formation seems to some to secure the theory against falsification by making it tautologous. Boys are sexually attracted to their mothers; if they express such an attraction, good; if on the contrary they behave as though their mothers were detestable, this conduct only indicates a reaction against their own forbidden desires, and again the claim holds good; so it is true no matter what. But *is* this "no matter what" being claimed? There is, after all, an alternative to both love and hate, a large range of conduct which would falsify the thesis; in the language of the schools, contraries have been mistaken for contradictories. That everything is either black or not black is necessarily true; but that everything is either black or white is easily falsified, and so formulates an empirical content. On the other hand, suppose the view that all dreams express the fulfillment of a wish is so construed that, when no other wish can be disclosed, the dream analyst concludes that the dreamer wished to prove the analyst mistaken; then what possible dream *can* in fact show him to be mistaken? Plainly, how dream wishes are to be identified requires fuller specification, not only to decide whether the view in question is correct, but even to decide just what the view is: a semantic approximation is necessary to achieve an epistemic one. Whether sufficient closure is provided elsewhere in the psychoanalytic theory of dreams is another and more complicated question.

But the concept of tautology itself belongs, after all, to a reconstructed logic; the statements to which the concept is applied may, in the logic-in-use, still be sensitive to empirical findings. That every day it either rains or doesn't rain remains true in a land of perpetual drizzle and fog; but it is not as useful a tautology there as in other climes. Systems of classifications are a matter of convention, but (as was pointed out in §9), they are not therefore arbitrary. The same holds true of those laws which might be said to be a matter of convention—in connection with notations, for example, or with scales of measurement (see §22). Indeed, we may say that there is a conventional element in every law, for a law is given to us, not as an abstract meaning, but in a specific formulation or set of formulations. These formulations constitute a selection from an open set of alternatives, all equivalent up to the degree of closure of the law in question. Which selection is made is a matter of convention. Yet the selection may well result from empirical considerations; and, of course, that the selection is to be made from a particular set of alternatives is also an empirical matter. Whether Euclidean or some other geometry is to be used in the characterization of physical space may well be conventional, as Poincaré tirelessly argued. But a choice here commits us to other decisions in the measurement of time intervals and of forces which we may be reluctant to make; and the commitment is thrust upon us by empirical findings.

What I have been getting at is that most laws, if not all, can be regarded both as empirical and as conventional. A reconstruction which fixes the status of a particular law either as a factual statement on the one hand or as a definition or rule on the other is likely to betray a premature closure. It must be recognized, moreover, that it is the function of the law which is decisive here, not its form. With regard to the question so often discussed whether Newton's laws are definitions or not, Toulmin (*133*:89–90) points out incisively: "The laws themselves do not do anything; it is we who do things with them, and there are several different kinds of things we can do with their help. . . . It is not that the laws have an ambiguous or hazy status: it is that physicists are versatile in the applications to which they put the laws." That the laws are capable of this range of uses is just what I have called functional ambiguity; and though meanings are always open to some degree, the status of the laws is "hazy" only in the sense that they do not fit into the molds of a reconstructed logic which insists that they be used only as conventions or only as allegations of fact.

Since Hume, empiricists have supposed all statements to be classifiable as either "analytic" or "synthetic" according to whether they formulated relations of ideas or matters of fact, and so are certifiable or not merely by reference to the rules of language. In recent years Quine and other logicians have raised serious doubts whether "analytic" and related concepts can be given exact definitions: such concepts seem to be subject to an ineradicable external vagueness. But in speaking of laws as being both empirical and conventional, I am less concerned with the openness of the predicate applied to them than with the uncertainty in the subject of the predicate. Saying flatly that a certain law is synthetic (or, equally, analytic) obscures the fact that every utterance of the law has its own use, that not all these uses are necessarily alike in their dependence on fact, and hence that the construction of a single usage for the proposition may fail to do justice to the meanings actually at work.

Specifically, it seems to be a pattern in science that as inquiry proceeds, and especially as theory is developed, the empirical analysis of a phenomenon is transformed into the structure of a meaning. What at an earlier stage of knowledge was seen as a contingent matter of fact about our subject becomes a necessary constituent of our conceptualization of the subject. We first learn that acids yield a high concentration of hydrogen ions, then come to think of the chemistry in such a way that "yielding a high concentration of hydrogen ions" is what "acid" means. I believe that this pattern is what is sound in the rationalist view of science as a quest for essences or intelligible forms to be incorporated, if we are successful, in definitions. A set of laws of economic behavior may be taken to define "economic man", or laws of politics to define "political man". We may say either that the laws are necessarily true of their constructed subjects, and it is an empirical question how far the constructions resemble real men; or else that it is human beings that the laws were about from the first, and what is empirical is the content of the laws. If laws are regarded as definitional, they are spoken of as "real" definitions rather than "nominal" to convey this empirical involvement.

Similar considerations apply to the use of laws as rules of inference instead of as premises. Like a definition, a rule is conventional; but we choose the convention for a reason, and the reason lies in empirical fact.

PRIORITY

From this standpoint we might say that concepts like "analytic" have also an internal vagueness: laws could be said to be more or less analytic according to their most usual or most important uses. Kant conceived of a priori judgments in an absolute way as those wholly independent of experience, grounding their universality and necessity (if they are not merely tautologous) in the fixed structure of the knowing mind. If we look instead at the changing structure of knowledge itself, or at what has come to be called "the structure of the language of science", a very different conception emerges. Every actual use of a scientific law is in a specific context, in which the law is embedded in a whole network of propositions which help fix its content for that use. The system as a whole is empirical, a posteriori; the law itself can be said to be only more or less so according to the way in which it usually functions in such systems. "In the practice of scientific research," the mathematician Weyl has pointed out (*137*:153–154), "the clear-cut division into *a priori* and *a posteriori* in the Kantian sense is absent, and in its place we have a rich scale of gradations of stability." We may speak of the *degree of priority* of a law as the measure of its analyticity, as it were, expressed by the scientist's reluctance to abandon or even to modify the law in the ongoing of inquiry.

A law is wholly analytic, and thus absolutely a priori, only if it is affirmed regardless of what happens. But in the history of science few such laws are to be found, even in mathematics. As knowledge grows, laws are progressively changed and quite often replaced altogether. Terms like "hypothesis", "law", "rule", "principle", and "axiom" mark, in some of their usages, increasing degrees of priority attached to the propositions which they name. The degree is a matter of the comprehensiveness of the field, of the scope, or of the range of the laws, as well as of the weight of evidence sustaining them in the theories in which they play a part. The content of a scientific law is not isolable as an abstract pattern of events; to understand the law we must look also to the patterns of inquiry in which it is used.

§13. Types of Laws

Laws may be classified in a variety of ways, ways which I classify in turn on the basis of C. W. Morris's famous trilogy of the "syntactic", "semantic", and "pragmatic" dimensions of signs. These dimensions concern the relations of signs to one another, to their referents, and to their users, and so correspond, respectively, to the form, content, and use of laws. I believe that these three modes of classification are in order of increasing importance, both for methodology and for science itself. It is the use which fixes the content, and the content in turn determines the form.

One might be tempted to say, on the contrary, that it is the content of a law which is responsible for the uses to which it can be put, and that the form sets limits to the content to be found in it. But to say this is to confuse the order of knowing with the order of nature, as Aristotle would put it—to confuse how we come to appreciate the significance of a law with how the law comes to have that significance. Words mean something, it cannot too often be repeated, only because men mean something by them. If a scientific law is thought of as a product of scientific inquiry and not of divine promulgation, it acquires content in the process by which it is arrived at. Something found must have existed before the search, but it cannot have the status and role of a "finding" apart from the search. The planets moved before Newton, and moved always as he later found them to move; in *this* sense they always obeyed Newton's laws. But "obeyed" is a manner of speaking. A scientific law is not a timeless logical essence on which from time to time the mind of the scientist lays hold; it is a constituent of a real, historical scientific enterprise, and shares in the purposiveness of that enterprise. Laws are discovered, to be sure, but they become laws in the discovery and in the subsequent validation. Wives are married; but we do not marry wives, save bigamously; we marry women who become wives only in the marriage. The notion that the law was always there waiting to be discovered is on a par with the myth of the true, predestined mate. The fact is that marriages are *not* made in heaven, nor are scientific discoveries.

Even more marked, I think, than the dependence of content on use is the dependence of form on use. How we say something, in science at any rate, is chiefly a matter of just what it is that we have to say, what we intend by the saying. The form of a law is not something already fixed by events but depends on the formulation we choose to give the law, and that formulation in turn depends on what we want to do with the law. Many scientific laws, for example, have the form of "minimal" principles: the law states that some magnitude or other always assumes a minimal value. (Thus a light beam passing through several media of different densities is refracted so as to follow the path which takes the least time.) Other laws have the form of "conservation" principles, in which some quantity remains constant (angular momentum, for instance). Yet, whether a particular law is to be regarded as a minimum law or a conservation law is a matter of choice, as J. G. Kemeny has pointed out. It is a matter of the formulation we choose for the law, not something settled apart from our purposes. We cannot speak of "the" content or "the" form of a scientific law without placing it, at least implicitly, in some particular context of discovery, justification, or use.

FORM

With this understanding, we may look briefly at some of the more commonly distinguished types of laws. First, a classification that may be applied to scientific generalizations, without regard to whether they satisfy all the conditions necessary to their being laws.

A *simple generalization* is one which moves from a set of statements of the form xRy to a generalization of the form $A(R)B$, where x and y are members of A and B, respectively. Observations have disclosed a certain relationship between paired individuals, or, say, between earlier and later states of the same individual. The simple generalization formulates the classes for which the relation is affirmed to hold quite generally. It is the product of a simple induction from some to all of an appropriately specified kind. A number of instances are known, and we generalize from them to all the instances of what we are prepared to call "the same kind". More fully, the form of the generalization is: "For all x and y, if x is of the kind A (has the property A) and stands in the relation R to y, then y is of the kind B (has the property B)." For example, we may wish to consider, on the basis of a number of clinical cases, the generalization that all mothers of autistic children are overprotective. Often the relation is just identity, so that the simple generalization has the form that all A's are B's: "For all x and y, if x is an A and is identical with y, y is a B"; that is, if x is an A, it is a B. For example, experimental

animals may have more quickly solved certain problems in the laboratory when the amount of food with which they were rewarded was increased; we might then generalize to all the animals of the species, or
to all problems of a certain kind, or to all rewards, or to all of some other
things.

It is clear that the predictions that are formally allowed by such generalizations, taken by themselves, are quite uncontrolled. They are the
expectations which correspond, on a less primitive level, to those operative in the formation of a habit. For Hume, nothing other than the workings of habit underlies the whole inductive process. Yet the question is
inescapable whether a particular habit is a good one. As Russell pointed
out, the chicken which has learned to come quickly when it is called to
be fed will also, in due course, come quickly to get its head chopped off.
Simple generalization plays a part in all cognition, and can be identified
in all the more complex types of generalization; but in itself it yields
knowledge of only a very low order.

A second type is *extensional generalization*, which moves from statements of the form $A(R)B$ to a generalization of the form $U(R)V$, where
A and B are classes included in U and V, respectively. Here we are
generalizing, not over individuals, but over kinds; we are saying, not
that all the individuals of a certain kind will be like those instances we
have observed, but that individuals of other kinds will be like those of
the observed kinds. The generalization has been extended in range and
scope. A simple generalization, for example, concludes from a few determinations of the melting point of some substance that the determined
temperature is *the* melting point, that is, that all samples of the substance
will melt at the determined temperature; an extensional generalization
would be one concluding that other (specified) substances also have melting points, or that all samples of the substance in question will exhibit
other specific constancies. The example is Reichenbach's, who speaks in
this connection of "cross induction", the induction being made from a
sequence whose elements are themselves inductions.

What is called the argument by analogy can often be reconstructed in
this form. A simple generalization relating A and B is extended to cover
cases of another kind, say C and D, because C is like A and D is like B.
More accurately, the "likeness" in question consists precisely in the
fact that when the "like" elements are grouped to form a new kind—

the U and V of the extensional generalization—the result finds scientific warrant. When the generalization fails, we say that the cases were not "really alike". It is true, in a sense, that where simple generalization relies on generic uniformity, extensional generalization turns to specific resemblances. But everything in the world resembles everything else, just as it differs from everything else. There is always an analogy to be drawn, and every analogy breaks down somewhere. The question is always whether just *that* likeness justifies an extension of what is known about one sort of case to the other. (The use of analogy will be further considered in §§30 and 31.)

What remains true is that extensional generalizations have greater warrant (generally speaking!) than simple generalizations. For the cross induction is supported by all the evidence which sustains the simple inductions on which it is based. The weight of the evidence is not a matter of sheer addition, to be sure. What is particularly significant is that a *variety* of cases can be adduced to support the conclusion. If problem solving by certain samples of rats, primates, and humans is found to exhibit a particular pattern, we are more encouraged to conclude that this represents a law of learning than if even a larger number of cases drawn from only one of those populations had exhibited the pattern in question. But a heterogeneous population to start with might still have provided us with no more than a simple generalization. What counts is that the constituent kinds are themselves "natural classes" figuring in warranted generalizations on their own.

A third type is *intermediate generalization*. Here we move from a statement of the form $A(R)C$ to two statements, $A(R')B$ and $B(R'')C$. An intermediary has been found between A and C, which resolves their relationship into two subsidiary ones. Such an intermediary is often said to account for the linkage between A and B; accordingly, we may say that intermediate generalizations are *explanatory in the weak sense*. Most familiar are the cases where the intermediate is a missing causal link: peyote produces visions because it contains a compound of lysergic acid, which is the hallucinogenic agent. Often, however, the intermediate generalization selects a subclass from the original one which has a stronger association with the second class than the original one did: A and B together are more highly correlated with C than is A alone. As the correlation gets higher, we tend to think of B as explaining the connection. People with meaningful surnames (like "Baker" and "Miller") are more likely than others to have succeeded in their professions because such names reflect a higher probability of membership in the more favored native white Protestant elements of the population. Trace findings are often important because of the intermediate generalizations which they suggest.

Finally, *theoretical generalizations* move from a set of statements of the form $A(R)B$ to one of the form $\alpha(R)\beta$, where A and B are members of α and β, respectively. (Note that in extensional generalization A and B are subclasses of the new classes, not members of them.) A fuller discussion of the relation between theories and laws will be undertaken in §34. Here it may be enough to remark that the theoretical generalization conceptualizes kinds, as the other sorts of generalization conceptualize individuals. It is usually a set of intermediate generalizations that serves as material for the theoretical one. The latter may thus be spoken of as *explanatory in the strong sense*, explaining laws rather than events, which the laws in turn (weakly) explain (see also §§38 and 39).

Theoretical generalizations are often said to be of a "higher level" than others, since they are "about" other generalizations, just as these are "about" individual cases. The notion of "level" will also be discussed below. It may be noted here that it is often confused with the *degree* of the generalization: the extensiveness of its field, range, or scope. All of the four sorts of generalization distinguished above may be formulated in varying degrees of generality, not only the extensional generalization. We raise the degree by looking for the weakest conditions under which the generalization would still hold, or for the minimal changes that must be made in the generalization for it to hold under wider conditions. We may find something—say, "delusional systems"—to be characteristic of schizophrenia, then consider whether it might not apply to all the functional psychoses; and to achieve this greater generality we may find it necessary to replace the characteristic by a less specific one, like "disturbances in reality-testing functions". In behavioral science, unfortunately, it has often happened that great generality is achieved at the cost of trivializing the generalization. No doubt all societies impose "controls" on their members; but for fruitful social theory—in the present state of our knowledge, at any rate—it appears that this very general concept of "controls" must be replaced by the more specific categories of law, government, custom, morality, religion, and the like. What can be said in these terms is much less general, to be sure; but it may well be much more promising for the extension of our understanding.

CONTENT

Among the types of laws distinguished on the basis of their content, of particular interest to behavioral science are *temporal laws*. These are laws in which time appears as a "real variable"; in a law which is affirmed as holding "at all times", time is said to occur only as an "apparent variable"—it does not itself enter into the content of what is being affirmed. Temporal laws are sometimes contrasted with what are called "simultaneity laws", like statements of causal connections; or better, with "atemporal laws", like those in which one magnitude is stated to be a determinate function of certain other magnitudes. Three sorts of temporal laws may in turn be distinguished.

Interval laws are those which state a relation between events separated by a distinct time interval. They are sometimes called "diachronic" as opposed to "synchronic" laws. Examples abound in psychoanalysis—for instance, in the role assigned to early traumas, or in connection with the concept of regression. Indeed, any explanation which makes reference to the effect of memory involves interval laws. It is not to be supposed, however, that interval laws occur only in behavioral science; in physics for an instance, the phenomena of hysteresis, as in metal fatigue, are in the usual formulations governed by interval laws. It is important to recognize that interval laws do not necessarily affirm the occurrence of action-at-a-distance in time; nothing is said in such laws themselves about the possibility of their replacement by or deduction from atemporal laws. The fact that we explain some action by reference to what the actor remembers does not preclude a subsequent explanation of the memory in terms of processes at work at the time of the action itself.

Genetic laws are temporal laws stated, not in terms of some fixed time interval, but in terms of the "age" of the event: its distance in time from an appropriate zero-point. They are sometimes also called "directional" laws as contrasted with "functional" ones, or "developmental" as against "equilibrium" laws. In psychoanalysis, the developmental sequence of oral, anal, and genital stages is presumably governed by genetic laws, and such laws are also involved in the phenomena of fixation and transference. Michels' "iron law of oligarchy" is a genetic law, formulating what happens to certain organizations as time goes on; the doctrines of Spengler and Toynbee similarly enunciate various genetic laws. Genetic laws are not necessarily limited to behavioral science. In biology, genetic laws are widespread, applying to the development of organs and tissues, of individual organisms, or of whole species. The second law of thermodynamics in physics (that in a closed system entropy always increases), is also a genetic law. As with interval laws, genetic laws in themselves do not necessarily preclude the possibility of their subsequent replacement by atemporal ones. Biological growth, for instance, is beginning to be understood in terms of a sequence of chemical controls, each determining the workings of its immediate successor.

Pattern laws are genetic laws referred to some zero point in time. Aging, for example, considered generally, is describable by genetic laws; for a particular individual, it manifests a pattern in his life history, with the date of his birth as the zero. In the same way, the evolution of a particular species—say, the horse—describes a pattern, though an account of the evolutionary process as such is likely to consist of genetic laws. The generalizations of Marx and Comte concerning the succession of stages in human history also exemplify what I am calling pattern laws (if, of course, they constitute laws at all). Theories of the expanding universe which postulate the explosion of a primeval "cosmic atom" involve pattern laws, as contrasted with "steady-state" theories. In short, pattern laws, if they are nomological at all, result from the application of genetic laws to a situation sufficiently particularized to allow for the fixing of a zero point.

It may be remarked that in history, as a constituent discipline of behavioral science, all three sorts of temporal laws occur, as well as atemporal ones. By and large it would appear that the order in which they have just been introduced above is also one of decreasing validity. Historians often have occasion to recognize the effect of tradition or something else in a nation's past; they may also have some reason to distinguish between events characteristic of the early and late stages, say, of a republic or an empire; but over-all historical patterns seem at present almost wholly speculative in nature. As for atemporal laws, it would probably be said that these fall outside the domain of history proper, but are borrowings from one or another of the sciences of man, the business of the historian with them being only to supply the particular facts to which they are to be applied. I shall return to some questions of the nature of historical explanation in §42.

What I want to insist on is that temporal laws are not to be objected to merely because they are temporal. Behavioral science can certainly do with all the laws that it can get. Knowledge of constancies that involve time intervals or successions is, so far as this feature is concerned, as serviceable for prediction, explanation, and control as is any other sort of knowledge. To be sure, atemporal laws may allow us to deduce the temporal ones, and so may tell us all that these can tell and more besides: the laws of planetary motion allow us to predict that eclipses will occur at certain regular intervals, as well as a good deal else. But half a loaf is still bread, especially to a man who has been subsisting on crumbs.

Moreover, whether temporal laws are always replaceable by atemporal ones is a question of fact, not of logical or metaphysical necessity; we cannot say a priori how time is woven into the fabric of events. What *can* be said from a methodological point of view is, as Bergmann has pointed out, that what is temporal is not a subject-matter (like child psychology, say) but rather our knowledge of that subject-matter at a particular time, as expressed in the laws at which we have arrived. There is no Bergsonian cleavage between matter and memory, corresponding to that between space and time, whereby geometry is the key to the understanding of the physical world and the flow of events is the key to the understanding of human consciousness. Genetic, evolutionary, or historical approaches have whatever scientific worth empirical evidence and argument can give them. They are not unscientific, nor somehow of a lower scientific standing; but neither is any of them, on the other hand, the sole avenue to truth in the study of man.

Another classification of laws on the basis of their content concerns their relation to causality.

Taxonomic laws assert the existence of certain stable natural kinds. These are the "identifications" spoken of in §11. They mark out substances or systems to be taken as units in subsequent inquiry. Sometimes they are called "syndromatic" laws, after the grouping of concurrent symptoms in the characterization of a disease. The various properties of a taxonomic entity are thought of as bound together in being effects of a single cause (as in the case of a disease), or in acting jointly to cause some effect (as in classifications of personality or character). I should prefer to say that the togetherness consists in the concurrence of the signs as elements in any laws or theories, causal or otherwise. What is important is that the taxonomy, if it serves the ends of inquiry rather than other purposes (the so-called "practical" ones), is through and through nomological. Taxonomies are formulated in the early stages of inquiry, just as hypotheses are; but like hypotheses, in the course of inquiry they are tested, confirmed, revised, or replaced. Only when their usefulness has been established may we speak of them as incorporating taxonomic laws. Setting forth a taxonomy is not a device by which ignorance hopes that knowledge will accrue; the taxonomy is an investment of capital in hand—it takes money to breed money. The great taxonomic naturalists of the eighteenth and early nineteenth centuries, like Linnaeus and Cuvier, knew quite a good deal, and only thereby enabled their successors to know more, as Mendeleev's periodic table prepared for the Bohr atom only because of the knowledge of chemistry incorporated in the table.

Statistical laws both presuppose and are presupposed by taxonomies, formulating correlations both among taxonomic entities and among characteristics which are therefore grouped into unitary elements. *Causal laws* are usually distinguished from statistical ones as stating invariable relationships: the correlation must not only be 1, but allow no exceptions whatever: for example, a sequence of A's and non-A's so constructed that the nth occurrence of a non-A is followed by n A's yields a probability of 1 for the occurrence of an A (this is the limit of the relative frequencies); but because it has an infinite number of exceptions it cannot, as it stands, correspond to a causal law. (We could say that a causal law is at work in producing, without exception, just this pattern.) In addition, a causal law involves a vanishingly small time interval: the cause precedes the effect in order of occurrence, while the effect follows it immediately—a point already appreciated by Kant in the early applications of the differential and integral calculus.

Causal laws, it must be said, are not at all so important in science as philosophers of science have often assumed. The ordered simultaneity which they affirm, if it can be made precise at all, is in any case a very special type of constancy. Atemporal and therefore noncausal laws are easily at least as important as the causal ones, for the purposes of science itself. The temporal sequence of cause and effect is much more likely to claim our attention when our concern is with the control of future outcomes. We want to know the cause of a disease so that we may prevent and cure it, but the ends of biological science might be served as well and better by laws and theories which formulate abstract functional relationships rather than concrete causal connections. The role of statistical laws will be considered in §§28 and 29.

Laws are also sometimes classified on the basis of the sorts of terms which occur in them. For instance, M. Mandelbaum has distinguished between "global" and "abstractive" laws according to whether or not they contain collective terms (§10)—that is, whether they concern whole systems or only elements which can appear as components in a variety of systems. The status of global laws is closely bound up with that of methodological individualism. Mill (94:573) held flatly that "human beings in society have no properties but those which are derived from, and may be resolved into, the laws of the nature of individual man. In social phenomena the composition of causes is the universal law." This is a view with which Freud seems to have agreed, that societal laws are to be derived from those of psychology, while Durkheim, Weber, and others insisted on the autonomy of the science of society. But on this issue, like that of the status of temporal laws, methodology must content itself with pointing out only that the question is an empirical one, not logical. If global laws can be formulated which succeed in describing, predicting, or explaining social phenomena, well and good; and if such laws can be shown to be derivable from others concerning only persons and acts abstracted from social systems or situations, also well and good. What is not of much scientific worth is only the continuing dialectical debate as to what must be impossible or necessary a priori.

USE

One of the most important differentiations among laws is that based directly on the way in which they arise and function in inquiry. On this basis, *descriptive generalizations* are contrasted with *theoretical laws* (or simply "laws" taken in a narrow sense). They have also been called

"experimental laws" or "(merely) empirical laws" (better would be
"empiric", as in medicine, for all laws are empirical in the usual sense in
which this is opposed to the logical or to what transcends experience
altogether). Descriptive generalizations stem from fairly direct observations, and so are on a comparatively low level of abstraction. They deal
with the phenotype rather than with the underlying constitution responsible for the appearances. In Dewey's terms, they are generic propositions with direct existential import, as contrasted with universal propositions of an abstract if—then form. Descriptive generalizations inform us
what manner of creature we may expect to encounter on our travels
without purporting to lay bare the nature of the beast.

Such a descriptive law is usually arrived at by simple induction, or at
most by way of extensional generalization from other descriptive laws.
As intermediates are identified it moves in the direction of theoretical
generalization. In itself, it has no explanatory force, or at most only in
the weak sense. ("This camel has two humps because it is a Bactrian
camel, not a dromedary; all Bactrian camels have two.") By the same
token, it is only weakly predictive. Not having any reason for the generalization beyond its instances already observed, we do not know
whether it is indeed a law or only an accidental, and so a merely apparent, constancy. The so-called "Bode's Law" gives a formula for the dis-
tances of the planets which holds very well for the first seven, and was
even useful in the discovery of the asteroids; but it fails miserably for
Neptune and Pluto, which were discovered by calculations based on
Newton's laws.

It is the capacity for prediction and explanation which makes the distinction between descriptive and theoretical laws so significant. Yet the
difference between them is, after all, a matter of degree. The phenotypes
described may involve subtle and indirect observations, as with descriptive generalizations about the distribution of blood types or immunities
in various ethnic groups. Constructs and even some theoretical terms
may play a part, as in the empirical studies of constitutions and the
political process by Aristotle and Machiavelli and their modern successors. The descriptive generalization may be corroborated or corrected
by its relation to other laws even if it does not have a place in a fully
explicit theory: knowing that the color of animals is a geographic variable, European naturalists might have been reluctant to conclude that all

swans are white even before the discovery of black ones in Australia. And as inquiry proceeds, descriptive generalizations may gradually be transformed and combined into full-fledged theories, as natural history gave way to biology, or as the descriptive astronomy of the stellar universe from Herschel on led by continuous stages to cosmological models satisfying the Einstein field equations.

§14. Laws in Behavioral Science

DESIRABILITY

The first question that arises in connection with laws in behavioral science is whether the study of man is concerned with discovering and formulating laws at all. (The corollary question whether, in that case, it is deserving of the name of science may be set aside for the moment.) Some time ago the view was strongly urged, especially by Dilthey and Weber, that the student of cultural phenomena, of man and his works, is concerned with the concrete individual as contrasted with the abstract universal which they took to be the referent of general laws. Explanation and understanding are directed to "particular, historically given configurations"; we achieve such understanding by relating what is given to other individual configurations, not by subsuming it under a nomological universal. To be sure, the relation sought may be a causal one, but it is the concrete determination of one individual by another which is important, not the abstract relationship. The question of causality, says Weber (135:78–79), "is not a question of the subsumption of the event under some general rubric as a representative case but of its imputation as a consequence of some constellation." A knowledge of laws is of value for "the cultural sciences" so far and only so far as "it facilitates and renders possible the causal imputation to their concrete causes of those components of a phenomenon the individuality of which is culturally significant."

As Weber develops it, this position does not imply a repudiation of the search for laws in the field of human behavior. It does not deny an interest in such laws, but insists only that the interest is not an intrinsic one: it is instrumental to the achievement of other goals. The establishment of regularities is a means rather than an end; we want to discover the abstract universal, but only in order to understand the concrete individual. Note that for the performance of this function noncausal laws may also serve. Whatever be said about the nature of understanding and explanation (§§38 and 39), we must acknowledge at least the potential contribution of any knowledge of a stable connection among events. Asked a question about some problem of child behavior, the clinician will immediately counter with the question, "How old is the child?" Known regularities of development and growth bear on the interpretation of the individual case even though our knowledge may not extend to the causal connections responsible for the regularity. Even abstract formulations are not, just for that reason, "devoid of content", as Weber supposes (*135*:80); it is only that their application to concreta requires a more complex specification. The more abstract law does not lead away from "the richness of reality" but is, on the contrary, richer in meaning.

What is more to the point, I believe, is that the relation between the means and ends of scientific endeavor has here been misconceived. Neither means nor ends are absolute: the end sought is not an ultimate destination but a temporary resting place; the means to it is not something merely to be traversed but itself partakes of the value in the journey. A scientist may well be interested in coming to know a generalization so that he can understand particulars; but equally, the particular may be of scientific significance to him because of the contribution it makes to his quest for generality. In the conventional idiom, a scientist is concerned with both facts and laws, and with each of them, in some measure, because of the light which it can throw on the other. In any case, the use of generalizations as means to the understanding of particulars rather than as scientific ends in themselves does not distinguish "the cultural sciences" from the natural sciences—by no means (if I may be permitted the expression)! Geology and meteorology are chiefly concerned, after all, with *this* earth and air, at particular times and places, and apply the laws of physics and chemistry to "particular historically given configurations". Among scientists, the historians and clinical psychologists are not a breed apart merely because their scientific interest centers on particulars; what counts is how they move to and from the center.

POSSIBILITY

Quite as extensive a debate—and an even more futile one—has been carried on over the related issue whether scientific laws governing human behavior can be formulated at all.

Stemming from the view just discussed, that "the cultural sciences" focus on particulars, is the argument that there can be no laws here because each individual studied is unique, while laws deal precisely with what is common to many instances. I believe that both premises are true; but the conclusion does not follow from them. Of course every individual case is unique; on the Leibnizian principle of "the identity of indiscernibles"—that things which cannot be differentiated from each other are in fact one and the same thing—uniqueness is no more than a restatement of individuality. But every particular studied in physical or biological science is also an individual, also unique. Laws in whatever science group individuals together only on the basis of a similarity in some respect or other, not on the basis of identity (or the group would have only one member). Laws do deal with what is common to many, but uniqueness does not imply that *nothing* is shared with other individuals, only that *not everything* is common to them. A law requires repeatability, for it formulates a constancy of recurrence; but what recurs is not one and the same instance—for this kind of recurrence is contradictory—but another instance sufficiently like the former ones to serve the purposes of the generalization of which it is an instance. And this requirement applies to laws about human beings as to laws about anything else.

Yet the argument continues with the insistence that the study of man is interested precisely in what differentiates one person or one historical situation from others, not in what is shared with others. But what must not be forgotten is that differences are understood and explained—even appreciated—only by reference somewhere to similarities: how we conceive of an individual is the product of generalizations. This is the role of the identifications discussed in §11; emphasis on this role, as I see it, is not a subtlety of reconstructed logic but a straightforward recognition of something essential in the logic-in-use by historians, clinicians, and other inquirers into the unique particular. The psychoanalyst Heinz Hartmann reminds us of "the very great number of actual observations on which we base, in every individual case, the interpretations of an aspect of a person's character, symptoms, and so on. . . . Every single clinical 'case' represents, for research, hundreds of data of *observed regularities*, and in hundreds of respects" (in *61*:21 n; emphasis mine). To understand a person or a particular configuration of events is to know something of what *kind* of person or happening it is;

if we have no generalizations to draw on, no kinds are available to us for knowledge of individuals.

Moreover, such knowledge serves in turn as a basis for further generalizations. Every particular is representative—the problem is always to ascertain what it represents. It is ironic that romanticism conceived of love as unalterably fixed on the unique individual ("Had it any been but she, and that very face . . . "); yet the Platonism from which it drew its inspiration looked on the individual as a pathway to the universal. Indeed, what is seen as truly an individual precisely thereby becomes a type—a paradox made familiar in the arts. Perhaps for this reason, history and depth psychology have an affinity to literature—not because the characters and events of fiction are so particularized, but just the contrary, because of the artistry with which in literature as in myth a universal significance is made manifest in a concrete particular. What is important about the Oedipus legend—whether for anthropologist, historian, or psychologist—is not the individual of the legend but the shared reality which its helps uncover.

I certainly do not mean to say that knowledge of an individual case, however deep or comprehensive, in itself justifies the enunciation of a general law. To say this would be to commit what Jerome Bruner has aptly called "the fallacy of the dramatic instance". The individual case does not validate the generalization but guides its formulation and testing; the case provides meaning, not truth. In this sense we may speak of a *paradigm*, a particular case considered as representative for a generalization, whose content is thereby being made manifest. Such a paradigm is not unlike what Bacon in his *Novum Organum* called "ostensive instances"—"those which show the nature under investigation naked, in an exalted condition, or in the highest degree of power; freed from impediments, or at least by its strength predominating over and suppressing them." The paradigm is a device for specifying meaning with respect to internal vagueness, being presented as the clearest instance of the general category. In this respect the paradigm functions like an ideal type, but is an actuality rather than an abstract construction, an individual to be generalized rather than a concept already generic in form. The emphasis on the importance to behavioral science of coming to understand real particulars is, I believe, a healthy one, for often the scholar preoccupied with historical movements, forces, and institutions rather than with the lives of men is more likely to be writing fiction than is the novelist. But for science, what is rooted in the particularity of fact comes to flower in the generalizations of theory—or else it fails to seed.

Quite another traditional argument against the possibility of laws in behavioral science is based on the historical importance of the trigger mechanism: "In human affairs the smallest causes may produce the greatest effects, and the real application of scientific method is out of the question" (64:761). The classical example is Pascal's, with reference to Cleopatra's nose—had it been a quarter of an inch longer, the history of the world would have been different. The trouble with such examples is that they so temptingly invite the fallacy of the dramatic instance mentioned above. No doubt, any number of striking cases of this kind can be listed freely; but even a whole flock of swallows does not make a summer. It is one thing to say that not all events follow a foreseeable pattern; it is quite another to say that none do. No finite number of instances will establish the negative, while even one positive case refutes it. It is not the formal logic or lack of it that concerns me. The fact is that in numberless instances every day we can and do recognize patterns in human behavior. If we did not, as B. F. Skinner has remarked, "we could scarcely be effective in dealing with human affairs" (quoted by Scriven in 39:332).

Of more methodological interest is the point that trigger mechanisms, far from ruling out the possibility of laws, presuppose them. They consist in each case of causal sequences: "For want of a nail the shoe was lost, for want of a shoe the horse was lost, . . . " To be sure, the question is not whether there *are* regularities but whether it is possible for us to discover and formulate them. But I do not see that the disproportion between cause and effect, which constitutes the trigger mechanism, in itself makes it impossible for us to identify any triggers or to anticipate the consequences of their being pulled. That one thing leads to another is the basis of many counsels of prudence, and some of these counsels are even justified by experience—as most adolescents at last come to realize. Just such disproportionate effects of the way of a man with a maid are among the most firmly based and widely known generalizations about human affairs.

It must be admitted, on the other hand, that the causal sequences for which the trigger effect of Cleopatra's nose is the paradigm are so subtle and complex as to make tracing them quite hopeless. But we are not restricted to causal laws, and statistical laws governing whole classes of such cases are very far from hopeless. On the contrary, a great many are already available, on the level of descriptive generalizations if not of theoretical laws. The trivialities that trigger a suicide are no doubt unidentifiable in particular cases, but many factors of considerable statistical significance can be and have been identified. Similarly, a chance word or gesture by a candidate may gain or lose thousands of votes; but to acknowledge that this trigger is cocked is not to say that an astute campaign manager is wholly ignorant of how to win elections. Even if forecasts were always impossible, at least conditional predictions could be made as to what *would* happen under specifiable sets of circumstances, although we do not know which set will actually obtain. If what happens is seldom foreseen, at least it is not always surprising.

At bottom, the situation is the same whether we are concerned with human affairs or with processes involving the rest of nature. Accidents happen everywhere—in the fall of meteors as in the rise of heroes. And historical accidents are no less subject to causal determination than are those outside the range of human interests. The point has been clearly stated by C. Frankel (47:359): "An 'accident' in history is an event whose causes lie outside the particular causal sequence under examination, but whose effects become part of that sequence. And in calling it an accident we mean only to say that we cannot explain it from the point of view of this sequence; we do not mean that it is inexplicable, or that it is not part of any causal sequence." Accidents set limits to our knowledge at any given time, or rather, they are defined by those limits as seen in the perspective of a given interest. But as the frontiers of knowledge expand, what was once an act of God comes to be seen as belonging to the domain of natural law (the fall of rain or the onset of a disease). Indeed, the accidental may itself provide the focus for the research by which the domain is extended, as in current studies in astronomy of novae and supernovae. The notorious instability and variability of human affairs need not plunge behavioral science into despair: we might yet make virtues of unhappy necessities. The discovery of large numbers of variable stars gave the final blow to the myth of the unchanging heavens; but the variability itself at last revealed an underlying constancy, in the period-luminosity law for the Cepheids, and so provided us with a yardstick for the universe.

FREE WILL

There is another argument against the possibility of a behavioral science, one on which over the centuries a literature has accumulated as dubious as it is vast. I refer to the argument from "free will": we cannot formulate laws governing human behavior because human beings are free to choose for themselves what they will do. I am reluctant to add even a line to this futile discussion, but the omission of the point would, I suppose, be a glaring one; for behavioral science I believe that the argument is of importance chiefly as subject-matter for psychological and sociological examination as to why the argument is so persistently made and so firmly adhered to.

Plainly, scientific laws do not "govern" events in any way at all significantly comparable to the way in which statutes "govern" the actions of men. There is nothing to be enforced, nothing to be violated (save our own preconceived ideas about presumed regularities). And in any empirically useful sense that I have ever been able to understand, "freedom" is no whit incompatible with the workings of natural law. We cannot void a contract freely entered upon merely on the ground that we were caused to sign by our heredity and environment; we do not escape the compulsions of psychopathology or of politics merely by insisting that nothing whatever causes us to act as we do. The distinction between free choice and behavior that is compelled is drawn *within* the domain of causation, not between that domain and something presumed to lie outside it. A free choice is not uncaused, but one whose causes include in significant measure the aspirations and knowledge of the man who is choosing. And I see no reason a priori why choices freely made should persistently refuse to exhibit any regularities whatever, even in a statistical sense. Nothing compels my poker companions to bluff, but I flatter myself that I can sometimes predict when they will.

DETERMINISM

Quite the opposite view has also been current for a century or so, namely, that human affairs are so completely determined, at least in their general outlines, as to confer inevitability on the future course of events. We might call this view *apocalyptic determinism*, for it is associated with various philosophies of history which purport to reveal our inexorable fate. Let us grant, for the sake of argument, that comprehensive historical laws have indeed been established. What the historicist philosophies fail to appreciate is that the sense in which a law shows the future to be determined by the past by no means implies that something impels us along a preexistent path. The law might very well state only that one variable is a determinate function of another. We could then formulate the inverse function and reverse the order of "dependence" of the variables; we would not wish to say that the future made the past inevitable, yet it would determine it in the same sense as in the usual direction. To be sure, B is inevitable if A is true and the law "If A then B" is also true; the two premises together logically necessitate the conclusion. But this is not to say that the law itself formulates a logically necessary connection between A and B, or even a relation of causal necessity between them. The law might be a statistical one, for example; or if not, its validity might be construed in statistical terms. In either case there would be a real possibility that B would not occur even if A did.

More generally, laws formulate what would happen under various sets of conditions. The historical situation sets limits to the conditions which can obtain, and therefore to the eventualities that might ensue; to insist that these limits are so narrow as to allow for only one possibility is to beg the very question at issue. That choice is limited surely does not imply that there is no choice at all. At any given juncture in human affairs there are some things that we might do while others are simply out of the question. We can dismantle nuclear weapons or explode them; we cannot recall the radiation already released. History fixes the alternatives that confront us, and the laws of history fix the consequences that each would have. It does not follow from the existence of just any laws of human behavior that there are no alternatives to the unfolding of a predetermined pattern; what is required for this conclusion are laws that specifically affirm the existence of such a pattern, what I called "pattern laws". The point at issue is precisely whether we are justified in concluding that historical laws are of *this* sort and not some other—as though we can no more prevent a nation from declining when "its time has come" than we can put a halt to the aging of an individual organism. The example may be more instructive than historicists would like: geriatrics does not defy the laws of biology but applies them, to understand—and in increasing measure to control—the process of aging.

Underlying the doctrine of historical inevitability is, I believe, a confusion as to the sense in which the scientific enterprise presupposes a fixed order among events. The progress of science may be broadly viewed as a movement from empirical fact to rational theory. The scientist is not content with knowing what goes on in the world, though he begins with such knowledge. He wants to discover what *must* be true, not just what happens to be true at a particular time and place, or many of them. To understand an event, Spinoza and other rationalists would say, is to see why it happens, to see it, that is, as a necessary consequence of the workings of general principles. For methodology it may be enough to say that the scientist labors to transform descriptive generalizations into laws, and isolated laws in turn into systematic theories. Now determinism is often conceived as an essential component of the scientific outlook: the search for laws and for their unification in theory is taken to embody the belief that everything that happens must happen just as and when it does, the belief that the cosmos is a single fixed world order. Behavioral science, if it is truly scientific, is therefore committed—so the argument runs—to the corresponding belief about events in the human domain.

But scientific inquiry is always specific and limited. We do not study "the world", but some special and usually very restricted portion or aspect of it—even cosmologists have specific and limited concerns if they are scientists rather than metaphysicians. The context of inquiry, by which the objectives of an inquiry are defined, is always concrete and particular whatever the abstractness and generality of its subject-matter —Newton and Einstein had each of them a particular set of observations and hypotheses to try to unify and explain. Beliefs about the world as a whole are not involved, therefore, but only beliefs about the specific subject-matter of the inquiry. It is not "the uniformity of nature" which is invoked, but at most only the uniformity of the characters and events which concern us then and there.

Moreover, though the scientist, we may agree, is not content with brute fact, he need not suppose that it can be wholly explained away. He needs to find only enough rational determination in the fact to get on with, that is, enough to enable him to proceed to the next level of understanding and explanation. "All that an ardent scientist has to believe," Conant (22:166) rightly points out, "is that the lowering of the degree of empiricism can go on indefinitely, not infinitely." More would be of no use to him. When Kant propounds his transcendental deduction of the category of causality he establishes, let us suppose, that the human mind is so constituted that it cannot conceive of events save as effects of causes. But to be told that everything has a cause is more than a scientist engaged in a particular inquiry bargained for; he would be quite content with the knowledge that the events which interest him are enmeshed in a causal network. But indeed, even that knowledge is either futile or unnecessary: futile because it cannot tell him *what* the causes are, and unnecessary if he already knows them.

METHODOLOGICAL DETERMINISM

The point is that for science the restricted determinism of which I have been speaking is not a premise but a presupposition, not a superlaw ("the Principle of Determinism") which the scientist applies to discover other laws, but a perspective within which he sees himself as an explorer bent on discovery. We may call it *methodological determinism*, to distinguish it from its doctrinal or metaphysical form. Methodological determinism states only that laws are worth looking for here, not that they surely *exist* here, and surely not that they necessarily exist always and everywhere. This is the standpoint from which Reichenbach offers his justification for induction. The fisherman need not know nor even believe that there are fish in the stream; it is enough if he knows that his bait and tackle will allow him to catch them if there are any. I would add, it is even enough if he just enjoys fishing; there are worse ways for a man to spend his time, whether he catches anything or not.

One other question concerning laws in behavioral science may be mentioned as involving both metaphysical and methodological considerations. This is the question whether such laws are necessarily reducible to the laws of physics and chemistry, or at least to those of biology. An affirmative answer to this question, as a matter of doctrine, seems to be like an acceptance of doctrinal determinism in being both unwarranted and scientifically useless. As a methodological presupposition, however, it provides a valuable perspective in which the behavioral scientist can see continuing possibilities for turning to his own use the findings of other sciences. But the significance of such possibilities appears only as they are actualized; otherwise their affirmation expresses only a hope. There are behavioral scientists whose claim that "ultimately" what they are asserting is derivable from the laws of physics or of biology is rather like the profligate's assurance to his creditors that eventually he will come into a large inheritance. What he says may be true; but the creditors are scarcely to be blamed for insisting on "a little something on account". Freud was convinced that his findings would sooner or later be formulable on a strictly biological basis; it was not, however, his materialist metaphysics that gave his work importance, but the significance of his findings in their own terms. It may well be that the psychologist can derive the whole of his discipline from neurology, biochemistry, and the rest; it is not destructive skepticism but productive pragmatism to say, "I'd like to see him do it!"

Chapter IV

EXPERIMENT

§15. The Process of Observation

An observation in science is first of all something done, an act performed by the scientist; only thereby is it something seen, a product of the process in which the scientist is engaged. As process, observation is a part of what Nagel calls "controlled investigation". Scientific observation is deliberate search, carried out with care and forethought, as contrasted with the casual and largely passive perceptions of everyday life. It is this deliberateness and control of the process of observation that is distinctive of science, not merely the use of special instruments (important as they are)—save as this use is itself indicative of forethought and care. Tycho Brahe was one of the greatest of astronomical observers though he had no telescope; Darwin also relied heavily on the naked eye; De Toqueville was a superb observer without any of the data-gathering devices of contemporary social research. In behavioral science, observation is less likely to involve special instruments than special circumstances—say, like those of the psychoanalytic-interview situation,

126

Above all, "observation" means that special care is being taken: the root meaning of the word is not just "to see", but "to watch over". The scientist observes his data with the tireless passion and energy of an anxious mother.

Much of the forethought that goes into scientific observation is directed toward making accessible what otherwise could not be seen, or if seen, would not be noticed. Special care is taken to ensure that the scientist will be able to see what he is looking for if it is there to be seen. Only when this condition is satisfied can negative results have scientific significance; and negative results may be of profound importance, marking—as the Michelson-Morley experiment did—the breakdown of expectations based on received doctrine. Observation is purposive behavior, directed toward ends that lie beyond the act of observation itself: the aim is to secure materials that will play a part in other phases of inquiry, like the formation and validation of hypotheses. When observation is thought of as passive exposure to perception, its instrumentality is left out of account. The scientist becomes a voyeur, finding satisfaction in the unproductive experience of just looking at nature. No doubt there is always some gratification in uncovering secrets, exposing what is hidden; but the scientific motivation is more mature in its demands. In science, observation is a search for what is hidden, not just because it *is* hidden, but because its exposure will facilitate an intimate, sustained, and productive relationship with the world.

INTERSUBJECTIVITY

To be able to serve these ends, observation must meet certain conditions. "Repeatability" is often spoken of here as a requirement for scientific acceptability. I believe that this is a mistaken specification, or, at best, a misleading one. Many important scientific observations take place on special occasions whose recurrence is incidental to their scientific significance. Of particular importance to behavioral science are special events like clinical outbursts, disasters, and war crises, as well as regularly recurrent ones like elections or rain dances; and for other sciences, important observations may be made in connection with eclipses, earthquakes, or the birth of quintuplets. Of course, when such events happen again we can observe them again, but we cannot repeat the observations at will. And the recurrences can be expected to differ in ways relevant to the purposes of the observation—the core of soundness in the misplaced emphasis on the "uniqueness" of the subject-matter of behavioral science (§14). The child asks the magician to "do it again", not to subject him to scientific test, but to enjoy once more the encounter with the miraculous. For the scientist, repetition is a device to improve the quality of observation, but not the only device, and not necessarily the best.

The methodological importance of what is called repeatability is, I think, made more plain by its restatement as *intersubjectivity*. A scientific observation could have been made by any other observer so situated: nature plays no favorites, but exposes herself promiscuously. The intersubjective becomes the mark of objectivity, for it testifies that the observation is uncontaminated by any factors save those common to all observers. Whether a distortion common to all men can nevertheless be said to yield something objective is a philosophical question that has no bearing on the conduct of the human enterprise of science. The methodological question is always limited to whether what is reported as an observation can be used in subsequent inquiry even if the particular observer is no longer a part of the context. I ask "Do you see what I see?" to help decide whether what I see is to be explained by self-knowledge or by knowledge of the presumed object.

ERROR

It is usual to refer in this connection to the so-called "human equation", much better designated as the "human factor". The logical significance of an observation is conditioned by psychological factors that have played a part in determining the outcome of the process. Wishful thinking, for example, has its counterpart in wishful seeing. Certain experiments on extrasensory perception, for instance, were afterwards shown to have yielded apparently positive results because of the direction of the quite honest clerical errors made by recorders hopeful of such a result; similarly, it is notorious that arithmetical mistakes on income-tax returns are almost invariably in favor of the taxpayer. Other studies have revealed the effect of social pressure not only on what we believe but quite literally on what we see. ("Do you see yonder cloud that's almost in shape of a camel?" "By the mass, and 'tis like a camel, indeed." "Methinks it is like a weasel." "It is backed like a weasel." "Or like a whale?" "Very like a whale." Polonius may have been more honest than politic.) Observers must be trained to observe scientifically, and the very discipline which they undergo may itself subject them to trained incapacities that will produce distortions in other contexts. The "law of the instrument" (§4) may be as much at work in the process of observation as in other phases of inquiry.

The difficulties in assessing the significance of observations do not stem only from the personal, idiosyncratic failings of the observer, but may be rooted in features intrinsic to the process of observation itself. A century ago Augustus De Morgan, one of the founders of mathematical logic, and more sensitive to the problems of the empirical sciences than most of his successors today, called attention to various ways in which we may confuse properties of our observations with what we suppose we have observed (see *64*:409 ff.). Instead of *A* causing *B*, it may be our observations on *A* that cause *B*, as is illustrated by the famous Hawthorne experiments, where changes in the productivity of workers under varying conditions were at last understood to have resulted just from the fact that the workers knew they were subjects of investigation. Or, *A* may produce only our observation of *B*, which would otherwise occur without being observed, as is illustrated in the apparent increased incidence of psychosis in modern urban life, which may be attributable only to the higher frequency with which it is diagnosed and reported. Or, our observation of *A* may cause our observation of *B*, as in the attempt to assess the effect of psychotherapy by using the appraisals made by the patients themselves. Or, our observation of *A* may be necessary to the observation of *B*, although in fact it is *B* that causes *A*—illustrated in the relation between the manifest and latent content of a dream from the standpoint of the dreamer. Like all skilled performances, observation is by no means as simple as it looks.

There are several general procedures by which errors of observation are taken into account. These procedures are said to constitute *controls* of the observation: they are efforts responsive to the effects of the particular context or observer, designed to minimize error in assessing the significance of what has been observed.

First, we may institute procedures to *insulate* the observation, separating it from the factors that would otherwise produce error. The training of observers and the setting up of experimental situations as contexts of the observation are largely insulating devices. Special instruments may be employed, like one-way windows, or the intent if not the fact of observation may in other ways be concealed from human subjects. Astronomical observatories are located where the air is clear, and far from city lights, perhaps even in outer space. Questionnaires are pretested to eliminate ambiguities or unintended implications; and so endlessly.

Second, we may attempt to *cancel* error where its elimination is out of the question. Observations of a child's behavior, for example, except in very special circumstances, are inevitably colored by the emotional involvements with the child of those who have the most opportunity to observe him: parents, siblings, teachers, and friends. But the very multiplicity of observers may to some extent cancel out the effect of particular relationships. In general, statistical devices may be employed where there is reason to expect a great number of errors more or less independent of one another, for in that case errors in opposite directions are likely to compensate for each other. An interesting compensatory device for the human factor is reported by Darwin, who tells us that he kept a separate notebook to record observations counter to his theory, lest he overlook or underestimate them.

In most cases, however, errors of observation can neither be prevented nor canceled out. What is still possible is to *discount* the error, make ourselves aware of its direction, and perhaps even of its extent, and take it into account in our treatment of the observational data. In observing the shape of an object we might try to insulate against errors of perspective by viewing it from a point directly above its center; in fact we learn early to make use of the laws of perspective in interpreting what we see from any angle: coins look round as we discount the elliptical shapes they usually in fact present. Reaction times of observers can be measured and corrected for, just as astronomers correct the observed time of, say, eclipses by taking into account the time it takes for light from the event to reach us (this kind of correction was in fact the basis of the first determination of the velocity of light). In general, we *standardize* instruments and contexts of observation, not in order to eliminate an error but rather to give it a fixed and known value, on the basis of which we can shift at will what we choose to call the "zero point".

WHAT IS OBSERVED

Setting aside the treatment of error—whether it is prevented, canceled, or discounted—what is it that is observed? A usual statement goes that observations are only of matters of fact, while laws and theories are products of conceptual processes. There is undoubtedly an important distinction here. Facts remain fixed through time in a way in which theories definitely do not (of course as time passes situations change, but it remains a fact that the situation *was* such-and-such at an earlier time). And a particular set of facts may play a part in a wide variety of laws and theories. For these reasons, as Jevons (*64*:414) pointed out, errors of fact are more "mischievous" than mistaken theories, often much more difficult to identify and correct. Yet I believe that the difference between facts and theories lies in the ways in which they function in inquiry rather than in the processes by which we arrive at them, in their use rather than their origin. All observation involves theorizing, and—for science, at any rate—perception is impossible without conceptual processes. It is hard to improve on Norwood Hanson's (*54*:7) formulation: "There is more to seeing than meets the eyeball."

There is an empiricist tradition, from Hume through Mill to Russell, in which a distinction is made between "hard" and "soft" data, according to whether they are purely observational or contain an inferential element. The basis of scientific knowledge is taken to be a "reading" or protocol which does not interpret but merely records a perceptual content. Positivists like Pearson and Mach, and Carnap in his early work, all proposed a reconstruction of knowledge on a phenomenalistic basis (Mach's book on this subject is called *The Analysis of Sensations*). What we observe are bare shapes, sounds, colors, and textures, which are then organized and interpreted as the familiar objects and events of experience. The contents of observation itself are free from conceptual contamination. Nietzsche's label for this philosophical doctrine is not, I think, unjust; he called it *"the dogma of immaculate perception"*.

The fact is that no human perception *is* immaculate, certainly no perception of any significance for science. Observation is already cognition, not just material for subsequent knowledge, and the possibility of error is as ever-present in this cognitive process as in the more obviously inferential ones. Seeing is believing because we do not just see something:

we see *that* something is the case. The perception apprehends a significant structure, or rather, a structure which becomes significant in the
apprehension, acquiring what Dewey calls a "funded meaning". We take
what we perceive as being of a certain kind, bringing an abstract concept
to the perceptual situation and subsuming the concrete given under it.
Because of this tacit predication, the eye with which we see is itself the
mind's eye, or it would be indeed unseeing. We feel impelled to put a
second metaphorical eye behind the real one only because of a reconstruction according to which first something without meaning is seen,
which is then interpreted as having a certain significance—a Kantian
intuition on which the faculty of understanding then goes to work. But
observation is already the work of understanding: the photoelectric cell
does not *see* anything at all in the same sense as we do. The uninterpreted
intuition or bare sensation is not the beginning of perception but the end
product of a subsequent analysis, a reconstructed accessory after the fact.

It will not do to say that all this is only a matter of psychology, not of
the logic of the cognitive process. For it is surely a logical requirement
that what is observed be formulable in propositions, which can serve as
premises for subsequent inferences. But the language in which observational propositions are stated is itself inferential in character. As Popper
(*111*:59 n) has urged, there is no purely "phenomenal language" distinguishable from a "theoretical language", no way to talk about something sensed and not interpreted. Mill (*94*:420) argued that "what is
needful, in order that the fact, supposed to be observed, may safely be
received as true . . . is that it be an observation, not an inference." But
shortly thereafter (*94*:422) he recognized that "we cannot describe a
fact without implying more than the fact . . . To describe it is to affirm
a connection between it and every other thing which is either denoted or
connoted by any of the terms used." Even if perception itself were
immaculate, the perceptual report exposes us to sin, as a necessary consequence of the way in which language works (see §7). Benjamin Lee
Whorf (*139*) has put forward the suggestive thesis that the very structure
of a language makes for certain segmentations and interpretations of
experience. And there have been some experimental indications that perceptual discriminations, say of colors, are affected by the vocabulary
available for labeling the differences.

After the moment of the observer's birth no observation can be undertaken in all innocence. We always know something already, and this knowledge is intimately involved in what we come to know next, whether by observation or in any other way. We see what we expect to see, what we believe we have every reason for seeing, and while this expectancy can make for observational error it is also responsible for veridical perception. The Japanese do not hear the difference between *l* and *r* because in their language these sounds are not contrastive: the difference makes no difference to the meaning of any Japanese words in which they might occur. This indifference distorts their perception of spoken English, but by the same token allows for easy identifications in spoken Japanese. We do not make proper observations by stripping ourselves of theories—which is impossible, in any case—but rather by making use of the theories appropriate to the observational context. Where special instruments or experimental situations are involved in the observation, it is quite clear that theories must play a part, at least in order to discount the errors that may have been introduced by the observational devices themselves. Chromosomes are so called not because they are themselves such markedly colored bodies, but because of the deep stain they take in the processes employed to make them visible. But theories are also at work even in the simplest and most direct observations.

For we do not observe "everything that is there to be seen". An observation is *made*; it is the product of an active choice, not of a passive exposure. Observing is a goal-directed behavior; an observational report is significant on the basis of a presumed relation to the goal. Color is an index of significant differences of structure and function in various types of both stars and algae but not of mushrooms or of mammals (including humans). To include color among the observational data in all these sorts of cases equally is thereby to make certain hypotheses about the facts, and not merely to report "just the facts". Data are always *data for* some hypothesis or other; if, as the etymology suggests, they are what is given, the observer must have hypotheses to be eligible to receive them. In his *Theory of Data* Clyde Coombs proposes that the term "data" be used for observations already interpreted in some particular way. I am saying that there are no other sorts of observations, though often the interpretation at work is far from explicit and clear. The profound importance of Coombs's analysis is that no one interpretation is necessitated by what is observed; there are always many ways of mapping behavior into data, as he puts it. But without some mapping or other the process of observation is of no scientific significance. To speak of observations as yielding "facts" is only to point to the objective locus of their status and function as data; but to perform their function they must be, as Coombs says in a Kantian idiom, "in part a product of the mind of the observer".

What has just been said is what I also take to be the burden of Dewey's repeated insistence that the perceptual and conceptual materials of knowledge are instituted always in "functional correlativity" with each other. Theories are as much involved in the determination of fact as facts are in establishing a theory. When a fall of meteorites was reported to the French Academy toward the end of the eighteenth century, the datum that stones sometimes fall from the sky was dismissed as "a superstition unworthy of these enlightened times". We ourselves, of course, are *really* enlightened, but we are no less dependent on theory for distinguishing between fact and superstition. The example given is one of a large class of what might be called *cryptic data*: those which, in a given state of science, are hard to make sense of in the light of the theories current at that time. Not uncommonly it is the cryptic data that provide a point of departure for significant theoretical advance. The rate of precession of the perihelion of Mercury was inexplicable on the basis of Newtonian mechanics, as was the negative result of the Michelson-Morley experiment; both were eventually accounted for, in terms of the general and special theories of relativity. On the other hand, some cryptic data turn out to be errors of observation or interpretation; they are cryptic only because there is really nothing there to be explained, save the process of observation itself. The Martian canals may be taken as an example, if, as is now generally thought, they are the product of an optical illusion characteristic of visual perception pushed to its limits.

Even greater importance in the history of science attaches to what might be called *invisible data*, those which are recognized as data only conjointly with the acceptance of the theory explaining them. They are not Bacon's "clandestine instances", which embody some characteristic only in the most rudimentary and therefore inconspicuous form. On the contrary, invisible data are retrospectively seen to be perfectly obvious and even striking manifestations. Freud's clinical observations of hysteria in males were dismissed as absurd (the word *hysteria* itself is from the Greek for *womb*), as were his accounts of infantile sexuality, since everyone "knew" sexuality begins only at puberty; today both of Freud's observations can easily be made by most wives and all mothers. The "paradigm observer" has been described by Hanson (*54*:30) as "not the man who sees and reports what all normal observers see and report, but the man who sees in familiar objects what no one else has seen before". Intersubjectivity is still called for, but it is achieved only after the fact.

In some cases data are invisible because a scientific dogma makes for a simple refusal even to look at them: none so blind as those who will not see. Galileo's colleagues refused to look through his telescope at the moons of Jupiter which he had discovered—a case which today is often cited (with what justice is debatable) by those interested in telepathy and related matters. Whatever the scientific merit of particular findings, it cannot be denied that in general what is most responsible for invisible data is the force of preconceived opinion. "This it is," Mill (*94*:508) has remarked, "which, in all ages, has made the whole race of mankind, and every separate section of it, for the most part unobservant of all facts, however abundant, even when passing under their own eyes, which are contradictory to any first appearance or any received tenet."

It is not our conceptions only which both limit and inform the process of observation. *Instruments* of observation are also of enormous significance for the course of inquiry as a whole. The state of knowledge at any particular time is profoundly affected, not only by the techniques of gathering data then current, but also by the technology for doing so. It was more than the nineteenth century's pride in its technological achievement which impelled Jevons (*64*:272) to proclaim that "the invention of an instrument has usually marked, if it has not made, an epoch". I believe that the history of science bears him out to the full. His statement is as true for behavioral science as it is for physics and biology. In 1903, for example, "the experimental training of a rat in a maze led at once to a long series of studies in the evolution of animal intelligence with the maze as the observational instrument" (E. G. Boring in *46*:193). Similar importance attaches to such observational devices and situations as, say, free association, communication nets, and opinion polls. In sum, in making an observation we are not passive but active; and we are doing something, not only with our eyes and our minds, but also with our lips, hands, feet—and guts.

§16. *Observation in Behavioral Science*

INTERACTION

Most of the problems of observation in behavioral science (and some problems of theorizing too) stem from the shared humanity of the scientist and his subject-matter, or rather from the richer and more specific commonalities to which the abstraction "humanity" points. The act of observation affects the person being observed, directly or indirectly, and to a degree which is often of the same order of magnitude as the phenomena which the scientist is interested in observing. In the classic Hawthorne studies the effect of the process of observation altogether masked the effects of the other variables initially discriminated. Such effects cannot be attributed to merely psychological factors of no logical significance; they *are* psychological, but so is the subject-matter, and this fact is essential to the logic of the situation. What we are confronted with here is comparable to the case in quantum mechanics so often subjected to methodological analysis: the beam of light necessary to the observation of a subatomic particle must inescapably alter the particle's position or momentum. This effect has nothing to do with an alleged subjectivity of observation itself; it is a consequence of the laws of physics. The effect of the behavioral scientist on his subject-matter confronts him with problems which are not made any easier by generalizations about the universal applicability of "the scientific method".

For some time, for example, there has been a tendency for experiments on attitude change—as Irving Janis has pointed out to me—to be described (and no doubt conceptualized) in terms of stimuli provided by "E" (the experimenter) and the reactions to them of "S" (the subject), as though one were tracing the transmission of mechanical forces through a gear box; but in fact human beings were interacting with one another, and in ways significantly dependent on their specific humanity. Thus the transference phenomenon involved in the attitudes of student subjects to faculty experimenters, or perhaps of the suburban housewife to the pollster, cannot safely be ignored. On a broader scale, the phenomenon of self-fulfilling predictions (as well as self-defeating ones) poses methodological difficulties which must be faced. At the very least, the behavioral scientist must constantly cope with restrictions imposed on his studies as defenses against their anticipated undesirable consequences, whether he is investigating sex patterns, decision making, economic institutions, or something which requires access to classified materials.

All these difficulties are real and important; yet I cannot but feel—perhaps because I need not face them myself—that they are far from insuperable. The behavioral scientist deals with them by the several devices for imposing controls on observation spoken of in §15. Some steps can be taken to insulate the observation, though some contamination is always to be expected. The thermometer inserted into a liquid to measure the temperature of the liquid changes that temperature itself; but the thermometer can first be heated or cooled so as to minimize the effect, and there are even ways to measure the temperature from a distance. Statistical devices and appropriate experimental designs can allow the effect of the observation to be canceled out, or nearly so, though to be sure this is not always easy. A corps of psychoanalysts cannot very well observe the same subject so as to cancel out the effects of their own probing; yet the fact that psychoanalysts of different schools consistently report characteristically different findings—if it be a fact—is suggestive, and might be put to good use scientifically. And the influence of the observer might be so controlled as to be discounted rather than prevented or canceled, just as every teacher already knows that students do not perform on important examinations "as well as was to be expected", and accordingly discounts the effect of tension (I have myself concluded that there is no way to prevent this effect, and I shrink from what is involved in canceling it). The self-fulfilling prediction can be subjected to test if its own workings can be assessed as a second-order effect: the election-eve poll might be read by only a small proportion of the voters, and of these only a small fraction in turn might be sufficiently undecided to be affected by it.

In short, while I have no wish to minimize the problems posed by the effect of the observer on the behavior observed, I see no reason to doubt that the behavioral scientist can continue to live with these problems. I believe that more difficult problems arise from the reverse effect of the subject-matter on the observation, for this effect is both more difficult to recognize and more difficult to subject to controls. I am human, said the poet, nothing human is foreign to me; self-awareness requires no less an admission and self-esteem no less an aspiration on the part of the behavioral scientist. But the more involved he is with his subject-matter, the more likely it is that his observations will be affected by the involvement. Countertransference may come to be as important as the more easily observed transference: the patient's admiration for his analyst may at last be perceived as the beginnings of a grasp on reality. And the participant observer may invest so much in the participation as to create vested interests which subvert the scientific ones, robbing them of their autonomy, and perhaps destroying them altogether. In one famous case an anthropologist who succeeded in having himself initiated as a shaman afterwards refused to divulge his secrets to the colleagues of his earlier calling. Like every agent whose work is to spy on his fellows, the behavioral scientist must learn to suspect his own loyalty first of all and to keep it under careful surveillance.

But indeed, in every science, whatever the subject-matter, emotional investments play a part and may override the scientific interest; and for that matter, the passion for truth is just that: a passion. Hobbes remarks somewhere that if our interests were as much involved in geometry as in politics its foundations also would be subject to as bitter dispute. The history of mathematics suggests that he is mistaken only in the conditional. So far as concerns the process of observation, the involvements of the scientist are especially disquieting, for, as we have seen, his interests are intrinsic to the significance of the process. Observations are always molded by prior conceptions, and when the observations concern matters on which there is strong feeling, it may be more appropriate to speak of preconceptions or even prejudices. "If even on physical facts, and these of the most obvious character, the observing faculties of mankind can be to this degree the passive slaves of their preconceived impressions, we need not be surprised," says Mill (*94*:509), "that this should be so lamentably true as all experience attests it to be, on things more nearly connected with their stronger feelings—on moral, social, and religious subjects." In a word, the scientist has *values*, and for the behavioral scientist the subject-matter gives his values an unavoidable relevance. The distortions of observation which may result are eliminated or canceled only with the greatest difficulty. Discounting them by making them explicit and by incorporating the scientist's values in the scope of his study is rather more promising. But a discussion of this matter must be postponed to §§43 and 45.

LEVELS OF INTERPRETATION

Still another sort of problem arises from the common humanity of the behavioral scientist and his subject-matter. It is that behavior has meaning to the person engaging in it as well as to the observer, and the two meanings do not at all necessarily coincide. In §4 these meanings were distinguished as "act meaning" and "action meaning". An act (as contrasted with an action) is a succession of biophysical events whose meaning lies in the actor's purposes, or in the goal to which the act is directed. Acts themselves are rarely observed, save in time-motion studies, or in disciplines like phonetics and kinesics; normally we do not observe motions but performances, we do not hear phonemes but words, we do not see bodily movements but gestures. An action is an act considered in the perspective in which it has meaning for the actor; the biophysical process here has psychological and social dimensions. What we observe are actions, but the observation rests on inferences and reconstructions.

In this relation is the root of the difficulty. Because the behavioral scientist shares the act meanings of those whose behavior he is studying —because he speaks the same language, as it were—it seems to him as though action is directly observed, without the mediation of hypotheses. Yet that meanings are shared is always only a presumption, and observational data have no more validity than attaches to that presumption. The unfortunate fact is that the relation between acts and actions is by no means a constant one even for a given actor, to say nothing of different persons, groups, or cultures. Lasswell has referred to this difficulty as the problem of "index instability". A particular act may have a variety of act meanings, and so constitute correspondingly different actions— as American soldiers discovered on their first dates with British girls. On the other hand, a variety of acts may have the same meaning and so constitute the same action—as the same word may be written in either print or script even though these do not in the least resemble one another. (In another connection William James gives the example of "Pas de le Rhone que nous", which can be taken in English for "Paddle your own canoe".) When the behavioral scientist "sees" what is going on, he is in fact making interpretations which require independent validation.

The situation is further complicated by the fact that an action meaning is quite distinct both from the act meaning and from the scientist's hypothesis as to the act meaning. An action meaning attaches to an action —something already interpreted—when the action is put into the framework of the scientist's theory of its occurrence. When a behavioral scientist is said to "understand" a political event, a culture pattern, or a neurotic symptom, say, two things are involved. First, he has interpreted certain movements as having a particular meaning for the actors: marking the ballot was a vote, bowing was a gesture of deference, washing the hands was a ritual of purification. Here he has reconstructed an act meaning, and his reconstruction has provided him with the subject-matter for his theorizing. But second, he interprets the vote as a resurgence of nationalism, the gesture as a recognition of membership in the leisure class, or the ritual as an obsessive symptom of a compulsion neurosis. These meanings are for the observer, not for the actor, and are not to be confused with the observer's hypotheses as to the meaning for the actor.

The point is that both levels of interpretation enter into what the behavioral scientist takes to be observational data. That act meanings are involved in what is observed has been recognized by all but the strictest behaviorists; the part played by action meaning in constituting data has not received the attention it deserves. "Even at the stage of description," Freud (quoted in *20*:65) once pointed out, "it is not possible to avoid applying certain abstract ideas to the material in hand, ideas derived from somewhere or other but certainly not from the new observations alone." What we see when we look at behavior may be bare acts, or purposive actions, or events having a theoretical significance. All three may present themselves as observational data, but all three are also inferential, though it is not uncommon to draw the line dividing observation from inference, or data from theory, between the first two, or even between the second and third. In the actual situation of inquiry into behavior, however the labels are used, determinations of act meanings and of action meanings enter into the data just as do descriptions of biophysical processes. The situation ascribed in the following to psychoanalysis holds, I think, quite generally: "What we are used to call 'clinical findings' in psychoanalysis is determined not only by observable data but also by explicit or implicit assumptions. They make our findings meaningful [action meaning] by assigning them a place in the framework of our hypotheses. Without these assumptions not even a simple statement concerning the interaction of conscious and unconscious motivating factors in the broadest sense could ever be made" (55:16).

INTROSPECTION AND IDENTIFICATION

In physical science, act meaning plays no part, just because of the subject-matter, and even in biological science its application is restricted. The question arises whether the role of act meaning in behavioral science affords opportunities for special methods of observation. I believe that there are indeed two: introspection and identification.

It seems to me undeniable that a valuable part of the data for behavioral science is provided by self-observation. I do not see how one can disagree with Colby's (20:5) remark that "in investigating persons there are advantages to being a person". Thereby we are given continuous access to the subject-matter; and though some of it may remain inaccessible (what we are ourselves unaware of), and all of it remains uncertain (for we may be mistaken in what we think we have introspectively observed), it is far from being true for these reasons that therefore none of the data so obtained are of any scientific worth. The argument that introspective data fail to meet the test of intersubjectivity is to me quite unconvincing. It is true that you cannot experience my anger. But if this proposition is not a sheer tautology (what you experience is *your* experience), *I* can not experience my anger either—afterwards. Both you and I need corroborative evidence, and for both of us the evidence is indirect, though we are each likely to rely on evidence from different sources. The same is true, however, when we come to agree on an external perception; we need additional evidence, and each of us will find it in his own perspective. As was pointed out earlier, it is not repeatability that is called for, but the instituting of controls. It must be admitted, however, that doing this is not as easy as it seems: it takes skill and effort to introspect in a way that is scientifically useful. Not many can manage, like Freud, to interpret their own dreams without outside help.

It is by way of identification that introspective materials assume particular importance: the village idiot finds the strayed horse by asking himself where he would go if *he* were a horse—and there it is! We look within to arrive at the act meanings of the behavior of others, assuming that the act has for them the meaning it would have for us if we were to perform it. Sociologists like Cooley, Znaniecki, Sorokin, MacIver, and others refer in this connection to sharing "states of mind", to "vicarious experience", to "intimately comprehensible" connections, to "imaginative reconstructions" (see *1*, which I am following closely). It used to be fashionable to speak here of *verstehen* (understanding) as a method peculiarly appropriate to the study of man. What characterizes this operation, according to the useful account given by T. Abel (though in the present terminology), is that the connection between act and action is established by reference to the act meanings the observer himself would attach to the act in comparable circumstances. I understand the act when I see it as though it were the outer form of my own corresponding action.

There is indeed a sense in which understanding is the goal of all science, a sense which will be explored below in connection with the pattern model of explanation (§38). But "verstehen" cannot be identified with understanding in *this* sense. For in this sense understanding is the apprehension of an action meaning, the significance which attaches to an action in the light of some appropriate theory, whereas "verstehen" is the apprehension of an act meaning, the significance which attaches to an act in the light of the goals and purposes of those performing it. "Verstehen" does not explain human behavior except in so far as it transforms biophysical processes into actions with psychological and social meaning. It interprets behavior so that the behavior constitutes something *to be* explained, in other than the physical and biological terms appropriate to the bare movements alone. The process of "verstehen" consists in internalizing the observed movements, and applying to them "behavior maxims", that is, "generalizations of direct personal experience derived from introspection". These maxims formulate "emotional connections" ("I hate him because he attacks me"), which form the basis of our interpretation of the observed acts. But the maxims allow us at best only to interpret the behavior, not to explain it. Through "verstehen" I apprehend a murder as an act of revenge ("If he had done it to me, I would have killed him myself"). But a theory of motivation, and the part played by revenge in such a theory, is not even suggested.

The interpretation of acts through identifications is to my mind of fundamental importance for behavioral science. Without this process, it would be as though every communication we receive is a cryptogram, not interpreted but decoded, by procedures of the kind that might be carried out by electronic computers. We *can* proceed in this way, but the fact is that we do so only seldom, and there is no good reason why we should do so always. Yet the operation of "verstehen" is as inferential and problematic as are those of cryptanalysis. Its outcome is familiar and, generally speaking, reliable; but it does not constitute its own validation. For action meaning, "verstehen" is quite irrelevant— unless it be assumed that human beings are endowed with the gift of being able to explain all their own actions, though they may be ignorant of what causes them so much as to sneeze. And for act meaning, "verstehen" provides hypotheses but not verifications. It is easy, however, to deceive ourselves on this score, for, as Abel points out, when we have related what is observed to our personal experience, our curiosity is likely to be satisfied, and familiarity serves in place of genuine explanation. We feel that we understand why someone did something when we see it as no more inexplicable than our own behavior, that is, when we share an act meaning. But we know why the someone did the something only in the psychological sense of "for what purpose", not in the scientific sense of "for what reason"; in short, we apprehend motives but not causes. This apprehension too, however, can be a valuable datum.

A similar assessment can be made of the method of participant observation. The participant does not get evidence of a distinctive kind, but is in a favorable position to get the evidence (*51*:51). Act meanings are more easily accessible to him because he himself shares them. On the other hand, it may also happen that his own involvement distorts his observations, as was pointed out earlier; this distortion may well occur even when the observations are introspective, perhaps especially then ("I tell you, I'm *not* angry, I'm not!"). And for action meaning the participant is no more favorably placed than is any other theorist.

There is in many methodologies a certain imperiousness which is especially marked in the position they take on the methods of introspection and identification. It is held that such methods are mandatory or else that they are prohibited, that behavioral science *must* use them or that it definitely must *not*. These attitudes are perhaps related to the defensive incorporation and exclusion spoken of in §4, and also find expression with regard to such matters as the place of mathematics in behavioral science, or the place of animal experimentation in the study of man. On these questions I do not see that methodology is provided with any Tablets of the Law, that it can lay down commandments of "Thou shalt" or "Thou shalt not" to mark out the way of life for the scientist. The methods we have been discussing have whatever place the working scientist can find for them; their usefulness depends entirely on the use he puts them to. The methodologist who lays down the Law would do well to remember the hope expressed by Moses, that every man become himself a prophet.

§17. *Functions of Experiment*

Basically, experimentation is a process of observation, to be carried out in a situation especially brought about for that purpose. The great astronomer Herschel characterized experiment as nothing other than "active observation", which is indeed what it is in astronomy. But no scientific observation, as we have seen, is wholly passive; how much the scientist intervenes before or during the process of observation is a matter of degree. Correspondingly, there is no sharp distinction between observation and experiment, only a series of gradations and intermediates. The biologist who studies bacteria by staining them and mounting them on slides is not ordinarily thought of as performing an experiment; yet his intervention is of a different sort, and requires different controls, than do observations made on the living organism. The behavioral scientist, merely by bringing a subject into his office for interview, may already be introducing conditions relevant to what he should expect to observe, and so is to some degree experimenting.

WHAT EXPERIMENT CAN DO

In this broad sense, the importance of experiment for empirical science can scarcely be exaggerated. Poincaré (in *140*: 31) says of it that it is "the sole source of truth; it alone can teach us anything new". That science did not develop further in the cultures of ancient Greece, India, and China seems to be traceable at least in part to similar failings in all three. They suffered no lack in their powers of reason or in their exercise of those powers, both speculatively and in the disciplined patterns of mathematics; observation also was often both acute and diligent. But observation was limited to superficial data, that is, to what was most easily available; and it was not carried out in a controlled and systematic way so as to maximize its bearing on the products of reason. Not until the culture made it possible for a man who worked with his hands and a man who exercised his mind to be united in a single person, or united, at any rate, in a shared enterprise, did science embark on its fantastically accelerated growth.

It is experimentation that expresses the basic empiricism of science. The scientist cannot lead us into nature's secret retreats unless he will risk having her slam the door in his face; experiment knocks on the door. The cardinal principle of experimentation is that we must accept the outcome whether or not it is to our liking. It is wiser not to ask the lady if we cannot believe in her reply, though wisdom may also dictate a number of careful replications. "It is necessary to obliterate one's opinions, as well as that of others, when facing the decisions of the experiment," the physiologist Claude Bernard has said (quoted by Duhem in 38:236); "we must accept the results of the experiment just as they present themselves with all that is unforeseen and accidental in them." Students often make use of "Fudge's factor" (it goes by many names): the number by which the observed result must be multiplied to obtain the magnitude specified in the laboratory manual; alas, there are working scientists who are also given to comparable, though of course less blatant, "adjustments". Telepathists need to warm up, or they become fatigued, or else some distraction intervenes; accordingly, whatever part of the sequence of trials is unacceptable may be discarded. I once saw a great probability theorist roll dice to obtain a sequence to illustrate a lecture, then decide that the outcome was not sufficiently "random" to be illustrative! By submitting to the judgment of experiment we correct the presumption of the demand that the world conform to our expectations.

In the study of man, experiment has only recently begun to play any significant role. For some time, thinking about human behavior has been largely speculative, its cognitive style belletristic. So far as there was concern with matters of fact, it allowed at best only for empirical generalizations, since laws are hard to come by without experiments to determine, by the varying of conditions, what is essential in the observed relationships. Even in recent philosophy of science and in the reconstructed logics associated with it, experiment has not been given the attention it deserves; modern logical empiricism has been more logical than empirical, and in a formalist perspective experiment does not loom large. Yet a multiplicity of cognitive styles must be recognized, and it must be acknowledged that each may have its own contribution to make to the scientific enterprise. Not all scientists have what Charles Peirce called the "laboratory mind", and a variety of skills and temperaments enter into inquiry. There are scientists for whom theory is important only because of the new experiments it suggests, and others who view experimentation only as a procedure for generating and verifying theory. The history of science honors many names of both kinds, and those of other scientists as well, distinguished for the accuracy of their observations, the subtlety of their mathematical analyses, or the sweep of their simplifying syntheses. In our Father's house there are many mansions.

I believe that this old truth has a new importance because in contemporary behavioral science the attitude toward experimentation is in danger of becoming a kind of ritualism (65:104), as though the laying on of hands can itself effect a cure of diseased ideas. As with all rituals, the emphasis passes from content to form, from substantive questions to procedural ones, and virtue comes to be localized in the proper performance of fixed act sequences. Particular techniques are identified with "the scientific method", and inquiries in which those techniques are not employed are then dismissed as having no scientific significance. No doubt there are few if any behavioral scientists who would subscribe explicitly to any such notions; but it seems to me that the presence of these notions can be recognized from time to time in the training of students, in the formation of research policy, and in the assessment of other inquiries. Observation remains basic to all science, but not all observation must be carried out by fully developed experimentation. This is as true for physical and biological science as for behavioral science; there are many important disciplines, with distinguished achievements to their credit, in which experiments have played a relatively minor role: astronomy and oceanography, paleontology and physical anthropology, archaeology and linguistics, to mention only a few.

In short, experiment does a great deal for the scientist—more, perhaps, than he could hope for otherwise—but this is not to say that he cannot live without it. The place of experiment in any acceptable reconstructed logic must depend on a realistic appraisal of the functions of experiment in inquiry. These functions are no more—and no less!—than to provide occasions for "controlled observation", as Nagel (*103*:452 ff.) calls it. Experimental observation, says R. A. Fisher, virtually the founder of the self-conscious and explicit design of experiments, is "only experience carefully planned in advance". This simple phrase makes reference to the two most general and fundamental traits of scientific inquiry—the empiricism and the rationality in inquiries that conform to logical canons—and it also hints at how the two traits merge into one in what they characterize. Experiment is the consummation of the marriage of reason and experience, and though it is not in itself the life of the mind, it is the most passionate and fruitful expression of our intellectual life and loves.

What experiment can do is to minimize the errors of observation that are inseparable from casual encounters, or at any rate from unplanned ones. The experimenter knows what he is letting himself in for, and is in a position to judge soberly whether (and in what respects) the game was worth the candle. Where errors are not prevented, experiment facilitates their detection and correction, prepares us to make the best of what we get, enables us to discern the virtues behind the necessities of human frailty. By experiment we are empowered to observe under rare and special circumstances of our own choosing; and we choose them in the hope of thereby enriching our experience. Experiment is the device by which we strip appearances from reality, and by putting matters to a test, distinguish dependent from independent variables. And by design, our ingenuity works to maximize the information that can be extracted from recalcitrant data.

KINDS OF EXPERIMENT

In a word—but there is no one word to describe what experimental inquiry achieves. Different experiments do different things; we need not always remain at the level of generality which arrives at a single function answering to the general concept of experiment. Reconstructed logics too often achieve an elegant simplicity, not by identifying the one in the many, but by refusing the name of logic to the many specifics of inquiry that may lie outside the logic's predetermined generalities. Here are some of the many things that experiments do, some of the many kinds of experiments that can be recognized when they are classified according to their functions.

Some experiments are *methodological* (so-called): they serve to develop or to improve some particular technique of inquiry. Typically, we already know the relevant facts and laws concerning the ostensible subject-matter of a methodological experiment; the outcome of the experiment tells us something new only about a certain way of getting at such knowledge in other cases. If the results of applying the technique are contrary to our expectations, we alter our beliefs, not about the subject-matter, but instead about the techniques employed or the circumstances of their employment. Instruments of observation or measurement must be standardized and calibrated; the operations by which these results are achieved constitute methodological experiments. Carbon dating must be applied to materials of known antiquity in order to be made useful subsequently in establishing the age of other materials of unknown or uncertain date; tests of creativity or of latent homosexuality must be standardized against known populations.

It is not uncommon, to be sure, for an experiment to be called "methodological" when the experimenter must otherwise confess that it has performed no useful function whatever; thereby the label has taken on a questionable tinge. Yet there is no doubt that methodological experiments in the sense discussed above are frequent and important in science. It might even be said that every experiment is to some degree a methodological one, enhancing by its success our confidence in or our mastery of a certain technique, or directing attention by its failure to the possibility that the technique was at fault, rather than the theoretical or other presuppositions.

A certain type of methodological experiment is sufficiently important to deserve its own name: the *pilot study*, also known as a "pretest". Such an experiment is designed to establish the magnitudes of certain variables that will play a part in a major experiment that is being planned—for instance, how much time should be allowed for the performance of a task by the subjects. Or it may aim at determining whether certain contaminating factors are sufficiently strong to obscure the effect to be studied in the major experiment—for instance, whether the subject's response in the experimental situation will vary significantly with the sex of the observer. Unfortunately, too often what is called a "pretest" is only a pretext, whereby the experimenter guilty of poor planning, sloppy execution, or crude analysis tries to save face by presenting his work as a "pilot study". At best, calling such activity a pretest amounts to saying that if someone else were to do the experiment that ought to have been done, but wasn't, we might learn something. A pilot study properly so-called needs as much care and forethought as any other experiment. Listening to a musician tune his instrument is far from an esthetic experience, but it is also very different in both substance and function from hearing a poor performance.

Another type of experiment is the *heuristic* one. It is designed to generate ideas, to provide leads for further inquiry or to open up new lines of investigation. The first experiments with the running of mazes or with free association may have been of this type. Often a heuristic experiment makes use of models (in one of the many senses of this term—see §30), in the hope of uncovering fruitful analogies, as has been exemplified in recent years by the construction of artifacts which simulate purposive and even intelligent behavior. All experiments, to be sure, may be called heuristic, for all are forward-looking; if they tell us anything, they provide some answer to the question "what next?" Partly for this reason, the label "heuristic", like the terms "methodological experiment" and "pilot study", is used to cover up poor experimentation—it is easy to pretend to having achieved at least this much, that we now know what *not* to do next. Yet this pretense should not diminish our appreciation of what can be contributed by genuinely heuristic studies.

A special kind of heuristic experiment may be called *exploratory*. It is frankly intended just to see what would happen if ——. Often it is associated with a new technique, which is tried on a wide variety of problems and subject-matters until the most promising sorts of applications become apparent. (See, for instance, the early history of radioactivity.) An exploratory experiment may be conducted to determine a range of outcomes with the systematic variation of some parameter, as in fixing the optimal dosage of a drug. Or it may be conducted according to a trial-and-error pattern to exhaust some set of possibilities. In general, an exploratory experiment invites serendipity, the chance discovery; it is part of what we do to deserve being lucky. The so-called space "probes" nicely illustrate exploratory as well as methodological experiments; and perhaps I will be forgiven for also calling them pilot studies.

Probably the most common experiments in actual scientific contexts are those we might call *fact-finding*, aiming at the determination of some particular magnitude or property of a relatively well-defined object or situation. This type of experiment is exemplified by the administration of an intelligence test or the conducting of an opinion poll. The term "fact" in this connection may be misleading, for often what experiments of this sort aim at is the determination of a constancy that may be formulated as a universal law rather than as a particular matter of fact. An experiment designed to measure the velocity of transmission of nerve impulses, for instance, or one to determine maturation sequences in infancy, may be called a fact-finding experiment, though the knowledge obtained is by no means restricted in application to the particular subject of the experiment. It is true, however, that the generalization beyond the experimental context depends also on premises not yielded by the experimental findings themselves.

Boundary experiments are explicitly associated with some set of laws and consist of fact-finding inquiries designed to fix the range of application of the laws, particularly with regard to extreme conditions. In behavioral science such experiments are exemplified by studies of sleeplessness, sensory deprivation, perceptual thresholds, and the like. Much of the significance of boundary experiments depends on what is already known about phenomena more centrally subject to the laws in question; we may say they are experiments that aim at reducing both internal and external vagueness. They determine what happens at the limits of the conditions specified in the laws, and contribute also to a fuller specification of these conditions.

Simulation experiments are experiments on a model: they are designed to learn what will happen under certain "real" conditions related in a definite way to the experimental ones. A wind tunnel, for instance, is an apparatus for simulation experiments, and quite a comparable function is performed by college aptitude tests. In both sorts of cases a certain prediction is to be made concerning later performance. Every experiment, of course, is predictive in one way or another—if its outcome has no application outside the immediate situation it loses all experimental significance: to experiment is to try something out with an eye to its later use. In the case of simulation we try it out on situations significantly different from those we really have in mind, but so selected or designed that we can take account of the difference. We simulate when more realistic experiments are, as Helmer and Rescher point out (56:35), too costly, or physically or morally impossible, or when the real situation is too complex. In behavioral science, so-called "operational gaming", which is a type of simulation experiment, has been applied to military tactics, cold-war problems, bargaining situations, industrial competition, and the like. In all simulation experiments the fundamental problem is that of "scaling"—that is, "the translation of results from a simulation model to the real world" (56:40). A ship, plane, building, or bridge that is well designed in miniature will not meet full-scale requirements if we overlook the fact that surfaces increase with the square of the linear dimensions while volumes and masses increase with the cube. Corresponding problems of scaling are especially important in behavioral-science experiments where laboratory conditions may provide only miniature motivations and conflicts (see §19).

The usual discussion of experiment in philosophy of science focuses on only one type, which we may call the *nomological experiment*. This is one which aims at establishing a law, at proving or disproving some hypothesis or other. Sometimes a merely empirical generalization is in question, as in much of the experimentation on various types of extrasensory perception. More typically, the attempt is to transform an empirical generalization into a law in the narrow sense (§13), that is, to identify what is both necessary and sufficient for the empirically given connection, by varying the experimental conditions. Until we have "added the evidence of experiment to that of simple observation", Mill says (94:252–253), we have "only proved invariable antecedence within the limits of experience, but not unconditional antecedence or causation." The nomological experiment is designed to bring out what is essential to a certain effect. The visiting Frenchman who confided in turn that the Empire State Building, Central Park, and the Staten Island Ferry each reminded him of a beautiful woman at last explained, "Everything does!" Phenomena are not usually so accommodating in providing us with their explanations; it is here that nomological experiment comes into play.

By far the most familiar type of nomological experiment is that called a *crucial experiment*. Two or more alternative explanations for some phenomenon are available, each being compatible with the empirically given data; the crucial experiment is designed to yield results that can be accounted for by only one of the alternatives, which is thereby shown to be "the correct explanation". The frequency with which such experiments are discussed in methodological literature is quite disproportionate to their rarity in actual scientific practice (though not to their importance when they do occur). As I. M. Copi (*25*) has pointed out in a beautifully lucid discussion, different interpretations of the experimental findings are always possible; to insist that a particular test is crucial to the correctness of a proposed explanation may very well amount to a begging of the question. Only in fairy tales do Cinderellas have a unique size in footwear, and thieves clap their hands to their heads on hearing the shout that the thief's hat is burning. In sober fact the crucial experiment does not conclusively establish one alternative while making the others absolutely untenable; at most it only alters the balance of probabilities. The issue is always how much trouble we are willing to go to, how much else we are willing to question or to assume, in order to adhere to the chosen alternative.

The logic of the situation is that "an experiment can never condemn an isolated hypothesis" (Duhem in *38*:238). It is always a whole network of hypotheses, a comprehensive theory, that is involved. Newton argued for the existence of an absolute space on the basis of what happens when a pail of water is rotated: the water slowly rises to the rim and gradually subsides when the pail is suddenly stopped. But Ernst Mach argued that the water is rotating relative to the stars, not in absolute space. That distant heavenly bodies are responsible for inertial mass may be implausible, but it is *possible*, and is an explanation that the experiment itself does not rule out; and if Einstein is right, it is the explanation to be preferred. When experiments are explicitly planned and interpreted in the light of comprehensive theories, rather than more restricted hypotheses, they may be called *theoretical experiments*. Often they are as simple—and as profound—as that one of Newton's, or as some of those performed by Galileo; but they may also be as complex as the observation during total eclipse of the bending of starlight in the sun's gravitational field, which is one of the important experimental tests of the general theory of relativity.

I believe the widespread view to be mistaken that in behavioral science theoretical experiments are not to be found because in this area

there are allegedly no sufficiently rich and sufficiently precise theories
to lend themselves to experimentation. I am inclined to think, rather, that
theoretical experiments are too frequent, if anything—that is, that too
many experiments in behavioral science call for so large a number of
supporting hypotheses for their interpretation that the significance of the
specific experimental findings is obscured. So far as theory is concerned,
my impression is—though it is an impression only!—that the behavioral
scientist suffers less from poverty than from an embarrassment of
riches. Theoretical experiments are not the only ones by which science
advances, even theoretical science; and though such experiments may be
the most important ones considered singly, their contribution may well
be matched or even outweighed by the cumulative effect of other types.
Not every experiment need be designed with an eye to the Nobel prize.
The belief that every soldier carries a marshal's baton in his knapsack
may heighten morale, but it is not to be forgotten that every marshal
needs an army of soldiers behind him.

There is another kind of experiment, those which serve the purposes
of science only indirectly, by way of training future researchers or by
contributing to the further education either of the scientist himself or
of the general public. I call them *illustrative experiments*. They do not add
to the knowledge already available somewhere, but only to what is
known by the specific audience to which they are presented. (This limitation may also apply unintentionally to other types of experiments;
here, the situation is correctly understood from the beginning.) The
classroom repetition of an experiment which is important either historically or in the current state of the discipline is an example of an
illustrative experiment, as is any replication undertaken by a scientist in
the spirit of wanting to see for himself how it comes out.

Sometimes illustrative experiments are, as it were, enactments of a
metaphor, dramatizations of a more or less suggestive analogy. Several
rats, caged alone, were trained to obtain pellets of food by pressing a
lever on the opposite side of the cage from the food slot. When two rats
were put into the same cage, the food released was devoured by one rat
before the other animal, pressing the lever, could reach it. Soon both
were waiting at the food slot, and neither worked the lever, till at last
one frantically pressed the lever many times over, then rushed back in

time to get a few pellets which were as yet uneaten. Such an experiment may invite much comment from the standpoint of various social and economic philosophies, and might be taken to illustrate the breakdown of production under severe competition, the exploitation of labor, surplus value, class conflict, and I don't know what else; but plainly, it proves nothing about these matters. In general, illustrative experiments may be contrasted with the *probative experiments* which do provide evidence for specific factual predictions, hypotheses, or general theories. Unfortunately, illustrative experiments are often mistaken for probative ones; in particular, it is often thought that an experiment *proves* a certain theory when it does no more than provide another instance, clear-cut and compelling, of just the sort of fact which it is the business of the theory to explain. The best that can be said for such unrecognized illustrative experiments is that they sometimes do have heuristic value.

Finally, there is a type of experiment which has an altogether "practical" aim, so-called, as contrasted with a scientific one. It may be called a *trial run*, and consists in a provisional application of some selected means to an end outside inquiry. The trial run is illustrated by the tentative application in a limited context of the outcome of a piece of market research or operations research, or by the testing on selected patients of a new drug or therapeutic method. It is like the pilot study in looking to a later and more extensive undertaking, but here the latter is not itself also an experiment. And the trial run is like the simulation experiment in making predictions about a large-scale phenomenon from studies in the small, but here the small-scale situation is not something simulated but is itself a situation of the kind in question. The trial run is only sticking one's toe in the water before plunging in.

The dozen or so types of experiment I have just surveyed are by no means mutually exclusive: a given experiment might simultaneously exemplify several different types. Nor is the list at all exhaustive; more types can be distinguished the more refined our classification of the functions which experimentation can perform. The important point is to recognize that there are many methods and stages of inquiry, and that in each of them experiment may have various roles to play. What these roles are must be determined, not on the basis of some preferred reconstructed logic, but on the basis of the logic-in-use in science itself.

§18. *The Structure of Experiment*

In the performance of every experiment, a dialectic of action and passion is at work. The experimenter is active in seeking out, designing, and constructing the experimental situation, in doing the experiment, and in making something of it. But he is passive in accepting the outcome of the experiment whether or not it accords with his expectations. After all the planning and preparation, a time comes when the voice of the experimenter is stilled while nature speaks. All the experimenter's actions only make ready for this moment of truth in which he is wholly passive, his mind receptive and yielding. He has come to his Sinai and stands mute as a voice proclaims, "Hear, O Israel!" The experiment is apocalyptic, a drama of revelation; but it does not end in a motionless tableau. What has been revealed becomes at once a matter for interpretation and commentary, generalization and reconstruction. The experimenter becomes active once more. He must mix his labor with the truth which has been given him, that it may become truly his.

GENERALIZATION

First, the outcome of the experiment must be subjected to *correction*. That there are dangers in this process does not relieve the experimenter of the necessity to carry it out. We may so "correct" the results of the experiment as to destroy their significance; we may "adjust" the data, not to the truth, but to our own preconceptions. Bad cooking may destroy both nutriment and savor, yet we are not thereby constrained to subsist on raw meat. Some corrections of the experimental data are always called for, and making them is an essential part of the experimental method. The experiment yields always only a number of isolated points in our attribute space. The curve that we fit to these points—as Poincaré has emphasized (*140*:32)—does not, in general, pass through them but only somewhere near them. The raw data are treated as an approximation to what the experiment "really" shows; we correct them by transforming them to what they would be (in our judgment) if they were not approximate but exact. Our judgment may be in error; but there is no doubt that there is error also in taking the results at face value, just as they come before us.

What was said earlier (§15) about errors of observation applies also to observation carried out in an experimental setting. We try first to insulate the experiment from sources of error, so far as these are already known to us and subject to control. We may cancel certain errors by suitable replications and appropriate statistical analyses. An important part of the task of experimental design is to allow for the cancellation of error, for instance by recombining certain elements so that errors are made first in one direction, then in the reverse direction, or so that the same error is made in both the test group and the control group. And finally, we attempt to discount error which cannot be prevented or canceled out, by measuring its direction and amount and subsequently making the corresponding correction of the data.

It is this possibility of discounting error that is usually aimed at by the *standardization* of the experimental conditions. Such standardization, however, can easily be given an undue emphasis; it is "often thoughtlessly advocated as a panacea," R. A. Fisher (*43*:100) points out. An equivalent amount of care and attention given to preventing or to canceling error may be more rewarding than efforts to hold constant a factor afterwards to be discounted. Moreover, rigidly fixed experimental conditions exact the price of limiting the information yielded by the experiment to just that narrow range of application. On the other hand, "we may," Fisher continues, "by deliberately varying in each case some of the conditions of the experiment, achieve a wider inductive basis for our conclusions, without in any degree impairing their precision". By arranging the materials of the experiment according to the factors known to be at work, and by using techniques of analysis of variance, we make the sources of error themselves part of the subject of the experiment.

For what we wish to do is not only to correct the experimental data but also to *generalize* from them. The curve that we fit to the observed points is a continuous one, and the line we trace to connect the observations itself represents a generalization. The something that empowers us to make this inference is just what constitutes a good experiment. A good experiment, says Poincaré (*140*:32), is one that "informs us of something besides an isolated fact; it is that which enables us to foresee, that is, which enables us to generalize". We have reason to believe that what we have found in the experiment's results, suitably interpreted and corrected, we will find again, and always, under the conditions for which the experiment provides a sufficient specification.

The problem is to be able to say just what these conditions are, to distinguish between the experimental variables and the unwanted ones that are also represented in the actual findings. Particularly does this discrimination become problematic when the latter variation is not a random one but systematic (§23). We may say that the planning of an experiment is directed primarily at facilitating the making of just this distinction, afterwards, between the significant and the "contaminating" factors. The occurrences of highly anomalous events, prodigies of nature, geniuses, psychotics, deviants of all sorts, are sometimes spoken of as "nature's experiments". There is no doubt that they may be of considerable scientific interest, constituting, as they do, a source of what I have called "cryptic data". But they differ from genuine experiments just in this, that they preclude the possibility of instituting the controls necessary to specifying the conditions which will warrant generalization.

YIELD

The design of experiments has another and closely related task: to maximize the information yield per unit of research cost. It is an essential characteristic of experimentation, says Fisher (*43*: 18–19), that it is carried out with limited resources. Even if the act of cognition itself be conceived as the commerce of a disembodied intellect with abstract ideas, no one, surely, can apply this conception to the experimental operations which make the cognition possible. Experiments necessarily involve expenditures of energy, time, money, and materials; I do not see how the interests of either inquiry or logic are served by pretending otherwise. Planning an experiment is always a matter of allocating scarce resources. We must decide, therefore, which sources of error (or "causes of disturbance", as Fisher calls them) should deliberately be ignored, and which should be given care and attention; and for these we must also ascertain the extent to which it is worthwhile to take the trouble to diminish their magnitude. It is pointless to conceive of a good experiment as one which takes account of every possible source of error. Such perfection is not to be found even in Heaven; whatever God was trying to prove by the creation of man, I rather imagine that the results are inconclusive.

In his *Theory of Data* (*24*: ch. 2) Clyde Coombs has used in this connection the suggestive idioms of information theory: "One might regard

a psychological experiment as a communication system between a subject and an experimenter. . . . On *a priori* grounds, one would expect
that the higher the channel capacity the better, but this is certainly not
true. One pays a price for data, not only in financial terms, but in wear
and tear on the organism at the source. A method with too high an information capacity may, through boredom and fatigue, result in a decrease
in the information transmitted. Furthermore, the potential variety of
messages from the organism may not be great, in which case a more
powerful method is inefficient. . . . Ideally, a method of collecting data
should be selected which matches the information content in the source
but is not such a burden as to generate noise. These criteria may be in
conflict with each other, or with constraints imposed by the stimulus
material, or by the method of analysis to be used, or with practical considerations like time and money." I venture to say that in behavioral
science, at any rate, poor experiments are more often the result of trying
to find out too much than too little. You get what you pay for, and bar-
gains are as much to be distrusted in research as anywhere else.

FACTORS

Methodologists, unfortunately, have sometimes tried to make logical
virtues out of practical necessities. "The great method of experiment,"
it used to be said (*64*:417), "consists in removing, one at a time, each
of those conditions which may be imagined to have an influence on the
result." The obvious difficulty with this one-factor theory, already
recognized in its classic formulations, is its assumption that the various
conditions are independent. A famous set of experiments was once carried out to determine what produced ovulation in the rabbit. One after
another a series of possible causative agents was eliminated—various
hormones, nerve impulses, and so on—and still the rabbit ovulated, till
at last it was recognized that when one source of stimulation is blocked
others become effective. The rabbit, if I may say so, does not put all her
eggs in one basket, and the experimenter would be well advised to follow
her example.

Even when the assumption of independence is not made, we are usually
not in a position to say how the several factors are dependent on one
another, and especially not in a position to say that their covariation is
expressible by some simple function. Indeed, we are usually ignorant as

to which of the factors will utlimately turn out to be the really important ones. For these reasons, Fisher points out (*43*:91–92), the one-factor theory is more appropriate to expositions of what is already known than to laboratory practice in actual research. It is an interesting speculation how far our reconstructed logics are affected by the circumstance that those who create them usually have a professional responsibility as educators. We spend so much time or have so great an emotional investment in explaining things to students that the characteristics of this pedagogical endeavor may insensibly enter into our conceptions of the scientific explanation of things (§38).

In fact, we test one factor at a time "not because to do so is an ideal scientific procedure, but because to test them simultaneously would sometimes be too troublesome, or too costly". Indeed, even the choice of which factors to investigate is made "not because we anticipate that the laws of nature can be expressed with any particular simplicity in terms of these variables, but because they are variables which can be controlled or measured with comparative ease" (*43*:92). An awareness of such determinants of experimental design is important for a proper assessment of what has been achieved and what yet remains to be done. The awareness is even more important, perhaps, because an explicit statement of the assumptions underlying the design—the "practical" as well as the scientific assumptions—allows them to be critically appraised, and possibly replaced by more realistic ones. Thereby the potentialities of the experimental situation can be more fully realized. We may find it as expedient to investigate several variables simultaneously as to study their effects singly, or it may turn out to be more worthwhile to direct our efforts to controlling or measuring a particular factor than to experiment forthwith on those which are more manageable.

THE CONCEPTUAL FRAME

What all this comes to is that the experimental method is inseparable from the development and application of hypotheses and theories. For these are needed to tell us when we can generalize from the experimental situation, what controls must be imposed, what corrections are afterwards to be made. Without such conceptual guides, the physical operations themselves remain haphazard or wholly problematic in significance ("This proves something, but I don't know what!"). We may speak of the *conceptual frame* of an experiment as embodying all the ideation that enters into its design and interpretation. In actual scientific practice, every experiment is performed within a conceptual frame. To be sure, this may be modified as the experiment goes forward, and may be clearly recognized and understood only retrospectively; but it is at work throughout. And, the conceptual frame is less important for some types of experiments than for others—exploratory experiments may be in search of a frame, heuristic ones may be looking for fruitful changes in it, and illustrative experiments may be so routine that the conceptual frame scarcely comes into the focus of attention. Nevertheless it is essential to experimentation as such.

So true is this that experiment can more easily dispense with physical operations than with the perspectives that give these meaning. The so-called *thought experiment* (Gedankenexperiment) is one which is performed entirely within the conceptual frame itself. "Imagine," we say, "what would happen if ——"; merely conceiving the operations may be enough for us to be able to conceive their outcome. The work of many scientists, from Galileo to Einstein, is full of experiments of this type; significantly, both of these men made immeasurable contributions to the conceptual frame of experimental science.

The same physical operations may constitute a different experiment if in the meantime the conceptual frame in which they are performed has changed. An experiment may accordingly be subjected to a *secondary analysis*—that is, analysis in a new conceptual frame—which may give it a very different and often much greater significance. A secondary analysis is one of the recurrent features associated with serendipity. An experiment is performed for some particular purpose that it fails to achieve; but incidentally some other finding appears which is then recognized as being of the utmost importance if only the whole experiment is differently conceived. The events described in the dissertation on roast pig are not so far removed from the patterns of scientific discovery; a disastrous experiment may still be made to yield a scientific return if we don't mind poking about in the ashes of our expectations. I am reminded of what John von Neumann replied when he was asked whether the scientists who exploded the first atom bomb were not afraid that the whole earth might be caught up in the chain reaction. "Oh," said he, "if that had happened, it would have been so completely at variance with all we know of nuclear physics and quantum mechanics that it would have given us a great deal of food for thought!" It would, in fact, have provided someone with a wholly new conceptual frame.

In sum, "theory dominates the experimental work from its initial planning up to the finishing touches in the laboratory" (*111*:107) It guides us in the decisions as to what to observe and under what conditions, what factors are worth investigating and which are to be controlled. It tells us what errors may be expected and how they are to be dealt with. It is essential in making the actual observations of the outcome, for "without theory it is impossible to regulate a single instrument or to interpret a single reading" (Duhem in *38*:237). Above all, theory is necessary to give significance to the experimental findings. For a properly designed experiment—unless it is wholly exploratory in nature—"it is always needful to forecast all possible results of the experiment, and to have decided without ambiguity what interpretation shall be placed upon each one of them. Further, we must know by what argument this interpretation is to be sustained" (*43*:12). Even the exploratory experiment calls upon theory to make sense of what the exploration has discovered. Whether in a particular state of science we would be well advised to do more theorizing or more experimentation is one of those existential dilemmas (§4) which it is fruitless to try to resolve. The fact is that we cannot do either of these things well without doing the other even better—or having someone else do it for us. The meeting place between theory and experiment is one of those dangerous intersections at which neither vehicle is allowed to proceed till the other has gone by; the remarkable thing is that traffic moves most freely only when both roads are well-traveled.

§19. Experiment in Behavioral Science

The question whether experimentation in behavioral science is worthwhile, or even possible, is beclouded by the vagueness of the term "experiment".

MANIPULATIONS

In particular, it is not always clear whether or not the conception of experiment requires actual manipulation and transformation of the ma-

terials to be observed. I have tried to put emphasis, not on this requirement, but on that of instituting controls. Experimentation, when it is
conceived sufficiently broadly to do justice to its various functions, consists in making observations in circumstances so arranged or interpreted
that we have justification for analyzing out the factors relevant to our
particular inquiry. We are not merely taking what comes, but going
after what we want and taking steps to make sure we get it—or at least,
to maximize our chances of getting it. These steps are not always manipulative in character. They may be a matter of making appropriate selec-
tions, as in constituting a test group and a control group; or they may
involve appropriate ways of processing the raw data, as in the application of techniques of multivariate analysis. In this broad sense, experiment is deliberate, controlled observation-interpretation. I am not
troubled by the result that certain possible distinctions are dissolved in
this usage. Where called for, we may speak of *manipulative experiments*
to direct attention to the importance of the physical operations on the
subject-matter that are prerequisite to making the observations.

It is worth noting, however, that the usual emphasis on manipulation
derives from the characteristics of the logic-in-use in an earlier state of
science (2:4). The mathematics and statistics of the eighteenth and
nineteenth centuries could conveniently manage only two changing variables at a time, and the ideal experiment was therefore conceived as an
experiment in which all the variables but two were held constant. One,
the "independent variable", was then manipulated, while observations
were made on the other, the "dependent variable". This was the practical basis of the classical one-factor theory of experiment mentioned in
the preceding section. But contemporary mathematics no longer imposes
this constraint, and manipulation—whether to hold "everything else"
constant, or to introduce changes in the one factor—is correspondingly
no longer absolutely essential. Reconstructed logic is still occupied
largely in catching up with the developments in statistical theory and
technique of the early decades of this century. It has scarcely begun, it
seems to me, to take account of the revolutionary changes in the logic-
in-use by present-day scientists that have been brought about by the
fantastic developments in the capacities of computers and of the whole
new data-processing technology.

VERBAL EXPERIMENTS

From the standpoint of behavioral science, manipulation itself must be more broadly conceived than one often finds in these discussions. Experiments in physical and biological science evoke, alas, an image of a mass of brass and glass as different as can be imagined from anything to be found in the human condition. But the child poking at an ant with a blade of grass is also performing a manipulative experiment, as much as is a physicist shooting ions through a rarefied gas. Merely providing a stimulus that would otherwise not be acting, or not acting then and there, is also a type of manipulation of the observational materials. Thus, questionnaires, tests, and interviews—all of which are so widespread in contemporary behavioral science—must all be regarded as experiments, and even as manipulative ones. The argument that the behavioral scientist cannot experiment because his subject-matter does not lend itself to manipulation is embarassingly superficial, and simultaneously underestimates both the recalcitrance of physical materials and the docility of human subjects.

The reluctance to recognize such *verbal experiments* as truly experimental, or at any rate, the reluctance to allow them scientific validity, stems, I think, from the prejudice that their data are pejoratively subjective. For my part, I have no hesitation whatever in agreeing with the dictum that "to find out a person's thoughts we must sometimes ask him a question" (*83*:205). What the answer reports is subjective in some appropriate sense, to be sure. But the fact that *that* answer is given is as objective a datum as any which scientific observation can yield. To be sure, the sounds or marks by which the answer is conveyed must be interpreted as having a certain meaning. But there are always interpretations to be made of every datum, and even when these are arrived at by way of identification, in the process of "verstehen", they may still have scientific worth, as I have urged in §16. What is troublesome is that the act meaning of a verbal response does not, in general, coincide with its action meaning, and that its latent content may be very different from the manifest one. But this difference is itself accessible to observation and inference, and in any case is not always a significant difference in the particular context of inquiry. We know what to make of it when the lady protests too much, and it is also worth remembering that the line following reads, "Oh, but she'll keep her word."

SOCIAL EXPERIMENTS

There is a type of manipulative experiment in behavioral science where the changes are produced, not by the scientist's intervention, but by that of the policy maker or practitioner. Daniel Katz (*42A*:78–79) calls it a "natural experiment", but this designation makes it too easily confused with the anomalies often referred to as "nature's experiments"; better might be the label *social experiment*, though this might wrongly suggest that the change was made for the sake of experimentation, which is true very seldom, if ever. Whatever they are called, and whatever their motivation, such interventions as the evacuation of London's children during the blitz, the relocation of California's Japanese, or the desegregation of schools in the southern United States, can serve as experiments in behavioral science, and have in fact been subjected to intensive study as such. The great advantage of such experiments, as Katz points out, is that the manipulation of the variables is much more powerful than would otherwise be possible or even desirable, and the changes produced much more clear and drastic. On the other hand, the problem of controls is likely to be a much more serious one, for "we generally lack a control group whose comparability to the experimental group is assured".

The recognition of the possibility of studying various social processes in the conceptual frame of an experiment helps to put into perspective the experimental role of *survey* techniques. Rensis Likert has pointed out (*83*:250–251) that behavioral scientists often speak of "surveys *or* experiments, as though it were a question of one or the other; but in many research problems the best work can be done only by using both interdependently". A survey can usefully precede and follow a social experiment, as, for instance, in the course of an election campaign, which can be viewed as an experiment on attitudes and opinions. The survey measures what changes have occurred, and may also be able to throw light on the reasons for their occurrence. Often the sample interview survey is, as Likert says, "the best way of securing the accurate measurements that are required when using the experimental method". It is not the business of methodology to pass judgment on the effectiveness of specific scientific techniques, like polling or depth interviews. But I might, perhaps, appropriately express the opinion that Likert is certainly right, as it seems to me, in calling attention to the place of such techniques in the experimental method.

FIELD AND LABORATORY

Much of behavioral science is occupied with *field studies*, that is, with direct or indirect observation of behavior in the circumstances in which it occurs without any significant intervention on the part of the observer. Of course, in his role as consulting expert the behavioral scientist may be taking some part in a social experiment. We should not overlook the opportunities for genuine and important scientific work afforded by this social role, in spite of the fact that in some quarters it is cynically—and foolishly—looked down upon as invariably the corruption of the scientific impulse by the taste of power (see §45).

When the scientist intervenes in the context of behavior as it is given, and for the specific purpose of experimentation, we may speak of a *field experiment*. This may be contrasted with a *laboratory experiment*, in which the context as well as the behavior pattern is subjected to controls. Plainly, the distinction is very much a matter of degree. Its usefulness depends largely on the extent to which the subject being experimented on is responsive to those features of the context that have been controlled. The difference between field and laboratory experiments is therefore least likely to be important for physical science, more so for biological science: some animals, for instance, will not breed in captivity, so that their courtship and mating patterns cannot easily be subjected to laboratory experiment. When it comes to human beings, such difficulties scarcely need elaboration.

Wherever experiments can be performed they are preferred to field studies, for they allow us to study precisely those factors in which we are most interested, and to differentiate between the dependent and the independent variables. And wherever laboratory experiments can be performed they are preferred to field experiments, for they allow us more readily to subject to controls whatever factors we choose, and to subject the others to more subtle variation. The question is recurrently raised, however, whether experimentation is possible in behavioral science at all.

On this matter my own attitude is that of the backwoodsman who, asked whether he believed in baptism, replied, "Believe in it? Man, I've seen it done!" Yet there certainly are distinctive difficulties.

Among these, the most commonly spoken of are the complexity and variability of social phenomena, as described, for instance, by Mill (94:574): "the impossibility of ascertaining and taking note of all the facts of the case, and (those facts being in a perpetual state of change) [the situation that] before sufficient time had elapsed to ascertain the result of the experiment, some material circumstances would always have ceased to be the same". The complexity, to be sure, is real. Simplistic explanations of social phenomena in terms of just sex, or economic interests, geography, climate, or whatever, have achieved only a heuristic suggestiveness at best, and then only when formulated in global terms; for most specific acts and events such explanations are quite futile.

Science, however, is never a matter of "taking note of all the facts of the case". We confine ourselves always only to those that are significant for our particular problem. In Eddington's famous example, the movement of an elephant down a grassy hillside is treated as the motion of a certain mass down an inclined plane, with a determinate coefficient of friction. We work, that is to say, at some level of abstraction, and to abstract from certain factors is nothing other than to ignore them. The contemporary theory of games is startling in its generality and power precisely because its abstract formulations bypass so much of the complexity of rules and play which, *as players*, we have become accustomed to regarding as the significant features of the game; but it remains true that these features are unimportant for the solution of the problems which the theory poses. The complexities of which we each take account as we react in social situations are not necessarily to be reflected in a scientific account of what we are doing and why we do it. In short, the argument that we cannot experiment in behavioral science because the problems are too complex is no more than a blanket rationalization of our ignorance as to what experiments to perform, and how to go about performing them.

Similar considerations apply to the argument that "before sufficient time had elapsed to ascertain the result of the experiment, some material circumstance would always have ceased to be the same". It is perfectly true that the facts studied in behavioral science are in a perpetual state of change, but so are the facts studied in any other science. What we need for knowledge is not permanence but persistence, not the absolutely unchanging but rather changes sufficiently slow or limited for patterns to be recognizable. That we have not succeeded in identifying the patterns we are seeking does not validate the argument that there are none because change is perpetual. Some changes are not significant for the particular problem being investigated, and others are only variations on a persistent theme. The monkeys at their typewriters would *not* produce all the world's literature, if only because they would develop habits instead of endlessly striking the keys at random. Every clinician knows how rigid and recurrent certain human behavior patterns can be. Experimentation in behavioral science may face greater difficulties in trying to produce changes in certain variables than in trying to hold others constant.

More serious than the fact that circumstances do not remain the same during the course of the experiment is the consideration that they are likely to differ from case to case; how, then, can we generalize from any experimental finding? The problem is nicely illustrated by the psychoanalyst's task of interpreting dream symbols. Every such interpretation put before the patient is by way of being an experiment. But there is no dictionary of symbols, nor can one be constructed; the meaning depends on the particular associations brought forward by just that patient in just those circumstances. The variability extends even to the interpreter: a Viennese analyst with a limited knowledge of English is reported to have spent many futile hours trying to understand why a patient dreamed of keeping birds in his office when the recounted dream concerned putting something in the pigeonholes in his desk. But that act meanings vary does not imply that action meanings are impossible to assign. Interpretations may be carried out in accord with more or less determinate criteria of correctness, and may then disclose certain regularities of content. An experiment on human beings must take account of the fact that the same acts performed by other human beings might well have different meanings, but when the "sameness" of a response is conceived with this fact in mind, it may well turn out that every subject will respond to the experimental situation in the same way. An international group of subjects will answer differently when shown a stone and asked what they call it; but none of them will mistake it for bread.

Another difficulty distinctive of behavioral-science experiments arises from the effect on the subjects of their role *as* subjects. The mere fact that they are being studied, and by just that experimenter in just that situation, may significantly affect their performance. I know of one case where a group of students was subjected to what they thought was an interview for employment as subjects but which was actually the experiment itself; during the course of the "interview" they were repeatedly offered dry crackers from a bowl standing nearby, the interest of the study being to determine the point at which they would resist the mild social pressure to accept hospitality. To the experimenter's dismay, each of them ate every cracker in the bowl. As they later explained, "I thought I was supposed to be cooperative!" It is not only laboratory experiments which encounter this difficulty: even in field experiments subjects may identify themselves as subjects, and perform in accord with what they see as the requirements of that role. This was dramatically evidenced in the Hawthorne studies, where "it was the 'artificial' social aspects of the experimental conditions set up for measurement which produced the increases in group productivity" (*42A*:101).

In this respect as in so many others, the distinction between laboratory and field experiments is a matter of degree. But so also—and this is the important point—is the distinction between experimental contexts of either kind and what is called "real life". "One is always playing some role in relation to some situation—whether the situation be that of the laboratory, of everyday life, or of the interview. The real problem is to determine the kind of situation which will liberate the attitudes being studied." (*83*:206). The difficulty being discussed, in other words, is not intrinsic to the experimental method as such but belongs to every technique of observation in which the subject knows or suspects that he is being observed. But this difficulty is far from being an insuperable one. The subject may not know that he is a subject, as in a field experiment carried out under the guise of a substantive operation (army trainees and college sophomores are undoubtedly the most widely used subjects for behavioral-science experiments because they never know what's going on anyway). The subjects may not care that they are subjects because far stronger motivations have been tapped, as in social experiments. The effect of the experimental situation may already be known and so discounted, as in many laboratory experiments. And the effect itself may be made matter for inquiry and subsequently subjected to controls, as is true of numberless methodological experiments.

I believe that the most serious problem which confronts behavioral-science experiments, especially in the laboratory, is that the motivations brought into play are relatively weak as compared with those we would like to investigate: it is tautological that the strong ones are those which actually determine most of our behavior. The experimenter must remember that he is working with human beings, whose deeper feelings, beliefs, and attitudes are not to be trifled with. As has been said of the researchers on atomic weapons, those fellows better not forget that they're playing with dynamite! No amount of "cooling off the mark" after he has been victimized in an experimental situation quite disposes of the scruples which many of us might have, unless we are convinced that what was done "didn't really hurt him" (and even that it didn't may not suffice). But the only way to be sure of avoiding serious consequences is to exclude from the experiment any serious motivational forces. A generation ago there was much interest in the question whether hypnosis could produce any behavior contrary to what the subject is "really willing" to do. Experiments were cited in which the experimenter's professional colleagues, one after the other, were hypnotized into stealing a dollar from him, till a critic freely confessed that he would have no reluctance whatever in doing the same thing himself, without hypnosis. In the same vein an investigation into reports that a therapist had been using hypnosis to seduce a number of his female patients concluded that while the seductions were indubitable there was quite insufficient evidence of hypnosis.

SIGNIFICANCE

Yet it would be a mistake, I believe, to take the position that experiments are so "artificial" as necessarily to deny them any generalized significance. The experimental situation is not to be contrasted with "real life" but at most only with everyday life. The laboratory is also a real place, though perhaps an unusual one for the subject to find himself in, and the experiment is conducted by real people. The impersonal professionalism of these people is, after all, no different from what the subject encounters daily in probably the majority of his miscalled "interpersonal relations", and the things he is asked to do are probably no more unintelligible or distasteful than a great many of the actions demanded of him by governments, employers, teachers, and wives. But however different the experimental situation is from others, the experimental situation may still provide a ground for generalization. What is needed is not that it be wholly like the other situations, but only that it not be so wholly unlike that we do not know how to relate it to these others. As was pointed out by Leon Festinger, himself a most ingenious experimenter in behavioral science, "It matters not whether such a situation would ever be encountered in real life. . . . The possibility of application to a real-life situation arises when one knows enough about these relationships to be able to make predictions concerning a real-life situation after measurement and diagnosis of the state of affairs there." (*42A*:139) The difficulty that must be surmounted is identical with what was mentioned earlier as the scaling problem; I shall return to it in connection with models (§§32 and 33).

Here as elsewhere in methodology, the dialectical level of discussion seems to be of dubious worth. Whatever arguments can be advanced to show that experimentation *is* possible in behavioral science do not themselves provide solutions for the real problems which such experimentation constantly faces. On the other hand, arguments purporting to show that the experimental method cannot be applied to a human subject-matter do not detract one whit from what has already been achieved—which, for my part, I find impressive—or from what is being discovered in on-going experimental inquiry. In connection with this subject perhaps more than with any other in methodology, I am tempted to reverse one of Marx's famous theses on Feuerbach: Philosophers have hitherto been occupied with trying to change the world of science; the thing is, however, to understand it.

Chapter V

MEASUREMENT

§20   *Functions of Measurement*
§21   *The Structure of Measurement*
§22   *Scales*
§23   *Validity*
§24   *Measurement in Behavioral Science*

§20. *Functions of Measurement*

One of the subjects of Kinsey's study of sexual behavior in the human male afterwards complained bitterly of the injury to his masculine ego. "No matter what I told him," he explained, "he just looked me straight in the eye and asked, 'How many times?' " In so far as the objection is well-taken it rests on the "no matter what". Plainly the subject felt that *what* he had done was incomparably more significant than the frequency of its performance; there are surely cases where this attitude is justified, even if it is scientific significance which is in question. The principle, "Let's get it down to something we can count!" does not always formulate the best research strategy; "Let's see now, what have we here?" may point to a more promising program. Measurement, in short, is not an end in itself. Its scientific worth can be appreciated only in an instrumentalist perspective, in which we ask what ends measurement is intended to serve, what role it is called upon to play in the scientific situation, what functions it performs in inquiry.

QUANTITY AND QUALITY

The failure to recognize this instrumentality of measurement makes for a kind of *mystique of quantity*, which responds to numbers as though they were the repositories of occult powers. I say "as though", for I do not mean to insist that this mystique always has the same roots as the belief in numerology, gematria, and other esoteric doctrines. The effect, however, is quite similar, just as the great emphasis on definitions may resemble a faith in the power of the word. The mystique of quantity is an exaggerated regard for the significance of measurement, just because it is quantitative, without regard either to what has been measured or to what can subsequently be done with the measure. Number is treated as having an intrinsic scientific value.

The nineteenth century, I believe, was particularly subject to this mystique, but it is still to be found among us. Lord Kelvin was very possibly not himself a victim, but he has often been quoted in defense of what amounts to that point of view: "When you can measure what you are speaking about, and express it in numbers, you know something about it; but when you cannot measure it, when you cannot express it in numbers, your knowledge is of a meager and unsatisfactory kind: it may be the beginning of knowledge, but you have scarcely, in your thoughts, advanced to the stage of science, whatever the matter may be" (*Popular Lectures* I 73). A similar viewpoint was formulated in the dictum that "science advances in the last decimal place". Counting and measuring were regarded as the necessary conditions for scientific progress. It is suggestive that for the nineteenth-century physicists there seemed little left to do except to extend the laws already discovered to ever greater degrees of exactness, though in the biological and behavioral sciences that was scarcely the situation, and by the turn of the century it was clearly no longer the situation in physics either. The contemporary mystique of quantity owes much, I think, to the law of the instrument: we have developed such subtle and powerful techniques of measurement that using them comes to seem all that is worthwhile.

In the history of science qualitative and quantitative considerations have worked hand in hand. Consider the development of the atomic theory, for instance. The world is full of many qualitatively different things, but very early, in both India and Greece, the idea was arrived at that they are all composed of the same stuff and differ only quantitatively, in the number and arrangement of their constituent particles. Ships and shoes, sealing-wax and cabbages, all consist of the same atoms (kings were regarded as special beings for a long time after). Qualitative differences among atoms, however, were then brought into the account: things are unlike, not only because of the numbers of atoms they contain or the parts of space they fill, but also because of the kind of atoms of which they are composed. But the atoms themselves, it turned out, combined in definite proportions, and differed again on a quantitative basis of relative weight. There were subatomic particles, essentially all alike, or at most of two kinds—protons and electrons—and the differences among atoms depended on the number of these which they contained, or their place within the atom. Then an ever increasing variety of such particles was identified, so that qualitative considerations were reinstated; and now again the attempt is being made to reduce this bewildering variety to an underlying uniformity, a field or whatever, manifesting itself in quantitatively different forms. The One and the Many alternate their roles in serving as the goal of the scientific quest. The drama needs adversaries, but in life we cannot be sure for very long which is hero and which is villain.

As Helmer and Rescher (56) pointed out in their discussion of the "inexact sciences", exactness is not as important for scientific status as is objectivity, or better, intersubjectivity. The questions before us are always, "How can we learn more than we know now?" and "How can we become more sure of what we already think we know?" In the answers to these questions measurement surely plays a part, and a very large one; but it is by no means the only method of extending or solidifying our knowledge.

WHAT MEASUREMENT PERMITS

If we ask just what it is that measurement allows us to achieve, one answer that immediately presents itself relates to the technology of an industrial civilization. The products of that technology must be engineered to within fairly narrow limits of tolerance if they are to work at all, particularly if systems of production and distribution call for freely interchangeable parts. Measurement, in a word, is a device for *standardization*, by which we are assured of equivalences among objects of diverse origin. This is the sense that is uppermost in a usage like "a measure of grain": measurement allows us to know what quantity we are getting, and to get and give just what is called for.

A second function of measurement, one which shows its scientific importance, is to make possible more subtle discriminations and correspondingly more precise descriptions. Consider the difference between a vocabulary of color words, however extensive, and the specification of colors by wave-length, or the difference between the vocabulary of olive sizes ("mammoth", "colossal", and the rest) and numerical indices of size or weight. We assign numerals to represent properties because, among other reasons, "such assignment enables us to distinguish easily and minutely between different but similar properties" (*13*:132). In turn, on this basis we can arrive at unambiguous classifications. Categories like "senior citizen", "well-to-do", or "feeble-minded" are obviously more difficult to put to scientific use than the corresponding numerical specifications of age, income, or intelligence. The vagueness of the qualitative classes invites misunderstanding and disagreement; but "when description gives way to measurement, calculation replaces debate," as S. S. Stevens has put it. This opinion is reminiscent of Leibniz's remarks in the seventeenth century, wherein he looked forward to a universal language of ideas, a symbolic logic as it were, in which all propositions could be precisely formulated. With such a symbolism, said he, metaphysicians would no longer engage in fierce and endless controversy, but, putting their arms on each other's shoulders in friendliest fashion, they would say, "Come, let us calculate!" His hopes, I am afraid, have not been realized, for modern logic only gives metaphysicians something else to argue about. But it is certainly true that quantitative specifications allow us to bring our scientific disagreements to a sharper and more illuminating focus.

For unambiguously detailed classifications allow us to state more subtle laws and more precisely formulated laws. Knowing that one thing "depends on" another is of incomparably less scientific worth than being able to say to just what extent changes in the first correspond to changes in the second. That growth curves are exponentials tells us much more than is contained in statements like "the size of an organism depends on its age"; but we cannot say what form a function has without some sort of measures of the variables it relates. And by making such measurements we can also perform discriminatory verifications among competing hypotheses or theories. The physics of both Newton and Einstein predict a precession of the perihelion of the planet Mercury; but Newton's is only about half the observed value, while Einstein's is very near that value. Incidentally, Newton delayed publication of his work for some eighteen years because his calculations did not fit the motions of the moon, till new and corrected measures of the earth's size yielded an acceptable fit from his theory.

THE USE OF MATHEMATICAL TECHNIQUES

More important than any of the considerations so far mentioned, though perhaps not wholly distinct from them, is that measurement makes it possible to apply to inquiry available mathematical techniques, whether for purposes of verification, prediction, or explanation. Jevons (64:456), in warning us that scientific knowledge is never absolutely exact, speaks of "a prevailing impression that when once mathematical formulae have been successfully applied to a branch of science, this portion of knowledge assumes a new nature, and admits of reasoning of a higher character than those sciences which are still unmathematical". I confess that I share this impression, provided that mathematics is broadly enough conceived (to include, for instance, nonquantitative logical calculi). What is involved is rather different, to my mind, from the effect Plato alleges in his *Laws*, that "arithmetic stirs up him who is by nature sleepy and dull, and makes him quick to learn, retentive and shrewd". What *is* true is that, as Plato continues, "aided by art divine he makes progress quite beyond his natural powers". Mathematics, that is to say, does not develop the scientist's powers but puts its own powers at his disposal; it allows the scientist to do wonders in spite of being sleepy and dull. To create the mathematics is, of course, another matter; but with its creation something of the genius of the mathematician himself is made available to every schoolboy. Today, a schoolboy can easily solve problems that would have given pause to Newton and Archimedes, and can do it because they *did* pause long enough to show us how.

But neither mathematics nor measurement must be identified with the treatment of quantity, as will appear below. For the present it is enough to recognize that even the use of quantitative mathematics is not restricted in application to theories or laws that are themselves quantitative in character. The theory of evolution as Darwin originally formulated it was not a particularly quantitative one; yet in establishing it Darwin made many counts of species (for instance, of seeds in a bird's crop), performed anatomical measurements, and used other quantitative data, like occurrences of individual variations or data about geographical distributions. In general, even if we are working with qualitative variables, the frequencies of their occurrence may be of importance to our inquiry, and these constitute a corresponding set of quantitative variables. Similarly, the reliability of a classification into qualitative categories may itself be a quantitative matter. No problem is a purely qualitative one in its own nature; we may always approach it in quantitative terms.

We may; but *can* we always do so? Are there not some things which are intrinsically unmeasurable, and are these not particularly to be found in the subject-matter of behavioral science? For my part, I answer these questions with an unequivocal "No". A detailed discussion of the issues must plainly follow and not precede a sketch of just what constitutes measurement (§24). Proleptically, I would say that whether we can measure something depends, not on that thing, but on how we have conceptualized it, on our knowledge of it, above all on the skill and ingenuity which we can bring to bear on the process of measurement which our inquiry can put to use. I believe that Nagel is right in saying of measurement that, from a larger point of view, it can be regarded as "the delimitation and fixation of our ideas of things" (in *27*:7). To say of something that it is incapable of being measured is like saying of it that it is knowable only up to a point, that our ideas of it must inevitably remain indeterminate. I have no wish to enter upon a discussion of philosophical views—either epistemological or metaphysical: like Kant's principle of the axioms of intuition, which purports to guarantee a priori that every possible object of knowledge is quantitative; or like Bergson's view that mathematics leads only to contradictions when applied to the flow of experience itself. For the purposes of science it suffices if measurability is treated as a methodological presupposition. That this treatment suffices means that it is worthwhile to suppose that we *can* measure, till our failures discourage us; and even then, our scientific impulse may keep us from discouraging others by promulgating the rationalization that we ourselves failed to do it only because it can't be done.

§21. The Structure of Measurement

Measurement, in most general terms, can be regarded as the assignment of numbers to objects (or events or situations) in accord with some rule. The property of the objects which determines the assignment according to that rule is called a *magnitude*, the measurable attribute; the number assigned to a particular object is called its *measure*, the amount or degree of its magnitude. It is to be noted that the rule defines both the magnitude and the measure. A procedure of measurement not only determines an amount, but also fixes what it is an amount *of*. We do not first identify some magnitude, then go about devising some way to measure it. As operationists have long insisted, what is measured and how we measure it are determined jointly. Operationists may have given undue emphasis to the "how" as against the "what", but this emphasis is a healthy corrective to the naive idea that magnitudes can be conceived quite independently of procedures for determining their measure in particular cases.

MAPPING THE DATA

That numbers are assigned to the objects is usually expressed by saying that the objects are *mapped* into an abstract space of some determinate structure. Mapping requires that a relationship shall have been established between the objects and the numbers so that to each object there corresponds exactly one number, one point in the abstract space. In general, several objects may be mapped onto the same point. When the objects are so selected that the rule of assignment permits only one object to be mapped onto any point, we speak of a one-to-one correspondence; usually, the word "correspondence" by itself is employed in this sense. Now, we are free to establish whatever correspondence we choose, but having done so we must abide by the consequences—otherwise we have not in fact "established" a correspondence, or "laid down a rule" for the assignment. Given the objects and a problematic situation in which they assume significance, we find that some rules of assignment are vastly more useful than others for dealing with the problem at hand. The task of measurement is that of devising a useful rule and exploring the properties of the assignment so as to be able to put it to use.

The space into which the objects are mapped need not consist of numbers. Generally speaking, it would be more accurate to say that what is assigned to each object is a *numeral* rather than a number. The rule of assignment determines certain relationships among the numerals, and it is this pattern of relationships which constitutes the abstract space. Only in certain special types of measurement does this pattern coincide with the pattern of familiar relationships among the numbers themselves. Serious blunders in the interpretation and use of measurements result from tacitly assuming this coincidence in cases where it by no means exists, that is, assuming that the numerals assigned stand in all the relations which hold among the numbers they designate. The only decisive feature of all measurements, as Weyl (*137*:144) points out, is "symbolic representation". Measurement "permits things (relative to the assumed measuring basis [the assignment rule]) to be represented conceptually, by means of symbols." The point to this representation is that manipulation of the symbols in terms of those relationships among them which the assignment has made significant will reveal corresponding relationships among the objects to which they have been assigned. We use numerals so as to be able to take advantage of systems of relationships already known and clearly understood.

ORDERS

The simplest form of assignment, basic to most other types of measurement, is one which establishes an *order* among the objects. We begin with a well-defined set of objects, that is, a set for which a criterion of membership has been specified so that, given an object, we can come to a decision—at least in principle—whether or not it is a member of the set. Now the order which we wish to establish among the objects is not a property of the set as such. A group of people at a cocktail party, say, is still one and the same group whatever order we take them in: order of volubility, of alcoholic capacity, or of position on the political spectrum. An order is constituted only by a relation which holds among the members of the set, like being less talkative, or more thirsty, or further to the right politically. The set is said to be the *field* of the relation; it is that which is being ordered *by* the relation.

To establish an order a relation must first of all be asymmetrical: if it holds between two members of the set in a certain direction—that is, *from* one *to* the other—it cannot also hold between them in the reverse direction. The parental relation, for example, is an asymmetrical one: if x is the parent of y, it cannot also happen that y is the parent of x. There are, of course, relations which always hold in both directions, like the sibling relation; these are called "symmetrical". And there are also relations, the "nonsymmetrical" ones, which are sometimes reversible and sometimes not, like the relation of loving, for the love may or may not be requited. All ordering relations must be asymmetrical, but only in the field being ordered; whether the relation ever holds simultaneously in both directions among objects outside the field is irrelevant.

Secondly, an ordering relation must be *transitive:* if it holds between two members, the second of which has the relation to a third, then the first must also stand in that relation to the third. Ancestor-of, for example, is a transitive relation: if x is an ancestor of y and y of z, then x is also an ancestor of z. There are relations which never exhibit this structure, like the relation of father-of: if x is the father of y and y of z, then x cannot also be the father of z but only the grandfather. Such relations are called "intransitive". And there are also "nontransitive" relations, which are sometimes carried over in this sense, sometimes not; the friends of my friends are sometimes my friends as well, but by no means always. As before, only in the field must the ordering relation be transitive.

Every relation which is both asymmetrical and transitive establishes an order. It is called a *partial order*, for not all the members of the set may stand in the relation to each other. If in addition every two members of the set are indeed related in one direction or the other, the relation is said to be *connected*, and to establish a *complete order*. Suppose, for instance, that the members of a committee arrive at a meeting one at a time; then they can be ordered by the relation "more punctual than": if x arrived before y, y could not have arrived before x; if x arrived before y and y before z, then x also arrived before z; and of any two members x and y, either x arrived before y or y arrived before x. The earliest to arrive stands first in this order (is most punctual), then the next to arrive, and so till the last. If some members of the committee were absent altogether, then the order is only a partial one for the committee as a whole; the relative punctuality of the absent members is quite indeterminate.

Thus we may assign numerals as a measure of punctuality according to any rule which satisfies the condition that if x arrived before y he must be assigned a larger numeral than that assigned to y (that is, one designating a larger number). Similarly, assigning a smaller numeral to x than to y would give a measure of tardiness. The space onto which the members of the committee are being mapped on the basis of their relative punctuality is constituted only by the relations of greater and less among these numerals, as defined by the designated numbers. Instead of numerals we could as well have used, say, letters of the alphabet, it being understood that these stand in relations of precedence according to what is usually called the alphabetical order (or according to any other fixed order). These two measures are essentially indistinguishable; both establish the very same order of relative punctuality. Which specific numerals we use, or whether we use numerals at all rather than letters of the alphabet, is a matter only of notation.

When an order has been established, we are no longer restricted to so-called absolute terms, that is, those which simply make a predication of a property, like "heavy" or "punctual". We can apply comparatives—"heavier" or "more punctual"—on the basis of the order. But the fact that our English grammar often constructs comparatives by combining with the absolute term separate terms like "more" and "less" may be misleading. For this grammatical form suggests that there is some magnitude—weight or punctuality—which has a measure of quite a different sort, an *amount*; and that the measure on which the comparative is based derives from the fact that one object has a larger amount, more of the attribute, than the other. This implication may sometimes be true, but in general it is false. We may say that one thing is heavier than another because we have first determined just how much each of them weighs, then compared the numbers which represent their weights. But we might also just have hefted them simultaneously, so that we have no knowledge of anything other than their comparative weights. Similarly, we might see that one color is yellower than another without knowing how much yellow each has in it, or even—and this is the important point—without having any clear idea of what might be meant by the "amount of yellow" in a color. In general, measures of amounts are constructed on the basis of orders, as we shall see, rather than the other way around.

It must also be emphasized that the order of a set of objects is something which we impose on them. We take them in a certain order; the order is not given by or found in the objects themselves. (This point is obscured by the familiarity and usefulness of certain orders—for instance, spatial and temporal ones; as we become habituated to them, they are experienced as so compelling that we imagine the order to be imposed on us from without. Yet a reader of Hebrew or Chinese would take the letters on this page, for example, in quite another order than we do, as might a typographer or a proofreader.) What is to be found actually there among the objects is the ordering relation, which actually has the required properties. Whether a particular relation is or is not asymmetrical is not for us to decide but only to discover, for it depends on the facts of the case, not on our whim. But it is we who select the ordering relation, and we are free to choose what we will. The letters "g", "l", "o", "c", "i" can be ordered alphabetically, by their frequency of occurrence in the English language, by their position on the page or on the typewriter keyboard, so as to spell a word, or in any other way we like. And in selecting the relation, we also define it with sufficient closure so that it can be used to establish an order. We may, for instance, choose to define absence from the meeting as the minimal degree of punctuality, rather than as leaving comparative punctuality indeterminate. Only, as always, we must abide by the consequences of the choices we have made.

Suppose that with a given ordering relation there are objects in the field which, though not standing in that relation to each other, share with each other all their relations of that kind with other objects—that is, if x has that relation to z so does y, and vice versa, and if z has it to x, it has it to y as well, and vice versa. In our example of relative punctuality this would be the situation if two members of the committee came to the meeting together; the two of them would be more punctual than the same other members, and less punctual than the same other members (different sets of same others). In such a case we say that the relation establishes a *weak order*. The assignment of numbers no longer determines a strict one-to-one correspondence, because the same number is assigned to any two objects related as x and y above. Such objects are said to stand in an *equivalence relation* to each other: their relationship is symmetrical and transitive. That things equivalent to the same thing are equivalent to each other follows immediately. Identity, equality, and synonymy are all examples of equivalence relations. In general, every weak order determines an equivalence relation, constructed by combining the ordering relation with its converse (the same relation in the reverse direction). The most familiar example is the arithmetical one: if *x* is greater than or equal to *y* and *y* is greater than or equal to *x* then *x* and *y* are equal. As before, amounts or "sizes" are not presupposed but on the contrary are derived from such relations. If we know of two members of the committee that each of them is at least as punctual as the other, it follows that they must have arrived at the meeting at the same time.

Weak orders and partial orders are often confused with one another, with disastrous effect. If the order of two objects is indeterminate, this relation by no means justifies the conclusion that they occupy the same position in the order, that is, that they are equivalent. Not being able to express a preference between two alternatives, for instance, is very different from being able to judge that they are equally preferable—a point which is very important in the measurement of utilities. The setting up of an equivalence relation often also encounters difficulty in establishing transitivity. Each of two colors, for instance, might be judged to be at least as yellow as the other; it does not follow that they are of the same shade of yellow. It may happen that *x* is indistinguishable in this respect from *y* and *y* in turn from *z*, yet the difference between *x* and *z* may be readily apparent.

On the basis of a genuine equivalence relation we can construct *equivalence classes* (also called "abstractive sets"); they consist of objects all equivalent to one another, and containing every object (in the field) which is equivalent to any member of the class. With respect to the relation of relative punctuality, for example, each equivalence class consists of committeemen who all arrived together. An equivalence class may, of course, have only one member in it; if all of them are such unit classes, the order is a strong one. In a weak order there are equivalence classes with more than one member; the equivalence classes themselves, however, are always strongly ordered.

Counting may now be seen as a type of measurement: it is a way of assigning numbers to objects. The objects being measured are classes; we number the individuals only in order to be able to assign a measure to the class which they compose. When we count, we are always determining how many things there are of a certain *kind*. The procedure is rather more complicated than familiarity makes it appear to be. To start with, the objects in the class to be counted must be ordered in some way—we must count first this one, then that one, and so on. It is true that the count arrived at will be the same no matter in what order we do the counting, but some order or other is nevertheless needed. The numbers to be used for the measurement are also ordered, and in a particular way, according to increasing size—a point not appreciated by very young children, who "count" at first by reciting the numbers they know in a random sequence, or beginning with their favorites, or the like. Now a one-to-one correspondence is established, the object which is first in the series of objects being associated in some way—by a mark or tally, or by being moved to one side, or otherwise—with the first member of the number series, the next object with the next number, and so to the end The strict correspondence is necessary to ensure that every object is counted and that none is counted more than once. (The one-to-one correspondence, by the way, does not presuppose the number *one;* it is a matter only of identity or diversity.) The rule of counting is then that the last number corresponding to a member of the class is assigned to the class as its measure; it is the number of objects in the class, the magnitude measured being known as the *cardinality* of the class.

This sketch of the procedure is still oversimplified. It assumes, for instance, that we can always identify the "next" object in the ordered series, so that we can assign to it the next number. This assumption is false, for example, if the objects to be counted are the fractions between zero and one, and they are ordered as usual according to size, since between any two fractions there is always another; there is, however, a way of ordering the fractions so that this condition is met. And we have assumed also that the series to be counted comes to an end; there are other ways of measuring cardinality which do not rest on this assumption, nor is it true that classes whose members taken in some order never come to an end are all of the same "size", that is, have the same measure assigned to their cardinality (some infinities are bigger than others). Moreover, because correspondence is transitive, we often count, not by assigning numbers to the members of the class to be counted, but to the members of some corresponding class. The word "calculus", in fact, is said to derive from the word for the pebbles which were heaped up one by one as soldiers or sheep filed by to be counted; the pebbles could then be counted, or measured in some other way.

That objects can be counted, or ordered with respect to some attribute, does not suffice to enable us to measure a magnitude in such a way that we can usefully perform whatever arithmetical operations we choose on the numbers assigned. We may be able to answer questions of more or less, and even to say how many objects in the field have a greater or smaller magnitude than some given object, without being able to say how much each of them has, or that one has twice as much as another, and so on. For this purpose, the procedures of measurement must satisfy other conditions as well. A particular type of measurement which achieves this end—one which for some time was mistakenly regarded as the only type to do so (see §22)—is that known as *additive measurement*. A brief examination of it may bring into relief a number of important features of measurement in general.

Consider a set of objects which has been ordered by some relation. Now suppose that we can find or devise an operation which can be performed on the objects so as to satisfy a certain set of requirements. Let us call this operation *combination;* it will afterwards be seen to correspond to the operation of addition on the assigned numbers, but it is of the utmost importance not to confuse the physical combination of objects with the arithmetical addition of the numbers assigned to them, even though the two operations will be seen to have the same logical structure. The purpose of the requirements, in fact, is precisely to ensure this sameness of structure. The requirements to be met by the way of combining objects that has been adopted for the measurement are four. (1) First, the operation must be *commutative:* when two objects are combined the outcome must be the same regardless of which object is taken first. (2) It must be *associative:* the outcome must be the same regardless of how the combined objects are grouped—that is, the result of combining an object with the combination of two others must be the same as combining with the third the combination of the first two. (3) The operation must be *incremental* with respect to the ordering relation: if two objects are equivalent with respect to that relation, then the combination of either of them with some third object is no longer equivalent to the other one but precedes it in the order established by the relation. (4) Finally, the operation must satisfy a requirement of *equalities:* if two equivalent objects are each combined with objects equivalent to one another, the outcomes must be equivalent.

The measurement of weight by a balance provides a simple illustration. Let a set of objects be ordered according to which one depresses its side when they are placed on the two pans of the balance. This sorting provides a (weak) order: experience shows it to be asymmetrical and transitive, under suitable conditions; and when the two objects balance one another they are equivalent. The combining operation to be employed consists in putting the two objects on the same pan. Again, experience shows that the four requirements for an additive operation are satisfied. Take, for example, just the last one: if two objects balance one another, as do two other objects, then one from each pair placed together on a pan will balance the other two on the other pan. We then say that this way of combining objects for weighing is an additive operation. It has the same structure as the operation of addition.

More precisely, two relations are *isomorphic* to one another if a one-to-one correspondence can be established between their fields in such a way that whenever the first relation holds between two objects then the second relation holds between the corresponding objects, and vice versa. So defined, isomorphism is an equivalence relation—it is symmetrical and transitive. A *structure* is an equivalence class of isomorphs. It is in this sense that the relation which an object has to two others by virtue of being their combination has the same structure as the relation of number to two others when it is their sum.

The profound importance of this fact is that it allows us to assign numbers in the weighing procedure so that they can meaningfully be added to one another (and therefore also subtracted, multiplied, and divided), for the sum of two numbers is precisely the number which would be assigned to the combination of any two objects to which the numbers added would be respectively assigned. To say, for example, that an object x has twice the weight of an object y means that x is equivalent in weight to the combination of y with any object equivalent to y, and therefore also, by the properties of the combining operation, to the combination of any two objects equivalent to y; in other words, the number assigned to x is twice as great as that assigned to y.

STANDARDS

To fix these numbers what is needed is only that a *standard* of measurement be specified. A particular object, say a cube of platinum, is chosen and called a "kilogram" or "pound" or whatever (this is a matter of notation). This object constitutes or defines the unit of measurement. To say that something weighs one gram would then mean that the combination of a thousand objects each equivalent to it in weight would in turn be equivalent in weight to the standard kilogram, the platinum cube. The interpretation of all other weight assignments is thereby also fixed. It is worth noting, however, that this relation holds only when the numbers assigned are rationals—either whole numbers or ratios of whole numbers. That something weighs two-thirds of a gram, for instance, means that it weighs as much as the combination of any two objects equivalent to one another and such that the combination of three members of their equivalence class would weigh one gram. But no such interpretation can be given if we were to assign for the weight of an object a number like $\sqrt{2}$. It is for precisely this reason that such numbers were called "incommensurables". I shall return to this point shortly.

The choice of the standard of measurement is a matter of convention; but it is not an arbitrary choice. Suppose we had chosen as our standard a cube of iron rather than platinum. Then, as the iron rusted, all other objects would become lighter in weight, and subsequently, if the rust blew away, even heavier than before. It is important that the literal truth of this statement be recognized, for how much an object weighs is determined by its relation to the standard—this is precisely what is meant by the standard's being the standard. Yet we would prefer to say that only the standard has changed in weight. We can, indeed, say so; properly construed, this statement would be equivalent in meaning to the preceding statement that everything else has changed its weight in a systematic way. The difference between the two is a matter only of "descriptive simplicity" (§36). We can choose whatever standard we like; but whether we really like what we have chosen depends on what the facts disclose as to its own susceptibility to change.

In actually carrying out measurements we seldom make any direct use of the standard itself. Instead, we rely on some *secondary standard*, like the set of brass weights to be found in any laboratory. The secondary standard is presumed to be equivalent to the standard, and therefore, by the transitivity of equivalence, to be capable of providing measures relative to the standard itself. This presumption, however, must be checked; the process of doing so is called *calibration*. Its purpose, as G. E. Mount (in *98*:17) has stated clearly, is "to equate the number assignments, which are made on a given occasion, to the number assignments that would be made of the same things on any similar occasion with the same instructions." To achieve this purpose it is not only the secondary standard that must be calibrated, but the instrument as well. For instance, if the instructions for weighing with a balance do not distinguish between the left and right pans (but only discriminate them as "one pan" and "the other pan"), the balance must be calibrated so as to justify this indifference: two equivalent objects must continue to balance one another when they interchange pans, or else a correction must be introduced. Often the secondary standard is built into the instrument, and the two are calibrated together, as in weighing with a spring rather than a balance.

FUNDAMENTAL AND DERIVED MEASUREMENT

Once certain measurements have been made, on their basis we can establish the measurement of other magnitudes. Campbell (*12*) distinguishes these two sorts of measurement as "fundamental" and "derived". A *fundamental* measurement is one which presupposes no others, save those which consist in establishing an order or making a count; a *derived* measurement is one which is carried out by making use of laws, logical or empirical, relating to fundamental measures. The simpler case is that in which the laws involved are purely logical; in that case the derived measure is a *calculation* from the fundamental ones—calculation being, as Campbell has pointed out, nothing other than the "deduction of propositions from numerical laws". For example, given ways of measuring mass and volume, we can introduce a measure of density, which is simply mass per unit volume. It is in the course of such calculations that measurement may make good use of irrational numbers and even of imaginaries.

Many derived measurements proceed on the basis of empirical connections with an already established measure. Stevens speaks in this context of an "indicant" as "a presumed effect or correlate" of some phenomenon in which we are interested; "as soon as we learn the quantitative relation between the indicant and the object of our interest, the indicant can be calibrated and used to measure the phenomenon". In this capacity the indicant is often known in behavioral science as an *index*. We may know, for instance, or have reason to believe, that the morale of a group is reflected in the effectiveness of its performance of group tasks; if we have some way of measuring this effectiveness—say by the frequency and speed with which success is achieved—we may use it as a derived measure of group morale. In such cases, the value of this derived measure or index will depend on its empirical connections in turn with other measures of morale.

An important application of derived measurement is for the specification of meaning of a concept for cases outside the range covered by its fundamental measurement. There is an illuminating discussion of this point in Hempel (*58*:71-73). We cannot determine the weight of the individual molecules of a gas by the balance procedure alone; but we can do so with the help of Avogadro's law that equal volumes of all gases, at the same pressure and temperature, contain equal numbers of molecules. This sort of difficulty, it may be said, is "only a practical one"; but in measurement practicality is everything. Moreover, there are many cases where there are theoretical reasons why the fundamental measurement cannot be applied, though derived measures may be used. We cannot measure with the mercury theormometer temperatures greater than the boiling point of mercury itself, but the theory of heat makes other measures possible. As laws move from merely empirical generalizations to theories, there are likely to be corresponding changes in the methods used for measurement of the magnitudes which figure in the laws. The observation that things expand when heated underlies the ordinary thermometer; but the theory of heat requires—and makes possible—the introduction of a thermodynamic scale.

Throughout the process of measurement, as we have seen, laws are presupposed; it is their discovery which makes the measurement possible. Laws are involved in establishing an order—for instance, the generalization that a certain relation is indeed transitive; in establishing an additive scale—for instance, that a certain operation is indeed commutative; or in establishing a derived measure—for instance, that a certain variable is indeed an index of the magnitude to be measured. It is this fact, that measurements embody within themselves whole systems of laws, which is at bottom what makes measurement of such scientific significance. "When we measure a property," Campbell says (*13*:133–134), "the numeral which we assign to represent it is assigned as the result of experimental laws; the assignment implies laws. . . . We should expect to find that other laws could be discovered relating the numerals so assigned to each other or to something else. . . . It is because true measurement is essential to the discovery of laws that it is of such vital importance to science."

§22. Scales

Measurement has been described as the assignment of numbers according to a rule, what the numbers are assigned to being called a "magnitude" and each number its "measure" in a particular case. A *scale* of measurement, Stevens has suggested, may be identified as the rule of assignment, the principle by which a measure is determined for any given magnitude. Of course, the term "scale" is sometimes used to refer to the measuring instrument, and sometimes even to the standard of measurement. In this section it will be taken as a designation of the logical structure of the procedure of assignment. This scale specifies, in effect, in what respects the numerical relation among the measures is isomorphic to some corresponding relation among the magnitudes. Otherwise put, the scale determines what operations among the numbers assigned in a measurement will yield results significant for what is being measured. It tells us, in a word, how to interpret the numbers arrived at in a measurement. The value of a particular scale, then, as of measurement in general, consists in the mathematics which it allows us to employ in the course of our inquiry.

What mathematical transformations measurements can be subjected to depends on the scale in terms of which they were arrived at. But it plainly depends also on the available mathematics. There is no advantage in using a scale that allows operations that we do not know how to perform, while a scale that precludes known operations tautologically leaves something to be desired. The insistence on the use of certain scales of measurement, therefore, depends on the state of mathematics at the time. As Kemeny has explained (*75*:154–155), "A numerical theory will enable us to use powerful mathematical methods usuallly taken from the calculus. A theory that is stated in terms of a simple ordering requires a much more intricate mathematical treatment. . . . The real reason for preferring a numerical scale is mathematical convenience. We may also foresee the day when, with the development of mathematics, numerical scales will become much less important than they are now considered." The law of the instrument is thus of particular importance in measurement. We tend to think that certain procedures are required by the subject-matter when in fact the situation is only that those procedures are the ones most readily available to us. It is for this reason that the development of new scales and techniques of measurement can be so valuable.

The laws that are presupposed in a procedure of measurement are embodied in the scale. Coombs has rightly emphasized that every scale is a theory, not "merely" a matter of definition. In developing a scale for a particular purpose (not just abstractly), discovery plays as much of a role as does invention. Suppose, for example, that a person's preferences among a given set of alternatives are empirically disclosed to be non-transitive. We might choose to regard his preferences as inconsistent, and adopt a scale for the measurement of his utilities which implies that they *can* be ordered. In doing so, we have committed ourselves to certain conceptions of rationality as well as of values and their behavioral expression; if these conceptions turn out to be untenable, our scale of measurement is correspondingly brought into question. Another example, also from utility theory, is provided by Arrow's postulate of "the independence of irrelevant alternatives". This postulate is violated by the housewife who wishes to purchase poultry, is informed that she may have either duck or goose, and says that she prefers duck; when the butcher returns from the cooler and tells her that there is also turkey, she replies, "In that case, I'll take goose"! Such preference scales do occur, and not just with geese; but theorists are by no means agreed on how these choices are to be analyzed.

Many more different scales of measurement are in use, or available for use, than is sometimes realized. In particular, traditional discussions of the subject by methodologists have often left the impression that there are only two scales, corresponding to so-called "intensive" and "extensive" measurement, although in fact there are several scales of each type, as will appear shortly. Coombs has listed a dozen or so different

scales; I shall sketch the properties of some of the more important ones
(which itself implies a scale of measurement), following closely Coombs's
account. They are presented in order of increasing strength (a measurement again!)— that is, in order of how much can be done with them, and
correspondingly, how much they presuppose, how much is to be established about what is being measured before a selected scale can be applied
in the measurement.

SCALES OF INTENSIVE MEASUREMENT

The simplest of all scales is the *nominal scale*, where numbers are assigned only as labels or names. A particular galaxy is identified as
"M 31" or "NGC 224", according to its listing by Messier or in the
New General Catalogue; it is also known as "the Great Nebula in
Andromeda". The set of words has the same denotation as the numerical
expressions. Such assignment of numbers constitutes a measurement only
as a limiting case, for the only relation among the numbers of a nominal
scale which is isomorphic to one among the objects to which they are
assigned is the relation of identity and difference: no two numbers are
assigned to the same object, and no two objects have the same number
assigned to them. That numerals occur in the name does not make the
assignment mathematical any more than saying "Let $x =$ the murderer"
makes criminal detection a matter of mathematics. For a nominal scale
the assignment of any particular number to an object imposes no constraints whatever on the assignments to other objects, beyond the requirement that *that* number is not to be used again. Any two numbers
can be interchanged without affecting anything but the notation.

Yet nominal scales have their uses, and are likely to become even more
common in the future, especially in behavioral science. For the processing
of large amounts of data, especially with the help of computers, may require the identification of a great many individuals, and the free invention
of arbitrary names taxes our imagination if not the actual resources of
our language. All-digit dialing is a consequence of just such pressures;
social-security numbers, the numbering of checking accounts and credit
cards, and countless (!) other such devices have a similar origin and
function. Yet nominal scales are not without substantive significance—
they may facilitate the establishment of taxonomies. Indeed, the numbers

of a nominal scale are often assigned with a classification in mind—for instance, for football or baseball players, according to the position in which they play, or for addresses, which are even on one side of the street and odd on the other.

In a *partially ordered scale* the assignment of a number to a particular object provides either an upper or a lower bound to the numbers that can be assigned to some of the other objects in the field. That is, certain objects are so related in terms of the magnitude being measured that one of them must be assigned a lower number than the other (or a higher one, as the case may be). But other pairs of objects may be quite incomparable in this respect—it will be recalled that incomparability is by no means the same as an equivalence, or weak ordering. Often such incomparability results from the fact that the magnitude is made up of two or more distinct attributes, which may allow for relations in opposite directions simultaneously. People may be partially ordered by size, but there will be many cases where height, weight, and girth do not all relate the same way: *a* may be taller than *b*, but *b* may be more solidly built—which is "larger"?

In general, a partially ordered scale orders some relatively homogeneous subset of the field; of course, that it *is* homogeneous may not be known independently of just this fact that it is capable of being so ordered. Reviewers may assign from one to four stars to a movie as a measure of its entertainment value, but differentiations must also be introduced between, say, "adult" and "family" pictures, or between musicals and serious dramas. Even granting the objectivity of an assessment of quality, it is surely quite another problem to compare across genres. In the same way, Hubble assigned the letters "a", "b", and "c" to galaxies according to the degree of their openness, but also distinguished elliptical, irregular, spiral, and barred spiral galaxies, the comparisons as to openness being made within each type but not (or at least, not as easily) between galaxies of different types. In behavioral science, we may wish to order, say, the masculinity of various interests and occupations: flower-arranging or hunting, being a decorator or being a lumberjack. But cross-cultural differences may be crucial—in some fortunate societies women perform the physical labor while men are occupied with esthetic concerns.

In an *ordinal scale* the assignment of any one number fixes an upper or a lower bound for all the other numbers to be assigned. The ordering is complete, though it may be a weak one, with the same number being assigned to two or more objects. The simplest cases are those in which numbers that are chiefly used as though they belong to a nominal scale in fact reflect a certain order among the objects, one that determines the order in which they are to be labeled. The serial numbers of a manufactured product, for instance, are essentially only devices for identification; yet a higher serial number also indicates a later date of manufacture. Similarly, the numbering of the galaxies in the New General Catalogue in fact proceeds in the order of their right ascension, their longitude on the celestial sphere. Such incidental orderings, as it were, are quite common among nominal scales, since these scales attempt to apply names "systematically". When it is this system which is the basis of their use, they constitute ordinal scales.

The magnitude measured by an ordinal scale is sometimes known as a "serial attribute" or just a "serial" (Lazarsfeld). The objects are so ordered as to be put into a series, for every ordinal scale is isomorphic with the relation of earlier-than among an appropriate set of time points. In general, such a series has only an arbitrary origin, though of course in a given field there may well be a first member with respect to the ordering relation. For example, hurricanes are named alphabetically, the first of the season being given a name beginning with "A"; comets are similarly named by the year of their discovery, with alphabetical suffixes to indicate the order of their discovery that year. In discrete series (those in which it is always possible to speak of "the next member" of the series), objects may be identified by the number of "generations" or steps separating them from some arbitrary beginning point. Yet these steps are not to be conceived as units of measurement in the sense of the scales to be mentioned below. Hurricane Karen occurred later in the season than Hurricane Jessica, and was the second one after Hurricane Iona; but there is no saying how much later than the preceding one each occurred, nor even whether one time interval was greater or less than the other.

In the usual application of ordinal scales, a "standard series" is provided or constructed, measures being assigned to other objects according to their relation to appropriate members of the standard series. The usual example (I might almost say, the standard example) is the Mohs scale of hardness. Minerals are ordered by the relation "capable of producing a scratch", so that if one mineral can scratch another but not conversely, it is assigned a higher number than the other. In the Mohs scale, talc, a very soft mineral, is arbitrarily assigned the number 1, gypsum 2, and so on up to diamond 10. That a particular mineral has a hardness of, say, 1.5, means that it is harder than talc, but softer than gypsum. We can *not* say, however, that its hardness is "halfway between" the other two.

Suppose we have a scale to measure the morality of behavior, with the standard series "depraved", "immoral", "decent", "conscientious", and "saintly". Although there may be no doubt about the order in which these categories are to be put (granting that we know how to apply them in a particular case), there may be grave doubt indeed about how near to moral perfection each of them stands. We do not know whether there is a greater moral advance in progressing from "immorality" to "decency" than from "decency" to "conscientiousness": is it harder to give up a favorite vice or to be scrupulous in avoiding a whole set of sins which are not particularly tempting? If such questions can be answered, the scale is not merely an ordinal one, but constitutes an *ordered metric*. Not only are the objects ordered, but the intervals between them are also ordered, at least partially.

Chess players are classified as "beginners", "C players", "B players", "A players", "experts", "masters", and "grandmasters". The presumption is that a player of a given rank can usually defeat a player of any lower rank. Differences between the skills characteristic of adjoining ranks can also be compared on the same basis. Suppose that masters defeat experts more often than they are defeated by grandmasters; then we may say that their superiority to experts is greater than their inferiority to grandmasters, and we are on the way to establishing an ordered metric. To take another example, a preference scale may have been established among a set of alternatives a, b, c, and so on, in that order of increasing preference. We now offer a choice between b and the tossing of a coin to decide between a and c. If b is preferred to the coin tossing, we may say that it is more to be preferred over a than c is over b, and if the coin tossing is preferred then the interval between a and b is less than that between b and c. Assigning numbers to indicate preferability is then subject to the constraint that, when numbers are assigned to the two adjacent objects that are furthest apart, a pair of numbers is fixed for every other object, one an upper bound and the other a lower bound to the number which may be assigned to it.

The use of any of the four scales so far discussed—nominal, partially ordered, ordinal, and ordered metric—is sometimes called "intensive" or "qualitative" measurement. It is intensive because it allows us to determine at most a degree rather than an amount, qualitative because it permits us to answer questions of more or less but not questions of how much or how many. The term "scaling" is also sometimes used in this connection, in contrast to "measuring", in a sense which restricts the latter to quantitative procedures. More often, however, the imputation of "scalability" to a magnitude means that it is unidimensional, that is, that objects are capable of being completely and not just partially ordered on that basis.

There is another scale sometimes classified as a type of intensive measurement, though it is no longer only qualitative. It is the *interval scale*, which provides equal intervals from some arbitrary origin. The assignment of two numbers to any two objects fixes the numbers for all the other objects. The initial twofold assignment corresponds to selecting both an origin and a unit of measurement. Thus the Centigrade scale of temperature is an interval scale: 0 and 100 are arbitrarily assigned to the freezing point and the boiling point of water; the temperature range between these is divided into a hundred equal intervals known as "degrees Centigrade". Arithmetical operations cannot be performed, to be sure, on the assigned numbers themselves. A temperature of 20°C can not be said to be twice as high as one of 10°C. The Fahrenheit scale is also an interval scale though with different origin and unit (0°F is the temperature of an equal mixture by weight of salt and snow), and on the Fahrenheit scale the ratio of those same two temperatures (20°C and 10°C) would be less than 7 to 5 rather than 2 to 1. But arithmetical operations *can* be performed on *differences* between temperatures: it is twice as far from 0°C to 20°C as it is from 0°C to 10°C, and this statement remains true when those temperatures are measured instead on the Fahrenheit scale (they correspond to 32°F, 50°F, and 68°F).

An important example of an interval scale is that constructed by von Neumann and Morgenstern for the measurement of utilities. Suppose we have a preference ordering among a set of alternatives *a*, *b*, *c*, and so on; as before. As in the case of an ordered metric, making a choice between *b* on the one hand, and on the other hand the tossing of a coin to decide between *a* and *c*, tells us whether the interval between *a* and *b* is greater or less than the interval between *b* and *c*. Now imagine that we use a loaded coin, loaded in a way known to the person making the choice. We are asking whether he prefers *b* outright, or a certain probability *p* of getting *c* together with the probability $(1 - p)$ of getting *a*. Now *p* is varied until these alternatives (either *b* or else the gamble on *a* and *c*) are equivalent as to preferability. Then *p* may be taken as a measure of the "utility" (preferability) of *b*. This number is fixed only up to a linear transformation—that is, the origin and unit of measurement may be arbitrarily selected. (The measure is *p* itself when *a* is taken as 0, and *c* as 1.) But differences in utilities remain in constant ratio whatever selection is made.

SCALES OF EXTENSIVE MEASUREMENT

A *ratio scale* is one which provides equal intervals, but with a zero point which is no longer arbitrary. All the numbers assigned can be multiplied by a constant without affecting anything but the notation, for this corresponds only to changing the unit—we measure length in inches rather than feet when we multiply all the measures by 12. But we cannot *add* a constant to all the measures, for this introduces an arbitrary zero point, and we would have only an interval scale. With a ratio scale, the assignment of a number to just one object fixes the assignments for all the others. The one assignment determines the unit, and the zero point is given by the operations of measurement themselves. Differences between temperatures constitute a ratio scale (though the temperatures themselves are measured by interval scales), for a difference of zero is not subject to arbitrary definition. Thus, differences in temperature provide a basis for the measurement of amount of heat: a calorie, for instance, is the amount of heat necessary to raise the temperature of 1 gram of water by 1°C.

Since the zero point is fixed, the numbers themselves represent fixed differences, whose ratios remain constant regardless of the arbitrary choice of unit. They may therefore be subjected to whatever arithmetical operations we wish. Otherwise put, ratio scales are isomorphic with the measurement of cardinality itself: measurement by a ratio scale has the same structure as counting the number of units to be found in a given magnitude. The measure assigned to the magnitude is nothing other than this count. It is for this reason that such measures can be added and subtracted, multiplied and divided. Ratio scales might suggestively be called "cardinal scales" to connote this isomorphism, especially by contrast with ordinal scales, which are isomorphic with the ordinal numbers. A horse which came in second in one race and third in another has nothing to do, we may suppose, with being fifth; but a bettor who won two dollars in one race and three dollars in another has indeed something to do with five dollars—it is the amount he can afford to lose on the next race.

Measurement with ratio scales constitutes what is called "extensive" measurement, though this term is sometimes used so as to include also interval scales. The additive measurement discussed in the last section yields a ratio scale. This fact is easily seen in Campbell's formulation of such measurement as proceeding by the construction of a "standard series". We begin with a standard object a, then continue the series with $a + a'$, $a + a' + a''$, and so on, where the primed objects are all equivalent to a (and so to one another), and the symbol "$+$" stands for a combining operation satisfying the additive conditions previously stated. The cardinal numbers are successively assigned to the members of this series, so that each number after 1 is in fact the number of units equivalent to the combination-object in the series. Ratio scales, however, need not be arrived at in this way, but may be constructed, as we have seen, in terms of the differences in an interval scale, and in other ways as well.

It is to be remembered that, if measurement in general is the mapping of objects into an abstract space, the range of possibilities is basically limited only by our imagination and ingenuity in constructing such spaces. The act of measuring does not consist merely in applying a yardstick of some sort, but also in devising the stick to be applied. As has happened over and over again in the history of science, the most abstract and even bizarre mathematics has afterwards turned out to have a homely and concrete application. Of special interest to behavioral scientists might be, for instance, an axiom of measurement formulated by Archimedes and bearing his name. For any two magnitudes a and b, with measures x and y, respectively, if x is greater than 0 and less than y then there is some number n such that nx is greater than y; if this n does not exist in a given case, we say that a is "infinitesimal" with respect to b, or that *b* is "incomparably greater" than *a*. In our own time the mathematician Hilbert has constructed abstract spaces in which this axiom is not satisfied. It may be that non-Archimedean measures are called for in the treatment of utilities, where they might correspond to "supreme" or "absolute" values. There is no room, I believe, for the mystique of quantity; but a sense of awe and wonder at the resources of mathematics may enable us at last even to number the clouds by wisdom.

§23. *Validity*

The root meaning of the word "validity" is the same as that of the word "value": both derive from a term meaning strength. The validity of a measurement consists in what it is able to accomplish, or more accurately, in what *we* are able to do with it. Plainly, this "what" depends on the context of the measurement's use. Validity is not determined just by the instrument and scale of measurement, nor even also by the "intrinsic nature" of the magnitude being measured. We must take into account as well the functions in inquiry which the measurement is intended to perform, or with respect to which—whether by intention or not—its validity is being assessed. The basic question is always whether the measures have been so arrived at that they can serve effectively as means to the given end.

The usual characterization of a valid measurement is that it is one which "measures what it purports to measure" (*63*:109). Whether it does so is in turn established in two fundamentally different ways, though which is relevant may vary from case to case, and the distinction is seldom a sharp one even for a single context. Briefly, one is a matter of definition, the other of empirical connections.

A measurement may succeed in measuring what it purports to measure because the procedure itself plays an important part in specifying the meaning of the term naming the magnitude in question. The rules for assigning the numbers embody, as it is usually put, an operational definition for the magnitude. If the meaning of "intelligence" (as a term of psychology rather than of everyday discourse) is specified by reference to certain tests, there can be no question that those tests do indeed measure what is called "intelligence". Unfortunately, it often happens that what is claimed to be a specification of meaning does not in fact perform that role. What we are given is a pseudo definition (§8): the term is not always used subsequently in ways that are fixed by what was claimed to be its definition. The danger is that we succumb to what Coombs (in *42A*:476) calls "operationism in reverse", that is, "endowing the measures with all the meanings associated with the concept". This fallacy is less tempting when the measurement is validated only by its empirical connections with other indicants of the magnitude. Such validation is known as "prediction to a criterion" or as "test prediction". Here the validity of a measurement is a matter of the success with which the measures obtained in particular cases allow us to predict the measures that would be arrived at by other procedures and in other contexts. The intelligence test, for example, is validated in the degree to which the IQ score enables us to predict scholastic achievement, or performance in other problem-solving situations. In general, however, validity involves both definitional and predictive considerations, particularly when the measurement is of a magnitude which is conceptualized not only in descriptive generalizations but in some theory as well.

ERRORS

Now a measurement may measure what it purports to measure, yet do so badly. Its outcome may fail to be as useful as it would be if the numbers assigned were only somewhat different, or if at least the procedure were always to assign very nearly identical numbers whenever it is carried out. Validity, in a word, demands that the measurement be relatively free of *error*. The error of a measurement is itself a measure of our failure to achieve what we aspired to; validity is a matter of the scientific significance of our aspiration. No human aspirations ever are wholly achieved; no measurement is quite free from error. Yet as human beings we may reasonably hope—and as scientists earnestly labor—to reduce error to a minimum.

One source of error is inherent to the measuring instrument. For every instrument there is a limit to the discriminations it can make. Differences that fall below this limit are not recognized, and objects that differ thus slightly are measured as equivalent. That we can speak with empirical meaning of such "immeasurable" differences results from the fact that they are not in a strict sense immeasurable, but only unmeasured by the procedure in question. They may be identified retrospectively, as more refined techniques of measurement are developed. Or, the existence of differences below the limits of discrimination of the measuring instrument or procedure may also be revealed by the breakdown of the transitivity of equivalence. By the axiom of Archimedes, no matter how small the differences are between apparently equivalent objects, the cumulation of these differences must eventually become large enough to be detectible. The discriminating power of an instrument or procedure of measurement is known as its *sensitivity*. One source of error, then, is insufficient sensitivity.

A second type of error consists in the fact that when a measurement is repeated it does not, in general, yield identical results. There is inevitably a certain amount of variation among the outcomes of repeated measurements; these are said to be subject to a "random fluctuation". Each measurement may thus be conceived as having two components, the first corresponding to the magnitude being measured and the second consisting of a positive or negative deviation produced by other and uncontrolled factors. The smaller these deviations, the more reliable the measurement is said to be; *reliability*, in other words, is in turn a measure of the extent to which a measurement remains constant as it is repeated under conditions taken to be constant. Among these conditions, the observer making the measurement is of particular importance, especially in behavioral science. Accordingly, reliability is often interpreted as a kind of intersubjectivity: the agreement of different observers on the measures to be assigned in particular cases. But changes in the circumstance of measurement other than the identity of the person making the measurement are also involved in reliability.

The existence of random fluctuations is as inescapable a feature of the process of measurement as is the existence of a limit to the discriminations that can be made in the process. With greater care in the performance of the measurement the random variation may be expected to decrease, as shots carefully aimed at a bullseye are likely to be less widely dispersed than if they were just roughly directed to the target. But even Robin Hood cannot split arrows indefinitely—some random variation always remains. As a result, an increase in the sensitivity of a measurement does not always have the effect of reducing its error. Such reduction takes place only when the inherent error, or lack of sensitivity, is large relative to the random error. "Increasing the sensitiveness of the instrument beyond a certain point, unless the fluctuations can be diminished to a corresponding extent, may simply result in making measurement impossible, because the effect to be observed is swamped by chance variations" (*121*:130–131).

The variations that occur are not always nicely divided between positive and negative deviations. Imagine, for instance, a series of measurements of length made with a yardstick which has not been properly calibrated but is in fact somewhat too short, as compared with the standard of length. Then, although the measures would, as always, show some random variation, the errors would tend on the whole to be on the positive side—measured lengths would be too great significantly more often than they would be too small. Or consider what would result if the incidence of crime, say, were measured by reference to police records in the weeks preceding an election campaign for a reform administration, or contrariwise, during a period when "the fix is in". In all such cases, we speak of a *systematic error*, as contrasted with the error due to random fluctuations. Here the deviations are not random but tend to one direction or the other, as the case may be, according to the particular distorting factor which is at work.

But to be able to speak of a systematic error we must be able to identify such a distorting factor. A measurement which is free of systematic error is said to be *accurate* (not to be confused with "precise", an attribute which depends on sensitivity, as well as on reliability). But the accuracy of a measurement is plainly a matter of what it is we presume ourselves to be measuring. If we are interested in the incidence, not of crime, but of arrests or of convictions, the effect of the election campaign is no longer a systematic error but part of what we are measuring. What is random error and what is systematic error, in other words, depends on what we are taking into account in the assignment and interpretation of our measures. As Coombs has put it (*23*:484), "the measurement theory assumed in analyzing data becomes a part of those data, and such portions of the data which are incompatible with the *a priori* abstract system are rejected and regarded as constituting [random] error variance." A systematic error, in short, is one due to a factor whose effect was presumed to be already incorporated in the theory of that measurement; effects due to other factors are called random.

THE "TRUE" MEASURE AND THE SIGNIFICANT FIGURE

Whether error is systematic or random, whether it is due to lack of sensitivity or lack of reliability, the very concept of error presupposes a concept of truth—or so it would appear. Whenever we speak of an error in measurement we apparently imply a contrast with a measure which is free from error. The validity of measurement is often conceived in these terms (or rather, misconceived, as I shall urge): a valid measurement is thought of as one which is true to the actual magnitude being measured. I call this conception *the fiction of the true measure*. Metaphysically, it has both a realist and an idealist version. For the realist, facts are absolutely determinate in themselves, whatever may characterize our knowledge of them, so that objects and events are wholly definite as to both quality and quantity. For the idealist, what is given in experience is always an approximation to an absolutely determinate abstract entity, which alone is the proper objective of genuine knowledge. Both views, however, recognize that all actual measurements fall short of the determinateness of what they each conceive as the reality. It is for this reason that I speak of their conception as a fiction. What they call the "true measure" is what *would* result *if* we were to perform a measurement entirely free from error. But this is just what we cannot perform. "Such an ideal does not actually exist," as Campbell (*12*:137) points out; "there is no experimental method of assigning numerals in a manner which is free from error."

From the standpoint of an empiricist, therefore, the "true measure" cannot have its meaning specified in these terms. For this specification amounts to explaining what we experience by reference to something which lies outside experience. To be sure, we correct measurements, reduce their error; but we do so always only up to a point. Reference to what would happen if only our measurements were not subject to any error at all is only a manner of speaking; it does not give empirical meaning to "true measure" but itself calls for empirical specification. In the words of Hume, "the notion of any correction beyond what we have instruments and art to make is a mere fiction of the mind, and useless as well as incomprehensible (*Treatise* I 2 iv). What we *can* say is something along the following lines. As we increase the sensitivity, reliability, and accuracy of our measurement of some magnitude, we find (or hope to find) that the measures increasingly exhibit a convergence toward some particular value. This value can usefully be dealt with as the mathematical limit toward which the measures tend. The "true measure" of the magnitude is nothing other than this limit. In some such way as this we can specify the meaning of validity in terms of the outcomes of actual measurements, rather than talking as though we compare these measurements with something which is not, and can never become, accessible.

Measurements *are* corrected and errors *are* reduced. There is no objection to speaking of this process as a successive approximation to the "real value" of the magnitude we seek, provided this idiom does not incline us to take literally the fiction of the true measure. That one measure is closer to the real value than another may mean simply that it deviates less than the other does from the limit of an unending sequence of such measures. Another fiction, however, may well be involved in the notion of the endless replication of a measurement. The point is only that the improvement must be judged in relation to data that are, or at least could become, available, rather than in relation to an inaccessible truth about what is being measured. Such data are by no means confined to the results of additional measurements. They consist to a significant degree in the effectiveness of the measure in question in performing whatever roles in inquiry are assigned to it, as it enters into, or is applied in conjunction with, various laws and theories. Instead of saying that a new procedure or instrument of measurement is an improvement over the old because it comes closer to the "real value" of the magnitude, it may be less misleading to say that it is an improvement because the "true measure" specified in its terms is more useful scientifically than the old "truth" was. In general, "we choose our scales so that certain empirical laws receive an expression as intuitive and/or as mathematically simple as possible. . . . If our theoretical structure changes or expands, then we frequently change our scales. . . . It is merely another figure of speech to describe these successive steps as approximations to a true or valid scale. . . . In itself no scale is more valid than any other" (Bergmann and Spence in *91*:264).

One of the reasons why the fiction of the true measure is important methodologically, and not only philosophically, is that it tends to overemphasize the value of precision. If improving measurement means approximating more closely to the truth, we are tempted to suppose that the more precise the measure is the better it is, for it is then closer to the absolutely determinate "fact" we are seeking to know. This exaggerated importance attached to precision is, I think, a part of what I have called the mystique of quantity. Round numbers are not nearly as impressive as those carried out to several decimal places; the latter are felt to be intrinsically more scientific, a perception which is perhaps strengthened just by the label "the exact sciences". In the instrumentalist perspectives in which I am viewing methodology (§6), the value of precision is seen differently according to the different functions which the measurement is to perform and the different respects in which it is adapted to the performance.

It not infrequently happens that because it is felt that an imprecise measurement is of no scientific worth, a degree of precision is claimed quite beyond what is allowed by the sensitivity of the instrument, the scale employed, or other limitations of the procedure. Such *false precision*, as we may call it, is exemplified by a purportedly exact count of a class which is only vaguely specified. The number of people in the United States suffering from "mental illness" surely could not be stated exactly even if we had at our disposal the relevant data, for it is not clear just what is to be counted; we cannot assign an exact number even to the beds occupied by such patients, though this is a somewhat less vague class, without a specification of the criteria of admission and discharge used in the various hospitals and institutions, and perhaps the criteria used by the various administrators and clinicians in each. It also happens, more often than one would wish, that measures of different degrees of precision are combined, and then there is claimed for the combination, not the least degree of precision among its components, but the greatest. Such a practice may have its uses in filing expense accounts, but it does even more violence to the intellectual virtues than to the moral ones.

False precision is the result of rather obvious blunders. More subtle, and correspondingly more widespread, is the mistake of *pointless precision*, the use of more exact measures than can be taken advantage of in the situation. I think that Ritchie (*121*:113) is quite right in his judgment that "it is really just as bad technique to make a measurement more accurately than is necessary as it is to make it not accurately enough". I have always been impressed with the frequency with which in scientific practice, especially in the so-called "exact sciences", use is made of approximations, and even of determinations of no more than "order of magnitude". The anxiety of many behavioral scientists to be precise in their measures is often, in my opinion, an overanxiousness, possibly reflecting a lack of assurance of the scientific worth of their endeavors. Loose approximations can, of course, be misleading, and even disastrous, but they can also be of enormous heuristic as well as practical value. The question is always whether the differences among the various possible precise values are significant for the problem at hand; this question is as relevant to scientific interests as to any others. If it is answered in the negative, the differences may be and should be glossed over in an approximation. When we know that all the propositions within certain limits are effectively equivalent, as Campbell (*12*:186) puts it, and that the approximate proposition lies within these limits, the use of the approximation is completely justified.

Measurement, I have said, is fundamentally the coordination to objects of a symbolic system, usually a numerical one. The point of view which I have been presenting with regard to the validity of measurement comes to this, that you can do what you like with the numbers assigned, provided that you know what you are doing and are prepared to accept the consequences. Among these consequences is the circumstance that the result either of a measuring procedure or of a mathematical manipulation of the measures may consist of numbers which cannot be brought back into any useful relationship with the original objects or with any others. A set of measures accurate to within one decimal place only (say because of the limits of sensitivity of the measuring instrument) can be multiplied or divided so as to yield numbers with three, four, or even a dozen digits after the decimal point. Only the first, however, is said to be a *significant figure;* the others do not answer to any feature of the situation itself but only of our own representation of it. "Measurement is never better than the empirical operations by which it is carried out," Stevens has said. Nor is it any better, I would add, than the conceptual operations, so to speak, which it involves. Ritchie (*121*:131) has wisely warned against the temptation "to make up for bad experiments by fancy calculations". Mathematics can spare us the painful necessity of doing our own thinking, but we must pay for the privilege by taking pains with our thinking both before and after the mathematics comes into play.

I recall a childhood puzzle which takes advantage of just this necessity. Three men registered at a hotel, paying ten dollars each for their rooms. The clerk, later realizing that the three rooms constituted a suite, for which the charge was only twenty-five dollars, gave five dollars to the bellhop to refund to the guests. Since five dollars is not evenly divisible by three, as well as for other less subtle reasons, the bellhop kept two dollars for himself and returned only three dollars as a refund. On his way back he calculated as follows. "They each paid ten dollars, making thirty dollars in all. I returned three dollars, or one dollar to each of them, so they each really paid nine. Now three times nine is twenty-seven, and two dollars I kept, making twenty-nine. Where is the thirtieth dollar?" Of course, if his two dollars is subtracted from the twenty-seven, not added, the remainder is twenty-five, the amount paid to the hotel. We are quite free to add the numbers if we wish, but not to expect the sum to represent anything in the situation. What is missing in the bellhop's manipulations is not the dollar but good sense; his logic was no better than his morals.

§24. *Measurement in Behavioral Science*

QUALITY AND QUANTITY

Possibly more widespread than the mystique of quantity, and certainly more pernicious in its effect, especially on behavioral science, is a corresponding *mystique of quality*. This mystique, like its counterpart, also subscribes to the magic of numbers, only it views their occult powers as a kind of black magic, effective only for evil ends, and seducing us into giving up our souls for what, after all, is nothing but dross. In this perspective, knowledge—and particularly, knowledge of human beings—consists in the apprehension of qualities, which in their very nature elude the net of number, however fine its mesh. As my friends at the University of Michigan have sometimes formulated this view, "If you can measure it, that ain't it!" For the student of human behavior, at any rate—so the view goes—measurement is pointless at best, and at worst, a hopeless distortion or obfuscation of what is really important. The exact sciences belong to the study of nature, not of man. Yet, on the face of it, disciplines like demography and economics make considerable use of mathematical methods and quantitative specifications, while, as Helmer and others have emphasized, there are many physical sciences—or at least, many parts of them—in which qualitative considerations predominate. What lies behind the mystique of quality?

To start with, every measurement involves some degree of abstraction: certain things are necessarily omitted in the numerical description, for this is always based on a determinate set of properties and relations to the exclusion of others. A specification of weight tells us nothing about size or density, for instance, which may nevertheless be involved in the quality of "massiveness". Yet this is only to say that no single quantitative description tells us everything; but is this not equally true of any single qualitative description? What is crucial is that the quantitative account includes all that is contained in the *corresponding* qualitative one. There is much that we do not know about a day in June when we are told that the temperature was 72°; but surely we know as much as if we had been told only that it was "warm". When we speak of the day as "rare"—excellent and pleasurable—we are not contrasting a quality with a quantity, but referring to a whole set of qualities for which, singly or in combination, quantitative specifications might conceivably be given. The argument that even if they *were* given, they would still leave something out, seems to me a straightforward self-contradiction. And the position that they cannot in fact be given strikes me as no more than a begging of the question.

The point is that both quality and quantity are misconceived when they are taken to be antithetical or even alternative. Quantities are *of* qualities, and a measured quality *has* just the magnitude expressed in its measure. In a less metaphysical idiom, we could say that whether something is identified as a quality or as a quantity depends on how we choose to represent it in our symbolism. Predicates not assigned in terms of a scale (or perhaps, not in terms of an extensive scale, at any rate) specify qualities; when an appropriate scale has been introduced, we identify their referents as quantities. Conversely, we may begin with a set of measures, then introduce labels which mark out qualities, that is, properties considered apart from their scaling. The transformation of quantity into quality, or conversely, is a semantic or logical process, not a matter of ontology. The vocabulary of "hot" and "cold" has no other denotation than that which belongs to the temperature scale; color words do not name something other in the furniture of the world than is named by the specifications of wave length. (Of course, the *sensation* of blue is something different from the color. It is not itself a quality but a perceptual event or process which we conveniently describe by reference to the quality; but it can equivalently be described as the sensation of light of such-and-such a wavelength.)

WHAT IS NOT MEASURED

The notion that measurement inevitably leaves something out, in a sense in which the omission is sinful, stems, I think, partly from this: that very often—especially in behavioral science—our measures *do* omit properties and relations which are important in the conceptual frame within which we see the subject-matter. The intelligence measured by the IQ test, for instance, may fail to include such capacities as creativity, or the sort of thing that is called "practical good sense". It does not therefore follow that it is a poor measure, but only that we would be making poor use of it if we were to interpret it so inclusively. The criticisms which are usually made of such tests—and not by laymen only —amount, for the most part, to nothing more than the insistence that the tests do not measure everything we might like to think of as an intellectual capacity. The mystique of quality comes into play when this probable truth is taken as premise for the dubious conclusion that therefore the tests measure nothing significant at all. The limitations to which every measure is subject are first interpreted as shortcomings, and then generalized into a condemnation of measurement as such.

This condemnation also derives in part from a basic confusion between knowing something and having an experience of it. It is one thing to know that the day is warm, and another to feel its warmth. Though the cognitive process itself is an experience, as richly concrete as any other, *what* is known is something abstract, formulable in a proposition. We know and can state that such and such is the case, but no limited set of propositions can exhaust the content of an experience of the situation. Now qualities are usually thought of as being objects of direct experience, while quantities are supposed to be arrived at only in symbolically mediated cognitions. Hence measurement is decried as yielding only a bare abstraction which falls far short of a qualitative description.

But that quantities are only known and qualities only experienced is a wholly unwarranted notion. We can directly experience numerosity and even the specific cardinality, if it is not too great or if the elements are appropriately grouped, as every card player can testify. And on the other hand, we can have indirect, symbolically mediated cognitions of quality, as in our knowledge of whether a particular turtle is male or female—a fact which is likely to be a matter of direct experience only for herpetologists or for other turtles. What *is* true is that having an experience allows for a great deal of knowledge, while the cognition that some proposition is true consists precisely in knowing *that* proposition, not an indefinite set of other (and logically independent) propositions as well. But by the same token, having the experience does not consist in knowing anything whatever, at least in the sense of "knowing" relevant to the scientific context; it only provides an occasion for cognitions, and evidence of some sort (by no means conclusive) for their warrant. We are back to the argument that a measurement does not tell us everything; but neither does just one qualitative description.

The argument goes further, however. It is alleged that measurement not only leaves out something important but even denies its existence. Essential qualitative differences are swallowed up in the sameness of quantity. What is most distinctive of the human personality—that it is individualized—is just what is denied when we set about to fix the psyche in a set of measures. But such a view naively mistakes mathematical equalities for strict identities, and misinterprets the affirmation of a measured equivalence between two objects as the allegation that they are in fact one and the same object. A sameness is indeed being asserted, but it is a sameness only of the formal, structural properties which answer to the scale and procedures of the measurement. The force of what Nagel (*103*:137) calls "the petulant criticism of science" lies largely in "the interpretation of equations as the literal identification of different qualitative continua, and as the attribution of intrinsic, nonrelational common characters to diverse subject matter". As for sameness, qualitative descriptions could also be said to group individuals into classes defined by the possession of the common quality. It is the numerical description which has the advantage here, I think, since it makes explicit how abstract the commonality is.

THE POWER OF MEASUREMENT

I believe that the deepest roots of the mystique of quality, especially with regard to behavioral science, lie in the circumstance that measurements play various roles in human affairs which by no means always accord with our values. One of the most important social functions of measurement, as I have already pointed out, is that of standardization. But while we recognize the value of standardizing things, we feel degraded in having our own measure taken. The resistance to being standardized ourselves is, if I may say so, wholly just; would that such resistance were more widespread and more effective! But it is not measurement which is corrosive of our personality. To make that diagnosis is to confuse the study of values with the process of valuation, and to project onto the objects known, traits which belong only to the quest for knowledge. Measuring a value does not "reduce it to a number", in any sense which in the least depreciates its worth. When we assign a number to some aspect of behavior, we have not thereby robbed the behavior of its human significance. We have concerned ourselves only with the significance of the behavior for science, and this is likely to have been enhanced by the measurement.

The rub is that the science may then be used in ways inimical to our values. Measurement of behavior adds immeasurably to the effectiveness of various instruments of social control. The more exactly our responses are known, the more easily they can be manipulated. A latent distrust and even an overt hostility against the application of measurement to human subject-matters is, in this perspective, quite understandable. But this is not to say that it is justifiable. The mystique of quality may be rooted in the morality which insists that man be treated as an end in himself, and not merely as a means for political, military, or commercial aggrandizement. But the moral impulse is here misdirected. It is not the science which is sinful, but the use to which it is put. That knowledge is power does not give the victims of power a stake in ignorance. The irony is that the mystique of quality secretly recognizes how much can be achieved by a quantitative approach, and opposes it for just that reason. But we have tasted of the fruit of the Tree, and there is no road back to innocence. What we must do is not to resist the growth of knowledge of human behavior, but to use what we know so as to preserve and to enhance our precious humanity.

INCOMMENSURABLES

There remain to be considered three problems of measurement in behavioral science which are more specific in nature.

One of the basic characteristics of human behavior is that it is purposive. Now purposes, and their corresponding goals and values, are far from being as single and as simple as measurement seems to require. It is not only that they vary from person to person and from time to time; they are also so interwoven with one another that in any given context several of them will almost surely be involved simultaneously. Power, gain, and glory—the classical trilogy of Hobbes—are less likely to command a single-minded loyalty than a dedication which is responsive to all three or to none of them. In choosing a home, a job, a wife, or just the lead to the next trick, a variety of considerations are likely to play a part; how can they be combined to allow for a measurement of the desirability of the various alternatives that might be chosen? For different values are incommensurable with one another: how can freedom be measured against security, stability of family or community life against industrial development, a soul that is lost against a world that is gained?

There is no doubt that measurement faces real difficulties here, but the situation need not be prejudged as hopeless. For specific purposes, bases of comparison among different values can often be found (*118*:158 ff). Such indices as money costs or energy consumed may be useful as derived measures, without the implication that their own value is interchangeable with the one which is being measured. Of more general bearing is the consideration that measurement is not limited to scalars, that is, magnitudes which are subject to a simple ordering. We may also use vectors and other multidimensional measures. A man might choose a job or a house by first weighing separately a number of component desiderata (salary, working conditions, and prospects; or rental, size, and location), and then by somehow summing the results, as though the components were reducible to a common measure. But he does not choose his friends by summing his appraisals of component traits and habits; he reacts, rather, to the personality as a whole. This *configurational method*, as we may call it, is probably more widely applicable in behavioral science than the *method of summation* relying wholly on scalar measures and some (hopefully) appropriate system of weightings.

JUDGES

But here a new difficulty arises, for usually the configurational method is applied by making use of human "judges". Measures of complex situations which do not easily lend themselves to scalar quantification—like the effectiveness of a psychotherapeutic technique, or the influence of a political boss—are most often arrived at with the help of a "human yard-stick". Estimates are made by a panel of presumably competent observers, and some suitable statistical combination of these is then taken as the measure of the magnitude in question. As a result, the scientist using such a measure is describing "not the behavior of his subjects, but rather the behavior of the group composed of his subjects *and* of his judges" (Bergmann and Spence in *91*:259–260). This combination does not, however, make such measurement subjective, in any pejorative sense. All measurement yields, not a property intrinsic to the object being measured taken in isolation, but a relation between that object and the others serving as standards of measurement. When the relation is to other human beings, or even to the observer himself, it is not therefore a subjective one. As always, everything hinges on the controls which can be instituted, and on the sensitivity and reliability with which the discriminating judgments are being made.

THE QUANTITATIVE IDIOM

There are some who argue against the possibility of any significant measurement in behavioral science on the ground that we cannot in these matters define an operation of combination that will have the structure of arithmetical addition. Now, impossibilities are in the nature of the case difficult to demonstrate, and in science the history of such claims is an inglorious one: over and over what one period was convinced just couldn't be done was subsequently accomplished—though, to be sure, usually in a rather different form than was originally conceived. But suppose this be granted: that nothing important in human behavior is subject to additive operations. Such operations, as we have seen, are not absolutely necessary to extensive measurement. But suppose that even this be granted: that we cannot hope to use ratio scales on a distinctively human subject-matter. The resources of measurement are by no means thereby exhausted. "Systematic study can be carried on in the social sciences as elsewhere by many devices which are less precise than strict quantitative measurement but nonetheless far better than unaided individual judgment. . . . There is a direct line of logical continuity from qualitative classification to the most rigorous forms of measurement, by way of intermediate devices of systematic ratings, ranking scales, multi-dimensional classifications, typologies, and simple quantitative indices. In this wider sense of 'measurement', social phenomena are being measured every day" (Lazarsfeld and Barton in *83*:155). Particularly noteworthy in this connection, I think, is the increasing use of types of mathematics not previously exploited for the purposes of behavioral science, as exemplified by von Neumann and Morgenstern's use of set theory in the analysis of rational decisions, or, more recently, Harary and Cartwright's application of graph theory to the analysis of organizational structures, as well as the use by many researchers of probability theory in the study of learning.

In my opinion, great as may be the difficulties of measurement in behavioral science, they are made greater both by being overestimated and, not infrequently, by being underestimated as well. It often happens that a *quantitative idiom* is used, not only without any actual measurements having been performed, but without any being projected, and even without any apparent awareness of what must be done before such measurements can be carried out. When the quantitative idiom is used by those who are unsympathetic if not downright hostile to the methods of measurement, the methodologist may be pardoned, perhaps, for feeling somewhat dismayed. Lawrence Kubie has made this point to his psychoanalytic colleagues, for example. Concepts like "depth of repression" and "strength of resistance", and in general, those pertaining to the "psychic economy", are almost always employed in a quantitative idiom; but a corresponding measure theory is almost wholly lacking. Kurt Lewin's "hodological geometry", whatever its shortcomings both from a logical and from an empirical standpoint, was at any rate an effort to provide a basis for talk about "life-space" and related ideas. I have no doubt that measurement can do much for the behavioral scientist, but only if he in turn does as much to deserve it.

THE DILEMMA

The great resources of mathematics, however, confront the behavioral scientist with a basic dilemma as he embarks on the enterprise of discovering or devising a procedure of measurement, a dilemma which has been clearly and forcibly stated by Coombs (23:488, 486): "If he chooses a strong axiom system, like a ratio or interval scale, he will put more into the data, he will have powerful mathematical and statistical tools available, he will be more likely to get a solution and it will be a simpler one. On the other hand, he will have more error variance, he will fit less of his data, and what he gets out will to a greater degree represent what he has put into the data by his assumptions. . . . The social scientist is faced by his dilemma when he chooses between *mapping* his data into a simple order and *asking* his data whether they satisfy a simple order." For this dilemma there is no general resolution; it is one of those existential dilemmas, like that between cultivating theory or experiment, with which the scientist simply learns to live. Only, his life becomes easier when he increases his awareness of the price that is being exacted of him as he makes his choices from moment to moment.

It is worth recognizing, too, that the situation is aggravated by the circumstance that measurement occurs in contexts of action other than those defined by the aims of scientific inquiry. We measure, that is to say, for a variety of reasons other than scientific ones; these impose their own requirements, which cannot always be made compatible with those stemming from our scientific interests. As Coombs has pointed out again (23:487), "society often requires that at least a simple order be imposed on an attribute [for instance, in deciding which commodity to purchase]. . . . This is the primary explanation of why the social scientist must so frequently be 'unscientific' and, in effect, be forced to treat his measurement theory or scale as 'right' in spite of his data." We need not come to a decision as to which purposes are the more important, or at least, we need not decide this in general, once for all. But it is important, I think, for the behavioral scientist to be clear in his own mind which purpose is primary for him in a given context, and what its requirements are. Too often, we ask how to measure something without raising the question of what we would do with the measurement if we had it. We want to know *how* without thinking of *why*. I hope I may say without impiety, seek ye first for what is right for your needs, and all these things shall be added to you as well.

STATISTICS

§25. *Functions of Statistics*

Measurement, we have seen, always has an element of error in it. The most exact description or prediction that a scientist can make is still only approximate. If, as sometimes happens, a perfect correspondence with observation does appear, it must be regarded as accidental, and, as Jevons (64:457) remarks, it "should give rise to suspicion rather than to satisfaction". Statistics is first of all a theory of error—not, to be sure, a theory of error in the concrete, since this will differ according to the procedures and circumstances of measurement, but a theory of the abstract or structural characteristics of error. The theory uses such characteristics to identify error, to measure its magnitude, and to provide ways of taking it into account. The great mathematician Gauss, one of the first to develop a theory of error, made characteristic use of it when he performed measurements to determine whether the geometry of physical space was indeed Euclidean (Gauss was also the first to conceive of a non-Euclidean geometry, though he did not publish his results). He measured the angles of a large triangle, some miles on a side, to deter-

mine whether its angular sum was indeed 180 degrees, and rightly concluded that if the sum differed from 180, it was by an amount less than
the error of his measurement. It is statistics, in the broadest sense, that
enables us to formulate scientific results in this cautious, qualified way.

UNITIES

Even if a particular measurement were quite free of error and wholly
exact, replications of the measurement would almost certainly fail to
yield always identical measures. Both our concepts and the contexts in
which they are applied are open to some extent: different observers will
have somewhat different conceptions, and will view somewhat differently what we call the "same" situation. To objectify the results of
inquiry we must provide some degree of intersubjective constancy. Here
is a second function for statistics to perform. Savage (*124*:154, 156) suggests that statistics might even be defined by this function as "the art of
dealing with vagueness and with interpersonal difference in decision
situations. . . . Statistics is largely devoted to exploiting similarities in
the judgments of certain classes of people and in seeking devices, notably
relevant observation, that tend to minimize their differences". A number
of observers each making his own estimate of a certain magnitude, or a
single observer making estimates on successive occasions, provide us
with a multiplicity of findings which we want to reduce to some underlying unity, or at least to a less divergent set.

In many cases the multiplicity belongs to the subject-matter, and only
derivatively to the observations made upon it. Inquiry may be directed
to a large class of objects and situations, sufficiently alike to be grouped
into one class, but nevertheless differing significantly from one another
even in the class character, to say nothing of other properties which may
be of importance to the inquiry. Whatever conclusions are reached will
hold, at best, only for some members of the class, not for all of them, and
even for these the conclusion will hold, in general, only to varying
degrees of approximation. Here, then, is another multiplicity to be reduced to some unity: what single description will best characterize a
heterogeneous class, and how good a description is it? There are multi-
plicities of measurements, of observers, and of objects, and questions of
this kind are raised by all three.

Suppose we are given a description or explanation intended to cover a large class of cases. The evidence supporting it can never be absolutely conclusive, and our confidence in it can never reasonably attain complete certitude. For usually the evidence will derive from only some of the instances within the range of the conclusion, and a degree of uncertainty will attach to the remaining cases—for instance, those which belong to the unobserved future. Even in the comparatively rare circumstances where our data are exhaustive (where we have examined every member of the population in which we are interested), the element of error in each datum cannot be left out of account in assessing the weight of the evidence supporting our conclusion. What is worse, it is also likely to happen that while some of the instances support our conclusion, others run counter to it, and the positive evidence must be weighed against the negative. Statistics thus also faces the task of assigning some degree of confirmation or of credibility to the conclusions that result from inquiry, in the light of the inconclusive evidence on which these are always based. We may say that statistics, in its broadest sense, consists of the ways of dealing with a multiplicity of data so as to determine what conclusions they support, and how much support they provide for each.

From this standpoint, statistics is often characterized today as dealing with the reasoning employed when we make decisions in the face of uncertainty. In these uncertain times it may not be too much to say that all our decisions are of this character, except possibly for those made in pure mathematics. At any rate, the decisions made by an empirical scientist at the conclusion of any inquiry are surely (if I may be permitted the adverb!) being made in the face of uncertainty. For no inquiry is in fact concluded; it is only terminated. There is always more to discover which might add to (or, alas, detract from) the justification for the decision reached.

Two sorts of uncertainty are to be distinguished. One is *risk*. We face a risk when we have knowledge of a law that operates but involves a random element. We are given a probability, but what the outcome will be in the case before us remains uncertain. The other type of uncertainty

may be called *statistical ignorance:* here we do not know what law is operative. We are ignorant, not necessarily of all the circumstances, but of
enough of the significant ones so that we cannot assign a determinate
probability to possible outcomes. The difference between these two sorts
of cases is illustrated by the decisions that must be reached if we find
ourselves in a card game with strangers (excluding the rational decision
not to play at all) : there is an element of risk intrinsic to the game, and a
quite different element of statistical ignorance about the players—their
skill, their style, and, of course, their honesty. As play proceeds, the element of risk remains fixed by the rules of the game, while the statistical
ignorance, hopefully, is gradually reduced.

It might be argued that the difference between the two types of uncertainty is not a fundamental one. We are never wholly ignorant of
relevant probabilities. Indeed, in my example, the fact that the other
players are strangers already evokes a certain set of expectations; and
these expectations have a rational foundation, as we have always been
taught. Contrariwise, risks are not so determinate as might initially
appear. We never know for sure what the probabilities are but only
make estimates of them; these estimates may be more or less in error—
and if we knew by how much, or at least in what direction, we would
not be making those estimates but better ones. Nevertheless, the distinction is of some methodological importance. Not infrequently, especially
in behavioral science, we unknowingly treat a situation of considerable
statistical ignorance as though it confronted us with determinate risks.
What is objectionable is not that we are making assumptions that go
beyond what we know; all assumptions have this character. The objection is that we are unaware of how much is being assumed. Ignorance is
being made the occasion for a pretense of knowledge rather than for further inquiry. If we do not know a probability, we do not know it;
ignorance is not a premise from which we may conclude that the probability is 1/2 or anything else. I shall speak shortly of the a priori interpretation of probability; but even here, as we shall see, there are conditions to be met for its application. The danger lies in assuming that these
conditions hold in a particular case without awareness even of what the
conditions are. Ignorance is bliss only until we must pay the price for
our mistakes.

QUALITY OF KNOWLEDGE

The view is widespread, though seldom made explicit, that statistical knowledge is not really knowledge at all but a kind of makeshift for the sake of action. The use of statistics is taken as a mark, rather, of the absence of knowledge. The statistical approach is treated as a counsel of desperation, to be followed only when all else fails. What it yields is deemed, at best, only second-best, something with which ignorance may console itself for its own shortcomings. This attitude derives, perhaps, from a Platonist theory of knowledge, according to which nothing is worthy of the name "knowledge" unless its truth is both universal and necessary. What is merely probable belongs to "opinion" rather than to knowledge; it is a useful counter in the business of everyday life but has no place in the treasury of science. In modern times it has been doctrinal determinism (§14) which has derogated statistical knowledge. Every event has its causes, and scientific knowledge is the apprehension of causal laws, by which the event can be seen as the necessary consequence of its antecedents. If only we knew enough about the coin we could predict the fall of "heads" or "tails"; we use probabilities instead only because of our ignorance.

In the last hundred years or so, the outlook has changed markedly, partly, perhaps, because of developments in physics, and partly because of the remarkable growth in statistical theory itself. There are many who now regard causal laws as simplifications of what are essentially statistical relations. That is the position skillfully defended by Reichenbach, for example (in *83*:122): "Causal laws are introduced by a process of schematization; we assume them to hold for ideal conditions, knowing that the inevitable 'errors of observation' will lead to deviations from the ideal. To speak here of 'errors' is a concession to apriorist philosophies, which insist that there is a strict law 'behind' the observed occurrences. It would correspond better to actual procedure to assert merely a high-percentage correlation, omitting any interpretation of deviations as errors, and then to proceed to the statement that the percentage of validating observations can be made higher by a suitable selection of relevant factors." Whatever account be given of the nature of scientific laws, statistical propositions must be seen as embodying knowledge in the fullest sense of the term. What they tell us is not necessarily something less but only something different from what is conveyed by other propositions. We may have learned more when we come to know a probability for a whole class of events than when we know with assurance only what a particular outcome will be.

But like every other kind of knowledge, statistical knowledge is not the product of spontaneous generation; it must have its parentage and nurture. Statistics is never in itself a source of knowledge. In these matters the mystique of quantity is especially widespread, as though a statistical formulation somehow provides its own content. The magic of numbers cannot produce cognitive rabbits out of truly empty hats. In common with all other branches of mathematics, statistics alone is but an instrument for transforming data, not for producing them. And when the data have been cast in statistical form, they are still data; they have not thereby been made into a scientific conclusion. The point to the statistical formulation and transformation is to enable us to extract all the information that the data contain, so that we can bring them to bear on the hypotheses for which they are data.

It is observation that remains the basic source of scientific information. We perform experiments and carry out measurements so that observations can be made in the most favorable circumstances and in ways that will maximize their yield. Statistics can be viewed as the general and abstract theory of this set of procedures. It is concerned with planning the acquisition of information, with processing it when acquired, and with applying it to the solution of the problems which motivated the inquiry. "Statistical procedure and experimental design are only two different aspects of the same whole," Fisher (*43*:3) has said, "and that whole comprises all the logical requirements of the complete process of adding to natural knowledge by experimentation." Mathematical statistics can, certainly, be cultivated for its own sake, that is to say, for the sake of the intrinsic intellectual and esthetic satisfactions which it affords. Nothing is further from my intention than to deny or in the very least to disparage this motivation, which I believe to be a fundamental part of the scientific impulse, including that expressed in the pursuit of behavioral science. But from the standpoint of methodology, statistics is wholly ancillary to empirical procedures. In the economy of the scientific enterprise it corresponds, not to mining or agriculture, but to manufacturing and commerce: the raw materials must be provided for it, perhaps in accord with its own demands, but then it converts these materials into useful products, so distributed as to stimulate the continued growth of the enterprise as a whole.

§26. *Probability and Induction*

Basic to the various operations of statistics is what is usually called the "theory of probability". I prefer to use the expression "calculus of probability" for the mathematical system, reserving the term "theory" for an interpretation of probability, a conception of its meaning and justification. The calculus can be developed, at least to a very great extent, quite independently of any particular theory. "Probability" can be taken as a primitive term of the calculus, undefined save by a set of postulates which specify its formal properties. The calculus itself does not give us any specific probabilities; these must be arrived at in other ways, and just how depends on the particular theory of probability to which we subscribe. What the calculus does is to enable us to transform given probabilities into other probabilities. It allows us to perform calculations, provided that we have been given data on which to base our calculations. It is in this respect quite like arithmetic. If we are told that a hen-and-a-half lays an egg-and-a-half in a day-and-a-half, we can compute the production of eggs by seven hens in seven days; but arithmetic itself tells us nothing about the pullulation of poultry—that information we must obtain elsewhere.

CALCULUS OF PROBABILITY

Following are some of the features of the calculus important to its application. They are here sketched very loosely; moreover, I present them without strict attention to the difference between a formal property of the calculus and an interpretation deriving from one or another of the usual theories of probability.

Probabilities apply directly to *classes* of events rather than to the individual cases of which the classes consist. (This feature is especially insisted on by the frequency theories, but is taken into account in some form by other views as well.) If we do speak of the probability of some special event, we are tacitly referring it to a class of events for which the probability is given or computable. Furthermore, the class in question is effectively infinite. We may distinguish only a finite set of alternatives to be considered, but each of them is then regarded as capable of recurring indefinitely often; the coin has only two sides, but it may be tossed over and over again. In particular, probability is not to be thought of as applying to subclasses only just large enough to allow for all the alternatives being considered. A probability of 1/4, for example, does *not* mean that one of every four cases is a "favorable" one (that is, the kind to which the probability is being assigned). On the contrary, a good many of the sets of four will have no favorable cases in them at all, while others will have two or three, or will even consist entirely of the favorable ones. This is the so-called "lumping" effect characteristic of random sequences: it has often been observed that for years we do not encounter a certain word, or hear a certain name mentioned, then suddenly encounter it two or three times within a week.

Probabilities are *relative* to some set of circumstances which serve to identify the class to which they are applied: if these circumstances change, then the probabilities, in general, will also be different. The probability of drawing certain cards obviously depends, for instance, on whether each card drawn is returned to the deck or laid aside, on whether the deck is stacked or thoroughly shuffled, on whether it has the usual composition or some other one. Reichenbach uses the term *reference class* in this connection, and has emphasized that probabilities associated with different reference classes are in no way directly comparable with one another. In many applications, the reference class in question is sufficiently clear and familiar that it need not be explicitly identified; but it is always an essential feature of the situation, and sometimes does require special attention. Any Southern Californian is a better weather forecaster than the chief meteorologist in New York, provided that each is forecasting his own local weather.

Probability measures are *normalized* to a scale between 0 and 1, inclusive: negative probabilities and those greater than unity are excluded by the rules of the calculus. The occurrence of such values marks an error of computation or of interpretation or both. Probabilities are often expressed by fractions or percents, as well as by the real numbers in the interval. Sometimes they are stated in the form of "odds": if the probability of a certain event is 1/3, for example, the odds against it are said to be 2 to 1. When Damon Runyon observed that in human affairs the odds are always 6 to 5, against, he implied that the probability of succeeding in our endeavours is never better than 5/11. The formulation in terms of odds presupposes the *law of the complement:* if the probability of occurrence of an event is p, the probability of its nonoccurrence is given by $1 - p$. In applying this law, we must be sure that we are in fact considering the nonoccurrence of the event, and not some special alternative to the event. If the favorable case is "white", the complementary probability applies to "any color other than white", and not, say, to "black" alone. And of course, it is assumed that the reference class remains the same: if the probability of sunshine in Los Angeles is p, we surely cannot say that $1 - p$ is the probability of overcast in New York.

When we have the separate probabilities of two events, the probability of occurrence of either one or the other is given by the sum of the two probabilities, provided that the events are mutually exclusive. Where the events are not exclusive, the *law of summation* is that the occurrence of at least one of the events is given by the sum of their separate probabilities minus the probability of their joint occurrence (as specified below). Ignoring the condition of exclusiveness is responsible for many errors. These are sometimes betrayed by the fact that the sum of the probabilities exceeds unity, but not always, and the error is even more vicious when it is less noticeable. In the frequency theories, the mistake may be described by saying that certain cases have been counted twice over. For example, the probability of drawing a face card is 3/13 and of a spade, 1/4; the probability of either a face card or a spade, however, is not the sum of these two, for in that case the jack, queen, and king of spades will have been counted once as face cards and once again as spades. Subtracting the probability of joint occurrence amounts here to canceling out one of the counts of these three cards.

The probability of occurrence of both of two events is given by the product of their separate probabilities, provided that the events are independent of one another. For the purposes of the calculus, independence need not be interpreted in causal terms. Two events are *statistically independent* of one another if the probability of occurrence of either of them is unchanged by the occurrence or nonoccurrence of the other. Otherwise put, the probability of one event remains the same when it is referred to a reference class changed only in this respect, that the occurrence of the other event is included in the specification of the class. Thus the probability that two spades will be drawn is simply the square of the probability that one is a spade, provided that the first card drawn is replaced in the deck, which is then shuffled. Otherwise, the circumstance that the first card is a spade has reduced the probability that the next card drawn will also be a spade—the two events are in this case not independent. The *law of the product* is that the probability of joint occurrence of two events is given by the probability of the first multiplied by the probability of the second in the circumstance that the first has already occurred. (When this circumstance is irrelevant, this formula is equivalent to multiplying the separate probabilities.)

I have already pointed out that a probability of, say, m/n, does not mean that of the first n cases m will be favorable ones; on the contrary, this is rather an unlikely outcome. The chances are somewhat better that in $2n$ cases, approximately $2m$ will be favorable, and this ratio becomes still more likely as the total number of cases considered increases. At the same time, the chances that the ratio will be exactly m/n are correspondingly lessened. This effect is usually described as the *law of large numbers* (Bernoulli's theorem), which may be stated as follows: if we take a sufficiently large number of cases, the observed ratio will always be closer to the probability than some preassigned degree of approximation. How large the number must be depends on the degree of approximation previously selected. That the observed ratio will have the exact value of the probable ratio, it is to be noted again, is increasingly improbable. This point played a historic part in the Dreyfus trial, where the prosecution argued that Dreyfus' correspondence must be in code because the frequency distribution of the letters of the alphabet contained in the correspondence deviated from what is "normal" for the French language. The testimony of Poincaré for the defense that the most probable distribution is highly improbable was not very convincing, in spite of its being correct. (Possibly a contributing factor was that Poincaré had identified himself on the stand as the greatest living expert on probability, a tactical error which he later justified to his friends by pointing out that he was under oath at the time.)

Under the designation of "the law of averages" the Bernoulli theorem is often grossly misapplied. It is mistakenly interpreted as implying that a preponderance of unfavorable cases in one part of a sequence must be "averaged out" in another part, which is then expected to have a correspondingly larger proportion of favorable cases. This error constitutes the so-called *gambler's fallacy*, the inference that a series of, say, "tails" makes it more likely that the next toss will come up "heads". (In fact, if anything, it is more rational to continue to bet on "tails", for the series of "tails" gives a slight basis for supposing the coin to be somewhat biased for that side.) What the inference overlooks is that each toss is quite independent of its predecessors. The coin has no memory of its past performances, and does not keep count so as to preserve its "average". Mathematically, whatever preponderance has been observed is of less and less significance as the number of cases increases—in effect, there is nothing to be "averaged out".

The calculus of probability, then, provides ways of transforming or combining given probabilities so as to arrive at others. But how we are "given" them to start with, and what we have learned when we have arrived at the others—these matters are not settled by the calculus itself but depend on its interpretation.

THEORIES OF PROBABILITY

Historically the earliest and in many ways the simplest interpretation is that provided by the a priori theory, which is also said to deal with *mathematical probability* in a narrow sense. Roughly speaking, a probability is here interpreted as the ratio of the favorable cases to the total number of alternatives. Its clearest application is to gambling games. Dice, cards, roulette, and the like are devices which present a fixed set of clear-cut alternatives. The odds for wagers placed on these alternatives, or combinations of them, are computable by direct applications of the calculus. An example will illustrate both the a priori method and the simple laws of the calculus.

Suppose that in a seven-card-stud game my first four cards are the deuce, trey, four, and five of spades. What are the odds that after I have been dealt three more cards I will have either a flush (five cards of the same suit) or a straight (five cards in numerical sequence, regardless of suit)?

Consider first the probability of making a flush. One of the remaining three cards must then be a spade. The probability that the next card to be dealt to me will be a spade is lessened by the fact that four of the spades have already been dealt to me—they are no longer among the alternatives open. Let us suppose that two other spades are showing in the other hands; these are also not available to me. The cards that have been dealt face down to other players need not enter our calculations; they will leave the results unchanged. It is true that there may be spades among them, but it is a matter of indifference to us whether the spades are there or are among the cards that remain in the deck after I have received my total of seven cards. What concerns us is only the proportion of spades outstanding in all the cards which are still unexposed. Let us suppose that I have seen a total of 17 cards, so that there are 7 spades left among 35 cards. The probability that the next card dealt to me will be a spade is then 7/35.

Now to make a flush I need not get a spade next; it suffices if any one of the three cards still to be dealt me is a spade, and more than one spade would be superfluous. It is simpler, then, to compute the probability of *not* making a flush, for this outcome occurs when all three cards are not spades, and the probability we are seeking is 1 minus this probability. By the law of the complement, the probability that the next card is not a spade is 28/35. If it is not a spade, there are then 34 cards remaining, of which 27 are not spades, so that the probability that neither of the first two is a spade is the product of these two fractions. For all three to fail, the probability is $28/35 \times 27/34 \times 26/33$, or very nearly 1/2. The probability of my making a flush is then 1 minus this value, or also 1/2, approximately.

To succeed in making a straight I need one of eight cards: the four aces and the four sixes. Let us suppose that three of the eight have already been exposed. Then there are 5 favorable alternatives among the remaining 35. The probability of my making a straight, by the same reasoning as above, is then $1 - (30/35 \times 29/34 \times 28/33)$, or approximately 3/8. By the law of summation, the probability of my making either a straight or a flush is the sum of the separate probabilities (in this case $1/2 + 3/8$) minus the probability of both occurring together. To simplify the computation of the latter, let us suppose that the two outcomes are independent. (In fact they are not, for the flush slightly increases the probability of the straight: if we know that one of the three cards in question is a spade, we know at least that it is not a deuce, trey, four, or five, which somewhat increases the probability that it is an ace or a six, provided that neither of these was among the spades already exposed.) On the assumption made, the joint probability is the product of the separate ones, or 3/16. The answer to our problem, then, is 11/16 approximately, or odds of somewhat less than 3 to 1 in my favor.

For the a priori theory, then, initial probabilities are arrived at by an analysis of the situation into its alternative outcomes; we count possibilities, and these are determined by the nature of the case. They need not be uncovered by observations specifically made for the purpose. It is crucial, however, that the alternatives be equally probable, or they must be given correspondingly different weights in the count. We must *not* say, for example, that the probability of drawing a spade is 1/3, because there are three possibilities: a spade, a club, or a red card. The last is twice as likely as either of the first two, since it contains within itself two alternatives of the same probability as the others. To avoid circularity, equiprobability must be determined in some way which does not depend on first arriving at the probability of each. What is usually employed is some form of the so-called "principle of indifference", roughly that alternatives may be treated as equiprobable unless we have knowledge of a difference between them judged to be relevant to their occurrence (or should we say, relevant to the *probability* of their occurrence?). Thus in practice, the equal distribution of weight within dice, the equality of angles separating the numbers on a roulette wheel, the equal size, thickness, and smoothness of cards in a deck, and so on, are taken to justify the usual assumptions of equiprobability.

The difficulty is, however, that not knowing a difference exists is by no means the same as knowing that no difference exists. The probability at which we arrive a priori may be grossly in error because of the effect of certain factors whose presence can be determined only by observation, or by inference from other empirical data. If experience supports the necessary assumptions, mathematical probabilities are by far the easiest to apply; but if we simply take it for granted that a given problem can be formulated as though it consisted of drawing cards from a well-shuffled deck, or colored balls from an urn, or the like, the mischief may already have been done.

Consider, for instance, the probability that two first cousins have the same last name. The a priori method might proceed as follows. There are four ways in which the cousins can be related: the two mothers are sisters, or the mother of one and the father of the other are sister and brother, or the other way around, or else the two fathers are brothers. Only in the last case do the cousins have the same last name, so the probability is 1/4. But a large number of assumptions are being made in this calculation, and some of them might well be false. It is being assumed, to start with, that a person always takes the last name of his father, which may not be true; that neither cousin is a married woman, or if so, that she does not take her husband's name; that two people would not have the same name unless they were related; that the sex ratio of the nubile population is equal; that the probability of someone's marrying is equally affected by the prior marriage of a brother as of a sister; and many others. For behavioral science especially, there are grave dangers in assuming out of hand that everything in human affairs can be represented as a game of chance. Mathematical probabilities are not to be applied casually. The behavioral scientist would do well to remind himself constantly that he is playing with strangers, with an unexamined deck, in a game of uncertain rules, as the twentieth-century physicist has already come to appreciate that *his* game is being played on a cloth untrue, with a twisted cue, and elliptical billiard balls.

In recent times a totally different perspective on probability has emerged into prominence, especially in connection with problems of human behavior involving rational choice and decision making. This is the *subjectivist* view, which may be said to deal with *personal* or *psychological probabilities*. Here probability is taken as a measure of degree of belief, as it were—an approach, not to certainty, but rather to certitude. It is not, however, a matter of *any* beliefs that are entertained, but rather of rational beliefs. We could say, indeed, that the subjectivist theories provide a definition of rationality of belief in terms of a consistent system of personal probability assignments. When a man arrives at a decision in a particular situation, there is operative, first, a set of values to which he aspires, and second, a set of probabilities which he assigns to the various possible outcomes of the acts among which he is choosing. The meaning of his probabilities is constituted by just the way in which his choices relate to his values on the one hand and to the alternatives presented in the situation on the other hand. Roughly speaking, the assignment of a probability expresses a willingness to place a wager at the corresponding odds. The calculus of probability is a device for achieving consistency in the wagers constituted by our actual choices. The probabilities with which it works are arrived at by ineluctably personal judgments.

Resistance to such theories is often based on prejudice against their forthright subjectivism more than on an awareness of their specific shortcomings. Their implications have been developed with subtlety and care, and provide plausible interpretations for a wide class of cases. In making decisions outside of actual gambling games we seldom do proceed, as a matter of fact, after the fashion of the a priori theories. The choice of a wife, a public policy, or a church may well entail assignments of probabilities to anticipated futures, but it is doubtful at best whether in matters of sex, politics, or religion we proceed by determining a set of equiprobable outcomes and then counting the proportion of favorable ones. (For that matter, neither do we appear to make counts of past performances, as is required by the frequency theories to be discussed shortly.) Instead of treating psychological probabilities as our personal estimates of a magnitude, the subjectivist theories take them to constitute the magnitude itself.

Psychological probabilities appear to play a particularly significant role in the following kind of situation. In the calculus of probability there is an important proposition known as "Bayes's theorem". It states that if there are several ways in which a certain outcome might have appeared—say, several causes which might each have produced a given effect—the probability of each is computed as follows. For all the possible alternatives, we multiply the probability that the cause in question would produce that effect by the so-called *antecedent probability* of occurrence of that cause, then divide by the sum of these products. Consider, for example, a set of suspects in a murder case; for each suspect there is one probability that he *could* have committed the crime, based on the evidence linking him with the act—opportunity, the weapon, a torn button, or the like; and there is an antecedent probability constituted by character and motivation. In the case of alternative hypotheses to explain a phenomenon, one probability concerns how good an explanation each would provide if it were true; the antecedent probability refers to the likelihood of its truth apart from the phenomenon it purports to explain. It is these antecedent probabilities which are generally admitted to be most difficult to determine, and for which the subjectivist theories insist that psychological probabilities are inescapable. There are other reconstructions of choice among competing hypotheses which do not make use of Bayes's theorem, precisely because of this difficulty, but the subjectivist makes the claim that antecedent probabilities are tacitly involved in these other reconstructions as well.

There is a third approach to probability which has the immediate advantage that its assignments are quite impersonal (though, of course, we each have our own estimates of the probability), so that intersubjectivity is assured from the outset. This approach is provided by the *frequency theories*, which may be said to define a *statistical* or *empirical probability*. For these theories, probability is applied not to classes but to sequences—that is, to classes whose members are taken in some determinate order, usually conceived as a temporal one. At any stage of the sequence, a certain ratio of favorable cases may be observed, their *relative frequency*; the probability is the *limit* of this frequency as the sequence is indefinitely extended. Such a definition provides a fairly direct interpretation of the probability calculus, and a simple application to those cases where the statistics of relative frequencies are available or can be made so. We do not need equiprobable alternatives as the apriorists do, nor are personal commitments or judgments involved in any essential way. Probability is thus not a measure of ignorance but one of knowledge, knowledge not of what is yet to come but rather of frequencies already observed.

This last is at the heart of the objections raised against frequency theories. The probability cannot be identified with the observed relative frequency but only with its limit as the sequence "goes to infinity". Otherwise we face the difficulty—apart from mathematical complications in the usual form of the calculus—that the ascription of probabilities would no longer have explanatory force (as in statements of trends and tendencies—see §12). Like theoretical concepts, probabilities "would not serve the purposes we require of them if statements about them could be translated into statements about directly observable frequencies" (*9*:167). On the other hand, our data never provide us with a limit but only with an actual frequency. What is more, we cannot even content ourselves with frequencies "in the long run"; it is obligatory to quote Keynes in this connection: "in the long run we shall all be dead" —and nowadays we add, "if not sooner!"

The problems for the frequency theory come to a head when we attempt to apply a probability, as we so often want to do, to a single case rather than to a whole sequence of cases, whether long or short. We ask, for instance, "What is the probability of a nuclear war in the next three years?" or, "What is the probability that this patient will attempt suicide during the course of therapy?" (These are meant as two distinct questions.) There is no sequence of nuclear wars to which we can look (such a sequence may even be an empirical impossibility); and if we look at a sequence of warlike situations, we would have to conclude that the probability is zero, for not one of them was in the required sense a nuclear war. As for the other probability, to be sure there have been many patients and many attempted suicides among them—too many, indeed, speaking methodologically as well as morally. For with which class of patients is the one in question to be grouped? A great range of probabilities can be assigned according to our choice. Though some classifications may give the effect of certain record performances in baseball ("most strikeouts by a left-handed pitcher in the third inning of a night game"), it is not easy to specify the criteria for a unique choice. The problems of the *single case* and the *choice of reference class* remain troublesome for frequency theories.

Each of the three theories of probability, then, has its own difficulties, though not necessarily insuperable ones, and none of them commands universal assent. For methodology it seems to me the part of wisdom, in the present state of thought at any rate, not to endorse any one of the three to the exclusion of the others. Each of them seems to be particularly suitable for its own distinctive class of problems. The behavioral scientist may find it useful to apply mathematical probability to the treatment of certain questions of heredity, for example; statistical probability for questions of growth and development; and psychological probability in connection with questions of choice and decision by the mature adult. We tend to use an a priori theory when the problem can be clearly structured in the appropriate way, a frequency theory when sufficiently extensive and reliable statistics are available, and a subjectivist theory in other cases, especially where personal values and assessments seem to play a crucial role.

For the appraisal of the probability of a hypothesis or theory, still other conceptions have been brought to bear. Two are especially noteworthy in contemporary philosophy of science. Reichenbach, who has been an ardent exponent of the frequency interpretation for all uses of probability, speaks in this connection of the *weight* to be assigned to a hypothesis, in terms of the relative frequency either of the verified consequences of the hypothesis among all its implications, or else of true hypotheses among all hypotheses of that class (though just which class is uncertain, as was indicated above). Carnap has developed in some detail a conception of *degree of confirmation* to be attached to a proposition with respect to a given set of other propositions, the premises from which it is inductively inferred. This degree is computed on the basis of the partial implication, as it were, which holds between premises and conclusion. The particular degree of confirmation assigned applies analytically, in terms of the definition of the "best estimate" to be made on the basis of the given evidence. Although the theory has been developed with precision and rigor, it has been worked out only for fully formalized and extremely simple systems, very far from adequate for the formulation of the content even of the so-called exact sciences, to say nothing of behavioral science. There is the further difficulty, as Braithwaite (9:196–197) put it, that "the extent to which a hypothesis would fit into the body of scientific knowledge is highly relevant to its claim for incorporation into such a body of knowledge, and it is difficult to see how a formal logic of 'confirmation' can help in the matter [beyond certain] obvious truisms."

INDUCTIVE INFERENCE

But here we come upon issues of more concern for the philosophy of science than for methodology (but see §38). What is beyond dispute is that in the course of the past century inductive logic has entered upon a new phase of development, contrasting markedly with what had been achieved from Aristotle through Bacon and Mill. What is new is not that we have now a "logic of discovery", in the sense of a set of routines for making discoveries (§2). What we have, rather, are procedures which provide a far better reconstruction of the process of discovery than was hitherto available. As Carnap has pointed out, the situation in this respect is no different from that in deductive logic: there are no routine ways of discovering deductive theorems, or proofs for them, any more than there are ways of discovering inductive hypotheses, or evidence for them. But there *are* ways of assessing the validity of a given proof, and now also, of assessing the weight of a given body of evidence.

What is new is that inductive logic is now generally agreed to rest on some theory of probability, however that be interpreted. The conclusions of an inductive inference are never established absolutely, but only to some degree or other. To just what degree depends, inescapably, on the premises from which it is inferred—that is, on the state of our knowledge. In Reichenbach's view, we are always to use the narrowest reference class for which we have reliable statistics. Carnap formulates a corresponding requirement to use "the total evidence available" (*16*:211). In either case, we proceed always from what we know, and probability remains our guide in science as it is in life. From the standpoint of methodology, the importance of probability theory is the reconstruction which it can provide for inductive inference. As for the philosophical problem of induction so much discussed since Hume, methodology can content itself with Peirce's postulate that the evidence bearing on the truth of any particular proposition will not indefinitely remain equally divided: the probability, weight, or degree of confirmation of any proposition is not forever indeterminate. The problem we actually face in scientific inquiry is not how we ever get any knowledge at all, but how we can best use what knowledge we have as the means to learn more of what we do not yet know.

It is the various patterns of inductive inference that are of methodological importance. Carnap distinguishes four sorts of cases in which such inferences are made: from a population to a sample of it, which he calls the "direct inference"; from a sample to its population, the "inverse inference"; from a sample to another sample, the "predictive inference"; and from a sample to an individual outside it, the "singular predictive inference". He regards the last as the basic one, and the others as reducible to it. In Reichenbach's treatment, it is the inverse inference, from a sample to the population, which is fundamental; he calls it "induction by simple enumeration". Whichever pattern we start from, we proceed on the basis of an "inductive method", so-called, like those specified by the "rule of Laplace", Fisher's "maximum likelihood" method, and so on. Details of these methods are beyond the scope of this book (and of its writer). But it may be appropriate here to note that there are indefinitely many such methods. In adopting one, we take into account, as Carnap has pointed out, truth-frequency of predictions, errors of estimates, simplicity of calculations called for, and perhaps also esthetic features. "Here, as anywhere else," he concludes with characteristic wisdom, "life is a process of never ending adjustment; there are no absolutes, neither absolutely certain knowledge about the world nor absolutely perfect methods of working in the world." Probability is king, but even the monarch is hedged about with constitutional restraints.

§27. *Statistical Description*

Many statistical manipulations fall into fixed patterns, and specifications can be given of just which calculations are to be performed and in what order. In a word, they can be laid out in formulas. Arriving at the value which the formula yields in a given case is a routine matter. In the machine idiom which is increasingly appropriate here, the calculation can be programmed into a series of determinate steps (though the steps may be conditional upon the outcome of previous steps of the calculation). But statistics has not performed its function in inquiry merely because a statistical formula has been applied. The formula organizes the calculation, but not the thinking that determines what is to be calculated and what is to be done with the results. The unthinking use of the formula may be called *cookbook statistics*, by which behavioral science especially is victimized. It is not enough for the lady of the house to be able to follow a recipe. There are questions of dietetics; considerations of economy (a famous recipe contains the instruction, "Throw in one duck, for flavor"); and the matter of esthetic and other values ("Better a dinner of herbs with love than a fatted ox with hatred").

Every application of a formula rests upon a set of substantive assumptions as to the nature of the problem, and a set of hypotheses as to what might be helpful for its solution. When a problem is to be treated statistically, a subsidiary problem is generated which must be dealt with first. It is usually known as the *structuring problem*: the task of setting up a model of the problematic situation, in terms of which a meaningful choice can be made of the statistical techniques to be applied and of the interpretations to be put upon their outcome. The solution of the structuring problem requires a specification of the alternatives into which the cases studied can fall; the type of distribution among those alternatives; the nature of their dependence, if any, on one another; the magnitude of the errors in the estimations on which the classification is based; the costs of these errors, on some appropriate scale of utilities; and of course, the bearing of the expected findings on the next stage of inquiry or action. In short, to know what we are doing when we use statistics we must know much more than statistics. The proper use of this instrument, as of any other, depends on a knowledge of the materials to which it will be applied, and something of the ends for which the application is, after all, only a means.

The simplest applications are those that serve the purpose of reducing a multiplicity of data to a manageable simplicity. We are confronted with a set of different measures of the same magnitude, or a set of estimates of it made by different observers, or a set of objects of various magnitudes; what we want is a simple way of characterizing the set as a whole, a single estimate or representative measure which can be used either as a basis of comparison with other sets or as a way of identifying a pattern of relations between their respective members. What is applied for these purposes is known as *descriptive statistics*. We postulate some determinate structure of the set to be described, then employ various measures, as appropriate, to estimate certain characteristics of that structure. Each type of measure is known as a *statistic*, and the characteristics estimated are known as the *parameters* of the described distribution. Whatever statistic is employed has its own distinctive properties, which are decisive for its appropriateness or otherwise, and for the proper interpretation of the measure it yields. Many errors in the application of statistics result from a failure to take these properties sufficiently into account. And in the case of descriptive statistics, there is an additional source of error in forgetting that the parameters estimated apply only to the distribution as a whole, not to the individual cases that make it up, and that among these cases there may be considerable variation from the description given.

CENTRAL TENDENCY

The statistics most often used for the purposes of description are those known as *measures of central tendency*, the various types of "averages". That there are various types is of fundamental importance, a fact not sufficiently appreciated by their average (!) user.

The most familiar statistic of central tendency is the *arithmetic mean*, usually referred to by the term "average". It consists of the sum of all the values divided by the number of the values that have been added together. The arithmetic mean has the property of minimizing variation among individual values. If we take the deviations from this mean, square them (an operation that, among other things, eliminates the difference between positive and negative deviations), then sum the squares, the result is smaller than if we had started with the deviations from any other value. It is in this sense that the arithmetic mean is so representative a statistic.

Suppose we are taking samples from a population and wish to predict the characteristics of the samples from what we know of the population as a whole (the "direct inference"). If there is no systematic error in our sampling procedure, so that variations in one direction or the other are equally probable, then the arithmetic mean is the most probable value to be expected. It is the most free from error if the factors making for error act equally in both directions. When a magnitude is subject to a purely random variation, its specific values appear in a population with frequencies characteristic of the so-called "normal distribution". The remarkable thing about the arithmetic mean is that, no matter how an attribute is distributed in a population (however far from "normal"), provided only that its variation remains within some definite bounds, the means of samples taken without bias from that population do tend to have an approximately normal distribution. This fact has been described as "one of the most elegant, powerful, and important results in the theory of probability" (*18*:187). By using the mean we have ensured that the bigger the error that we might make in our inference, the less likely we are to make it.

But however representative the arithmetic mean is, we are not to forget that it applies only to the population as a whole. No Vassar graduate has a family of 2.3 children. The mean itself, moreover, takes no account of the way in which the individual magnitudes are distributed. This fact may make it a wholly misleading statistic, when it is used, say, for the purposes of comparison of two groups. Consider, for instance, the income level of two populations; the mean incomes of the two may not differ significantly at all even though in one of them virtually the entire population is penniless but a few are millionaires, while in the other the income is fairly evenly distributed. To take another example, if we had a numerical measure of a person's level of anxiety or dejection at a particular time, or of the amount of hostility he is manifesting, the mean value over a period of time would not be a very useful diagnostic index of mental health: a few minutes of really acute anxiety, of suicidal depression, or of murderous rage may be more significant clinically than the preceding weeks of equanimity. The murderer has no right to complain of the label on the grounds that he killed only once in a lifetime.

Other means have other statistical properties. The *geometric mean* is arrived at by multiplying together all the individual values, and then, if the number of individuals is n, taking the nth root of the product. This statistic has the property of giving much less importance to extreme values than the arithmetic mean gives. If a set of three individuals has the values 2, 8, and 32, the geometric mean is 8 while the arithmetic mean is 14. The geometric mean is especially appropriate also where the comparison among individuals is more meaningful in terms of their ratios than their differences. In this example, we might wish to think of the largest value as only 4 times the middle one, rather than as exceeding the middle one by 24 (the numbers might represent, for instance, different stages of growth of a population which doubles itself at regular intervals).

The *harmonic mean*, which is the reciprocal (division into 1) of the arithmetic mean of the reciprocals, is useful in averaging rates of change, and other ratios. And still other means have been defined.

One of the most useful measures of central tendency is the *mode*. This is simply the most frequent value in the distribution. It remains stable under repeated sampling, and is obviously not affected at all by extreme values. A manufacturer on a small scale of shoes or clothing is not interested in mean sizes but in the modal one, so as to sell most of a limited product. A politician, too, may be more concerned with the mode of public opinion than with its mean; the latter might satisfy no one, while the mode, by definition, accords with the views of more people than any other. On the other hand, the mode—to apply the political metaphor—is governance by plurality: it is not a function of all the items, and not even of a majority of them, necessarily. Just what the mode is may vary with the interval chosen, the way in which the attribute space is subdivided into distinct classes. What is worse, "the" mode may not exist: several classes in the distribution may be equally numerous. In particular, bimodal distributions are not uncommon, and not only on the political spectrum. Here other measures are called for.

The *median* is a statistic which takes account of all the values, without being much influenced by the extremes. It is the value for which there are as many values below it as above. The median salary of a college professor, or the median cost of a psychoanalysis, is likely to be a more informative datum than the mean or the mode for these values. Defined as it is in terms of an ordering relation only, the median does not have any algebraic properties. It is especially useful, therefore, in connection with ordinal scales. An even-money wager that a horse will run in the money is a fair bet if his median performance is between third and fourth (only the first three horses are paid off); it is likely to be more than fair if that is his mean performance (he could never have been better than first but could easily have been worse than sixth); and it is most probably quite an unfair bet if that is his modal performance (it may be more frequent than any other and still be quite infrequent).

DISPERSION

None of the measures of central tendency tells us how the values from which it is computed are distributed. A statistic which does tell us something of the distribution is said to be a measure of *dispersion*. It specifies in some way how far the individual values depart from others or from the central tendency. The simplest specification that can be given is just the *range* of the distribution, the spread of extremes between which it lies. This leaves open just how the values are distributed within this range, but sometimes we have other reasons for supposing them to be evenly distributed within the extremes. Sometimes, too, it is precisely the extreme values which are of most significance: the losses which might be incurred by an insurance company, the load of a traffic or communication system, or the conduct implied by the apocryphal decoration, "Order of Chastity, Second Class".

By far the most commonly used measure of dispersion is the statistic known as the *variance*. This gives us, in effect, the mean departure of the individual values from their mean value. It is defined as the mean square deviation from the mean—that is, the mean of the square of each value minus the square of the mean value. (The squaring gives relatively greater prominence to the larger deviations.) It may be noted that the mean could in turn have been defined as the value which minimizes variance. To give the variance the same dimensionality as the values themselves, we usually deal with it by first taking its square root. This number, the square root of the variance, is known as the *standard deviation* of the distribution. It is a statistic which is relatively uninfluenced by fluctuations in sampling, and thus constitutes a fairly reliable representation of the dispersion. For normal distributions, approximately two-thirds of all the values are no further from the mean value than is given by the standard deviation.

Further consideration of the properties of the standard deviation, as well as of other descriptive statistics, would bring us quickly into matters of statistical technique rather than methodology. I leave the trees so to restore the forest to the focus of attention.

§28. Statistical Hypotheses

All inductive inference is based on samples. We wish to make a generalization about a whole class of cases and have observed only some of them, or we want to predict a future outcome on the basis of the past. Even if our conclusion concerns only one individual, or a set of individuals on all of whom we have made observations, the measurements we have taken are only a sample of all that might be made, and in assigning particular values to the measured magnitudes we are making an inference, based on that sample, of what other measurements would yield. We always know something and always grasp for more, and the grasping is part of the knowing. All hypotheses might be said to be statistical hypotheses in a broad sense; statistics has the task of assessing the weight of the evidence for a particular hypothesis contained in a given set of data.

SAMPLING PLANS

In basing an inference on a sample we are caught up in what appears to be a dilemma, which we may call the *paradox of sampling*. On the one hand, the sample is of no use to us if it is not truly representative of its population, if it is not a "fair" sample. On the other hand, to know that it *is* representative, we must know what the characteristics of the population are, so that we can judge whether the sample reflects them properly; but in that case, we have no need of the sample at all. The paradox is resolved by the consideration that the representativeness is not a property of the sample but rather of the procedure by which the sample is obtained, the *sampling plan*. And we can know—though never for sure—that this is an appropriate one without already knowing what we are trying to find out, the characteristics of the population. In any given case, the content of knowledge is validated by the method employed to arrive at it; but the method in general is grounded in its success in yielding the contents sought for. This situation can be compared with a corresponding "paradox of usage": we establish that a particular use of a word is correct by consulting the dictionary, but the dictionary itself is based on how words are in fact used.

A sampling plan has been described as "essentially a specification of what other samples might have been drawn and what the relative chances of selection were for any two possible samples". To know these we must indeed have some knowledge of the population, enough to make reasonable assumptions about the distribution within it of the attribute in which we are interested—the structuring problem must be solved though not necessarily in a unique and definitive way. As always, we must make use of some knowledge in order to get more. The decision as to what size the sample must be, for instance, is made on the basis of what Reichenbach calls "cross inductions": inferences from the adequacy of other samples drawn from thàt population, or from others similar to it in respects we are in a position to judge as relevant. A chemist is content to establish the boiling point of some substance on the basis of only two or three determinations, while two or three hundred may be quite insufficient to establish the boiling point, or tolerance for frustration, of human beings. The chemist's sampling suffices because we already know the relative invariance, from case to case, of the chemical properties of different specimens of the same substance. But different specimens of humanity vary quite markedly from one another in their behavior characteristics; the sample must be large enough to allow us to take account of this variance.

It is not only decisions as to sample size which must be based on antecedent knowledge, but also the choice of procedures for correcting and standardizing the data obtained by the sampling plan. Just as the results of every process of measurement require adjustment for their proper interpretation, so also do those of every sampling process. We use, not the raw mean of the observations, but some suitably adjusted or weighted mean. As Mosteller (97:33) has pointed out, "weighting a sample appropriately is no more fudging the data than is correcting a gas volume for barometric pressure". We cannot say whether a sample is a fair one or not without referring at least tacitly to the process by which it was obtained, and thereby to corresponding procedures for processing the data before basing upon it any inferences as to the population from which it was drawn. To take the simplest illustration, the very act of including an individual case in our sample may give it certain properties which must be discounted in subsequent inferences—that every person interviewed, for instance, shows a certain embarrassment or hostility in the interview is scarcely a basis for concluding that these are character traits of the population being sampled.

What is required is that the sampling plan should not be one which preferentially selects specimens differing from the rest of the population in some respect significant for the inquiry, or at any rate, that the higher probability of their being chosen be sufficiently determinate—and determinable!—so that it can be corrected for. We say otherwise that the sample is a *biased* one—the expected values in the sample differ from the true values of the parameters in the population being studied. The classic instance of the biased sample is provided by the ancient story of "one who in Pagan times was shown a temple with a picture of all the persons who had been saved from shipwreck, after paying their vows. When asked whether he did not now acknowledge the power of the gods, 'Ay,' he answered; 'but where are they painted that were drowned after their vows?' " It is clear that the bias of the sample has nothing to do necessarily with any prejudice of the observer; it is intrinsic to the sampling plan adopted. The bias may be a subtle one. Suppose, for instance, we are interested in determining the changing size of the American family. We might begin with a fair sample of the present population, find out from each person in the sample how many siblings he has, then how many his parents had, his grandparents, and so back to earlier generations. But this sampling plan is biased in favor of larger families in the past, for the larger the family the more likely it is to have left descendants in the present generation with which we began the sampling. And childless families in an earlier generation cannot be represented at all in our sample.

What is required of the sampling plan is not only an absence of bias in its samples (sometimes called "accuracy"), but also *stability*. To make use of the sample we need to know how likely it is that other samples produced by the same plan will yield essentially the same results. "The ability to assess stability fairly is as important as the ability to represent the population fairly" (97:18). Instability is most easily seen with regard to very small samples: they may be selected without any bias at all, but because of their size it may very well happen that repeated samples will show large differences among themselves. The use of unstable samples is a failing especially common in behavioral science, with its reliance on case studies, clinical observations, and the like. Even if the samples have been chosen without bias (rather than, say, because they are the most striking, or the most easily accessible), they often do not provide a basis for reliable generalizations about the entire population of cases which they are supposed to represent.

A sample is acceptably free from bias if it is a *random* one. Just what constitutes randomness is not universally agreed upon. The discussion is usually in terms of the characteristics of a sequence of cases. The distribution of "favorable" cases in the sequence (those in which we happen to be interested) is sometimes said to be random if it satisfies what von Mises called "the principle of the excluded gambling system", that is, if there is no way to select a subsequence (without reference to the favorable trait) that will yield a higher proportion of favorable cases than in the sequence as a whole. (We might, for example, bet on "black" every other time, or after two "reds" have appeared in succession, or otherwise systematically.) This principle, however, has been held by some to be self-contradictory when formulated strictly. Alonzo Church has characterized a sequence as random if no law can be formulated in a human language (that is, one subject to certain technical restrictions of finitude) which describes the sequence. However randomness be strictly defined, it is generally agreed that the members of a random sequence are statistically independent of one another (§26), and that the frequency of the favorable cases is unchanged when the sequence is regularly sectioned, or in other words, when the frequency is the same in any subsequence consisting of every *n*th member of the original sequence.

Like fairness, randomness is a property of the sampling plan rather than of a particular sample. A "random number", so-called, is in no way different from any other number; whether it is random cannot be determined at all by inspecting the number itself. What is random is the sequence of which it is a member, or rather, the particular way of arriving at that sequence. In practice, we use mechanical devices to construct such a sequence, like tossing a coin or dice. For if we were to construct the sequence by making a series of what we feel to be "arbitrary" choices, the result would almost surely not be random. We would fail to do justice to the "lumping" effect previously spoken of—for instance, we would be unlikely to allow, say, twelve favorable cases in a row, which will, however, appear in a random sequence—as will twenty in a row, or indeed any other number, if the sequence is long enough. There are machines which can beat human opponents at matching pennies, if the human player chooses "heads" or "tails" without using a mechanically random method (like tossing the coin itself); the machine takes advantage of the departure from randomness in human choices. Of course, mechanical methods need not be separately applied in each inquiry; tables of random numbers are available, themselves constructed by such methods (for instance, by counting the fluctuations in an electric current, which occur with a frequency of some thousands of times per second, then recording the last digit of the count).

It is the "lumping" effect which limits the usefulness of so-called "grab samples" (like taking a handful of beans from a sack, or the next ten patients to enter the clinic). Such samples are likely to be too homogeneous, and therefore also insufficiently stable. Suppose, for example, we wish to study what is said by patients during psychoanalysis. If we select one month's records, much may depend on whether it is a month near the beginning or near the end of the therapy. The records of an equal number of hours distributed throughout the whole course of the treatment would be much more representative. (Here, of course, the "lumping" is not random, but presumably follows a more or less determinate sequence set by the course of the therapy—for instance, as transference is built up and then broken.)

There are many different patterns which a sampling plan may follow. We may select our cases individually at random (in the example above, choosing separately the desired number of hours); we may sample by clusters (choosing one hour from each week or each month, say); we may construct a stratified sample, dividing the population into subclasses and sampling from each (choosing some hours from each phase of the psychoanalysis, according to our conception of what those phases are, or from each distinctive type of hour—for instance, those with marked abreactions or those showing deep resistance). There are still more patterns: probability samples, where each subclass enters the sample proportionately to its frequency in the population; multistage samples, one plan yielding an intermediate sample to which the same or another sampling plan is then applied; and various others. What is important is the recognition that each sampling plan calls for its own standardization, and its own way of computing stability. As with measurement, where there are many different scales that might be used, each having its own properties, sampling is not a simple, uniform procedure but one which varies from problem to problem, in ways that permit and even demand correspondingly different mathematical treatment.

HYPOTHESES

On the basis of a sample (or for whatever reason) we may formulate a *statistical hypothesis*, which has been defined by J. Neyman as any "assumption concerning the frequency functions of observable random variables". The hypothesis may be that a given parameter of the population has a certain value, or that its value falls in a certain range, or that certain variables are statistically independent of one another, or that the distribution is normal, or that it has some other specified characteristic, or that some other statistical statement is true. How such hypotheses are to be construed depends on the theory of probability that is invoked for the purpose. There are those who hold, for instance, that because statistical hypotheses tacitly refer to limits of infinite sequences (or at any rate, to "long runs"), they are not in the strict sense propositions at all, for no finite set of observations could falsify them. That an infinite sequence has a certain limit is logically compatible with the initial segment of the sequence, however long, having any value we choose. That a coin comes up "heads" the first ten times we toss it does not show it to be loaded; indeed, an unloaded coin is bound to come up "heads" ten times in a row sooner or later, and this occurrence at the beginning may simply be a case of "sooner".

On this view, the statistical hypothesis is to be thought of, not as a proposition, but as a procedural rule—a rule for constructing propositions or for inferring one proposition from another—as a "posit", to use Reichenbach's term, a commitment to a wager, or the like. It is crucial, however, that on any interpretation the acceptability of the hypothesis depends on the observed frequencies. The behavior of the coin may not strictly falsify the hypothesis that it is a fair coin, but it may well affect the wisdom of betting even money on the next toss. The hypothesis may not entail particular frequencies in finite samples, but it does assign probabilities of finding samples with specified frequencies. (See 9:131.) In the logic-in-use, however it be reconstructed, we test statistical hypotheses about a population by what is observed in the samples we have drawn from that population.

The weight of the evidence for or against a hypothesis, however, by no means depends solely on the frequencies themselves. Other hypotheses already established may be brought to bear, providing second-level probabilities concerning the observed frequencies on the assumption that the hypothesis in question is false. By this means, what Reichenbach has called "concatenations of evidence" are built up; a chain of probable inference may very well be stronger than its weakest link, stronger even than its strongest link. There is a beautiful example in the first chapter of Darwin's *Origin of Species;* because it is so much more representative of the logic-in-use in behavioral science than the mathematical deductions (of the type of Newton's *Principia*) so often cited by methodologists, I quote it here at length. Darwin is considering the hypothesis that all the breeds of domestic pigeons have a common origin in the rock pigeon, *Columba livia.* He argues:

If the several breeds are not varieties, and have not proceeded from the rock-pigeon, they must have descended from at least seven or eight aboriginal stocks; for it is impossible to make the present domestic breeds by the crossing of any lesser number. . . . The supposed aboriginal stocks must all have been rock-pigeons, that is, they did not breed or willingly perch on trees. But besides *C. livia,* with its geographical sub-species, only two or three other species of rock-pigeon are known; and these have not any of the characters of the domestic breeds. Hence the supposed aboriginal stocks must either still exist in the countries where they were originally domesticated, and yet be unknown to ornithologists; and this, considering their size, habits, and remarkable characters, seems improbable; or they must have become extinct in the wild state. But birds breeding on precipices, and good fliers, are unlikely to be exterminated; and the common rock-pigeon, which has the same habits with the domestic breeds, has not been exterminated even on several of the smaller British islets, or on the shores of the Mediterranean. Hence the supposed extermination of so many species having similar habits with the rock-pigeon seems a very rash assumption. Moreover, the several above-named domesticated breeds have been transported to all parts of the world, and, therefore, some of them must have been carried back

again into their native country; but not one has become wild or feral. . . .
Again, all recent experience shows that it is difficult to get wild animals to breed
freely under domestication; yet on the hypothesis of the multiple origin of our
pigeons, it must be assumed that at least seven or eight species were so thoroughly domesticated in ancient times by half-civilized man, as to be quite pro-
lific under confinement.

. . . The above-specified breeds, though agreeing generally with the wild
rock-pigeon in constitution, habits, voice, coloring, and in most parts of their
structure, yet are certainly highly abnormal in other parts. . . . Hence it must
be assumed not only that half-civilized man succeeded in thoroughly domesticat-
ing several species, but that he intentionally or by chance picked out extraordi-
narily abnormal species; and further, that these very species have since all
become extinct or unknown. So many strange contingencies are improbable in
the highest degree.

Some facts in regard to the coloring of pigeons well deserve consideration. . . .
We can understand these facts, on the well-known principle of reversion to
ancestral characters, if all the domestic breeds are descended from the rock-
pigeon. But if we deny this, we must make one of the two following highly improbable suppositions. Either, first, that all the several imagined aboriginal stocks
were colored and marked like the rock-pigeon, although no other existing species
is thus colored and marked, so that in each separate breed there might be a tendency to revert to the very same colors and markings. Or, secondly, that each
breed, even the purest, has within a dozen, or at most within a score, of generations, been crossed by the rock-pigeon. . . .

Lastly, the hybrids or mongrels from between all the breeds of the pigeon are
perfectly fertile, as I can state from my own observations, purposely made, on
the most distinct breeds. Now, hardly any cases have been ascertained with certainty of hybrids from two quite distinct species of animals being perfectly
fertile. . . .

From these several reasons, namely,—the improbability of man having for-
merly made seven or eight supposed species of pigeons to breed freely under
domestication;—these supposed species being quite unknown in a wild state,
and their not having become anywhere feral;—these species presenting certain
very abnormal characters, as compared with all other Columbidae, though so like
the rock-pigeon in most respects;—the occasional re-appearance of the blue
color and various black marks in all the breeds, both when kept pure and when
crossed;—and lastly, the mongrel offspring being perfectly fertile;—from
these several reasons taken together, we may safely conclude that all our domestic breeds are descended from the rock-pigeon or *Columba livia* with its geographical sub-species.

TESTS AND ERRORS

Note that throughout this argument Darwin relies on probability considerations, though without ever making these explicitly quantitative.
He uses the following expressions: "improbable", "unlikely", "a very
rash assumption", "improbable in the highest degree", "highly improb-

able", "hardly any cases have been ascertained with certainty", and finally, "we may safely conclude". Modern statistical theory and practice attempts to replace such expressions by others specifying numerical values, as measures of the support which given quantitative data provide for a given statistical hypothesis. When does the evidence permit us to say "we may safely conclude . . . ", or that the opposite conclusion is sufficiently improbable? A way of answering this sort of question is known as a *statistical test;* it consists of a rule prescribing, as Neyman puts it, "that we take action A when the sample point determined by observation falls within a specified category of points, and that we take action B in all other cases". On the face of it, a wide variety of such rules might be formulated. Which we choose, as in the case of any other rule of action, depends on the consequences for our values of acting in accord with the rule.

In making a decision of this kind, two sorts of errors are possible. One, known as the *error of the first kind* or *Type I error*, consists in rejecting the hypothesis being tested though in fact it is true. The other, the *error of the second kind* or *Type II error*, consists in accepting the hypothesis being tested though in fact it is false. In general, the two sorts of error have very different consequences for our values. For example, in the quality-control of a process of drug manufacture, much less is lost by rejecting a batch which in fact comes up to specifications, in spite of what a sampling indicated, than in accepting a batch which in fact is noxious, though the sample indicated otherwise. The situation may be the reverse in judging whether or not students have passed certain entrance examinations: the student mistakenly admitted will afterwards reveal his lack of aptitude, while the skills of the one mistakenly rejected may be lost to society forever.

A statistical hypothesis is usually so formulated that the more important error is of Type I. The negative form of a hypothesis is known as the *null hypothesis*, and states, for instance, that there is no dependency of one variable on another, or that there is no significant difference between two measures of some parameter. The Type I error then consists of mistakenly rejecting the null hypothesis, and the Type II error of mistakenly accepting it.

A given statistical test will in general be more sensitive to one type of error than to the other. The probability of occurrence of the Type I error when a given test is used is called the *significance level* of the test, or often, the "level of confidence" which it provides. Thus, the statement that a hypothesis is established "at the .05 level" may be interpreted as saying that the probability is .05 that the statistic employed would have at least the observed magnitude if the hypothesis were in fact false, that is, if the null hypothesis were the true one. The probability of detecting the falsehood of the null hypothesis when it is in fact false (which is the complement of the probability of the Type II error) is known as the *power* of the test. The power increases with the size of the sample—roughly speaking, in a larger sample "coincidence" becomes less probable.

It is important to note that the application of a statistical test to a hypothesis with respect to a given set of data depends in an essential way on the set of hypotheses taken to be alternatives to it. Such a set is always involved in the conclusion arrived at even when it is not explicitly mentioned. "Nothing, however improbable, can be judged a mere coincidence in virtue of its own probability, but only by comparison with the probability of something else" (*12*:263). Indeed, every specific event that occurs had, prior to its occurrence, a vanishingly small probability, as Charles Peirce pointed out. Every bridge hand dealt is quite as improbable as that in which each player has all thirteen cards of a suit. Yet in the latter case we might well suspect that the cards were stacked, or at any rate insufficiently shuffled, while we do not entertain such suspicions at every deal (discounting the paranoia of serious bridge players). The difference lies in the hypotheses regarded as alternatives. Sherlock Holmes understood this principle very well, in his repeated insistence that when we have eliminated all the possibilities but one, the one remaining, however improbable, must be the truth. His genius lay in recognizing possibilities that escaped such bunglers as Watson and the inspectors from Scotland Yard.

Here, as elsewhere in the use of statistics, which calculations are appropriate depends on how the problem has been structured. We proceed always on the basis of a set of assumptions, especially about the distribution in the population. The stronger these assumptions, the more powerful the statistical test that can be applied; on the other hand, the less extensive is the applicability of the particular solution of the structuring problem which has been decided upon. The difficulty is that we do not know, in general, whether large effects might not be produced by small departures from the conditions assumed for the appropriateness of the tests. (This is a point to which I shall return in the discussion of models, §32.) Recently there has been developed a set of statistical techniques, known as "nonparametric", which make no assumptions about distributions. They depend usually only on rankings rather than on fully arithmetical measures, and for that reason are particularly useful in behavioral science. But here we come once more on matters of technical, rather than broadly methodological, concern.

CORRELATION

Among the most familiar uses of statistics is that conveyed by the designation *explanatory statistics* (as contrasted with descriptive); they are often misused just because of their familiarity. Here calculations are made to determine the degree to which two sets of values *correlate* with one another, in the sense that variations in the one are matched by corresponding variations (in the same or opposite direction, respectively) in the other. The most usual measure is arrived at by computing the deviations from their means of sets of corresponding values, then taking the mean product of these, and dividing this product by the product of the two standard deviations. The result is the *coefficient of correlation;* it is 0 when there is no correlation at all between the two sets of values, 1 when they are perfectly correlated, and -1 when the correlation is perfect but inverse (one set of values rises as the other falls, and vice versa). The correlation is used in explanations by interpreting it to mean that the two sets of values do not just happen to agree in their variations, but do so because they are causally connected with one another.

Unfortunately, correlations seldom assume the extreme values, but fall somewhere in the middle range. Statistical tests must therefore be applied to rule out the null hypothesis, that the values are in fact uncorrelated. If it can be ruled out, the correlation is said to be "significant" (with respect to the significance and power of the test used). It must be remembered, however, that significant correlations may be the result, not of any real relation among the correlated values, but only of a similarity in the pattern of forces operative in the two cases. (Both sets, for instance, may be represented by a growth curve, exponential in both cases, though neither growth is in any way connected with the other.) And even where there *is* a causal connection, it may be quite indirect: both sets of values may be the effects of the same cause rather than one being the cause of the other. And the correlation itself gives us no way of distinguishing, in the case of a direct causal relation, which variable is cause and which is effect. In short, statistical tools are like any other: the more powerful they are, the greater the demands which they make on the care and intelligence of the user.

§29. Statistics in Behavioral Science

In recent years statistical theory has developed along lines that bring to the focus of attention actions rather than beliefs (see *124*:159 ff.). Problems are formulated in terms of what it is rational to do in a given situation, and not merely in terms of what it is rational to say under such circumstances. A number of new disciplines have sprung up—like decision theory, utility theory, and the theory of games—which draw upon and contribute to statistical methods. The contexts in which the scientist makes use of statistics may be viewed as choice-points in the flow of his behavior: the conduct of inquiry is, after all, a species of conduct. What emerges from every inquiry is a decision. The decision does not necessarily formulate some course of action to be pursued outside the context of inquiry, as a vulgarized pragmatism might insist; the action need not consist in the application of a scientific result to a "practical" problem. The scientific enterprise is itself a practical one—in it something important gets done, and we are interested in doing it well. Arriving at a scientific conclusion is a special case of reaching a decision, of making a choice among the alternatives which confront us in a problematic situation.

UTILITIES

Now, the rationality of a decision presupposes certain values. We choose one alternative rather than another because we prefer one outcome to another, and it is our expectation that the alternative chosen will have the preferred outcome. In this way there comes into play a system of "utilities"—the generic term often used for values, preferences, or desiderata of any kind in a decision-making situation. The decision is made according to what we expect will maximize the appropriate utility, or some sort of utility function. But since the outcome might not accord with our expectations, and thus affect our utilities adversely, and since, moreover, we may have occasion to reach a decision over and over again in comparable situations, strategic considerations enter. It may be better, for instance, never to make a certain choice even though it is usually the best one to make, if it entails a catastrophic result on the occasions when it is not best. This strategy embodies the principle of insurance: by not buying insurance we save the premium, and thus maximize our money holdings; but the savings may be dearly bought. There is always a question, however, of just what utilities are involved. Ambrose Bierce tells the fable of a determined insurance salesman to whom a prospect protested, "If you're so sure that my factory will burn down during the lifetime of the policy, why are you so anxious to sell me insurance?" The reply was: "Years ago the Company betrayed my sweetheart with a false promise of marriage; under an assumed name I have wormed my way into their confidence, and I have sworn revenge!"

Consider what is involved in arriving at an estimate of a particular magnitude, say the length of some object. We may suppose that some measurements have been made, and that the data yielded by them are available to us. The data do not tell us ineluctably what the length of the object is, for they speak a various language, and it is a foreign language to boot. We must interpret what is being said, and decide what to believe. (In a literal sense, this imperative is a basic problem for political science and political philosophy both: the voice of the people may be the voice of God, but the people do not speak with one voice, and God alone knows what they are saying; the pollster may be His vicar on earth, but here there can be no claim to infallibility.) In reaching a decision on the basis of the data we are, as it were, playing a game against Nature. This is not to say that it is "only a game", that is, that nothing important is at stake; nor is it implied that Nature is out to beat us. But there is a prize to be won—knowledge or truth—and a price to be paid for playing badly. The game has its own rules not of our making, what we call the laws of Nature and the facts of the case, which will determine our reward or punishment; but we are free to adopt what strategies we choose in accord with those rules.

Plainly, in order to make a rational decision as to the length of the object we must face a number of questions over and above those which are answered by a given set of measurements. What is the stake for which we are playing—that is, what will we do with our estimate when we have arrived at it, and what will it do for us in return? Is there always a winner, and how is he selected—that is, what defines the "best estimate" in this situation? Does the situation allow us to make more than one estimate—can any number of entries be submitted by each contestant? What is the cost of making an estimate—what box tops must accompany the entry? What price must be paid for an error, and how is an error defined? Is the price fixed, or does it vary with the size of the error? Can an error be corrected subsequently—are we playing touch-move or can a bad move be withdrawn? How will the prize be diminished by the range of the estimate made—do we win anything by estimating the length as lying between a thousandth of an inch and a thousand miles? How much will additional measurements cost? How long do we have to make up our minds? How much must be paid—in appropriate units of utility—for the use of a computer and other resources, both human and otherwise, available to the scientific enterprise?

These and similar questions cannot be set aside as extralogical, "merely practical" in import. They arise, whether or not they are explicitly formulated, in every actual context of inquiry—and science has no other locus. Many reconstructed logics seem to me to invite interpretation in theological terms: God is Truth, and every scientific quest brings the scientist either to salvation or to damnation. Nothing but Truth or Falsehood is at stake, nothing else is worth taking into account. But as Churchman (19:255) has pointed out, "if the chance of error alone were the sole basis for evaluating methods of inference, then we would never reach any decision, but would merely keep increasing the sample size indefinitely". Strictly speaking, even this alternative is not open to us, for accepting a finding as part of the data is itself a decision, even if we do not venture to make any inferences from the data. In acknowledging the premises we have committed ourselves as deeply as in drawing a conclusion from them. That a scientist has values, expressed in such commitments, is essential to the rational component of inquiry, just as having eyes and ears, or some sensory receptors, is essential to the empirical component. Some such values are presupposed by every statistical inquiry, though this is not to say that they cannot in turn be tested and corrected on the basis of inquiry (§44). With this understanding, I believe that Churchman is quite right in holding (*19*:257) that the criteria of correct inference from data are not fundamentally statistical in nature.

CRITERIA

What must enter into such criteria is a specification of the costs of reaching a decision, and of the losses incurred when the decision is a mistaken one. Of particular importance is the relative cost of errors of Type I and Type II. The scientist invests time and money in his experiments, and if his conclusions are erroneous, damage is likely to be done to society as well as to his own reputation (*18*:10). The scientist usually attaches a greater loss to accepting a falsehood than to failing to acknowledge a truth. As a result, there is a certain conservatism or inertia in the scientific enterprise, often rationalized as the healthy skepticism characteristic of the scientific temper. Behavioral science especially, I believe, suffers from this defense mechanism. My impression is that daring speculations are more likely to be made in, say, astrophysics or genetics than in, say, political science or economics.

No small part is played in behavioral science by the skills of "grantsmanship": there is an art of formulating research projects which are likely to be subsidized, and accorded deference by the Academy. Graduate students and young researchers play it safe, as prudence, indeed, dictates that they ought to do. Behavioral science might well profit if some of the resources available to it were frankly regarded as risk capital, to be invested in highly speculative ventures. Most of it, of course, would go down the drain, but fortunes are not made by the timid. Dorwin Cartwright has proposed that perhaps the only sensible definition of "basic research" is that which has a low probability of success, but which yields an enormous payoff when it is successful.

Even when utilities have been assigned in some acceptable way to scientific decision making, the problem still remains of what criteria to employ for choosing the strategy to be followed in the pursuit of these utilities. The one which is most famous, because of its role in the theory of games, is the so-called "minimax" criterion—acting so as to minimize the maximum loss which might be incurred. But as has been pointed out (*41*:158 n.) this criterion "is at the pessimistic end of a continuum of criteria. At the other end of this continuum is the 'minimin' criterion, which advises each experimenter to minimize his minimum risk. Here each experimenter acts as if this were the best of all possible worlds for him." It is clear that scientists may differ from one another in the utility they assign to risk taking; there may even be some few adventurous souls who assign it a positive utility. There will be differences in the evaluation by different scientists of the risks incurred by particular decisions, and differences in the utilities they associate with the expected outcomes. But what constitutes a good criterion for selecting strategies has been described as "the main gap in present-day statistical philosophy" (*18*:9).

VALUES

The upshot of this discussion is that logic is by no means as remote from ethics, in the broadest sense, as is commonly supposed. Charles Peirce argued that ethics was involved in logic because of the problem of the single case. On the frequency theory of probability, to which he subscribed, it is rational to act in accord with the probabilities only if the case before us is considered as a member of an infinite sequence of comparable cases. But no one of us will ever confront such a sequence. We are not being rational, therefore, unless we identify ourselves with the endless community of other decision makers. It is this ethical principle —making our own the interests of the whole of mankind—which Peirce insisted was basic to the logic of probability. Contemporary methodologists argue in a somewhat different fashion, but to the same effect. Thus Braithwaite (*9*:174) says: "The ultimate justification for any scientific belief will depend upon the main purpose for which we think scientifically —that of predicting and thereby controlling the future. The peculiarity of statistical reasoning is that it presupposes also at an early stage of the argument judgments as to what sort of future we want. In considering the rationale of such thinking we cannot avoid ethics breaking into inductive logic."

The main point underlying these arguments is that the distinction between facts and values cannot be drawn so sharply and so simply as is commonly supposed. Any conclusion as to what the facts are in a given case is the outcome of a process in which certain valuations also play an essential role. This point has been especially emphasized by Churchman (*19*:vii–viii): "The simplest question of fact in science requires for even an approximation, a judgment of value. . . . The science of ethics . . . is basic to the meaning of any question the experimental scientist raises. All the so-called 'facts' of science imply for their meaning a judgment of value." What is involved in this implication will be examined again in §43. For the present we may note that, if this line of analysis is sound, behavioral science is in a certain sense basic to all the others. Whatever its subject-matter, rational decision making is a part of human behavior, so that its theory, in so far as that theory goes beyond pure logic and mathematics, belongs to behavioral science. In a somewhat similar perspective, classical positivism made psychology basic to all science, by way of a phenomenalist epistemology: every scientific proposition reports or systematizes certain sensations, so that the theory of sensation becomes fundamental. But the nature of the dependence of other sciences on behavioral science must be formulated with some care. It is one thing to insist that we cannot fully understand the behavior of a scientist unless we know something of human behavior in general; it is quite another to suppose that by studying human behavior alone we can come to learn everything that any scientist is trying to find out. The first is almost a truism, but the second is a patent absurdity.

OBJECTIONS

What I have been discussing in these last few pages is the part played by behavioral science in statistical theory. What of the converse question—what part can statistics play in behavioral science? Historically, statistics developed out of a concern with certain problems of human behavior, those arising in connection with games of chance, insurance schemes, the recruitment and training of mass armies, and the like. Ironically, though statistical theory originally grew out of such contexts of application, more skepticism has been directed against its use in behavioral science than in physics or in biology.

The objections have come from two directions. The first is expressed in the familiar doctrine that human behavior is essentially unpredictable, because it is free. Stripped of its mystique, the doctrine rests, I believe, on two mistaken assumptions: that free choices are those which are uncaused, and that predictions can be based only on the knowledge of causal connections. Metaphysical freedom, if there be any such thing, is of no concern to the behavioral scientist, for by definition it marks the boundaries of his subject-matter, not its innermost essence. The other assumption is falsified by some of the earliest and most successful predictions human beings have ever made—I mean the astronomical ones—which were successful long before we had any knowledge of the causes at work (if, indeed, we have such knowledge even now!). It is true that there appears to be a certain random element in human behavior—what we call its "spontaneity" and such like—but there are certain stable patterns as well, constitutive of personality and character, and expressed in habits, institutions, customs, mores, and various other regularities of behavior. Even the random element lends itself to prediction, precisely by statistical techniques.

I believe that there is a core of soundness in the doctrine in question, a difficulty which confronts the behavioral scientist with a real methodological problem rather than a metaphysical puzzle. It is that predicting human behavior is itself a kind of behavior, which may have effects on what is being predicted. The feedback cannot always be ignored, and may even be of primary importance, as in the case of predictions made to a patient in the course of psychotherapy. But here also the use of statistics does not constitute the problem but may even help us to solve it. From a statistical point of view, the feedback may be analyzable as a second-order effect, or we may achieve a certain frequency of success with our predictions even though they are falsified in specific cases. What is also sound in the skeptical doctrine, I believe, is that behavior is a consequence both of the subjective probabilities of the actor (or his probability estimates) and of his utilities, so that predictions which replace either of these by our own—on the tacit assumption that they are the only ones possible to a rational being—are likely to be falsified. This again is a difficulty which is not intrinsic to the use of statistics for prediction, but one which, on the contrary, statistical theory can help us make explicit and cope with.

The second line of resistance to the role of statistics in behavioral science is not that it tries to do too much, but that it does too little. The aim of science is alleged to consist only in the discovery of universal laws, a viewpoint aptly designated "the nomothetic bias", while statistical correlations are said to fall far short of this universality. "However, a correlation coefficient is just as exact, that is to say, just as public and palpable in its meaning as a law. . . . And, in a sense, it has even more generality than the 'general' laws of nature which are observed under such meticulously specified conditions." (*91*:200). When we have discovered a significant correlation we have surely enlarged our knowledge, and not only with respect to the particularity of some specific matter of fact. True, the knowledge cannot be applied with certainty to every individual instance. But neither, with certainty, can laws which are not explicitly statistical in character—if we were to demand certainty we should have to say that we have no laws at all, but only some more or less eligible prospects for that title. And the approach to certainty increases as we move to larger populations of cases, satisfying various conditions of distribution—"that which is only probable when asserted of individual human beings indiscriminately selected, being certain when affirmed of the character and collective conduct of masses," as Mill (*94*:554) put it long ago.

In my opinion, the shortcomings—and they are many!—of the use of statistics in behavioral science are chiefly attributable to the tendency to forget that statistical techniques are tools of thought, and not substitutes for thought. As one of their influential users has emphasized, they "should be our servants in the investigation of psychological ideas. If we have no psychological ideas, we are not likely to discover anything interesting" (Thurstone, in *91*:277). In the proper use of statistical techniques, we turn to them because we have a need for them in the conduct of our inquiry, and not because they are there. And to recognize that they are tools of thought means to be aware also of the assumptions about our subject-matter which we make when we put a specific tool to use. In these perspectives, the reliance on statistics is no ground for embarrassment to the behavioral scientist. Whatever the techniques employed, it is not the study of man which is embarrassing, but the behavior which the study discloses. The behavioral scientist must acknowledge his share of responsibility for human folly—but let him rest content with his own share!

Chapter VII

MODELS

§30   *The Structure of Models*
§31   *Functions of Models*
§32   *Shortcomings of Models*
§33   *Models in Behavioral Science*

§30. *The Structure of Models*

One of the meanings of the term *model* is "something eminently worthy of imitation, an exemplar or ideal". I am inclined to think that this sense of the term is by no means irrelevant to its use in contemporary methodology. Those scientists who speak of their work as "model building" often give the impression that such an endeavor is the only true begetter of scientific knowledge, and that the construction and testing of models is itself the very model of modern scientific activity. They do so especially in behavioral science, and the emphasis on models is a characteristic feature of those schools or approaches to which the label "behavioral science" is applied in a narrow and distinctive sense, in contrast to what are regarded as more belletristic studies of man and his works. In short, models—to play on another meaning of the word—are much in fashion, though to say so is by no means to prejudge their scientific significance and worth. The words "model" and "mode" have, indeed, the same root; today, model building is science *à la mode*.

The fashion in question concerns one of the dimensions of cognitive style—roughly speaking, the use which is made of formal logic and mathematics. Note that this is a question of the style of thought, not merely of the style of presentation: Plato and Galileo both wrote dialogues, but with very different cognitive styles. Yet thought and its expression are surely not wholly unrelated to one another, and how scientific findings are formulated for incorporation into the body of knowledge often reflects stylistic traits of the thinking behind them. With this understanding, that it is not the manner of presentation itself which is decisive, we may identify the following cognitive styles in behavioral science. Of course, the differences between them are far from clear-cut; and we must remember that the classification is based on only one stylistic category—mathematization, as it were—so that quite other sets of styles could be discriminated as well.

1. The *literary* style. This cognitive style is likely to be occupied with individuals, particular persons or sets of events, case studies, clinical findings, and the like. A plot is unfolded—a behavior sequence is disclosed to have a certain significance. Act meaning rather than action meaning is fundamental. A person, a movement, or a whole culture is interpreted, but largely in terms of the specific purposes and perspectives of the actors, rather than in terms of the abstract and general categories of the scientist's own explanatory scheme. The autobiographies of Lincoln Steffens and Henry Adams, Freud's studies of Moses and Leonardo, some of De Toqueville, and much of the anthropological writing of the early decades of this century illustrate the variety of materials about human behavior that exhibit something of this style.

2. The *academic* style. This is much more abstract and general than the literary style. There is some attempt to be precise, but it is verbal rather than operational. Ordinary words are used in special senses, to constitute a technical vocabulary. Standard idioms in this vocabulary, together with certain recurrent metaphors, make up a jargon distinctive of a particular school, a special standpoint or approach to the subject-matter. The materials dealt with tend to be ideational rather than observational data, and their treatment tends to be highly theoretical, if not, indeed, purely speculative. System is introduced by way of great "prin-

ciples", applied over and over to specific cases, which illustrate the generalization rather than serve as proofs for it. The work of historical systematizers like Toynbee, essays in psychoanalytic theory, sociological treatises like those of Parsons or Veblen, and much of classical economics all exemplify the academic style (as does this book, by and large).

3. The *eristic* style. Here there is a strong interest in proof, and of specific propositions, rather than, as in the literary and academic styles, the aim only of exhibiting the cognitive possibilities in certain broad perspectives on the subject-matter. Experimental and statistical data become important. Attention is given to deductive relationships, logical derivations from propositions previously established or explicitly assumed, though proofs are sketched rather than rigorously laid out. The distinction is more or less clearly drawn between substantive, empirical statements and purely logical ones, like definitions and their tautological consequences. Definitions are frequent, and tend to be stated explicitly. In general, there is a considerable degree of awareness of what are thought to be the canons of "scientific method". This is perhaps the most pervasive style in twentieth-century behavioral science. Examples abound in the journals, except those which are frankly literary (in cognitive style), or those which are committed to one or another of the academic schools of thought. Pavlov and later behavioristic psychologists, Pareto, Keynes and his followers, Michels, Lasswell, and most contemporary linguists all exhibit what I am calling the eristic style.

4. The *symbolic* style. In the symbolic style, mathematics comes into its own. It is not, however, the rigor of mathematical demonstration which is significant, but the precision and power of mathematical ideas. The subject-matter is conceptualized from the outset in mathematical terms. Both problems and solutions are formulated, therefore, in a more or less artificial language; neologisms abound, and special notations are introduced for the purposes required by the context. The symbols are subjected to mathematically standardized transformations, though not in any over-all systematic fashion. Measurement is important, as providing the content for the mathematical forms which are employed. Statistical data do not serve, as in the eristic style, only as a body of evidence; they are processed so as to generate new hypotheses, and even new patterns of conceptualization. In this processing, computers and other instruments, both physical and ideational, are likely to play a major role. The symbolic style is characteristic of mathematical economics, psychometrics and

sociometrics, game-theoretic treatments of political problems, probabilistic approaches to learning theory, and so on.

5. The *postulational* style. This has many of the characteristics of the symbolic style, of which, indeed, it could be regarded as a special variant. It differs from the symbolic style in general only as logic differs from mathematics. The validity of proof is at the focus of attention here, rather than the content of the propositions which occur at the various steps. Emphasis is on the system as a whole, bound together by the chains of logical derivation. Rules for such derivations are explicitly formulated and applied. The foundation on which the whole system is erected is a set of propositions laid down to serve in just this way. These are the postulates; often they are also called "axioms", though in more strict usages this term is reserved for postulates whose truth can be established without appealing to anything beyond pure logic and mathematics. In general, postulates have an empirical content, and their truth is dependent on matters of fact. From the postulates theorems are derived, whose verification indirectly validates the postulates by which they are proved. Interest centers on the independence of the postulates from one another (none of them is a theorem of the system constituted by the rest), and on their mutual consistency (a proposition and its negation cannot both be derived from the set). What is wanted is the simplest set which will suffice for the derivation of the theorems in which we are interested, one which will allow for elegant proofs of the important propositions about the subject-matter. The postulational style is likely to be less demanding of extensive measurements, less bound to various quantitative scales. In behavioral science it has been most widely applied in the field of welfare economics, especially in connection with utility theory; but postulational methods have also been applied to such subject-matters as learning, communication, international relations, and kinship systems.

6. The *formal* style. This is very close to the postulational style, and indeed, presupposes the latter. The difference is that here the key terms are not given any interpretation; there is no reference to any specific empirical content. What is remarkable is that the validity of the derivations is not dependent upon any such content, but only upon the pattern of relationships holding among the symbols themselves—hence the designation "formal". In general, a number of different interpretations can be given to the formal system, with equal justification so far as the system itself is concerned. Thus Euclid's geometry can be developed in a purely

formal way; the "points" of which it speaks can be interpreted as ordered pairs of real numbers, "lines" as linear functions of such numbers, and so on; in that case the postulates of the geometry become axioms of arithmetic (algebra). On the other hand, "points" might be interpreted as intersections of hairlines, "lines" as paths of light rays, and so on, and whether the postulates are true then depends on matters of physical fact. In any case, a true interpretation (one in which the postulates are indeed true) yields true theorems as well. Because of the multiplicity of interpretations which it allows, a formal system has the immediate advantage of possible application to a variety of subject-matters, which are thereby shown to have the same formal structure. This style is as yet comparatively rare in behavioral science (or anywhere outside logic and mathematics, for that matter); an example is provided by Cartwright and Harary's theory of organization, which develops the mathematics of "graphs" or abstract relations, and which lends itself to various interpretations in terms of communication nets, structures of authority and influence, patterns of friendship, and such like.

I hope it is clear from the examples given that these various cognitive styles do not correspond to any classification of sciences according to subject-matter. The situation here is rather like that in the arts: the substance of a work of art, what is actually in the work, is indeed shaped by and perhaps even constituted by the style, but not the subject-matter, the point of departure for the artist's creation. A romanticist poem or expressionist painting may be more likely to have one subject-matter than another, but that same subject-matter can also be treated in quite other styles. More important, the cognitive styles presented above are by no means listed in order of scientific merit, unless this merit is tacitly defined by just such a stylistic requirement. From the standpoint of their contribution to the progress of inquiry there are good and bad specimens of each of the styles, whether for physical and biological science or for behavioral science. What might, perhaps, be said is that the list is in rough chronological order of development in any particular discipline. The use of mathematics and the construction of logical systems marks a certain coming of age; but many adults are still infantile in their behavior, and the most mature are those who know what children they remain.

MODELS AND THEORIES

The term "model" is often used loosely to refer to any scientific theory couched in the symbolic, postulational, or formal styles. I believe, however, that it is most appropriately applied only in connection with the last, or at most, with the last two. Broadly speaking, we may say that any system A is a model of a system B if the study of A is useful for the understanding of B without regard to any direct or indirect causal connection between A and B (49:36). For in that case, A must be like B in some respects: if we wanted to infer that because A has the property p then B has some other property q we would need to know that A and B are somehow connected, according to the specific relation between p and q, while to conclude that B also has the property p, we need only know that A and B are similar in appropriate ways even though in fact they have nothing to do with one another. On the other hand, just which ways are appropriate is already limited by the condition that *no* conditions are imposed on the physical relations between the two systems. The systems must therefore resemble one another as systems, that is, in ways which do not depend on the particular elements of which each consists, or else we would need to know just how elements of these particular kinds affect one another. The resemblance is in terms of the pattern or order exhibited in each system, the information which each contains, in the current idiom, rather than in terms of the configuration of mass and energy in which the information is embodied. In a word, when one system is a model of another they resemble one another in *form* and not in content.

More specifically, models are isomorphs of one another (§21). Both systems have the same structure, in the sense that whenever a relation holds between two elements of one system a corresponding relation holds between the corresponding elements of the other system. The systems need not stand in any causal connection, for what is required is only that the relations correspond, and to satisfy this requirement it is enough that we can *put* them into correspondence, that is, think of them as corresponding. Then, whether a system does or does not show a certain pattern in its own internal relations is plainly quite independent of what the other system shows. If there is an isomorphism, the systems significantly resemble one another only in their structural properties, additional resemblances, if any, being irrelevant.

The structural properties of a system are by definition those which would be shared by any other system isomorphic to the given one. Such properties are often called the "logical" properties of a system, in contrast to its "descriptive" properties, but this is a misleading usage. They are, to be sure, very abstract properties, for they concern only those features of relations which are wholly independent of what particular things stand in those relations. But structural properties are not "logical" as contrasted with "empirical". What structure a particular system has is a matter of fact, unless, to be sure, the system has been tacitly defined by reference to such properties. Thus the cardinal number of a class might be regarded as the structure of the relation of diversity (nonidentity) in the class, and how many members a class has is, in general, an empirical question. Similarly, it is an empirical question whether, say, the inheritance of property in a given society has the structure of a mathematical progression, like the sequence of positive integers.

We can now understand why the term "model" is sometimes used as a synonym for "theory", especially one which is couched in the postulational style. The model is conceived as a structure of symbols interpreted in certain ways, and what it is a model of is the subject-matter specified by the interpretation. Relations among the symbols are presumed to exhibit corresponding relations among the elements of the subject-matter. The theory is more or less abstract—that is, it neglects certain variables —and what it describes are certain more or less "ideal" entities, having an existence only in the context of the theory itself. What is hoped is that the system of such entities will be isomorphic, in appropriate respects, to the real system which provides the subject-matter for the theory. Some contemporary psychologists take the view that their subject-matter as a whole has a hopelessly complex structure, and so concentrate on the construction of "miniature systems" or "theorettes".

In my opinion, this sort of usage of the term "model" is of dubious worth, methodologically speaking. If "model" is coextensive with "theory", why not just say "theory", or if need be, "theory in postulational form"? In a strict sense, not all theories are in fact models: in general, we learn something about the subject-matter *from* the theory, but not by investigating properties *of* the theory. The theory *states* that the subject-matter has a certain structure, but the theory does not therefore necessarily *exhibit* that structure in itself. All theories make abstractions, to be sure, in the sense of treating as irrelevant some properties of their subject-matter. But not all of them abstract to the point of treating as relevant only the structural properties. Consider, for instance, the difference between the theory of evolution and a model which a geneticist might construct to study mathematically the rate of diffusion in a hypothetical population of a characteristic with a specified survival value. I think that at bottom the tendency to view all theories as models stems from an old-fashioned semantics, according to which a true proposition must have the same structure as the fact it affirms (the early Wittgenstein and Russell), and the still current but controversial realist epistemology, according to which theories offer ever more detailed and comprehensive pictures of reality (see §§33 and 35). I have grave doubts whether the working scientist is committed to either of these standpoints, to say nothing of both together; model building is only one of his cognitive strategies, and is not to be identified with the scientific enterprise as such.

ANALOGY AND METAPHOR

A more defensible usage views as models only those theories which explicitly direct attention to certain resemblances between the theoretical entities and the real subject-matter. With this usage in mind, models have been defined as "scientific metaphors". A metaphor, like an aphorism, condenses in a phrase a significant similarity (*49*:84). When the poet writes, "the morn, in russet mantle clad, walks o'er the dew of yon high eastern hill", he evokes awareness of a real resemblance, and such awarenesses may be made to serve the purposes of science. When they do serve in this way, we are likely to conceptualize the situation as involving the use of *analogy*. The scientist recognizes similarities that have previously escaped us, and systematizes them. Electricity exhibits a "flow"; there is a "current" exerting a certain pressure (the voltage), having a certain volume (the amperage), and so on. Analogies, it has been held, do more than merely lead to the formulation of theories, so that afterwards they may be removed and forgotten; they are "an utterly essential part of theories, without which theories would be completely valueless and unworthy of the name" (Campbell, *38*:297).

Theories are sometimes spoken of as models in acknowledgment of this analogical feature.

But just as it is questionable whether one should say that all language is metaphoric, though unquestionably meanings are extended by way of real or fancied resemblances, so also is it doubtful whether one should say that all theories are analogical merely because all of them note resemblances. Every theory groups together phenomena which, apart from the theory, would be thought to be significantly different; indeed, all predication classifies, and so alleges a similarity with regard to the class character. But the content of the theory does not consist merely in the statement of the resemblance, but also in the grounds it provides for recognizing the resemblance as a significant one. In some cases these grounds are constituted by other resemblances, and we can speak of an analogy; but not in all cases. The motion of the moon in its orbit is like the fall of the apple; the likeness, according to Newton, lies in the fact that they are both masses attracted to the earth in accord with the law of gravitation. But there the significant similarity ends, and there is no analogy to be drawn. The flow of an electric current, on the other hand, relates one resemblance to a number of others; it is the systematic elaboration of the resemblances which constitutes the analogy. A better example is perhaps provided by the familiar hydrodynamic metaphor in psychoanalysis, with the id as a reservoir having several "outlets" which can lower internal pressures, which in turn are countered by forces of repression, and so on. Freud also uses a societal analogy, with a "censor", an authoritarian "superego", internal "conflicts", and the like. No theory is to be condemned as "merely an analogy" just because it makes use of one. No two things in the world are wholly alike, so that every analogy, however close, can be pushed too far; on the other hand, no two things are wholly dissimilar, so that there is always an analogy to be drawn, if we choose to do so. The question to be considered in every case is whether or not there is something else to be learned from the analogy if we do choose to draw it.

KINDS OF MODELS

In these terms, a model might be said to be the embodiment of a structural analogy. The embodiment might be in a set of symbols (that is, in the conceptual structure they specify), or else in some actual physical system. Such models might be called *analogues*, as a generic term for both conceptual and physical isomorphs. These may be distinguished as *semantical* and *physical models*. As with analogue computers, a pattern is instituted on the basis of well-defined correspondences, and the properties of the pattern are then studied in order to learn something about the system to which it corresponds. In behavioral science, analogues are coming to command increasing attention, under such designations as "simulation", "operational gaming", and the like.

The strictest sense of the term "model" is associated with the formal style. Given a formal system, a model is constituted by any interpretation of the system which makes its postulates true. This is the sense in which the term is used by logicians, like Tarski and Suppes—"a non-linguistic entity in which a theory is satisfied"; it is the fundamental sense, by which other usages can be explicated. In the development of the formal disciplines, models have long been important as devices by which a system can be shown to be consistent, or at any rate, as consistent as some other system which serves as an interpretation for the first. (A contradictory system cannot have any nonlinguistic interpretation; and if a "dictionary" can be constructed to a second linguistic system, the first is contradictory only if the second is—it is in this way that non-Euclidean geometry was formally validated.) Models in this sense are also sometimes known as "structures"—for instance, in econometrics. We may call them *interpretive models* to make their origin explicit. The system being interpreted is sometimes also called a model, especially when the interpretation is another linguistic system; we may speak here of *formal models*. An interpretive model is thus a model *for* a theory, while a formal model is a model *of* a theory. Note that an interpretive model presupposes an explicitly stated formal theory; a semantical model provides or constitutes a theory. The semantical model corresponds to a subject-matter, a system of phenomena, while the interpretive model corresponds to a set of postulates or a system of equations, not specifically "about" anything.

We have thus distinguished five different senses in the confusing and often confused usage of the term "model": (1) any theory more strictly formulated than is characteristic of the literary, academic, or eristic cognitive styles, one presented with some degree of mathematical exactness and logical rigor; (2) a semantical model, presenting a conceptual analogue to some subject-matter; (3) a physical model, a nonlinguistic system analogous to some other being studied; (4) a formal model, a model *of* a theory which presents the latter purely as a structure of uninterpreted symbols; (5) an interpretive model, providing an interpretation *for* a formal theory. In the consideration both of the uses and of the shortcomings of models these distinctions will have to be kept in mind.

§31. *Functions of Models*

Many discussions of the role of models attribute to them functions that would be performed by any theory, whatever its style (§35). Thus models are said to provide "meaningful contexts within which specific findings can be located as significant details". That they do so is both true and important, but it is not distinctive of models. Every theory serves, in part, as a research directive; theory guides the collection of data and their subsequent analysis, by showing us beforehand where the data are to be fitted, and what we are to make of them when we get them. The word "data", it cannot too often be emphasized, is an incomplete term, like "later than"; there are only data *for* some hypothesis or other. Without a theory, however provisional or loosely formulated, there is only a miscellany of observations, having no significance either in themselves or over against the plenum of fact from which they have been arbitrarily or accidentally selected.

DATA ORGANIZATION

But the more ill-defined the theory, the more vague and uncertain is the significance it confers on data. Models have this merit, that they do not allow us to comfort ourselves with the notion that we are following up an "idea" when we are only moving from one observation to the next in the hope that something will turn up. Too often the hypotheses with which we work are at home only in the twilight regions of the mind, where their wavering outlines blend into a shadowy background. There they are safe from sudden exposure, and are free to swoop down for sustenance on whatever datum comes their way. Models are at any rate conscious, explicit, and definite; there is nothing ghostly in their appearance or manner; they look healthy even up to the very moment of their death.

I do not mean to minimize the importance of preconscious processes in the cognitive enterprise. But if the creative genius works with more than he knows, we ordinary mortals often know less than we think. The model saves us from a certain self-deception. Forced into the open, our ideas may flutter helplessly; but at least we can see what bloodless creatures they are. As inquiry proceeds, theories must be brought out into the open sooner or later; the model simply makes it sooner. In the Socratic metaphor, all thought is the conversation of the soul with itself. The creative imagination, in both scientist and artist, takes the form of a vigorous discussion with the boys in the back room; and there inevitably comes a time when someone says, "Put up or shut up!" It is at this moment that models are brought forward.

COGNITIVE STYLES

There are other functions attributed to models which more properly characterize any inquiry in the eristic and symbolic cognitive styles.

To start with, the model allows the scientist to make clear to others just what he has in mind. Science is a cooperative enterprise: every scientist is deeply dependent on his colleagues for criticism or corroboration of his findings. Moreover, science is a cumulative enterprise: the scientist builds on what others have already established, and contributes, in turn, a basis for still further construction. All this interdependence requires that scientists understand one another with as little uncertainty of meaning as can be. The communication of scientific ideas is not a matter merely of the sociology of science, but is intrinsic to its logic; as in art, the idea is nothing till it has found expression.

The literary and academic styles are scarcely if at all adequate for this communication. The literary style makes great demands on the reader's own capacity for imaginative interpretation. This reader's role is responsible for the vivid and compelling quality of that style: we share in the creative process of the scientist's reconstruction of the subject-matter. Unfortunately, there is no knowing just how much is in fact shared and how much is our own projection onto the data—or at any rate, such knowledge is not easy to come by. For this reason, among others, the literary style is thought to provide valuable materials for scientific treatment, but not to be scientific in itself. As for the academic style, systemic meanings make it difficult to detach any particular proposition from the matrix of the whole body of writing in which it is embedded, and the latter is usually vast and amorphous. This difficulty is characteristic, for instance, of those encountered in the attempt to construe psychoanalytic hypotheses in terms of learning theory and its data, or Marxist doctrines in terms of a "classless" political science. Though the symbolic style also has its own notations and idioms, their meaning is likely to be much more fully and explicitly specified.

Secondly, the eristic and especially the symbolic styles distinguish carefully between definitions and empirical propositions. Granted that this distinction cannot be drawn as sharply and as absolutely as has often been supposed; it remains true, nevertheless, that there are very significant differences in the degree of "priority" of propositions (§12). Certain propositions may command assent, not because of the overwhelming weight of evidence supporting them, but because of the usage of the terms in which they are formulated (even though this usage may in turn rest on empirical considerations). When this tendency is overlooked, we risk losing the substance of knowledge by grasping at its shadow. A mixture of tautologies and what have been called "heuristic slogans" is mistaken for a genuine theory, and a program is accepted as its own fulfillment. There is a certain kind of ambiguity, not uncommon in the literary and academic styles, in which a statement can be variously interpreted so as to have very different degrees of "priority": it is taken as a tautology to establish its truth, though in that sense it may be virtually lacking in empirical content, then taken as an empirical statement to give it significance, though in that sense it may be plainly false. Doctrines of human motivation underlying some of the classical political theories (for instance, that of Hobbes) suffer from this serious defect. It is one which models help us to avoid.

Explicit definitions have besides another valuable function. They may clarify and simplify relations among concepts, revealing an underlying order, and allowing for useful systematizations. This function has been performed with kinship terms, for example. Kinship systems depend, in general, on three parameters: sex, parentage, and the marital relation. Three terms, one for each of these parameters, will allow us to define all the kinship terms; but there must be three, and more would be super-fluous. Definitions have been used in this way to clarify, simplify, and systematize concepts in political science, economics, and other areas.

It is the postulational style that has recently excited so much interest and attention among behavioral scientists, and understandably so.

First of all, the postulational method provides us with a way of han-dling complex phenomena without introducing obviously artificial sim-plifications of the "other things being equal" type. We may lay down separate postulates for each of the various factors of the situation, and formulate explicitly whatever theories we might have as to how they interact. It then becomes a matter of deduction, or even of calculation, to determine the outcome in specific circumstances. This is the procedure followed in certain areas of economics, for instance.

In the second place, the construction of postulational systems reveals gaps in our knowledge. It allows us to identify the propositions that are needed for us to be able to derive the conclusions in which we are inter-ested: gaps in knowledge are revealed by the gaps in "proofs". This is one of the specific ways in which a carefully formulated theory can direct the search for data. For example, as economic inferences were made more rigorous, economists became increasingly interested in data bearing on motivations operative in the economy, in connection with such matters as attitudes toward risk, the value of gratifications lying in the future, or utilities not reflected in money prices.

The broadening of the conception of measurement to include the appli-cation of scales that are not fully quantitative has also been closely associ-ated with the use of the postulational style. For in this style we can apply the methods of mathematics even though we are not operating on numbers. The virtues of clarity, consistency, precision, and rigor become attainable with regard to subject-matters, like rational decision making, that might otherwise seem to preclude them. The whole development of the theory of games and much of utility theory illustrate this feature of the postulational style.

Perhaps the most important advantage conferred by the postulational style lies in its *deductive fertility*. It allows us to process our information so that we can squeeze out of our data a great deal of content not other-wise available to us, or at least not easily available. "It is the glory of geometry," Newton once said, "that from those few principles it is able to produce so many things." I remember how impressed I was to learn in elementary geometry that the volume of a sphere is given by $\frac{4}{3}\pi r^3$. That π should enter seemed to me clear from the fact that every cross section of a sphere is a circle; and that the radius must be cubed was understandable because we were dealing with a volume; but that the coefficient was $\frac{4}{3}$ I found mysterious and wonderful. A postulate system is the more valuable the richer it is in unanticipated consequences, for these show us how much more we know than we thought we did.

Of course, the conclusions deduced do not constitute knowledge unless and until the postulates from which they are derived are themselves known to be true. The validity of the proof assures us only that what we have is a theorem of the system; but the system itself must beseparately justified. It is just here that the postulational method shows itself so useful—in the process of verification of our hypotheses. It simplifies and shortens the process in that a verification of the postulates constitutes at once a verification of all the theorems that flow from them. Conversely, if any of the theorems is shown to be false, the postulate set as a whole (that is, the conjunction of the postulates, not each of them separately) is thereby falsified. Thus we can take advantage of very remote consequences to provide tests of our ideas. The literary and academic styles suffer from a certain vagueness and ambiguity so that we cannot say with assurance what are the logical consequences of a particular feature or component of a theory. In the postulational style we can settle unequivocally which particular theorems are doubtful when a particular postulate is questioned or replaced. And the rigor of the deductions can reveal hidden assumptions that actually play a role in our theory without having been explicitly formulated as part of it.

Finally, the postulational style makes possible an economical summary of our actual or anticipated findings. The postulates logically contain within themselves all the information embodied in the whole set of theorems which they entail. All the propositions of a theory are communicated in its postulates, somewhat in the way in which an indefinite multiplicity of facts is conveyed by the single law which governs them. To be sure, it is crucial that the content is only "logically" contained in the postulates: we have not learned the whole of mechanics in the few minutes it takes us to understand Newton's laws of motion. But what remains to be done is guided by the strict norms of logic and mathematics; exactly what the theory says is no longer a matter of personal judgment.

KINDS OF MODELS

All the advantages of models so far discussed apply to models, however, only in a very broad and loose sense. In a stricter sense, some similarity of structure between the model and its referent is called for, and this structural element has not yet entered into the discussion. We must ask what functions in inquiry are performed by the construction of isomorphic systems.

By far the oldest and the most widely used type of isomorph is the *physical model*. In the form of dolls, idols, effigies, and graven images of all sorts the physical model is as universal as magic and religion, from paleolithic rituals to the latest demonstrations against a losing football coach. A cognitive function is performed by the physical model in almost every branch of technology, from sewing to architecture and aeronautical engineering. In so far as it is an analogue, the model obeys the same laws as its original; but as a physical system in its own right it may differ in all sorts of ways—for instance, in scale—which give it distinctive advantages. Being more accessible and manipulable, it is well suited to the purposes of pedagogy—as exemplified by the planetarium, which may model the solar system or the cosmos. Because it is cheaper, safer, and faster, it allows for experimentation that would otherwise not be feasible. And by varying its construction or operation we can use it to trace out the consequences of alternative sets of assumptions, and so calculate an outcome or assess a theory. The potential contributions of physical models to behavioral science are only now beginning to be explored—for example, computer simulation of personality, or physical systems that model the economy or some part of it, and thus serve as analogue computers for the solution of problems in economics. Psychodrama (role playing) and operational gaming may also be regarded as the use of physical models, whose components are acts and events as well as objects.

The *semantical model* is a symbolic or conceptual analogue. By providing a clearly specified structure, it allows for the application of statistics and other mathematical tools. In general, these cannot be used unless certain requirements are satisfied; in the model we can decide just which conditions have been met. It is for this reason that an empirically given problem is so often replaced by one involving a certain way of drawing colored balls from suitably filled urns. The words "model" and "structure" are probably used more often in statistics than anywhere else, out-side, perhaps, the purely formal disciplines like logic and metamathe-matics. The construction of a semantical model also allows us to intro-duce the simplifying assumptions necessary to make our equations solv-able, while yet retaining a structural similarity to the original situation which the equations were intended to describe. This simplification is characteristic, for example, of the reformulation of economic bargain-ing or political negotiation as the play of a "game" in von Neumann's sense.

One of the great advantages of semantical models is that they allow a systematic exploitation of failure. Scientific advance depends as much on its misses as on its hits; if it did not, progress would be slow indeed, for error is much more frequent than truth. Learning in general is surely most effective when it profits from failure as much as from success. Now models are often used, not in the expectation of immediate success, but in the hope of successive identification of particular causes of failure, so that an acceptable theory can gradually be developed. "A good model," it has been said (*6*:40–41), "is often a member of a family whose mem-bers resemble one another in the possession of many common simplifying assumptions and subsidiary hypotheses, and differ from one another by the elimination or addition of one or several hypotheses or assumptions." A model is often worth knowing because of its family connections; if it is not capable itself of doing for us what is needful, it can introduce us to a relative who will be happy to oblige.

Formal models make for a flexibility of conceptualization in themselves, even without a family of variants. In making the model formal, we not only deliberately omit some variables which we may have reason to think are essential, but we also free our theory from the irrelevancies necessarily involved in any concrete embodiment of the structure. This is the great advantage Boltzmann attributed to what he called the "deduc-tive method": "Since the deductive method does not constantly mingle external pictures forced upon us by experience with inner ones that are arbitrarily chosen by us, it is far easiest for it to develop the latter clearly and free from contradictions. . . . Clarity suffers from a too early mingling with experience and is preserved most securely by the deduc-tive mode of representation" (in *27*:249–250). As a result, the formal model can suggest studies to determine what *is* relevant: certain things must be true in the concrete if they are to be capable of being represented by a particular abstract form. The abstractness of the formal model has the additional enormous advantage of extreme generality from the outset: a variety of matters may be so structured as to exhibit the identical form. Thus the transmission of ideas may reveal the same pattern as the spread of an epidemic (N. Rashevsky) or the diffusion of information (H. Simon).

The *interpretive model*, since it consists of a concrete instance of the abstract form, serves to suggest "at what points rules may be introduced for establishing correspondence between theoretical and experimental notions" (*103*:113). But its greatest merit is that it allows us to use what we know of one subject-matter to arrive at hypotheses concerning another subject-matter structurally similar to the first. The new area may provide an interpretive model for the old theory, as is illustrated by the work in recent decades on the structural similarities of computers and the nervous system. Interpretive models are thus peculiarly suited to interdisciplinary approaches, as the cybernetic model of mind in terms of feedbacks and the processing of information brings to a common focus the skills, knowledge, and interests of both psychologists and communication engineers. The hope is that ultimately two apparently distinct areas will be capable of being identified, or reduced to variants of a single underlying phenomenon, as optics and electromagnetism were eventually identified through the structural commonality formulated in Maxwell's equations. An interpretive model also serves to show that a more general theory still applies to an earlier, restricted domain, by showing that the latter may be construed as a particular model for the former. In this way, the construction of models also serves the ends of scientific explanation.

§32. *Shortcomings of Models*

Schools of thought in behavioral science today are often identifiable as much by the methods they apply as by the theories they espouse. There are the experimenters, those focusing on measurement, the devotees of statistics, the theoreticians, and now the model builders. Each method, to be sure, comprises a variety of techniques, some of which may stand opposed to one another. But underlying the variety in each case is a unity of purpose, in a perspective which sees that method as the most significant type of scientific activity. Verbal assent may be given to the truism that each of the methods has its place, but the commitment of practice, very often, is to the attitudes of defensive incorporation and exclusion (§4): *this* is the only thing worth doing. Of course, each of the methods does assign a place to the others: their function is to serve its own needs. For the experimenter, theory is of no concern except as it suggests experiments or guides their design and interpretation; the theoretician returns the compliment; and so for the rest. None of the methods is appreciated by the others in terms of its own problems and interests; each asks only, "What's in it for me?" This state of affairs is not limited to behavioral science, nor is it something new in the history of any of the sciences. But that the disease is pandemic does not make it any less virulent here and now.

Model building, though in some quarters it is still of questionable standing, is posing more and more of a challenge to the scientific Establishment in the study of man. Its aspirations command both my sympathy and respect, but these stop short of submission to a new orthodoxy. Like everything else human, science also can be spoiled by success. When one doctrine, method, or technique comes to be regarded as the sole repository of truth, or the one avenue to truth, for my part I have no doubt that it is truth which suffers. The danger is all the greater with respect to model building because so much else in our culture conspires to make of it the glass of fashion and the mould of form. Models seem peculiarly appropriate to a brave new world of computers, automation, and space technology, and to the astonishing status suddenly accorded the scientist in government, industry, and the military. It is easy to feel drawn to the wave of the future, and such tides are flowing strong today. Scientific caution, if not ordinary prudence, seems to me to be very much called for.

To be sure, every culture, every period of science, exhibits some style or other, and is subject to the norms of its own fashions. It is impossible to wear clothing of no style at all. If the current fashion dictates the building of models, and perhaps even the kind of models to be constructed, it is not for that reason alone to be condemned. I have nothing against the current mode, but I trust that it is not shamefully old-fashioned to be interested still in what lies underneath: glamor isn't everything. What I object to is both the blanket condemnation and the indiscriminate enthusiasm that are evoked by models. As with abstract expressionism in painting, I am afraid that model building is made too much a matter of principle, pro or con, and not enough a matter of the values, esthetic or scientific, achieved in the specific instance.

I believe, too, that there is not enough candor among scientists with regard to the part played in their endeavors by their own skills, interests, and temperaments. The tendency is to rationalize the working of these factors, in accord with the law of the instrument, by the conviction that what the scientist is able to do and would like to do is called for by the scientific situation or by the nature of science itself. It used to be said of the abstractionists that their style is a result of the fact that they cannot draw, but such criticism seems to me to be mistaken and, more important, misdirected. I ask, what is wrong, in either art or science, with a man's doing what he does best or enjoys most? The worth of the product must be assessed independently of the motivations which entered into its production. The harm is done when we misconceive the causes of our actions as reasons for them, and so seek to impose the same actions on others.

One of the functions of philosophy, as I see it, is this, that somebody must be willing to stand apart from the fashions in science, art, politics, or religion, and to say, "However . . . ". The intent of my head shaking with regard to models is neither to derogate what has been achieved nor to discourage further endeavor; to the contrary, I want to heighten awareness of possible shortcomings so as to make it easier to avoid them. A sober perspective on what can and cannot be achieved by models provides as little basis for wholesale rejection of model building today as for an exclusive preoccupation with it. The Zen master who was asked whether he believed in God replied, "If you do, I don't, and if you don't, I do." The errors of model building about to be discussed do not express my lack of faith in models; I present them as a way of saying "However . . . " to the blindly faithful.

OVEREMPHASIS ON SYMBOLS

To start with, I find it hard to resist the impression that part of the appeal of the model, a psychological basis for the great expectations it arouses, lies in an unconscious belief in the magic of symbols. The tradition of an omnipotent symbolism is an old and not always dishonorable one. The interest of philosophers from Leibniz to Russell and Wittgenstein in an "ideal language" played an important part in the development of symbolic logic, and even the occult doctrines running from Pythagoras through the Cabbalah and Kepler may have contributed to the recognition of the importance of mathematics for an understanding of nature. In the present century, symbols are everywhere at the focus of attention, and are widely thought to be in themselves great powers for good and evil. There is even recognizable what Philip Selznick has called a "cult of impression", complementing the nineteenth century's cult of expression: to produce and to be exposed to the right symbols is felt to be of great importance for everything from mental health to national security. The symbolic style is the style of the age. In physics, models have been important for a century or two; behavioral science, perhaps more sensitive to its milieu because of its subject-matter, may be drawn to model building as a response to the times.

Unfortunately, in behavioral science it is not uncommon that the symbolic style is only a mode of expression and not of thought. In a manner of speaking, it is often nothing but a manner of speaking. Definitions abound, but they are pseudo definitions: they do not specify the ways in which the defined terms are actually used in what follows. Elaborate notations often only codify the obvious, and though the symbols may be more economical and perhaps even more intelligible than the jargon of the literary and academic styles, what they achieve is hardly worth the trouble. By the use of the symbols a proposition is given the form of a scientifically useful statement, but not always the content. To introduce "x" as an abbreviation for a longer—and especially, a more prosaic— expression, then to say that $y = f(x)$, may be to present something which has the appearance of mathematics without the reality. As Braithwaite (9:366 n) has insisted, " 'No calculus without calculation.' . . . The essence of mathematics is not its symbolism but its methods of deduction." At best, such uses of the symbolic style may have some pedagogical value. Models of this kind, if the term can be allowed them at all, might be compared to illustrative experiments: we learn from them only what we already knew without their help.

OVEREMPHASIS ON FORM

There is a second failing, which is as sophisticated as this first one is naive. It consists in viewing models from the standpoint of a rationalist metaphysics, identifying the realm of truth with logical system and order. Here the influence of contemporary philosophy can perhaps be traced: even logical positivism has a strong undercurrent of rationalism in this sense, in spite of its overt epistemological empiricism. In particular, philosophy of science has been chiefly concerned with what must be true "in principle", while the ongoing of inquiry depends always on what is true in fact. Science advances on the basis, not of what is logically possible, but of what is actually available to it in the concrete problematic situation. "The statement that every proposition 'can' be expressed in mathematical form," Arrow (in *83*:130) has pointed out, "is doubtless true if we mean that there exists in some Platonic realm of being a mathematical expression of every given proposition, but it is not true if we mean that the mathematical expression in question can be given within the realms of mathematical theory now existing." A model is always possible, but it is not always useful in a given state of knowledge.

What limits its usefulness is not usually an inadequacy in our knowledge of mathematics or logic (though it is sometimes that) but rather an inadequacy in our knowledge of the subject-matter. The requirements of a model then impose a premature closure on our ideas. It is not that building the model deludes us into thinking we know something of which in fact we are ignorant—on the contrary, we may be using the model precisely in order to find out how much or how little of what we suspect is indeed true. The danger is that the model limits our awareness of unexplored possibilities of conceptualization. We tinker with the model when we might be better occupied with the subject-matter itself. In many areas of human behavior, our knowledge is on the level of folk wisdom (for instance, what Merriam has called "political prudence"); incorporating it in a model does not automatically give such knowledge scientific status. The maturity of our ideas is usually a matter of slow growth, which cannot be forced. The progress of inquiry often shapes our thinking in ways that were quite unanticipated at earlier stages. Closure is premature if it lays down the lines for our thinking to follow when we do not know enough to say even whether one direction or another is the more promising. Building a model, in short, may crystallize our thoughts at a stage when they are much better left in solution, to allow new compounds to precipitate.

But rationalism characteristically is more concerned with logical form than with empirical content. The model itself then becomes the object of interest, as means so often usurp the importance of the ends they are meant to serve. The failing I am speaking of is the tendency to engage in model building for its own sake. Candor must acknowledge the existence of this tendency, just as we recognize the corresponding tendencies to carry out experiments or to perform measurements only for the sake of experimenting or measuring. Kurt Lewin (*84*:12), who was very much concerned with the formalization or mathematization of psychology, took occasion to emphasize the purely instrumental role of these devices: "As psychologists, we are interested in finding new knowledge about, and deeper insight into, psychological processes. That is, and always has been, the guiding principle. Theory, mathematization, and formalization are tools for this purpose. Their value for psychology exists only in so far as they serve as means to fruitful progress in its subject-matter, and they should be applied, as complex tools always should, only when and where they help and do not hinder progress." I am saying only that whether models help is not something that can always be taken for granted.

OVERSIMPLIFICATION

When models are of no particular help, the failing which is chiefly responsible is likely to be oversimplification. Now this is a cheap and easy criticism to make, and I have no doubt that it is made far too often. Science always simplifies; its aim is not to reproduce the reality in all its complexity, but only to formulate what is essential for understanding, prediction, or control. That a model is simpler than the subject-matter being inquired into is as much a virtue as a fault, and is in any case inevitable. Yet a great deal depends on the considerations that led to the particular simplification that was made. It is one thing to ignore certain features of a complex reality on the hypothesis that what is being neglected is not essential, at least to a first approximation. It is quite another thing to follow the principle of "the drunkard's search" (§1), and to simplify in a particular way because then the model would be so much more elegant, or so much easier to work with. The game of "Let's pretend" is not in itself a purely childish pastime; under more impressive names it can be recognized as an enterprise of great scientific moment—

provided the gratifications of the fantasy world do not motivate a flight from reality.

It is unfortunate that this failing of models is conventionally known as "over-" simplification, with its suggestion that the trouble lies in having too much of a good thing. Some of the greatest achievements on the level of theory are remarkable precisely for their simplicity. The failing in question is rather that we have simplified in the wrong way, in the wrong places—not that we have gone too far but that we have moved in the wrong direction. The point is especially clear, I think, in connection with the use of statistics. Drawing colored balls from an urn or cards from a deck is a fantastic simplification of the actual mechanisms at work in, say, genetics or politics, but it may be an enormously useful simplification. On the other hand, the model may be an inappropriate one even for an actual game of cards. Culbertson once pointed out that the usual statistical analyses of plays at bridge are often inapplicable because the ordinary bridge shuffle is not sufficiently thorough to produce a random distribution; there have even been experts whose memories of previous deals allowed for successful finesses with a frequency so much above "chance" (as computed in the oversimplified model) that they were seriously suspected of cheating. Oversimplification might better be called "undercomplication": what is happening is only that something important is being overlooked.

The crucial point, it must be emphasized, is that what was neglected is something important for the purposes of that very model. There are always other things to be said about any situation, further knowledge to acquire. The point is that we are oversimplifying when what we say is not right even as far as it goes. The mathematical solution of a problem formulated in terms of the model may not be even an approximate solution to the corresponding problem in the real case. A mathematical theory of bluffing in games of incomplete information has been worked out by analyzing a model involving two players and three cards, and the results throw light on a variety of political and economic strategies. But a model for poker or politics which analyzed a game with seven players and fifty-two cards, but which assumed that the players have complete information, would be dangerously oversimplified; indeed, in such a model we could not talk about bluffing at all.

The difficulty is a familiar one in connection with physical models.

These characteristically involve a change in scale, and that difference may make some other and serious difference. As we move from the model to the full-scale phenomenon, a tenfold increase in linear dimensions increases surfaces a hundredfold and volumes by a factor of a thousand; the full-scale engine may need vastly more than ten times the horsepower of the engine that serves the model. Even this geometrical scaling is not so simple as it looks: in the non-Euclidean geometries there are no similar figures at all—two triangles, for instance, cannot have the same proportions and differ in area—and to assume the possibility is equivalent to presupposing that the geometry is Euclidean. Reichenbach illustrates both the elusiveness and the importance of these scaling assumptions by the Prussian drillmaster who slowly and painfully chins himself by one arm then barks to his squad, "Now *you* do it —ten times!" In behavioral science, the problem often arises in connection with the design and analysis of experiments involving motivations significantly weaker than those at work in the behavior in which we are interested. The criticism that a laboratory situation is an "artificial" one is justified only in so far as the charge can be defended that the model in terms of which the experiment is to be analyzed is oversimplified.

In short, a crude but more realistic set of hypotheses may serve the purposes of inquiry in particular cases far better than a refined but oversimplified model. This condition is especially likely when either we do not know what factors can safely be neglected, or when we cannot treat by the mathematics available to us for the model some factors which we already know to be important in that context of inquiry. "It is unphilosophical," Mill has said (94:583) (we would probably call it "unscientific"), "to construct a science out of a few of the agencies by which the phenomena are determined, and leave the rest to the routine of practice or the sagacity of conjecture. We either ought not to pretend to scientific forms, or we ought to study all the determining agencies equally, and endeavour, so far as it can be done, to include all of them within the pale of the science; else we shall infallibly bestow a disproportionate attention upon those which our theory takes into account, while we misestimate the rest, and probably underrate their importance."

I must repeat that such warnings do not constitute a blanket condemnation of model building. There are models which, happily, take into account all the factors that are important for the existent stage of inquiry, models which are then improved upon or are honorably retired as inquiry moves ahead. There are other models which, though they neglect something significant, nevertheless provide a sufficiently good approximation to be of considerable scientific worth. In still other cases, the model may be serviceable even though what it omits in its simplification makes a big difference, provided we know at least the direction in which the outcome in the model must be corrected in order to be applicable to the problem at hand. Even if the model provides us with only an upper or lower bound to an acceptable solution it may be enormously worthwhile. Not all simplifications are oversimplifications; but the danger is ever present, and must be faced.

OVEREMPHASIS ON RIGOR

Another failing of models—more accurately, of model builders—consists in an undue emphasis on exactness and rigor. Aristotle has often been cited in this connection for his remark that an educated man demands no more exactness then is allowed by the subject-matter being dealt with. Even though the statement to this effect occurs in the context of a concern with ethics, it is inappropriate, I think, to construe it as urging that the subject-matter itself imposes intrinsic limits on the exactness that can be obtained. Or if that is Aristotle's view, for my part I prefer the position taken by Kant in his principle of the axioms of intuition, that every object of experience has necessarily an extensive magnitude. There is no subject-matter that in itself precludes exactness of treatment. But the state of our knowledge and the techniques of observation and measurement available to us at any given time not only can but surely do impose such limits. Models are often improperly exact: they call for measures that we cannot in fact obtain, or that we would not know how to use if we did obtain them. For the time being, hedonic calculi, for instance, are to my mind incomparably less illuminating of human behavior than many mathematically cruder but empirically more subtle and sophisticated accounts of motivation.

To be sure, as I pointed out earlier, models themselves may free us from too great a reliance on purely quantitative measures, and encourage the use of a variety of other scales. On the other hand, there is a matter of rigor in deductions on which the model cannot easily compromise, and which may fetter our thought even more effectively than excessive demands of measurement. I believe that this drawback is often a feature of postulational models, and especially of formal ones. Many of these models, for all their rigor, have no remarkable deductive fertility: the ratio of significant theorems to the number of postulates and definitions is often disappointingly low. And where there is a deductive fertility, it cannot lightly be taken as a mark of a corresponding *heuristic fertility*: of being rich in implications for further observations, experiment, or conceptualization. Students of man and society like Veblen, Weber, and Freud, however mixed the reception accorded their ideas, are at any rate universally recognized to have been men who *had* ideas, even though their work was not conspicuous for the rigor of its deductions. In biological science, few theories have been of more importance than those associated with the basic concepts of evolution, of pathogenic germs, and of the cellular structure of living tissue; yet none of these theories was couched in a postulational or formal style. Even in physics, mathematical formulations and transformations are not inevitable concomitants of significant achievement. Faraday, for instance, "has made the most extensive additions to human knowledge without passing beyond common arithmetic" (*64*:579–580). Careful observation and shrewd even if unformalized inference have by no means outlived their day. I am not saying that there is any necessary antithesis between riches and rigor, but only that it would be equally wrong to take it for granted that there is necessarily a correspondence between them. If there *is* a choice to be made, for the empirical scientist there is in fact no choice but to go for the riches.

MAP READING

A fifth shortcoming or at least danger in the use of models may be called map reading: the failure to realize that the model is a particular mode of representation, so that not all its features correspond to some characteristic of its subject-matter. Historically, perhaps the most important instance of this error is the misconception of the relation between Euclidean geometry and physical space. The necessity which belongs to the geometry, in the relations of the theorems to the postulates, was misread for a necessity in the Euclidean constitution of space itself, as though something must be true of physical volumes because a corresponding proposition must be valid in the geometry. But that there are necessary relations within the model is not, in general, one of the structural features that make it a model. Such relations belong to what the model *is*, but not to what it is about. A model always has some irrelevant features, irrelevant, that is, to the isomorphism by virtue of which it is a model, as a map may have colors even though it is representative only by the sizes and shapes it depicts. What I am calling "map reading" consists in supposing that the British Empire is everywhere pink because the map so depicts it. It is, in a sense, the obverse of the error of over-simplification: instead of leaving out of the model something which should be in it, we read the model as containing something which in fact is not a part of it.

The dangers in this proceeding have been emphasized by Nagel, especially in connection with interpretive models. An inessential feature of the model, he warns (*103*:115), "may be mistakenly assumed to constitute an indispensable feature of the theory embedded in it. . . . In consequence the exploitation of the theory may be routed into un-profitable directions, and the pursuit of the pseudo-problems may dis-tract attention from the operative significance of the theory." Moreover, he points out (*103*:117), evidence in favor of a theory, however over-whelming, does not constitute proof of the physical existence of a par-ticular model for the theory, with all its various features. Map reading may even go so far as to result in the complete identification of a theory with a model for it (*103*:117 and *9*:93), a confusion facilitated by the usage which applies the term "model" indiscriminately to semantical, formal, and interpretive models. The theory is then mistakenly thought to deal with nothing other than the objects of the system constituting the interpretive model, with all their properties, whether or not these enter into the relevant structure. If a computer can serve as a model for a theory of the human brain, this has nothing to do with the fact that they both work by electric impulses, nor does it in the least justify the asser-tion that the brain is nothing other than a computer or that the artifact is nothing other than a thinking machine.

PICTORIAL REALISM

A model resembles what it models only in its structural properties: isomorphism is all that is demanded or, in general, supplied. Properties of a system which are irrelevant to its structure are thus also irrelevant to the status and function of the system as a model. They have been called (79:119) "exogenous" properties or variables, as contrasted with those which are "endogenous" to the system. The exogenous properties will be different, in general, in different interpretive models for the same theory. In any given case they may remain constant so long as the system is preserved, or they may be subject to change, provided only that these changes do not depend upon endogenous factors—we may give a political map any colors we choose so long as adjoining countries do not have the same color. The error of map reading just discussed consists in failing properly to draw the distinction between endogenous and exogenous properties, treating as relevant to the model some properties that are irrelevant.

Now it is easy to lose sight of the fundamental fact that the endogenous properties of a system are endogenous only relative to the perspective that brings the system into relationship with another system so that one can serve as a model for the other. In different perspectives, appropriate to other contexts or other "levels" of analysis, quite other properties may become relevant. A family, for example, may exhibit a hierarchical structure, and so serve as a model for, or be modeled by, a certain abstract geometrical system. Presumably it is a hierarchy in terms of relations like those of authority and influence; matters of affection, loyalty, esteem, and their like are here exogenous. But these latter relations may be as basic to the family pattern as are those essential to the model. What is more, each member of the family may be involved in authority relations with outsiders—the father with his employer, the children with their teachers, the mother with her priest—and these relations in turn may have an impact on domestic relations. We might even wish to consider each individual as having, not a unitary self, but an internal structure of authority—the superego over the id, for instance—so that again the original model would be inappropriate. The family, as a set of real human beings interacting with one another, transcends any model.

The point is that the model is not a picture of the family at all, but a device for the attainment or formulation of knowledge about it. "Thinking of scientific theories by means of models," Braithwaite (9:93) has said, "is always as-if thinking. . . . The price of the employment of models is eternal vigilance." The relaxation of the vigilance called for exposes us to the error of *pictorial realism*. Even though we correctly discriminate the endogenous properties of the model, we may misconceive them as constituting an image or likeness of what is being modeled. That the model can effectively perform its functions in inquiry is regarded as being due to, and hence a sign of, its being an accurate representation. To be sure, there *is* a similarity, structurally; the mistake of pictorial realism is forgetting that the similarity exists only in a given perspective, that it depends upon a particular mode of representation. The Mercator projection yields good maps even though it distorts the polar regions, and the distortion is endogenous to the model.

If a model is a scientific metaphor, pictorial realism takes the metaphor to be a literal statement. And the more well-grounded and familiar the metaphor is, the more likely it is to be taken literally. We think "That's what it is" instead of "That's what it's like". There are always similarities to be found. We seek those that will advance inquiry, or that will serve in some particular way, say for prediction or for control. But the service does not transform the similarity into an identity, and even partial identity is relative to the viewpoint. "The main object of physical science," Dirac has said, "is not the provision of pictures," and the question has aptly been put (*49*:178) whether we might not "go one step farther and say that knowledge of nature has no more to do with a model of nature than religion has to do with idols? Or to put it boldly: does the scientist observe the first part of the Third Commandment: 'Thou shalt not make unto thee any graven image'?" My answer would be that the model becomes an image only if that is how it is seen; an idol is constituted neither by its form nor by its substance, but by the idolatry of its worshipers.

The methodological moral to be drawn is this. Truth may be one, but if so, this proposition holds at best only for literal statements; there is no limit to the metaphors by which we can effectively convey what we know. To speak literally myself: if the model is not conceived as picturing reality, we can make good use of several models, even if they are not compatible with one another. The possibility emerges, as Boltzmann put it (in *27*:247), "that we can construct a system of pictures [sic] of the appearances in different ways. . . . Heretofore we held fast to the tenet that there could be only one truth: that errors were manifold, but truth unique. Given our present standpoint, this view must be opposed. . . . According to the one way of viewing things we turn our glance more to the unattainable ideal which is only a unitary one; according to the other way, we look to the multiplicity of what is attainable." Of course, it is one of the functions of theory to unite and systematize, to achieve ever greater unity in our conceptions (§35). But this need not be done by selecting some one of the models as the picture which only needs to be retouched to become a speaking likeness.

In short, the view that scientific achievement is marked only by our ability to formulate the truth about any subject-matter in a single comprehensive model—postulationally, and even formally, developed—is no more than a prejudice. That such models are rarely to be found, even in physical science, does not mean that scientists are either logically unsophisticated or indifferent to methodological requirements. The accusation means, rather, that methodologists are viewing science in terms of their own reconstructed logic and not in terms of the scientists' logic-in-use. Models are undeniably beautiful, and a man may justly be proud to be seen in their company. But they may have their hidden vices. The question is, after all, not only whether they are good to look at, but whether we can live happily with them.

§33. Models in Behavioral Science

A major difficulty with the symbolic, postulational, and formal styles in behavioral science is that they call for more closure than is usually available to start with. Concepts like "personality", "culture", and "ideology" are plainly of enormous importance in their respective disciplines; unfortunately, any single specification of their meaning in an explicit definition will probably have only a very limited application. It is easy, of course, to fake the closure: the usual terms can be replaced by symbols ("P", "C", "I") which are then allowed to appear in a variety of formulas. But when the symbols are interpreted, as eventually they must be in order to be brought into relation with observational data, their openness of meaning will become apparent once more.

ARTIFICIAL LANGUAGES

Artificial languages, like those of mathematics and symbolic logic, acquire empirical significance with the help of the natural languages. Even when it is operations that serve to specify meanings, the operations are usually verbally described, in ordinary discourse, rather than being performed then and there. Now, a vague term can be used to make another term less vague: I can explain that the symbol V standing between two propositions means that the first is true or the second is true or both, and this explanation is clear even though the word "or" which was used in the explanation is ambiguous as to whether or not *it* allows both to be true at once. All our instruments, however refined, have ultimately been produced by the human hand, for all its grossness. But for language to improve upon itself in this way we must know enough to be able to discriminate alternative possibilities of closure: semantic approximation leans on epistemic approximation as well as supports it (§12). Meanings become clear only when we know what we are talking about. Exact symbolisms in behavioral science suffer from the fact that their application depends on experience which is often unknowing, lacking in discernment, and only loosely circumscribed.

Arrow has pointed out (in *83*:130–131) that since language is itself a social phenomenon, "the multiple meanings of its symbols are very likely to be much better adapted to the conveying of social concepts than to those of the inanimate world". Our experience of the social world consists of talk to a large extent, and as participants in the social process we apprehend what is being said without much conscious reflection on meanings. It is not surprising, he continues, that the behavioral science to which mathematics has been most successfully applied is economics, for here "the individuals studied are engaged in relatively highly conscious calculating operations". They are themselves speaking the language of mathematics, as it were. In other areas of behavior, an artificial language may be doubly artificial: as a deliberate construction, but also as something feigned or fictitious. Like other devices contrived to fill what is thought to be a deficiency of nature, it may look even better than the real thing, but it is usually disappointing in its performance.

The myth of methodology and the semantic myth are nowhere more prominent, I am afraid, than in the preoccupation of behavioral science with its own language. But "the aim of a language," Simon (*79*:388) rightly reminds us, "is to say something—and not merely to say something about the language itself. Mathematical social science is, first and foremost, social science. If it is bad social science (*i.e.*, empirically false), the fact that it is good mathematics (*i.e.*, logically consistent) should provide little comfort." A strong emphasis on empirical materials is important to counteract the rationalist interest in form which is intrinsic to model building. As an onlooker I have often had the impression that what the behavioral scientist needs is more concern with his subject-matter and less concern with whether he is building a "Science". It is not merely cynicism, I trust, to observe that many students of man and his ways seem to have very little interest in—people! There can be no doubt that significant contributions have been made by scientists who were preoccupied with the workings of their instruments and techniques. But most scientific achievements, I venture to say, were attained by men who were fascinated by a particular subject-matter, and were prepared to use anything or to do anything that might satisfy their interest in the subject. The scientist exhibits something of the fixity of purpose and absorption with his subject of the hobbyist or collector, or even the lover: the successful one is not usually the man who prides himself on his technique, but the one who truly loves, and who won't take "no" for an answer.

EMPIRICISM

The division of labor within a scientific discipline may allow a theoretician to pursue his ends without himself providing the data by which the theory is shaped and tested. But the empirical materials must nevertheless constantly be in his mind. As attention focuses on the properties of a model, the data which it is to fit tend to become peripheral; by insensible degrees they are felt to be of only secondary importance, and at last are brushed aside as ugly facts capable of ruining a beautiful theory. The economist is often disdainful of the concreta of business administration, as the psychologist is of the gropings of psychotherapy, and I have even known political scientists who were wholly uninterested in the machinations of politics. To be sure, nobody can do everything, and in any case not all at once. But it is essential to preserve what Coombs calls "the integrity of the data"—that is, to make our models fit *them*, rather than assuming out of hand that behavior has just the properties needed for our models to be mathematically workable. Typical are such assumptions as that distributions are normal, functions are linear and continuous, operations are additive, relations binary, and forces independent in their action. That such assumptions may not correspond to the facts is not the point at all: an assumption need not be true to do its work effectively *as* an assumption. The point is that what is only affirmed as an assumption in the model may come to be asserted as a truth in the theory that emerges from the model, and mathematical needs come to be projected onto the facts as empirical discoveries.

KINDS OF MODELS

Models in behavioral science cannot be expected to fit the data exactly, and for two reasons, as Arrow (in *83*:151) has pointed out. First, some of the relevant variables are likely to have been omitted, as well as a great number of factors which may be individually insignificant but quite important in the aggregate. And second—what is especially true in behavioral science—the variables which are brought into the analysis are not likely to be measured with great exactness. Probabilistic considerations thus assume considerable importance; statistical formulations may usefully be built into the model rather than reserved for the treatment of the relations between the model and the data. (The model may predict that a certain proportion of experimental subjects will react in a given way, rather than make a flat prediction which is fulfilled in only some of the cases.) Models of learning and of choice behavior, for instance, have profitably taken this form. Classical mechanics, with its strict determinism, is not, after all, the only model for models to follow.

Among the behavioral-science models that have shown a great deal of heuristic as well as deductive fertility are those stemming from the theory of games. Of course, a "game" for this theory is not necessarily an amusement or diversion, but any activity with the structure of a contest, in which what one side decides to do depends on what it expects to be done by the other side. The specific content of the actions involved is irrelevant; all that matters is the payoff to the players associated with each possible combination of moves by the two sides. (In this way utility theory also enters into the analysis.) The game model thus serves for a wide variety of decision-making behavior, particularly where it is supposed that a rational choice is being made among alternative strategies of action. Accordingly, it has been applied to economic bargaining, political negotiation, the conduct of a hot or cold war, and even the battle of the sexes. Characteristic is the application of probability considerations to the choice of strategies: a player whose moves are strictly predictable can usually be taken advantage of by his opponent. What is especially remarkable about this class of models is that the mathematics used is essentially so elementary, while the behavior to which the models usefully apply is so subtle and complex.

Another group of models with far-reaching implications for behavioral science derives from cybernetics and information theory. The purposiveness of behavior can be simulated by artifacts ("automata" would thus be a misleading designation). Such a simulator is organized to reach and maintain a certain equilibrium on the basis of feedbacks indicating how far and in what direction its activity to that point departs from the pre-assigned condition. In more involved structures, goals themselves can be selected on the basis of still more general equilibrium conditions. In such models a place can also be provided for learning by allowing the probability of certain responses to be altered on the basis of the outcomes of their previous occurrences. The information whose processing provides models of various mental acts is itself only an abstract pattern. One might say: the computer does not understand instructions, it only follows them. Yet, as with all good models, the structural similarities are significant, and have generated ideas even with respect to such higher thought processes as insight. In my opinion, models of this kind are far more effective than philosophical dialectics in freeing behavioral science from the stultifications of both mechanistic materialism and mentalistic idealism. Mind involves not only matter or energy but also pattern or order, yet the latter is not a special substance whose analysis demands its own categories, language, and methods.

It would be rash indeed to attempt a priori to set limits on the fruitfulness of models in behavioral science. In the examples above, it is precisely the most distinctively human areas of conduct that are being vigorously studied by this method. Allport (*91*:157) may well be right that "the machine model in psychology had its origin not in clinical or social experience, but rather in adulation of the technological success of the physical sciences". That the behavioral scientist's interest in model building reflects the current fashion in science I have myself emphasized.

But throughout the history of science we can discern cognitive styles distinctive of the period. Fashion does not necessarily stand in the way of scientific achievement; it may even serve to give it form and color. An awareness of the danger that an established cognitive style may be repressive in its effect should not lead us to confuse mature emancipation with adolescent rebellion. The dangers are not in working with models, but in working with too few, and those too much alike, and above all, in belittling any efforts to work with anything else. That Euclid alone has looked on beauty bare is a romantic fiction.

THEORIES

§34. Theories and Laws

Whether or not theory formation is the most important and distinctive scientific activity, in one sense of the term "theory" this activity might well be regarded as the most important and distinctive for human beings. In this sense it stands for the symbolic dimension of experience, as opposed to the apprehension of brute fact. The content of our experience is not a succession of mere happenings, but a sequence of more or less meaningful events, meaningful both in themselves and in the patterns of their occurrence. They are consequential, that is—significant in their bearings on one another. With every action it is possible to associate a belief having the sense that the action taken will serve in that situation to fulfill the impulse which gave rise to the action, serve to satisfy the need or interest by which action was motivated. To be sure, the fact that a belief was in fact entertained by the actor may appear only in a retrospective analysis, or indeed not at all. It may be altogether a matter of an "as if", made no less fictional—though no less useful—by the designation "implicit belief". In this sense a habit might be said to in-

294

volve an implicit belief in a scientific law, or a succession to which we have been conditioned to respond as though it were necessary and universal.

THEORY, PRACTICE, FACT, AND LAWS

Human behavior not only supplements pure reflexes with learned habits, but also rises above habit to novel responses in unfamiliar situations, achieving creative solutions to problems never before confronted. These novel responses constitute the behavioral correlate of theorizing. A theory is a way of making sense of a disturbing situation so as to allow us most effectively to bring to bear our repertoire of habits, and even more important, to modify habits or discard them altogether, replacing them by new ones as the situation demands. In the reconstructed logic, accordingly, theory will appear as the device for interpreting, criticizing, and unifying established laws, modifying them to fit data unanticipated in their formulation, and guiding the enterprise of discovering new and more powerful generalizations. To engage in theorizing means not just to learn by experience but to take thought about what is there to be learned. To speak loosely, lower animals grasp scientific laws but never rise to the level of scientific theory. They learn *by* experience but not *from* it, for *from* learning requires symbolic constructions which can provide vicarious experience never actually undergone.

Theory is in this respect properly contrasted with practice, and "theoria" is contemplation viewed as something distinct from action. It is crucial, however, that the contrast makes sense only when referred to the context of the problematic situation in which we are taking thought. In an enlarged context, theorizing may be a very practical activity indeed and contemplation may be but another kind of action, neither passive nor disengaged. The criticism that a plan of action is "all right in theory but it won't work in practice" may well be a just one, but it must be properly understood. The theory may specify conditions which are not fulfilled in the particular case before us; the criticism then amounts to saying that the proposal is a good solution, but to another problem. A theory may even involve conditions which can never be fulfilled, because of the idealizations involved—perfect elasticity, frictionless motions, and the like. Then the criticism in question can only be to the effect that for the case at hand the assumed condition is an over-simplification, and that in this case the theory will not help to provide even an approximate solution. But unless in some cases the plan of action is of some use in solving our problem it is hard to know what is meant by the concession that it is "all right in theory". Theory is *of* practice, and must stand or fall with its practicality, provided only that the mode and contexts of its application are suitably specified.

A theory is a symbolic construction. Even those philosophies which regard natural laws as among the ingredients of which the world is composed are likely to shrink from including theories in these ultimate constituents. In some sense, theories are a human creation even though if sound they must somehow answer to what is in God's world. At any rate, that theories are symbolic means that they do not share the ineluctability of fact. Every fact is sufficient unto itself: it is just what it is. Now a theory, like any symbol, may also be taken as a matter of fact, a datum for the history of ideas or the sociology of knowledge. But in its function as a theory it reaches out beyond itself; the symbol gropes for its denotation or it ceases to be symbolic. The possibility of failure is intrinsic to its effort, and the aspiration to truth must be paid for by facing the ever-present risk of error, as the danger of death is the price exacted of life. A theory is therefore conjectural or hypothetical, contrasted in its uncertainty with a statement of "fact" as known truth: "after all, it's only a theory". Nevertheless, though error, to be sure, is of man's making, so, in the same sense, is truth—"nothing ventured, nothing gained" is also sound epistemology. Theories may, indeed, be better confirmed, more thoroughly validated, than some purely empirical generalizations or even some propositions about particular matters of fact.

Theory is thus contrasted both with practice and with fact; it also stands over against experience. Theoretical concepts are contrasted with observational ones (§7), and theoretical laws with empirical generalizations (§13). Though all conception involves the use of symbols, and is thereby distinguished from perception, in some cases the symbols relate directly to the perceptual materials while in other cases the relation is mediated by still further symbolic processes. The latter are the theoretical terms, whose meanings can be specified only by horizontal indications. (The difference need not be thought of as absolute; even if all terms are to some extent theoretical, the characterization makes sense since some terms are mediated by others and are in that relation more theoretical.) "Theoretical" thus means abstract, selecting from the materials of experience; but it also means conceptual (in a narrow sense), constructing from the selected materials something with no counterpart in experience at all. If we do speak of theoretical "entities", rather than of theoretical terms with characteristic uses, we must provide for such "entities" a shadowy realm of being or mode of subsistence. Similarly, theoretical laws are mediated by empirical generalizations which more directly relate to the facts. They are said to be on a higher "level", dealing with abstract kinds rather than concrete individuals, with theoretical entities rather than constituents of observable facts. They cannot therefore be said in any strict sense to describe the world, but serve rather to provide explanations for the truth of certain descriptions.

There are, then, theoretical terms, theoretical laws, and theories; each may be analyzed by reference to the other two, and the order of exposition is arbitrary. Concepts, judgments, and inferences are codeterminative, as Kant elaborated in some detail. What this relationship implies for methodology will be brought out, I hope, in what follows— that changes in any of the three inevitably make themselves felt in the others. In particular, a new theory requires its own terms and generates its own laws: the old concepts are not merely reorganized but reconstituted, the old laws not just corrected but given a new meaning. How and why this comes about is the central question to be explored.

We may say to start with that a theory is a system of laws. But the laws are altered by being brought into systematic connection with one another, as marriage relates two people who are never the same again. Each law takes up into itself something of the substance of the others. It is generalized, reformulated, or at any rate, reinterpreted. The theory is not the aggregate of the new laws but their connectedness, as a bridge consists of girders only in that the girders are joined together in a particular way. The theory explains the laws, not as something over and above them, but by giving each the strength and purpose which derives from the others. For my part, I would say that it is in the same sense that a law explains a fact: by relating it, not to an abstract entity (a "regularity" or "uniformity") but to other facts. What "governs" the particular is just this relationship to other particulars. Even if a philosophy of science holds that laws designate real universals it is not likely to construe theories in this way. I shall return shortly to some of the issues involved.

The system that constitutes a theory may be of two types. Where the two are distinguished they are often regarded as marking the earlier and later stages of theory formation. I prefer to view them as belonging to two different reconstructed logics (§§38 and 39). They represent not so much different theories as differences in the methodologist's rational reconstruction of theories. But even though each reconstruction were in principle applicable to all theories, in fact, I believe, some theories lend themselves more readily to the one and some to the other, so that, if we choose, we may speak of two sorts of theories without too gross a distortion.

A *concatenated* theory is one whose component laws enter into a network of relations so as to constitute an identifiable configuration or pattern. Most typically, they converge on some central point, each specifying one of the factors which plays a part in the phenomenon which the theory is to explain. (It has therefore been called a theory of the "factor type", as contrasted with the "law type" [*51*:117–119, 144–145].) This is especially likely to be true of a theory consisting of tendency statements, which attain closure only in their joint application. A law or fact is explained by a concatenated theory when its place in the pattern is made manifest. The "big bang" theory of cosmology, the theory of evolution, and the psychoanalytic theory of the neuroses may all be regarded as being of this type.

A *hierarchical* theory is one whose component laws are presented as deductions from a small set of basic principles. A law is explained by the demonstration that it is a logical consequence of these principles, and a fact is explained when it is shown to follow from these together with certain initial conditions. The hierarchy is a deductive pyramid, in which we rise to fewer and more general laws as we move from conclusions to the premises which entail them. Because of the fundamental role of deductive relations in hierarchical theories, these theories are especially suited to the postulational and even the formal style. Such a theory may then be described as consisting of: (1) a calculus, whose sentences contain names for the "theoretical entities" being dealt with and provide horizontal specifications of the meaning of these names; (2) a set of "coordinating definitions" giving the entities a vertical specification, a dictionary couched in observational terms; and (3) an interpretive model, a system of which the postulates of the calculus are true when they are interpreted as specified. (As I shall point out shortly, the process of coordination is emphasized in the instrumentalist conception of theories and the result-ant model is emphasized in the realist conception.) The theory of rela-tivity, Mendelian genetics, and Keynesian economics may be taken to exemplify hierarchical theories.

A somewhat similar distinction between two sorts of theories has been suggested by Einstein (35:53–54): "We can distinguish various kinds of theories in physics. Most of them are constructive. They attempt to build up a picture of the more complex phenomena out of the materials of a relatively simple formal scheme from which they start out. . . . Along with this most important class of theories there exists a second, which I will call 'principle-theories'. These employ the analytic, not the synthetic, method. The elements which form their basis and starting-point are not hypothetically constructed but empirically discovered ones, general characteristics of natural processes, principles that give rise to mathematically formulated criteria which the separate processes or the theoretical representations of them have to satisfy. . . . The advantages of the constructive theory are completeness, adaptability and clearness, those of the principle theory are logical perfection and security of the foundations."

Quite another classification of theories is based on characteristics of content rather than of form. Every theory may be said to demarcate an *explanatory shell* for the phenomena with which it deals. The shell around a given event is, as it were, a sphere containing whatever is referred to in the theory of that event. The contents of the shell constitute what is, from the standpoint of the theory, an effectively "isolated system". Such a system consists of the things that are both necessary and sufficient for an explanation, according to the theory, of the event in question. On this basis, we may distinguish *macro* or *molar theories* from *micro* or *molecular theories* according to the radius of the explanatory shell, as compared with the extensiveness of the sort of events being considered. The distinction is a matter of the range of the laws occurring in the theory (§12), the set of individuals to which they refer. Thus macro economics might be concerned with the workings of an economy or an industry, micro economics with the behavior of individual participants in the economic process. Similarly, a molar psychology considers a person as a whole, while a molecular psychology may focus on the interplay of habits or neural connections within the personality or organism.

In many quarters the position has been taken that micro theories are intrinsically more satisfactory. "It is often felt that only the discovery of a micro-theory affords real scientific understanding of any type of phenomenon, because only it gives us insight into the inner mechanism of the phenomenon, so to speak. Consequently, classes of events for which no micro-theory was available have frequently been viewed as not actually understood" (59:147). Underlying this position is what might be called the *principle of local determination:* the radius of the explanatory shell can be made indefinitely small. This principle is not identical with doctrinal determinism, though it implies the latter: where statistical theories are unavoidable the explanatory shell cannot be smaller than would allow for a statistically stable population. Local determination is determinism conjoined to a denial of action-at-a-distance in space or time: whatever happens anywhere is capable of being explained by reference to what is to be found then and there.

This point of view may well be involved in what Whitehead has called the fallacy of "simple location". It is not immediately and inescapably apparent—to me, at any rate—that a person, for example, must be conceived as localized within his skin, any more than that money must be conceived in terms of the local properties of the coin or currency. At any rate, I do not see that the principle of local determination is methodologically necessary, whatever metaphysical justifications for it might be given. Of course, economical explanations are to be preferred over those which introduce considerations that another theory can dispense with. But contracting the explanatory shell is by no means always a move in the direction of economy. It is not obvious that a neural explanation of Hamlet's behavior will inevitably be simpler than the Oedipal one. On the other hand, it is reasonable to expect that the former may be capable of explaining a great deal else besides. As with so many methodological disputes, I protest only against the denials each side would exact of the other, not against what each aspires to achieve for itself.

A classification of theories with which the preceding one is often confused is that into *field theories* and *monadic theories*. A theory may take as fundamental a system of relations among certain elements, explaining the elements by reference to these relations, or it may give primacy to the relata, explaining the relations by reference to the attributes of what they relate. (Leibniz's "monadology" is the most extreme antithesis to a field theory, since he repudiates relational propositions altogether: each of his monads mirrors within itself the whole universe.) Thus a theory of personality in terms of roles might be contrasted with a theory in which roles are explained by reference to sets of needs of the individual personalities participating in the social process. What makes a field theory depends, not on the range of the constituent laws, but on their scope—not on what things the laws are about, but on what the laws say about those things. Thus even a micro theory can be a field theory, as for instance when memory is dealt with in terms of reverberations in neural circuits rather than in terms of engrams: the stationary wave is a relational property of the system, not an attribute of any of its components. That field theories are necessarily more "scientific" is again a doctrine for which I do not see any methodological necessity, if this discrimination is separated from metaphysical preferences. There is no doubt, however, that the recent history of science, especially physics, puts field theories in a favorable light. What they can contribute to behavioral science remains to be seen.

Theories are often spoken of as being of a higher or a lower *level;* level can now be seen to refer to a variety of different characteristics of theories. It may be a matter of their range—for instance, whether they deal with human behavior, or with animal behavior in general. It may be a matter of scope—a theory of learning, or one of other kinds of behavior as well. The level of a theory often has to do with its abstractness, the length of the reduction chain connecting the theoretical terms with observable ones, as in the difference between behavioral theories and more strictly behavioristic ones. What is sometimes called the "level" of the theory depends on the length of the deductions in it, the steps between its "first principles" and the laws in which it finds application, as in the difference between the usual sociological theories and the typical "miniature theory" in psychology. Finally, a theory is sometimes said to be of a higher level as its explanatory shell has a smaller radius, so that micro theories are said to be of a higher level than macro theories.

In all these usages, the implication is that the "level" of the theory corresponds to its scientific standing. It is this implication that I have wished to counteract.

§35. Functions of Theories

Theory puts things known into a system. But this function is more than a matter of what the older positivism used to call "economy of thought" or "mental shorthand", and what today is expressed in terms of the storage and retrieval of information. It is true that the systematization effected by a theory does have the consequence of simplifying laws and introducing order into congeries of fact. But this is a by-product of a more basic function: to make sense of what would otherwise be inscrutable or unmeaning empirical findings. A theory is more than a synopsis of the moves that have been played in the game of nature; it also sets forth some idea of the rules of the game, by which the moves become intelligible. (The nature of explanation will be considered in the next chapter.)

In providing meaning, the theory also attests to truth. A hypothesis may be as much confirmed by fitting it into a theory as by fitting it to the facts. For it then enjoys the support provided by the evidence for all the other hypotheses of that theory. Just as a law is not only confirmed by factual data but also helps give the data factual status, so a theory is not only supported by established laws but also plays a part in establishing them. We may say both that psychoanalytic theory, for example, is supported by the symbolic fulfillment of wishes in dreams, and that it provides a basis for the interpretation of dreams as wish fulfillments. In the same way, Darwin found support in the fossil record, but only by interpreting fossils as something other than antediluvian remains.

THEORIES IN PROCESS

Theory, therefore, functions throughout inquiry, and does not come into its own only when inquiry is successfully concluded. It has a greater responsibility than that of an accessory after the fact: it guides the search for data, and for laws encompassing them. "Theories in physics," it has been said, "are constructions which serve primarily to integrate or organize into a single deductive system sets of empirical laws which previously were unrelated. . . . In psychology, on the other hand, theories serve primarily as a device to aid in the formulation of empirical laws. They consist in guesses as to how the uncontrolled or unknown factors in the system under study are related to the experimentally known variables." It is not surprising that this view was expressed by a psychologist (K. Spence in *91*:178–179). In his own field the role of theory in the process of inquiry is apparent to him; what he sees of another inquiry is not the process but only the product. How lush and lusty the grass looks, how green—from a sufficient distance! I do not believe that the role of theory in behavioral science is any different from what it is in physical or biological science. There are, of course, differences in the number, power, and weight of the theories which have been established concerning these different subject-matters; but everywhere, so it seems to me, theory works in essentially the same way.

What is important is that laws propagate when they are united in a theory: theory serves as matchmaker, midwife, and godfather all in one. This service is what is delicately known as the "heuristic" function of theory. To be sure, laws may also be produced by a kind of epistemic parthenogenesis, by direct inspection of the data, or by analogizing from a law already known—what I called "extensional generalization" (§13). But this becomes less and less likely as inquiry into a particular subject-matter proceeds. The more or less directly observable regularities are, almost tautologically, the first to be recognized; to go beyond them we must move from the observational materials to theoretical constructions. "At the present time, in the more highly developed sciences," says Campbell (*13*:88), "it is very unusual for a new law to be discovered or suggested simply by making experiments and observations and examining the results (although cases of this character occur from time to time); almost all advances in the formulation of new laws follow on the invention of theories to explain the old laws." This genesis is especially likely for the great breakthroughs in science. Conant (*22*:53) says flatly that "the history of science demonstrates beyond a doubt that the really revolutionary and significant advances come not from empiricism but from new theories". To be sure, theory will not generate new laws by explaining old ones till we have old ones to be explained. It is no part of my intent to urge that the time is ripe for behavioral science to abandon the direct search for laws of behavior and to occupy itself instead with developing theories of behavior. But where the behavioral scientist *is* occupied with theory, let him not settle for a purely Platonic relationship with what he already knows, in an elegant but possibly sterile system, but see to it, rather, that in the fullness of time the union is blessed.

It might well be said that the predicament of behavioral science is not the absence of theory but its proliferation. The history of science is undeniably a history of the successive replacement of poor theories by better ones, but advances depend on the way in which each takes account of the achievement of its predecessors. Much of the theorizing in behavioral science is not building on what has already been established so much as laying out new foundations, or even worse, producing only another set of blueprints. In an important sense, new scientific theories do not "refute" the old ones but somehow remake them; even scientific revolutions preserve some continuity with the old order of things. It is usual to speak here of "saving the appearances". In the classic example, the notion that the earth is flat has a grain of truth in it—the earth *looks* flat, and the hypothesis that it is in fact round must assign a sufficiently large radius of curvature to the earth to account for this look; it is crucial that plane geometry will fit to any desired degree of approximation a sufficiently small portion of the surface of a sphere.

This reconciliation, it might be urged, is again a matter of preserving the "integrity of the data". But laws, too, are carried over in some form. Sometimes the old laws are retained as special cases of the more general laws which play a part in the new theory. This mode of continuity is not the only one, however; old beliefs may be quite transformed by new knowledge—but transformed, not simply negated. Knowledge grows not only by accretion and the replacement of dubious elements by more sound ones, but also by digestion, the remaking of the old cognitive materials into the substance of a new theory. Hierarchical theories are typically improved by replacing some of their postulates with others, or by formulating a new set from which we can deduce the old one and other significant consequences as well. In the case of concatenated theories the pattern is sometimes extended, but more often it is changed in ways that reveal it to be a fragment of a larger and usually quite different pattern. The realization that some of the so-called "nebulae" are not really nebulous but enormously distant galaxies of stars in their own right not only generated new conceptions of the stellar universe, but also changed significantly the conception of our own Milky Way. Similarly, Freud's discernment that there is really a commonality between the lunatic, the lover, and the poet not only disclosed the method in madness but also altered our understanding of the workings of the unfrenzied imagination.

In general, we may say that knowledge grows in two ways: by *extension* and by *intension*. Growth by extension consists in this, that a relatively full explanation of a small region (of behavior, or of whatever the subject-matter may be) is then carried over to an explanation of adjoining regions. It is in this perspective that most studies of the conditioned reflex, for example, are viewed: when conditioning is sufficiently understood we may move on to more complex types of learning, then to other sorts of behavior seen as the products of learning. Growth by extension is implicit in the models or metaphors of science as an edifice, a mosaic, an erector set, or a jigsaw puzzle—it is built up piece by piece.

In growth by intension a partial explanation of a whole region is made more and more adequate. This growth type is characteristic, it seems to me, of the contributions of Darwin, Marx, and Freud, for example; it is not so much that they definitively explained a limited subject-matter which was afterwards enlarged, but that they laid out lines for subsequent theory and observation to follow, so as to yield a better understanding of the broad-scale phenomena which were their primary concern. Growth by intension is associated with such metaphors for the scientific enterprise as developing a photographic negative, bringing binoculars to a sharper focus, or gradually illuminating a darkened room—progress is not piecemeal but gradual on a larger scale.

Both sorts of growth, I believe, are involved in every theoretical advance, and for both concatenated and hierarchical theories. A new theory adds some knowledge, but it also transforms what was previously known, clarifies it, gives it new meaning as well as more confirmation. Before we had the new theory we did not quite know just *what* it was we knew. Paranoid systems and pseudoscientific doctrines, it has been pointed out (62:230), grow by extension only; they are essentially closed systems of thought even though additional beliefs can be annexed to them. In science, growth "is not simply adding on units to something already existing that remains unchanged in the process. The whole structure, the skeleton, changes with growth even though it remains recognizably similar to what it has been. The system of science would not be flexible unless its structure could change with increasing knowledge." The truism that theory organizes knowledge should not be allowed to conceal the equally important truth that it changes the content of knowledge as well as the form.

REALISM AND INSTRUMENTALISM

There is a widespread *realist* conception of scientific theory, in which it is regarded as a picture or map of the world. Conant (*22*:92–93) has suggested that this view, especially popular in the eighteenth and nineteenth centuries, embodies a mistaken analogy: "those who said they were investigating the structure of the universe imagined themselves as the equivalent of the early explorers and map makers". Scientific advance, in this conception, is thought to be a matter of extending the area of what is known; details may be filled in as time goes on, but significant changes occur only at the frontiers. Once a territory is discovered and mapped, we plant our flag on it, and it is ours forever.

If I may pursue the analogy, however, to make the territory truly ours we must live on it, colonize and develop it; thereby the face of the land will be changed, and new maps will be called for. This is the *instrumentalist* view of the nature of theories. We do something with them. They are tools of inquiry, and of reflective choice in problematic situations. In the pointed phrase of J. J. Thomson (quoted in *22*:91), a theory is "*a policy rather than a creed*". It serves to "suggest, stimulate, and direct experiment". To be sure, "its object is to connect or coordinate apparently diverse phenomena", but this object is achieved, not in a picture of the connection, but in the prescriptions by which we can move from one to the other. Properly speaking, instrumentalism is not an alternative to the realist conception, but a specification of what it means to picture reality. The map is a device by which we can get from place to place; its correspondence with the territory consists in the fact that it can be so used. The route which we are to follow need not be pictured; imagine instead that it is specified by a series of pairs of numbers —for each turn the distance to it, and the angle by which we must then change direction. The numbers can be expressed in binary digits, and represented by a bank of lights which are on or off according to whether the respective digit is 1 or 0. This pattern of lights will no longer in the least resemble the path, yet it is also a map, and entirely equivalent to the pictorial one. The point to the illustration is not merely that we should not confuse the endogenous and exogenous features of our model (§32), but that the endogenous features themselves are to be understood in terms of what they allow us to do with the model.

The objection has often been raised (for instance, by Maxwell in *41*:22), that instrumentalism cannot explain why a theory is successful, while realism "provides the very simple and cogent explanation that the entities referred to by well-confirmed theories exist". We may note first that a scientifically significant explanation of the success of a theory is provided only by another theory, which makes clear the respects in which the earlier one did or failed to do justice to the data. To explain that a certain theory works because what it says about the world is true may be very simple and cogent, though I do not see that it contributes very much to our understanding. But instrumentalism need not take issue with this sort of explanation. It emphasizes only that our reasons for affirming the existence of the entities in question often consist precisely in the fact that the theory referring to them is a successful one. The map is a good one because that *is* the shape of the territory, but we may have found that the territory has that shape in the course of making the map.

To be sure, this is not always the case: we may make direct observations. The objection continues that "it must be acutely embarrassing to instrumentalists when what was a 'purely' theoretical entity becomes, due to better instruments, etc., an observable one". Such changes in status are indeed recurrent and of some importance, as I pointed out earlier (§7); but I do not find them embarrassing. Quite apart from the fact that no entities are "purely observable" either, may we not say that the significance of the new status is that additional evidence has been provided for the theory, that the theory has been shown to be workable in another context or in another sort of way? A theory does not stand or fall with such observations of its "entities"; at any rate, there is no doubt that it may continue to play an important part in inquiry even if, from the standpoint of the realist, it is no more than a fiction.

What is of methodological importance here, as distinct from the more general philosophical questions that may arise, is that realism tends to put too much emphasis on the brute empirical determinants of theory. If a theory is essentially a picture of the reality, then to arrive at a sound theory we must concentrate on discovering how things are, rather than on inventing ways in which we can usefully conceptualize them. Many behavioral scientists are still given over to what is sometimes called Baconian induction: we survey the "facts" till the laws governing them are manifest, then find the simplest way to combine the laws into a comprehensive theory. The designation is somewhat unjust: Bacon himself characterizes the scientist as being neither wholly speculative and like a spider spinning his web from his own substance, nor wholly empirical and like an ant collecting data into a heap, but like the bee feeding on the nectar it gathers, digesting it, and so transmuting it into the purest honey. Nevertheless, philosophers of science from Bacon through Mill and beyond have on the whole leaned towards the ant; in behavioral science especially they have done so, perhaps as a reaction against the web spinning of continental Geisteswissenschaft.

But arriving at workable theories calls for the exercise of creative imagination, as has been emphasized by countless working scientists, from Einstein on down. We may perhaps speak of "discovering" laws, but theories must be said to be "invented" or "constructed". There is a class of puzzles which depend on the difficulty we all have in becoming aware of a mode of representation, which we project onto what is experienced as fact. The next number in the sequence 4, 14, 34, 42, · · · is 59; these are the express stops on the Eighth Avenue subway, as every New Yorker will tell you—if he thinks of it. The next letter in the sequence O, T, T, F, F, · · · is S; these are the initial letters of the number words "one", "two", "three", · · · . We have been tricked because we were looking for properties of the thing-in-itself, and not of something constituted by the forms of the knowing mind. Freeing ourselves from the illusion that knowledge is only the apprehension of facts, quite independent of the mode of representation, is what Kant called the Copernican revolution. It is essential, I believe, to appreciating the role of scientific theory.

I am not saying merely that the creative imagination plays a part in the *process* of theory formation, the context of discovery, but that it is also involved in the *product*, and so enters into the context of justification. It is tempting to suppose that the scientist exercises his inventiveness only in imagining what the reality might be so as to account for the observations; the theory is sound when he has hit upon that possibility which God chose to actualize. Thus Kekulé, in a famous burst of scientific imagination, conceived of the benzene ring as a possible way in which the atoms of benzene might be arranged in the molecule; and so they are. But the formation of a theory is not just the discovery of a hidden fact; the theory is a way of looking at the facts, of organizing and representing them. I am not saying that stereochemistry is a tissue of fictions, but that the spatial arrangements which are referred to in its theories may not be casually identified with those of ordinary observation. Similarly, the "orbit" of an electron can be understood only in the context of a particular atomic theory, and not identified with a planetary orbit, except for possibly being of a different shape and traversed by a much smaller body. A theory must somehow fit God's world, but in an important sense it creates a world of its own.

I shall turn shortly (§36) to the whole matter of the validation of theories; I do not wish to be misunderstood for a moment as depreciating the requirements imposed by the facts. The question is how those requirements make themselves felt. Aristotle characterized truth as saying of that which is that it is, and of that which is not that it is not. But there are ways and ways of saying. A theory does not just say something different from what is said by an observational statement; it says it differently—that is, the theory has a different role to perform in the usual contexts of its utterance. The difference between a theoretical and a descriptive formulation is, to my mind, very like that between a metaphorical and a literal statement. The metaphor is of the poet's own making, yet some metaphors are well-grounded and illuminating, while others are forced or contrived. Whether a metaphor is of the one sort or the other depends on the actual characteristics of what it is being applied to, but not in the relatively simple and straightforward way that marks the truth or falsehood of a literal statement. We may say that a theory is grounded in the facts, in a sense yet to be examined, but that it does not constitute a direct representation of the facts.

In this perspective, we need not look for *the* true theory, but countenance and even encourage various theories, and without thinking of them only as so many candidates for the single post to be filled. "Knowledge normally develops in a multiplicity of theories," Quine (*116*:251) has pointed out, "each with its limited utility. . . . These theories overlap very considerably, in their so-called logical laws and in much else, but that they add up to an integrated and consistent whole is only a worthy ideal and happily not a prerequisite of scientific progress." The aim of theorizing is to unify and systematize knowledge, but even in the happiest circumstances the aim is never completely attained. New knowledge is forever pouring in upon us, carrying with it new tasks for theory to perform. We need not expect of any one theory that it should be able to perform all these tasks, even within the limited domain of some special subject-matter. A reconstructed logic which presents science only as it would be if it fulfilled all its aspirations may obscure our understanding of science as it actually is. On this score I prefer the Jain logic of ancient India, with its doctrine of *syadvada:* that every proposition is true only up to a point, in a manner of speaking, in certain respects (this doctrine can be applied without inconsistency to the doctrine itself). We are familiar with *syadvada* in the Jain legend of the seven blind men and the elephant. I do not wish to say that scientists are blind; but humility is also an intellectual virtue—even with the best of theories we see through a glass darkly, and know only in part.

This whole instrumentalist view of theories—that their significance lies in the action they guide—is not to be confused with a vulgar pragmatism which conceives action so narrowly as to exclude the conduct of inquiry. On the contrary, the guidance which theory provides is chiefly and most directly for scientific activity—forming concepts and laws, conducting experiments, making measurements, providing explanations and predictions. Neither is the instrumentalist view to be confused with a strict positivism, for which only observation sentences have cognitive content, theories serving only to mediate between observations. On the contrary, in particular contexts of inquiry it may be observation sentences which are instrumental to the formation of theories, rather than the other way around. Theories are not just means to other ends, and certainly not just to ends outside the scientific enterprise, but they may also serve as ends in themselves—to provide understanding, which may be prized for its own sake. Only, to understand the world does not mean to hold in our hands the blueprints by which God created it, but some very human sketches by which we ourselves can find our way.

§36. *Validation of Theories*

It must be kept in mind that the validation of a theory—or of any other scientific belief—is not a matter of any official decision, the deliverance of a solemn judgment. Too often "Science" is Platonized, conceived as a single, self-contained entity, rather than as the outcome of the activities of countless individual scientists working in a wide variety of concrete and ever-changing contexts. At any given moment a particular theory will be accepted by some scientists, for some of their purposes, and not by other scientists, or not for other contexts of possible application. Even men of sound scientific judgment, as evinced by their own distinguished achievements, have often rejected theories, or expressed dissatisfaction with them, long after the views in question had won widespread acceptance—Huygens, for instance, was not satisfied by Newton's mechanics, and Einstein was doubtful of the underlying validity of quantum indeterminacy. In behavioral science, this state of affairs is the rule rather than the exception; very few theories are generally accepted.

We can, of course, reconstruct the situation in terms of the decisions that *ought* to be reached by anyone who confronts a given body of evidence. Explicit and precisely formulated criteria for such decisions are beginning to be worked out by Carnap and his followers. But it is recognized by everyone (almost everyone, I suppose I should say) that these are at present restricted to theories formulated only in very simple and fully formalized languages, so that they have no bearing on contemporary behavioral science, at any rate; and many philosophers of science (the proportion, I take it, is irrelevant) doubt whether such criteria will ever in fact be formulable in a generally usable way, whatever might be true in principle. The scientific situation seems to be more fluid and open. It seems impossible to formulate *all* the evidence and arguments that might be adduced to support or criticize a theory, even at a given stage of inquiry—that is, without regard to the fact that further evidence will be forthcoming later, for this fact would not affect the acceptability of the theory on the basis of the evidence at hand.

To be sure, it is not enough to say that there is an ineluctable component of good judgment in scientific decision making. Kant once urged that the faculty of judgment is indispensable because even where we have rules for its exercise, judgment is required to apply the right rules to particular cases—there can be no rule of law without courts and judges. But the question still remains what constitutes "good" judgment: a theory is not validated merely because it is accepted; rather, it is accepted—by scientists, at any rate—because it is believed to be validated. The normative question is still the basic one. Only, it should be clear what sort of norms are called for. The validation of a theory is not the act of granting an imprimatur but the act of deciding that the theory is worth being published, taught, and above all, applied—worth being acted on in contexts of inquiry or of other action. The acceptability of a theory will in any case be a matter of degree—more or less weight will be assigned to it, and it will always have a more or less limited range of justified application.

Norms of validation can be grouped according to the three major philosophical conceptions of truth: correspondence or semantical norms, coherence or syntactical norms, and pragmatic or functional norms. The first set is the basic one somehow; the others must be regarded as analyses or interpretations of correspondence. Science is governed fundamentally by the reality principle, its thought checked and controlled by the characteristics of the things it thinks about. There is in science a certain natural piety, a submission of the will to a world not of our making; we have learned that when nature is commanded our own will prevails only when we have first obeyed. The only alternative to the recognition that thought must be put into correspondence with its object, that thinking so does not make it so, is what Russell has aptly called the subjectivist madness. I hope that the instrumentalism I am espousing is in no way maddening.

NORMS OF CORRESPONDENCE

Truth itself is plainly useless as a criterion for the acceptability of a theory. When we are asked to justify our beliefs it is no good to answer that they are true, for the question obviously is, what makes us think so? We must proceed conversely, as Peirce insisted, and characterize truth as the outcome of the inquiry, suitably carried out. I do not say that this outcome is what is meant by truth, but that the meaning of truth does not constitute the criterion for its own attribution. We say that a theory is true if it "fits the facts", that is, if the predictions made on the basis of the theory are in fact fulfilled. Yet it cannot be forgotten that how we conceptualize facts in turn depends on the theories which play a part in their cognition. The circle here is not, so far as I can see, a vicious one, necessarily; it becomes vicious only if the facts are wholly constituted by the theory they are adduced to support, if they lack an observational core, and if the theory makes them out of whole cloth. The belief in witchcraft was illogical, not because it took for granted the existence of just the sort of facts it purported to explain, but because it provided such a poor explanation of the very real facts sometimes adduced in its support.

Every appeal to "the facts" rests on a bedrock of common sense, however fashionable it may be to disparage common sense. Every problematic situation occurs within the setting of what Mead called "the world that is there", a matrix of the unproblematic; every hypothesis is advanced on the basis of presuppositions. To be sure, these presuppositions have from time to time stood in the way of scientific advance, and progress has required the courage to thrust them aside. But wholesale skepticism is as sterile as uncritical acceptance of received doctrine. Every inquiry must start somewhere, and in scientific contexts it begins far beyond the Cartesian "I think, therefore I am". One of the early Fathers of the Church argued against the notion that the earth is round by complaining that, when its proponents are asked why people on the other side do not fall off, the reply is made that there is a force pressing inwards equally from all directions; now, he continued, when people caught in one absurdity defend it by piling up another, it is impossible to convince them rationally. If we smile at his argument, it is not because it is formally invalid. It is perfectly proper to criticize a theory by showing how much violence it does to what is already accepted as fact, even though in the end it is the latter that gives way.

We may say that what counts is the range of facts that the theory takes into account, and especially their heterogeneity. The argument just cited is to the effect that the theory is unacceptable because it is ad hoc. The facts supporting it are only those it was introduced to explain. We say today that such a theory has a low antecedent probability, but this expression does not tell us much more than the scholastic Latin. What they both say is that the theory is far-fetched, that it fits certain facts but only those, or at any rate, that we have no reason to expect that it will continue to fit the facts as we take more and more different sorts of facts into account. It is easy to overestimate the weight that accrues to a theory when it makes a successful prediction. A merely empirical generalization will also allow us to predict. What counts in the validation of a theory, so far as fitting the facts is concerned, is the convergence of the data brought to bear upon it, the concatenation of the evidence—beautifully illustrated, to my mind, in Ernest Jones's essay on *Symbolism*. In this way, the test of correspondence comes to be applied in terms of the relation of the theory to the rest of our knowledge, and it is norms of coherence that govern.

NORMS OF COHERENCE

Various pseudoscientific and unscientific doctrines fail largely because there is no way in which they can be fitted into the body of theory already established. This requirement is as important as that they fit their own sets of facts. "People have spoken of the 'shock of recognition', when some unknown phenomenon suddenly becomes familiar, being recognized as something already known. . . . There is also what one may call the 'click of relation', when widely different and separate phenomena suddenly fall into a pattern of relatedness, when they click into position. This is like the experience of truth, the feeling of wholeness, when the fragments have come together and form a whole body. Integration, like prediction, is a necessary test of a scientific theory" (*62:227*). There is, for example, considerable direct evidence for the existence of telepathy. But quite apart from the question whether such evidence is acceptable—whether adequate controls were instituted, whether the statistical analysis is sound, and so on—is the very weighty consideration that telepathy is wholly at variance with everything else we know about the transmission of information: unlike every other known type of disturbance, for instance, its propagation appears to be quite independent of the distance it traverses.

Yet plainly, we must not put too much reliance on the test of integration, or we preclude the possibility of any real breakthroughs in our thinking. Coherence is a conservative principle, which ruthlessly suppresses as rebellion any movement of thought which might make for a scientific revolution. The unyielding insistence that every new theory must fit those theories already established is characteristic of closed systems of thought, not of science. Indeed, premature integration is a species of premature closure, and an especially objectionable one. Moreover, norms of coherence are of doubtful worth when they are applied globally, as they are likely to be. Descartes's *Discourse on Method* was very much in the spirit of science when it counseled that problems must be broken down into parts small enough to be manageable. The work of analysis is at least as important as that of synthesis, and quite possibly has some claims to priority. We must be prepared to accept a usable explanation of what is going on *here*, even if we are quite unable to see how we could use that explanation anywhere else.

Nevertheless, the point remains that theories can not be validated as though they were wholly self-contained. It is simply a mistake, as Duhem and others have rightly insisted, to suppose that validation consists in confronting "the" theory with "the" observations. Other theories and facts are always involved—for instance, those bearing on the instruments of observation. We could say, indeed, that the whole of our knowledge is brought to bear, for there are no fixed boundaries of possible relevance to the acceptability of the theory, and especially none that can be drawn beforehand. Quite unexpected sources of verification or falsification are quite to be expected.

What must in any case be taken into account in assessing a theory is the set of alternatives to it in conjunction with which it is being considered. That a theory is validated does not mean that it is probable, in some appropriate sense, but only that it is more probable than the other possible explanations. At every stage of inquiry the scientist does what he can with the resources at his disposal; if it is objected that this thinking makes the acceptance of a particular theory only a temporary expedient, the reply immediately presents itself that all acceptances are only more or less temporary. Truth may be eternal, but science requires no more of a theory than that it be sufficient unto the day. Moreover, methodology cannot countenance assigning to alternative theories no more than a psychological significance, as though they affect the conclusion at which the scientist in fact arrives, but not the one at which he ought to arrive. For my part, I agree wholeheartedly with Feyerabend's remark (*41*:68 n) that "adherence to either the distinction between context of discovery (where alternatives are considered, but given a psychological function only) and context of justification (where they are not mentioned any more), or strict adherence to the axiomatic approach must be regarded as an arbitrary and very misleading restriction of methodological discussion: much of what has been called 'psychological' or 'historical' in past discussions of method is a very relevant part of the theory of test procedures."

The most widely applied norm of coherence is one internal to the theory itself; it is that of *simplicity*.

At the very outset a distinction must be drawn between what Reichenbach has called *descriptive* and *inductive* simplicity. The first is simplicity in the description itself, and the second in what is being described. Two theories of which one is descriptively simpler than the other are in fact equivalent in content. In Reichenbach's example, the theory that space is Euclidean, but that all bodies by which geometrical measurements might be made are subject to universal forces which systematically distort them, is, if the forces are properly chosen, strictly equivalent to the characterization of space by a non-Euclidean geometry without such forces at work. Whatever observations would support one of these descriptions would, by hypothesis, equally support the other description; they are empirically indistinguishable. Saying the contrary would be like saying that the expression "$a^2 + 2ab + b^2$" is different from "$(a + b)^2$" because one talks about the product of a and b, and the other about their sum. Descriptive simplicity as a desideratum of theories can easily be justified on the grounds of convenience in the handling of the theory itself. The advantages of a good notation are not inconsiderable. But descriptive simplicity is sometimes mistaken for the inductive type: that two descriptions are equivalent in content, hence that two formulations embody one and the same theory, is not always easy to recognize.

When one theory is inductively simpler than another, it is not just the formulations which differ but also what is being said in each. The content of one theory may be much more manageable mathematically than that of the other—for instance, it may concern only linear functions while the other calls for quadratics. The simplicity of a theory in the sense of manageability is relative to the state of mathematics, as Philipp Frank (*45*:351) has pointed out. Computer technology may also be relevant, and even just familiarity with the mathematics called for: as time goes on schoolboys learn what only savants could understand in an earlier era. But these considerations apply to what is simple *for* someone or other; a theory, however, may be simpler than another intrinsically, that is, without regard to how manageable someone finds them to be. A theory which makes reference to only two "entities" is in this sense simpler than one which invokes several dozen, as a sundial is simpler than a clock full of gears and springs, though most of us would find it much harder to adjust. Some progress in the exact analysis of such simplicity has been made by Nelson Goodman and others, but as is usual in contemporary logic—and perhaps inevitable at this stage of inquiry—the analysis applies only to formalized and simple (!) languages.

Frank (46:14) has also pointed out that the situation is complicated by the fact that what must be taken into account is the simplicity not only of the theory but also of "the whole discourse by which the theory is formulated", or as Bridgman puts it, not only of the "equations" but also of the "text". One can always sweep the dirt under the rug, and simplify a theory, or part of it, by introducing suitable complications elsewhere, as in the earlier example the universal forces allow us to keep Euclidean geometry. In the exact analysis this consideration perhaps enters by way of the circumstance that the simplicity of a proposition is relative to the structure of the whole language in which the proposition is formulated.

But as I have emphasized throughout, we need not have a perfectly precise notion of simplicity to make use of it. There is no doubt that some theories are simpler than others and can be recognized as such, even if we cannot say precisely why. The more serious problem is to justify the use of this attribute of theories as a norm, keeping in mind that we are speaking of simplicity of content, not just of form. Why should the simpler theory be the better one? The truth, one of Wilde's epigrams runs, is rarely pure and never simple; if this epigram itself is only a half truth, the insistence on simplicity may still be wholly mistaken. What is beyond dispute is the physicist Fresnel's remark that "Nature doesn't care about mathematical difficulties" (quoted in 121:114). Indeed, the argument can sometimes be made *against* a theory (for instance, a theory of human motivation) that the trouble with it is that it is too simple; Nature sometimes seems to prefer complexity. More realistically, both sorts of cases must be acknowledged. "If we study the history of science," says Poincaré (in *140*:35), "we see happen two inverse phenomena, so to speak. Sometimes simplicity hides under complex appearances; sometimes it is the simplicity which is apparent and which disguises extremely complicated realities." The progress of science is not always in the direction of the simpler theory.

The justification might be given for the norm of simplicity that the norm does not condemn complexity but only imposes on it the burden of proof. We are to introduce a complicating factor only if we have reason to expect error from its omission, and not if we just lack a reason for expecting error from the simpler treatment. On this interpretation, the norm of simplicity presents itself as another form of Occam's razor: variables are not to be multiplied beyond necessity. Here there is no metaphysical assumption about Nature's preferences, but an appeal to the same considerations of convenience that justify the choice of descriptive simplicity. Popper has urged an even stronger justification: the more complicated the theory the less it says, for the harder it is to falsify—the more likely it is that something in the theory will either make recalcitrant facts irrelevant, because they fail to satisfy certain conditions, or else reinterpret them so that they are no longer disconfirming. (The Marxist theory of history is a good example, I think.) "There is no need," Popper says (*111*:142), "for us to assume a 'principle of economy of thought' or anything of the kind. Simple statements, if knowledge is our object, are to be prized more highly than less simple ones because they tell us more; because their empirical content is greater; and because they are better testable." All things considered, perhaps the best methodological counsel as to the norm of simplicity is Whitehead's: "Seek simplicity and distrust it."

One other norm of coherence is that usually called the "esthetic". Whether or not a theory can be beautiful in the same sense as a work of art, there is no doubt that it can provide a comparable intrinsic pleasure in its contemplation. Euler's theorem, $e^{i\pi} + 1 = 0$, unites five fundamental mathematical constants with the most basic operations; this beautiful discovery is inscribed on Euler's tombstone. Various equations embodying empirical relationships, especially in modern physics, are generally acknowledged to have a comparable beauty. The beauty is in part a matter of their simplicity, both descriptive and inductive; but considerations of symmetry also enter, as has been emphasized by Einstein, Dirac, and many other scientists. The esthetic qualities of a theory admittedly play a more important part in the context of discovery than in that of justification, yet they have advanced our knowledge of nature since the time of Pythagoras: it would appear that God is an artist as well as a mathematician and engineer. The danger in the application of the esthetic norm is that it may close theory off from the facts—beauty is *not* truth, whatever the poet says. Nevertheless it has happened more than once that a theory was adhered to because of its simplicity and symmetry in spite of its disagreement with fact, then later observations and interpretations removed the disagreement. A scientist sometimes needs the courage, not only of his convictions, but also of his esthetic sensibilities. The esthetic norm, however, has little bearing on behavioral science in its present state, which may be characterized—without undue offense to anyone, I trust—as one of almost unrelieved ugliness.

PRAGMATIC NORMS

There remain the norms pertaining to the working of the theory, the effectiveness with which it performs the functions of theory. Let me say at once that success in what is usually called "practical" applications— that is, those outside the context of inquiry—is neither a necessary nor a sufficient condition for validation. It is no good saying to the economist, "If you're so smart, why ain't you rich?" or even more pointedly taunting the psychopathologist. Success in application is not a necessary condition, because the application may fail for many reasons external to the theory being applied—for instance, the conditions specified in the theory may not have been satisfied, like perfect competition in an economic theory, or the development of transference to the particular therapist in psychoanalysis. And it is not a sufficient condition, for the success may be due to factors external to the theory—for instance, the halting of a recession by the outbreak of war, or the cure of hysterical paralyses at religious shrines. To be sure, success or failure in practice raises certain presumptions; but what it contributes to validation must be carefully assessed in each case.

Setting aside the "practicality" of vulgar pragmatism, then, the pragmatic norms concern what the theory can do for science itself. The question is how effectively the theory serves our scientific purposes. Now these purposes are more varied than is sometimes recognized by methodologists, especially by those who are disinclined to view science as a concrete human enterprise. Thus the formulation of a scientific result need not always be regarded as an entry in the memory bank of some supercomputer, in which "Science" is stored as a set of propositions; it can also be regarded as a communication to scientific colleagues. In this perspective, *re*-discoveries can also be seen to have considerable importance, in the case of Mendel's work, for instance, and in many other cases in the history of science. A publication can also be the graveyard of ideas, as every academician knows; the locus of the life and work of scientific ideas is in men's minds, and not on the printed page. It is in men's hands too, as they build experimental apparatus or manipulate instruments of observation or measurement. It may even be that the distinction between "cerebral" knowledge and more deeply embedded "realization" can find application *within* scientific cognition, and not just in the contrast between science on the one hand, and art and action on the other. At any rate, the role that a theory plays in science is a matter not only of how it relates to other scientific propositions, with which the norms of coherence deal, but also of how it guides and stimulates the ongoing process of scientific inquiry.

From this standpoint, the value of a theory lies not only in the answers it gives but also in the new questions it raises. One might almost say that science is as much a search for questions as for answers. During the past several decades the exciting developments in behavioral science especially have not provided any notable solutions to problems of human behavior, but they have certainly opened up many new lines and techniques of investigation. In doing so they may not have contributed a great deal to growth by extension of our knowledge of man, which was more characteristic of the earlier decades of this century, but rather to growth by intension. New questions often arise, not only out of turning to new subject-matters, but also out of viewing old subject-matters in a new light. The value of a theory is heuristic—a designation which sometimes carries the unfortunate connotation that the theory is not good for anything else, as though there is so much better it could do. Frank has suggested (46:352) that the criterion of simplicity has actually served to pick out the "dynamic" theories, those that "proved to make science more fit to expand into unknown territory". Such theories appear to provide a simplification because they unify disparate phenomena (for instance, dreams, delusions, symptoms, and slips in psychoanalysis); new questions arise as each of these is seen in the light of the others.

More specifically, a good theory serves to explain old laws and to predict new ones. It may even serve as the condition for the acceptance of a generalization as a law, just as being subsumable under a law induces us to accept a datum as a "fact" (§11). "In the science of physics at least," Campbell (13:91) has remarked, "it would almost be more accurate to say that we believe our laws because they are consequences of our theories than to say that we believe our theories because they predict and explain true laws!" In this way, theory systematizes and unifies our knowledge. Kurt Lewin's metaphor is, I think, particularly apt: "The ultimate goal is to establish a network of highways and superhighways, so that any important point may be linked with any other. This network of highways will have to be adapted to the natural topography of the country and will thus itself be a mirror of its structure and of the position of its resources."

Thus we return to the norms of correspondence, yet in a way which indicates that correspondence alone is not the whole story. Even theories afterwards repudiated as downright false have had their part to play in their day, and may have played it well. "Perhaps the greatest difficulty of the historian of science qua historian [and of the methodologist too, I would say] lies in acquiring the proper and necessary sympathy for the plausibility of wrong ideas. The Aristotelian logic of motion, the geocentric planetary system, and the phlogiston theory . . . were all-powerful in their time, full of explanation and light, giving useful accord with observation and prediction of observation" (113:71 n). We must avoid the blunders both of claiming that today at last science has arrived at the truth and claiming that science never does get at the truth. The first is absurdly parochial, the second quite as absurd in supposing that "truth" can be given meaning in any other terms than by reference to scientific knowledge. Of course our present theories will be revised or discarded, just as their predecessors were; but this is not to say that there is no truth in them. Or rather, to say so is to make truth wholly irrelevant to the scientific enterprise. I should prefer to think of truth as itself a matter of degree—not the ever-receding horizon but the ground beneath our feet as we traverse it.

The problem of validation of a theory is too often discussed in the context of convincing even the most hardened skeptics, as though the problem is that of silencing critics. But scientists do more than criticize one another; they also provide each other with aid and comfort. It is not moral support which is in question here, but concrete help in specific tasks—sharing findings, techniques, ideas. A theory is validated, not by showing it to be invulnerable to criticism, but by putting it to good use, in one's own problems or in those of coworkers. Methodology, I believe, should say no more than this about a questionable theory: if you can do anything with it, go ahead. The fragmentation into schools so characteristic of behavioral science today can make for a healthy give-and-take, but only if the spirit of the encounters is not "Much good may it do you!" but rather, "May it do you much good!"

§37. *Theories in Behavioral Science*

BIASES

Many behavioral scientists, especially psychologists, believe that a satisfactory theory of human behavior must "ultimately" be a micro theory. To be "scientific" means to them to look to biology as the necessary foundation for social and psychological theory, and more particularly to the micro aspects of biology rather than to disciplines like ecology. That large-scale phenomena must be understood in terms of what is happening in the small has a certain plausibility, but I believe that the necessity is specious. We do sometimes explain in this way (as the behavior of gases on the basis of the motion of their molecules), but sometimes we explain in the reverse order (as the behavior of iron filings on the basis of the properties of a magnetic field). To the principle of autonomy of the conceptual base (§10) there corresponds a *principle of autonomy of the theoretical base*. Negatively put, it is that no type of theory defined by general attributes of form or content is in itself more scientific, methodologically more pure. The scientist *may* use whatever theories he *can* use. It is quite as "logical" to explain an employer's decision by reference to a theory of wages and prices as it is to explain an inflationary movement by reference to a theory of utilities governing choices of individual participants in the economy. It is my impression that both macro and micro economics have a certain respectability nowadays, but that in psychology and elsewhere in behavioral science methodological piety pushes most often towards micro theories.

I believe that one of the sources of this tendency is the image of the self as monadic. The principle of local determination may appear to us to be naturally and necessarily true of our own behavior, as a reflection of our sense of individuality and freedom. It is easier for us to accept a theory of behavior with complex predicates than one which introduces complex subjects for its propositions. The subject of a theory of behavior may be complicated, but not complex—it is just "me", a unitary self. Methodological individualism (§10) may then be invoked and misconceived as justifying a substantive doctrine, as though if we specify the meaning of collective terms by reference to individuals, it is really only individuals that we can meaningfully talk about. Moreover, the conceptual economy effected by contracting the explanatory shell insensibly gives rise to the absurd notion that if we haggle long enough we may have to pay nothing at all. There is such a thing as false economy too, and we get what we pay for.

Another source of theoretical bias here is what might be called *substantialism:* the search for entities and structures rather than for processes and functions. This point of view may be a continuation of nineteenth-century materialism, long abandoned by physical science but perhaps anachronistically still shaping the image of "science" for those engaged in the study of man. (There is always a certain lag in borrowed ideals: we never imitate our hero as he is but only as he was when he became our ideal.) The older categories of matter and energy have not yet been integrated in much of our thinking with the new category of information, so that order does not seem to us as real somehow as the materials which exhibit the order, and the message seems more ethereal than the channel by which it is transmitted. Quite apart from the level of its achievement, neuroanatomy in this perspective is a priori more scientific than the psychology of thought processes. What Whitehead called the fallacy of simple location, which I suggested might be involved in local determination, is here matched by his fallacy of "misplaced concreteness". Basically, this fallacy lies in the insistence that theoretical terms be interpretable as "ultimately" observational, when our instruments are sufficiently refined and ingenious; incomplete symbols with systemic meaning are felt to be not fully scientific.

There is also often at work in behavioral science a bias towards *physicalism*. The thesis of the unity of science as originally promulgated by Carnap and others seems to me entirely sound so far as it concerns the unity of method. Unfortunately, method is sometimes confused with specific techniques, and scientific status is then thought to be restricted to the use of techniques appropriate only to the subject-matter of physics. Similarly, the unity of terms is mistakenly thought to imply that the concepts of behavioral science must have their meanings specified in the terms of physics alone; this mistake lies in not recognizing that only observability is called for, and not the observable terms belonging to one science rather than another. But it is with respect to the unity of laws, and thus the construction of theories, that bias is most marked. What is at best a "regulative" principle in Kant's sense—a program and aspiration—is construed as "constitutive"—a criterion of scientific acceptability. It is thought that the laws of behavioral science must be such as can be deduced, ultimately, from those of physics, or they have not yet gotten at the truth. Pressure is then exerted to formulate laws which are already as close as possible to those of physical science.

This emphasis on what must be true "in principle" of the relations among the various sciences weakens the awareness of what is true of them in fact. For over a century there has been in vogue something like Auguste Comte's conception of the hierarchy of the sciences. Sociology rests on psychology, that in turn on biology, then biology on chemistry, and the entire structure finally on physics. Yet, "today no biological process is fully understood in terms of chemistry and physics. The facts are unknown to us. Few chemical properties are yet reduced to the physical relations of atomic constituents. The mathematics is too cumbersome. Physics itself wants a unified field theory and doubts determinism in atomic processes. So much for Comte's hierarchical unity of science" (Warren S. McCulloch in *46*:149). This situation is hardly one that justifies the insistence on formulating the laws of behavior only in such a way that they can be derived from those of biology. The hierarchical arrangement does make sense in terms of what one science can provide another—presuppositions, suppositions, and resources. Obviously, whatever help a science can get from the more "basic" ones— those on which it rests in the hierarchy—should certainly be taken advantage of; but it is hard to see why the less "basic" should be discouraged from trying to do anything on their own.

The dangers of substantialism and physicalism are well illustrated, I think, in contemporary psychiatry. Research on drug therapies and the physiology of the psychoses has already yielded some suggestive findings, and has opened many promising lines of further investigation. But many psychiatrists seem to view this undertaking in the perspectives of a Cartesian Dualism, dividing the categories of Body from those of Mind, and admitting only the first into the domain of science. What is overlooked is that psychological notions must still enter into scientific psychiatry by way of the concept of the illness and the standards of the cure. Suppose it were definitely established that the direct cause of schizophrenia is the concentration of a certain substance in the blood, or the formation of a certain structure in nerve cells or their connections. The effect of this cause, so far as it concerns psychiatry, would still be statable only in terms of macro behavior (for instance, that resulting from delusions of persecution). Nor would it follow that treatment necessarily requires the laying on of hands, whether by medicine or surgery. For the possibility would still be open that the substance or structure itself is produced or destroyed by various patterns of interpersonal behavior or communication (as in the familiar case of ulcers, so far as producing them is concerned, at any rate). Psychophysical dualism always encounters the problem of interaction between the two realms. What I find exciting about such developments as cybernetics and related disciplines is precisely that they have "helped to pull down the wall between the great world of physics and the ghetto of the mind" (46:155). Psychiatrists like Kenneth Colby have even begun to apply these ideas to such nonphysicalistic theories as psychoanalysis.

INTERACTION OF FACTORS

I confine myself here to mentioning only one other problem of theorizing in behavioral science, returning to the subject after considering the nature of explanation (§42).

In the present stage of our knowledge, human behavior is often seen as the outcome of the joint working of a number of distinct and often unrelated factors, as in the choice of a mate, or in the outbreak of war between nations. Consequently, two-variable causal laws are often inadequate, and important magnitudes are not scalable. In a sense, we know too much to be able to unify it in a single theory, and we do not know any of it with sufficient sureness. The problem of combining factors is not automatically solved by formulating the combination in terms of a field theory. We do not obtain such a theory merely by recognizing a multiplicity of factors and treating them as constituting a phase space, as Lewin has pointed out (in *91*:300). How the factors combine in their working must still be specified. "Rules of combination are not logically necessary principles. Even in the simple case where all factors are favorable, it does not *follow* that the combination of them will be favorable" (*51*:154). We need to know, not only the separate factors that are determinative of behavior, but also how they interact with one another. It is not always possible to advance step by step; to arrive at a good theory may call for as much boldness as imagination.

EXPLANATION

§38. The Pattern Model

DESCRIPTION, INTERPRETATION, AND EXPLANATION

We use the verb "to explain" in connection with very many different things. We may be said to explain ourselves, a dream, or a text; explain how to do something or other; explain why a particular event occurred or a certain law obtains; or explain for what reason a person or group acted as they did. Among these various explainings there is one set which it is comparatively easy to distinguish. I call it *semantic explanation:* making clear a meaning. I mean "meaning" in a very simple and straight-forward sense. I am not talking about the meaning of events, of actions, or of life, but about the meaning of words or other symbols (including acts as distinct from actions—see §4). A semantic explanation is a translation or paraphrase, a set of words having a meaning equivalent or similar to those being explained, but more easily or better understood. It is essential to semantic explanation that it serves as such only for

327

someone or other. What is intelligible to one person may not be so to another; one person may not need an explanation at all, and for another the explanation given may be inadequate. If the person to whom the explanation is addressed doesn't "get it", the meaning just has not been explained. A semantic explanation, as Dewey once said of education, is the outcome of a transaction, a sale: the sale is not made unless the customer actually buys.

Explanations which are not of meanings I call *scientific explanations* (other conditions must also be satisfied). These are not relative to the consumer, though they may be offered up for his acceptance. A statement offered as explaining a certain event, say, may in fact explain that event even though no one accepts the explanation. The difference between a semantic and a scientific explanation is in this respect like the difference between a statement's being clear and its being true. We cannot say that a statement is clear without at least tacitly indicating to *whom* it is clear. But if we say that the statement is true *for* someone or other, we mean only that he believes it, or has evidence for it, or something of the kind. We may also mean that he interprets it in such a way that the proposition it then designates is true; but then the truth of the stated proposition does not depend on him or on anyone else.

Certain explanations contain as components both semantic and scientific explanations; we may call them *interpretations*. They occur when what is being explained is viewed both as symbol and as fact; a statement has a meaning, but it is also an object or event occurring at a particular time and place. We interpret a speech by explaining its meaning, and by explaining also why it was made by that person who made it, and at that time; we interpret a dream by making manifest its latent content, and by explaining also why the dreamer produced the symbols he did. The scientific explanation may be suggested and supported by the semantic one, as in the case of dream analysis. But the relation between the two components of an interpretation may also be the reverse: we may understand *what* a person says because we know, from the context or in other ways, *why* he is saying it. Interpretation is of particular importance in behavioral science, because of the interplay between act meaning and action meaning; I shall return to it in §42. Hereafter, when I say "explanation" without a qualifier I shall mean scientific explanation, not semantic explanation or interpretation.

Explanation is often contrasted with *description*, as telling us, not merely what happens, but why. To explain a fact or a law is to give a reason for it; but just what constitutes a reason remains to be considered. The older positivism was unwilling to countenance reasons, because to the positivists the notion suggested something transcending empirical fact. For this reason they went so far as to hold that "laws simply describe, they never explain" (*106*:87). I think most contemporary philosophers of science (including positivists) would agree that laws do explain, and, in conjunction with other facts, do give reasons for particular occurrences. But this view does not necessarily imply that laws tell us anything other than how things happen.

The point is that descriptions may themselves be explanatory—the "how" may give us a "why" and not just a "what". For instance, we may describe certain prior events, and thereby provide a causal explanation, or we may describe certain intermediate events to explain why one produced another. An explanation does not tell us something of a different kind than a description does, but it tells us something else than the mere description of what it is explaining, and especially something appropriate to the context in which the explanation is to function. (See Scriven in *41*:175–176.) That scientific explanation is contextual does not mean, however, that its explanatory force depends on its audience, as in the case of semantic explanation. The point is rather that an explanation may be sound without being relevant; a good explanation is both. The same death may be explained both in physiological and in psychological terms: it was a case of poisoning, and also a case of suicide. Both are sound explanations, but they are certainly not equally good ones in a given context.

An explanation may be said to be a concatenated description. It does its work, not by invoking something beyond what might be described, but by putting one fact or law into relation with others. Because of the concatenation, each element of what is being described shines, as it were, with light reflected from all the others; it is because they come to a common focus that together they throw light on what is being explained. We see why something happens when we see better—in more detail, or in broader perspective—just what does happen. The difference between explanation and description may nevertheless be worth emphasizing to counter the illusion—not uncommon in psychology, according to

Kubie (in *61:65*)—that describing the same thing all over again, but in other terms, provides an explanation of it. A man is not incapable of work because he is lazy, incapable of love because he is selfish, or subject to compulsions because he is weak-willed. Such designations only describe what they purport to explain: they do not put it into relation with other processes or events.

It is significant that in the case of both semantic and scientific explanation we speak of "seeing" or "understanding" something which previously was obscure. Grasping a reason is in some ways like grasping a meaning (Peirce subsumes both under his category of Thirdness). The etymology of the word "explain" is to take out the folds, to make something level or even. An explanation makes something intelligible or comprehensible. It therefore provides us with a certain "intellectual satisfaction", as Braithwaite (*9:323*) calls it; its aim, says Campbell (*13:89*), is "the reconciliation with our intellectual desires of the perceptions forced on us by the external world of nature". Rationalism has its place in the scientific enterprise as does empiricism: the objects of sense are called upon to make sense.

But whether or not something has been made intelligible is not just a subjective matter. We may think we understand something without in fact understanding it. There is a difference between *having* an explanation and *seeing* it. In the case of semantic explanation, we do not have one unless and until we see it, but in the case of scientific explanation either the having or the seeing may occur without the other. That an explanation is often resisted when it is first offered is a commonplace of the history of science—men have it, but do not see it. The reverse is characteristic of the sort of explanations occurring in myth, paranoia, the occult "sciences", and the like. We may call them *runic explanations* —what they say has an explanatory ring, but they require a radically different interpretation. They provide a certain intellectual satisfaction, but it is one unwarranted by the actual state of affairs. Those who accept them only see an explanation, but do not have one. (I trust we need not trouble ourselves about the locution of seeing what is not there.)

Because both semantic and scientific explanation provide understanding, it is easy to confuse the second with the first—especially in behavioral science, where interpretation plays such an important part. A historical process, for instance, has been said to be understood if it is evident or plausible, by way of "psychological empathy". The trouble is, however, that "virtually always opposite historical processes are equally plausible" (E. Zilsel in *38*:721). The difficulty does not lie in the peculiar nature of history, but in the mistake of subjectifying explanation, treating truth like meaning, scientific explanation like semantic. It is just this confusion that characterizes runic explanations. In the early days of the Nazi regime a gang of thugs cornered a Jew and demanded of him who was responsible for Germany's troubles. "The Jews," he promptly replied, "and the bicycle riders."—"The bicycle riders! Why the bicycle riders?"—"Why the Jews?"

I believe that the confusion between semantic and scientific explanation also often underlies the great emphasis on familiarity as the basis of explanation. Familiarity helps us see an explanation, but it does not necessarily help us have one; it is fundamental to semantic explanation but may be quite unimportant for scientific explanation. Thus it has been said that the explanation of laws offered by theories is by way of "greater familiarity, essentially similar to that offered when a statement is translated from an unknown to a known language" (*13*:84; but see also *13*:77–78); here the comparison with semantic explanation is made explicit. Many scientists and philosophers have spoken of explanation as a process which "consists merely in analyzing our complicated systems into simpler systems in such a way that we recognize in the complicated system the interplay of elements already so familiar to us that we accept them as not needing explanation" (P. W. Bridgman, quoted in *103*:45). Such views are reminiscent of Russell's criticism of the old mechanists, that they thought that something was explained when it was shown to to be as unintelligible as what happens when one billiard ball strikes another.

But that familiarity cannot be the key to explanation should be apparent merely from the fact that it is inescapably relative to the person to whom the explanation is being offered: what is familiar to one man may be quite strange to another. A tourist can complain that everyone around him speaks a foreign language, but a scientist must be more objective. Scriven has pointed out (*41*:225) that the familiar is often not understood (rainbows, memory, or the appeal of music) while the unfamiliar may be very well understood (pure elements, the ideal gas, absolute zero). "On the other hand," he continues, "we do understand much of

what is familiar and so much explanation is reduction to the familiar."
It is understanding that remains fundamental, rather than familiarity.
What is needed is an account of understanding which is not merely psychological, in the sense in which a psychological account is invidiously distinguished from a logical one. We understand when we know the reason; that the reason is familiar may make it easier for us to know it, but its familiarity does not make it any more of a reason.

PATTERN AND DEDUCTION

Now, there are two accounts of the reasons which provide understanding, and thereby explanation. I call them the *pattern model* of explanation and the *deductive model*. Very roughly, we know the reason for something either when we can fit it into a known pattern, or else when we can deduce it from other known truths. Each of these models may well be universal in application—that is, each of them may provide an account of all the explanations which the other covers. From the nature of the whole pattern and some of its parts we can deduce the others; conversely, a deductive relationship might itself be viewed as constitutive of a cognitive pattern.

Yet, some cases of explanation may lend themselves more readily to one model and some to the other—for instance, explanations involving concatenated and hierarchical theories, respectively. The pattern model may more easily fit explanations in early stages of inquiry, and the deductive model explanations in later stages. Thus, it has been said that "when working with an individual patient an analyst . . . connects events into a pattern and intrinsically relates the pattern to other patterns. From these explanation sketches regarding individuals, generalizations regarding a class are attempted and lawlike explanations are formulated" (20:42). Perhaps, too, the various cognitive styles are not equally suited to each of the explanatory models—the literary, academic, and eristic styles may invite an account in terms of the pattern model, while the symbolic, postulational, and formal styles clearly suggest the deductive model. In any case, we must remember that we are dealing with a reconstructed logic. I put forward the two models, not to insist that there are two kinds of explanation—and especially not that in behavioral science the explanations are of a different kind from those in other sciences—but to acknowledge that there are two different reconstructions of explanation (different at least in formulation if not in substance), and that both may serve a useful purpose in methodology.

According to the pattern model, then, something is explained when it is so related to a set of other elements that together they constitute a unified system. We understand something by identifying it as a specific part in an organized whole. There is a figure consisting of a long vertical straight line with a short one branching upwards from it near the top, and a short curved line joining it on the same side near the bottom; the figure is meaningless until it is explained as representing a soldier with fixed bayonet, accompanied by his dog, disappearing around the corner of a building (the curved line is the dog's tail). We understand the figure by being brought to see the whole picture, of which what is to be explained is only a part. It is in this way that familiarity may come into play: the unknown is identified with something known, though not by way of its local properties but in terms of its place in a network of relations. "Why X?" "Because X is really nothing other than Y, and you know Y: it is a part of the old familiar Z!"

There is an extensive literature on cognitive patterns; gestalt psychologists, following the lead of Wertheimer, have carried out many investigations which seem to me of considerable significance for methodology, as well as for psychology itself. In most of the accounts, relationships are fundamental, as well as some notion of closure: wholeness, unity, or integration. The deductive model has the advantage of being formulated with incomparably greater exactness, but, as its proponents, I am sure, would be the first to agree, precision isn't everything. In my opinion, the effort to arrive at a more general and rigorous treatment of cognitive patterns is a most worthwhile endeavor; my impression is that considerable progress is now being made along various lines—in psychology, mathematics, linguistics, and perhaps in logic and philosophy as well. For the present, however, there is no doubt that the pattern model of explanation still leaves a great deal to be desired.

In Plato's account, the reason by which we understand and explain is a universal participated in by many particulars, which are thereby united in a single form. Aristotle, and most of his successors down to modern times, modified this view only to the extent of localizing the principle of explanation in the things themselves, as their essences or natures. Relations came into their own in science only in the seventeenth century or so, and in logic not until two centuries later. I believe that the importance assigned to relations is the gist of the opposition Lewin talked of between what he called the "Aristotelian and Galilean modes of thought". I do not mean to say, however, that the pattern model is more congenial to a modern philosophy of science, while the deductive model fits a Platonist or Aristotelian theory of knowledge: deductions, after all, can also be made from relational propositions, and the architectonic of forms, or of species and genera, is also a pattern.

Whatever the status of relational propositions in general, in the pattern model we explain by instituting or discovering relations. "In natural science," says Whitehead, "to explain means merely to discover interconnections." And for Dewey (28:511), "understanding or interpretation is a matter of the ordering of those materials that are ascertained to be facts; that is, determination of their relations". These relations may be of various different sorts: causal, purposive, mathematical, and perhaps other basic types, as well as various combinations and derivatives of these. The particular relations that hold constitute a pattern, and an element is explained by being shown to occupy the place that it does occupy in the pattern. We explain thunder by noting that a bolt of lightning heats the air through which it passes, which then expands, disturbing the air around it and thus setting up sound waves. We explain a surmise that a certain letter in the cryptogram is an M: because the letters following are ESSAGE, so that together they spell a word, and this word in turn combines meaningfully with its successor RECEIVED. We explain a sequence whose successive members are 2, 4, 8, and 16 by observing that these numbers are increasing powers of 2. Note that these explanations might be mistaken, and that in any case more detailed or more extensive patterns might be called for. We may explain the properties of a sample by the hypothesis that the population from which it was drawn has a certain distribution, but that hypothesis will not explain why this particular sample has those properties; to explain the latter we must place the sample in quite another pattern, treat it as a member of a different sequence.

The perception of a pattern is what gives the "click of relation" spoken of in connection with the norms of coherence for the validation of a theory (§36). The explanation is sound when everything falls into place. The perception that everything is just where it should be to complete the pattern is what gives us the intellectual satisfaction, the sense of closure, all the more satisfying because it was preceded by the tensions of perplexity. Rather than saying that we understand something when we have an explanation for it, the pattern model says that we have an explanation for something when we understand it. But this difference does not make the pattern model pejoratively psychological. The pattern model does indeed talk about psychological matters, but how else is knowledged to be conceived? Human knowledge cannot be anything other than an acquisition of the human mind, the product of human acts of knowing. The critical question is always whether the mere think-so (or feel-so) makes a statement so, and in the pattern model this is emphatically denied. The pattern is not constituted by our seeing it, but has its locus in a network of objective relations.

OBJECTIVITY

The test of objectivity is said to be prediction—if the alleged pattern *is* the pattern, we can expect to find such and such other elements in these and those places. But applying this test amounts to recasting our account in terms of the deductive model, as I shall indicate in §40. For the pattern model, objectivity consists essentially in this, that the pattern can be indefinitely filled in and extended: as we obtain more and more knowledge it continues to fall into place in this pattern, and the pattern itself has a place in a larger whole. This analysis of objectivity is the nub of Kant's answer to the question of what constitutes the difference between dreaming and waking, between appearance and reality. We cannot analyze the difference in terms that transcend experience, or we should never be able to draw the distinction. And we cannot analyze it in terms of specific contents, for whatever we can experience in waking life we can also dream of; whatever anything can really be, something else can also only appear to be. The difference is that the waking world hangs together in ways that the dream world does not: what happens in the waking world makes sense in relation to everything else that happens. Indeed, in waking life we can even make sense of dreams. If the dream world were coherent in its own terms, and if it provided a place for waking life as well, it would no longer be only a dream. Whatever has *all* the appearances of a certain thing, in every circumstance, in every relationship, really *is* just that certain thing.

THE COGNITIVE MAP

Not all explanation consists in fitting something into a pattern already given. The task of explanation is often to find or create a suitable pattern. To find or create it we need not always obtain new data. The scientific achievement—especially in the formation of theories—often consists in discovering new significance in the old data, giving them significance by ordering them differently, making manifest a new pattern. It is in this way that descriptions often play an explanatory role: they allow us to see relations which had previously escaped notice. "Understanding," says Scriven (*41*:193 n), "is roughly the perception of relationships and hence may be conveyed by any process which locates the puzzling phenomenon in a system of relations. . . . A description may enable us to supply a whole framework which we already understand, but of whose relevance we had been unaware. We deduce nothing; our understanding comes because we see the phenomenon for what it is, and are in a position to make other inferences from this realization." The explanation does its work by providing us with what has aptly been called a *cognitive map*, which tells us how things around us are laid out. Every explanatory pattern is a fragmentary map of a limited territory; we aim to fill in details, and to fit it together with other fragments. As we pursue these aims, moving always into new territories, we subject the map to continuous test. A sound explanation is one that grows on us as our knowledge grows.

§39. *The Deductive Model*

DEDUCTION AND PATTERN

The pattern model of explanation can be applied to systems of deductive relations as well as to patterns constituted by other sorts of relations. Wertheimer gives two examples.

We wish to explain why $(a + b)^2 = a^2 + 2ab + b^2$. Let a and b be represented by two line segments; than $a + b$ is represented by the line consisting of the two segments jointed together, and $(a + b)^2$ by the square having that line as side. Let lines be drawn across the square connecting

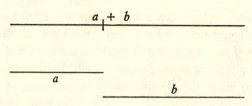

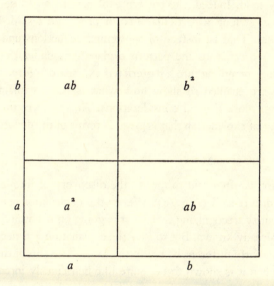

the points where the segments are joined. This produces two small squares, of different size, and two rectangles. One of these squares has a as side, the other b, and each rectangle has a for one side and b for the other. The large square is then seen to consist of four areas, one square representing a^2, another square representing b^2, and two rectangles each representing ab.

Again, we wish to explain why the sum of the first n integers is equal to $\frac{1}{2}n(n+1)$. The following is the method said to have been used by Gauss as a schoolboy. Rearrange the sequence into pairs, each consisting of the highest and the lowest number not already paired; thus, 1 is paired with n, 2 with $n-1$, 3 with $n-2$, and so on. The sum of each of these pairs is $n+1$, for this is the sum of the first pair, and in constructing the other pairs, whenever we increase the lower number by 1 we also decrease the higher number by 1. Now there are half as many pairs (including a half pair if n is odd) as there are numbers, and the sum of all of them is simply the number of pairs multiplied by the sum of each pair.

There is no doubt that Wertheimer's proposition and examples are illuminating, and for my part I am quite willing to acknowledge that they are of logical significance and not "merely psychological". Yet, a formal deduction of the equations may be quite as good an explanation of why they hold. Indeed, the pattern explanations given above can be regarded as sketching a particular line of proof, no less deductive for being informal. That is, instead of subsuming deductions under the pattern model, we can subsume pattern explanations under the deductive model. Fitting something into a pattern has explanatory force in so far as thereby we are enabled to show how what is being explained can be deduced from more general considerations. At any rate, the foregoing is the account of explanation that is given in terms of the deductive model.

GENERALITY AND SPECIALITY

Explanation is often said to mean "the discovery of like in unlike, of identity in difference" (*126*:18). We *see* the explanation when we discern the identity, recognizing that what is going on is nothing other than something already known. But to *have* the explanation it is necessary that what is apparently different be really the same. The slip of the tongue is explained when it is shown to be, quite like consciously intended words and actions, the expression of certain feelings and attitudes, just as the motion of the moon is explained by its being shown to be, like the fall of the apple, the resultant of gravitational forces. In both examples, the explanation consists in reducing a special case to a more general one; the identity in difference is the one in the many, the universal common to many particulars. "Laws explain our experience," says Campbell (*13*:79), "because they order it by referring particular instances to general principles; the explanation will be the more satisfactory the more general the principle, and the greater the number of particular instances that can be referred to it."

To say that particular instances are "referred" to general principles means this, that they are deducible from those principles together with something which serves to mark out whatever particular is in question. To explain something is to exhibit it as a special case of what is known in general. Socrates died because he was a man, and because all men are mortal; or because he threatened the social structure, and because all power elites . . . Why are men mortal? Because they are animals, and because all animals . . . ; and so on. These statements exemplify the essence of the deductive model of explanation, as developed with great care and detail by Hempel and Oppenheim and others. Thus they say (59:136), "an event is explained by subsuming it under general laws, i.e., by showing that it occurred in accordance with those laws, by virtue of the realization of certain specified antecedent conditions. . . . The explanation of a general regularity consists in subsuming it under another, more comprehensive regularity, under a more general law." We explain Y by adducing the principle that whenever X holds true then Y does, and adding that in the case of Y, X does hold true.

The various types of explanation—causal, motivational, functional, and so on (§42)—are differentiated by the nature of the general statements that serve, together with the particular antecedent conditions, as premises for the explanatory deductions. It is not the premises alone that explain, however, but the fact that what is to be explained follows from them. Only this following makes clear why something *must* be the case. A fact that is unexplained is merely contingent, and a law merely "empirical". The fact or law just happens to be thus and not otherwise; there is no reason for it—or better, if there is a reason we do not know what it is. That we do not know is what is meant by saying that something is unexplained. The explanation shows that, on the basis of what we already know, the something could not be otherwise. Whatever provides this element of necessity serves as an explanation. The great power of the deductive model consists in the clear and simple way in which the necessity is accounted for.

It is of enormous importance for methodology to recognize that in the deductive model the necessity does not lie in the premises but rather in the relation between the premises and the conclusion which they entail. The general principle adduced, therefore, need not be a causal law. If to give a reason for something is to show why the something must be so, we are not thereby limited to exhibiting the something as the effect of certain causes. What is required is a logical necessity, not a causal one;

an explanation in terms of purposes, for example, can be formulated in the deductive model just as well as can an explanation in terms of causes. (Why did he act that way? Because men act so as to maximize their expectations, and his subjective probabilities were such and such, his utilities so and so.) Indeed, even logical necessity may be too strict a requirement for explanation, as I shall point out below; it may be enough to show that, on certain premises, what is to be explained becomes very likely—it did not have to be this way, but the chances were that it would be.

The objection might be raised against the deductive model that it does not really explain "explanation" because it does not account for the feature of intelligibility. When an event has been explained we understand why it happened; its occurrence makes sense. Providing premises from which it can be deduced may not be enough to produce such understanding. According to the deductive model, this objection runs, we explain why x has the property G, say, by pointing out that x is a member of the class F and adducing the consideration that all F's are G. But this explanation may amount to no more than showing that the case to be explained belongs to a certain class of cases, all equally insusceptible of explanation. What we want to know is why the F's, including x, *are* G. From the premises given we can deduce that x has the property G, but its having the property has not been explained if we do not understand why those premises are true.

In my opinion, however, the objection is not well taken. In abstracting from the context of inquiry in which explanations function it loses sight of just what is to be explained in each context. There is always something else to be explained, but it is surely not true that we understand nothing until we understand everything. Explanations, like concepts and laws, have a certain openness (§41); in particular, every explanation is "intermediate", in the sense that it contains elements which are to be explained in turn. But its being intermediate does not mean that it cannot do its own work of explaining until it has itself been explained. There is a regress of explanations, but it is not a vicious one: we can explain A by reference to B even though B is not explained. The context may indeed make B problematic, in which case we must adduce some C; but this context is not to be confused with the one in which it is A that is to be explained, and for *this* explanation B might very well serve. There is a comparable nonvicious regress of evidence: the proposition p can provide evidence for q even though the evidence for p itself is not given. How do you know that q is true? Because p is. But how do you know that p is true? Because . . . a is true. This alphabet, however, has no beginning; we simply stop with what is unproblematic in that context. An explanation leaves something to be desired when there is something *more* to be explained—details to be filled in, a closer approximation arrived at, and so on. But it is no shortcoming of the explanation that there is something *else* to be explained. On the contrary, finality is a mark of runic explanations, not scientific ones; the road of inquiry is always open, and it reaches beyond the horizon.

In short, the fact that explanation, according to the deductive model, makes use of premises which are not axiomatic (so that they are to be deduced from still other premises) does not mean that the deduction does not contribute to our understanding of the conclusion. Even in the pattern model, understanding is a matter of the perception of relationships and not a matter of the perspicuity of the relata. We understand always in terms of something or other, and the question can always be raised how that something in turn is to be understood. It is true, however, that not just any premises will do. We do not explain why there is a lion in the garden, it has been remarked, by pointing out that in fact there are two of them there. From this statement we can certainly deduce that there is one, but surely our perplexity is at least as great as before. What is required is some generalization in the premises, or at any rate a tacit reference to a generalization. The event is explained by grouping it, not with just any set of events, but with a set that is nomologically bound together. In a word, we explain a fact by adducing the law which governs it.

LAW AND THEORY

It may well be that for the explanation of facts the pattern model often yields a more direct and natural account. We explain why there is a lion in the garden by pointing out that there is a circus nearby, from which it "must" have escaped, or that the house next door has just been rented by a lion tamer, or by a similar statement. But there are generalizations implicit here which allow the explanation to be also reconstructed in the deductive model. (Animals escape when they can, they prefer to walk on grass rather than on cement, and so on.) The more serious question is whether the explanation of laws rather than of particular facts is also a matter only of subsuming them under some more general principle, so that the explanation of laws is "an extension of the process involved in their formulation, a progress from the less to the more general. . . . I dissent altogether from this opinion," Campbell (13:79–80) has said flatly; "I do not believe that laws can ever be explained by inclusion in more general laws." What is needed is not more general laws as such, but theories. These do have a wider range of application, but what is significant is that the hypotheses of which theories consist are of a higher level than the laws which the theories explain (§§13 and 34).

The explanation of the law is provided by the circumstance that the law can be deduced from the theory. "All that is required for the higher-level hypotheses to provide an explanation is that they should be regarded as established and that the law should logically follow from them. It is scarcely too much to say that this is the whole truth about the explanation of scientific laws" (9:343). This last statement is, I am afraid, too much to say. The deductive model of explanation requires more of the premises than that they should be true and entail their conclusion. What more is required is not easy to state in a way that would win general acceptance. For my part, I believe that Campbell's formulation is as helpful as anything in more recent methodological discussion: "When we say the theory explains the laws we mean something additional to this mere logical deduction; the deduction is necessary to the truth of the theory, but it is not sufficient. What else do we require? I think the best answer we can give is that, in order that a theory may explain, we require it—to explain! We require that it shall add to our ideas, and that the ideas it adds shall be acceptable" (13:82–83).

Something of this requirement is involved, I suppose, in the characterization of the theory as being of a "higher level" than the laws it explains. The conjunction of two laws is plainly not an explanation for either of them, even though each can be deduced from the conjunction. But nothing has been added to our ideas by the conjunction. A theory explains because it is more than merely an aggregation of laws, or their notational unification. Though it is of greater range and scope than any of the laws it explains, it is not an extensional generalization of these laws, but a generalization of higher level: the law itself, rather than its instances, is shown to be a special case of a more general phenomenon. It is on this basis that models can make manifest the explanatory power of theories: the same formalism can be interpreted in terms of the several subject-matters covered by the theory. "The theory always explains laws," says Campbell (*13*:96), "by showing that if we imagine that the system to which those laws apply consists in some way of other systems to which some other known laws apply, then the laws can be deduced from the theory."

DEDUCIBILITY

Here again the pattern model of explanation may be useful. The theory explains, not just by virtue of the fact that it permits certain deductions, but because it institutes a more comprehensive pattern, of which the patterns constituted by the laws to be explained are recognizable components. It is by allowing such diverse phenomena to be fitted into a pattern that the theory provides understanding. Helmholtz once declared that "to understand a phenomenon means nothing else than to reduce it to the Newtonian laws". But on this assertion Philipp Frank (*44*:138) has commented, "It was completely forgotten that in Newton's own day his theory was looked upon as a set of abstract mathematical formulas, which needed a mechanical explanation to satisfy man's desire for causality. Newton himself recognized this need. . . . Men like Huygens and Leibniz never considered the Newtonian theory a physical explanation; they looked upon it as only a mathematical formula." On the other hand, it is important to reemphasize the difference between having an explanation and seeing it, between understanding in a logical sense and something which is psychologically satisfying. Deducibility may not in itself be enough for understanding; what more is required is that the explanatory premises be of a certain kind—nomological in the case of explaining facts, theoretical in the case of explaining laws. But when these conditions are met, "man's desire for causality" or for some other special type of explanation is of no particular logical relevance.

A far more serious objection to the deductive model is that deducibility is not only not a sufficient condition for explanation but that it is not even a necessary condition. There appear to be many explanations in

which laws do not occur as premises at all. The phenomenon to be
explained is just described, more fully or from a different point of view,
and this description serves as the explanation without any deductions
being made (Scriven in 41:193). (Consider, for example, an explanation of reproduction in some unfamiliar species—and not just for children either.) To be sure, it is not uncommon in these cases to say that
laws and deductions from them are "implicit" (as I did myself a little
while ago). But in the context of this issue such a claim may be begging
the question. It amounts to saying that we can reconstruct the explanation to fit the deductive model, but the issue is whether it would still be
explanatory if it were not so reconstructed.

What is more to the point is that there appear to be explanations
which cannot be reconstructed in this way. These are the *probabilistic
explanations*, in which statistical laws play a part, or perhaps even only
statistical data with no other laws than the tautologies of the probability
calculus. We may explain the properties of a sample by calling attention
to the distribution in the population from which it was drawn. This distribution does not entail that the sample *must* be what it was found to be,
but it does confer a certain probability on that finding, a probability that
may serve to explain it. There are, besides, the explanations, especially
common in behavioral science, which make use of quasi laws (§12),
those asserting something of "all cases for which an exceptional status
(in an ill-defined but clearly understood sense) cannot be claimed"
(56:11). Here again the premises do not entail the conclusion to be
explained, but only make it probable to some degree or other. Those who
believe that no laws are strictly universal, that all are statistical, and
that all are open to some extent just as are the more easily recognizable
quasi laws, would be, I suppose, dubious about any cases of strictly
deductive explanations. For the conclusion could be deduced only if the
premises were appropriately closed, and in that case they presumably
would not be such as "add to our ideas".

Hempel has acknowledged (41:137) that explanations adducing statistical generalizations must be conceived as inductive arguments. These
might still be fitted into the deductive model, however, with only slight
emendations. For in modern developments of inductive logic, following
Carnap, the circumstance that the conclusion has a certain degree of
confirmation with respect to the evidence adduced follows deductively

from the premises of the inductive inference. What is explained is then, not why the conclusion is true, but why it is probable. That elements are found to have atomic weights which differ from integral values is explained by reference to isotopes, which occur in nature in certain proportions; any particular sample, consisting of so very many atoms, is thus very likely to contain different isotopes in about those proportions. This explains our finding, though what follows with necessity is only that such a finding is very likely.

CONFIRMATION

In matters of detail, the deductive model still faces various difficulties arising from the logic of confirmation on which it relies. Take, for instance, "Hempel's paradox": The statement that all A's are B's is logically equivalent to the statement that all non-B's are non-A's. We might regard the first as confirmed if the examination of a great many A's shows them all to be B's, but it is hard to believe that it is equally confirmatory if we examine instead a great many non-B's and find them to be non-A's. To test whether all swans are white, we look at swans to see if they are white, but not at colored things to see if they are other than swans. Like the weight of evidence, the force of an explanation should not depend on the way in which the proposition is formulated. We need not consider here the various devices proposed to resolve the paradox or to specify formally what constitutes the nomological generalization required by an explanation. It is true that the deductive model calls for a certain amount of logical gadgetry to be workable, but the pattern model has not even been formulated with enough specificity for anyone to see what gadgets might be needed.

I do not mean to say that I agree wholly with that principle of Russell's which has dominated so much philosophy in our time: better to be definitely wrong than vaguely right. But many attacks on the deductive model, especially for explanations of human behavior, have been in the service of a certain obscurantism (pointed out by Brodbeck in *41*:272). Psychological understanding has been urged as all that is possible, or at least as an explanation much to be preferred to one with a logical base. Methodology, however, must insist, in my opinion, on a single standard of explanatory conduct; in the search for explanations the behavioral scientist is as much bound by logical commitments as are his more obviously respectable colleagues. Only, we must beware of confusing a particular reconstructed logic with the logic-in-use. The pattern model may be as useful a reconstruction of scientific explanation as the deductive one, and quite as free of "merely" psychological determinants. It is as easy to be prejudiced for the deductive model as against it, and often what presents itself to us as obscurantism is only a departure from the particular reconstruction that we have come to identify with reason itself.

§40. *Explanation and Prediction*

From the viewpoint of the pattern model the primary function of laws and theories is to provide understanding; from the viewpoint of the deductive model, it is to allow predictions. Yet a deductive explanation does provide understanding, or it would not serve as an explanation at all, and predictions play a part in the pattern model, as specifications of what is needed to fill in the pattern. In whichever way explanation is reconstructed, prediction is at least a possibility. In both models, laws serve to explain events and theories to explain laws; a good law allows us to predict new facts and a good theory new laws. At any rate, the success of the prediction in either case adds credibility to the beliefs which led to it, and a corresponding force to the explanations which they provide.

EXPLANATION WITHOUT PREDICTION

The question is whether the ability to predict is a necessary consequence of having a good explanation. Granted, for a moment, that if we can predict, so much the better for the explanation; but if an explanation does not allow predictions (as distinct from implying false ones), does it follow that it is unacceptable? "Yes" is the position taken by Hempel and Oppenheim. "An explanation is not fully adequate unless its explanans [what is doing the explaining], if taken account of in time, could have served as a basis for predicting the phenomenon under consideration" (59:138). Indeed, on their view "explanation" and "prediction" are two names for one logical fact: that two bits of knowledge, actual or potential, stand in a certain logical relation to one another.

"Scientific laws and theories have the function of establishing systematic connections among the data of our experience, so as to make possible the derivation of some of these data from others. According as, at the time of the derivation, the derived data are, or are not yet, known to have occurred, the derivation is referred to as explanation or as prediction. . . . Explanation and prediction have the same logical structure, namely that of a deductive systematization" (59:164).

Yet, if we look at the explanations which actually occur in science as well as in everyday life, and not only at what an ideal explanation would be or at what all explanations are "in principle", it appears that we often have explanations without being able to predict, that is, without being in a position where we could have predicted if only we had had the explanation in time.

In terms of the pattern model we may say that the pattern which provides the explanation does not uniquely determine its parts, so that a knowledge of the pattern as a whole and of some of its parts does not always enable us to predict the others. The explanation still explains even though it leaves open a range of possibilities, so that which possibility is actualized is knowable only after the fact. As in the interpretation of a work of art, our understanding is a matter of hindsight: we see why the work of art has the components that it does, but we could not have predicted on that basis what they would be. The theory of evolution explains highly specialized forms as produced by natural selection from a succession of less specialized ones, but the more highly specialized forms are predictable only in a general way. A symptom may be understood and explained as the manifestation of a conversion hysteria, but the knowledge on which such an explanation rests is not ordinarily enough to allow us to explain the patient's choice of that particular symptom, and is therefore not enough for us to have been able to predict it.

In terms of the deductive model the same point might be made by reference to the difference between necessary and sufficient conditions. Our knowledge, especially in behavioral science, is often limited to what is necessary for a certain kind of event to occur but does not comprise what is sufficient to produce it (Scriven in 41:186). In that case, what we can explain on the basis of that knowledge is not strictly deducible from it, and surely not predictable. In the earlier example the curved line was explained as representing the tail of the soldier's dog; the dog is necessary to the tail but not the tail to the dog. A certain neurosis might be explained as the result of a childhood trauma, but not all traumas produce a neurosis in later life; the neurosis is not predictable on the basis only of what serves to explain it. We may say that these are *partial* explanations, adducing some of the factors involved but not all of them, and that if only the explanations were complete then we could predict. Alas, most explanations, in behavioral science at any rate, are only partial; shall we say, because they do not allow for prediction, that they are not really explanations at all? An automobile accident is said to be due to defective brakes or to excessive speed or to a drunken driver; none of these things allow us to predict the accident, but in particular cases they may have considerable explanatory force (though, to be sure, in conjunction with the other factors assumed to be at work).

An explanation based on statistical laws allows for only statistical prediction at best, and the quality of the explanation may be much better than that of the prediction. It may be a perfectly acceptable explanation of why someone won at a game of chance that he was "lucky"—this means that his winning was not a matter of his skill nor of cheating; yet for just this reason there was no more basis for predicting that he would win than any of the other players, and possibly less. I do not see that it is necessarily unscientific to attribute importance to the role of chance in human affairs—in love or in war or in that peculiar combination of both which is politics—but the more important its role in explanations the more it limits predictability.

In addition to the facts that our explanations may be only partial, and that the laws and theories which they invoke are often statistical, another circumstance that limits predictability even though we have an explanation of sorts is the instability and variability of the subject-matter, its irregularity. In behavioral science, explanations often adduce large-scale and long-run factors—as with the causes of the Civil War, the rise of Fascism, or the decline of Rome. Yet the long-range predictions often are the most difficult to make. Methodologists have been misled, Nagel has pointed out, by "the tacit assumption that celestial mechanics is the paradigm of any science worthy of the name". In fact, he observes, it is not even a typical physical science; the circumstances that permit long-range predictions in astronomy are rare and special. It is not of much help in the conduct of inquiry, especially inquiry in behavioral science, to hold up the ideal of explanations having the predictive power of celestial mechanics. Why should behavioral science make demands on itself that are so seldom imposed in physics or biology? I think Scriven is quite right that "in place of the social scientists' favorite Myth of the Second Coming (of Newton), we should recognize the Reality of the Already-Arrived (Darwin); the paradigm of the explanatory but non-predictive scientist" (*Science*, Vol. *130*:477).

PREDICTION WITHOUT EXPLANATION

It might be, I suppose, that the ideal explanation from the standpoint of the philosopher of science (even if it is not a realistic ideal for the scientist himself) would be one that allowed for prediction. The converse, however, is surely questionable; predictions can be and often are made even though we are not in a position to explain what is being predicted. This capacity is characteristic of well-established empirical generalizations that have not yet been transformed into theoretical laws. Ancient astronomers made predictions of quality incomparably better than their explaining theories; even today the periods of certain pulsating stars are very well known even though we do not have any firm explanations of their behavior. Similarly, the course of a mental illness or the outcome of an election campaign might be predictable with far better grounds than are available for any explanation of these phenomena.

DIFFERENCES BETWEEN EXPLANATION AND PREDICTION

In recent years methodologists and philosophers of science have increasingly emphasized the difference between explanation and prediction. (See, for instance, *56*, Scriven in *41*, Israel Sheffler in *27*.) From a formal point of view a number of differences are readily apparent. Prediction involves a reference to the time of the assertion; of course, in a logical sense we can also predict the past (it is sometimes called "retrodiction"), but the state of knowledge at a particular time always enters into predictions in a way in which it does not enter into explanations. Further, explanations are always of an actuality (a fact or a law), even if they turn out to be wrong, while there is no corresponding actuality for an unsuccessful prediction. (It must be admitted, however, that the his-

tory of science provides a number of instances of explanations offered
for supposed phenomena which afterwards were shown to be nonexistent.) Moreover, an explanation establishes a certain conclusion as at
least more probable than its negation, and usually as highly probable,
whereas a prediction affirms only that a certain alternative is more probable than any other, though its probability may be rather low.

The most basic difference between explanation and prediction, however, is with respect to the grounds they each offer for their claims. An
explanation rests on a nomological or theoretical generalization, or on an
intelligible pattern, but a prediction need not have such a basis. I am not
speaking of guesses, even of those that rest on knowledge of which the
guesser is unaware. A prediction, as distinct from a guess, is reasoned—
a basis is put forward, some premise from which what is predicted is
being inferred. The point is that the basis may be a merely empirical
generalization. We can give a reason for making some specific prediction rather than another, but we may be able to give no reason other than
past successes for expecting the prediction to come true. Analyses of
voting behavior, for example, may have identified certain counties or
states as barometers of the political weather, thereby allowing the computer to make early predictions; but making predictions from them is
very different from having an explanation of the vote.

In short, explanations provide understanding, but we can predict without being able to understand, and we can understand without necessarily
being able to predict. It remains true that if we can predict successfully
on the basis of a certain explanation we have good reason, and perhaps
the best sort of reason, for accepting the explanation.

Whatever philosophical considerations might incline us otherwise,
emphasis on the difference between explanation and prediction is important for methodology. It may encourage efforts to improve specific techniques of prediction even in those areas—almost everywhere in behavioral
science—where well-developed explanations are lacking. It is perfectly
plain that sensitive clinicians, informed observers of the political scene,
shrewd economic analysts, scientists and practitioners of various sorts
with a nose for impending developments—all are capable of making more
successful predictions than can be derived from the explanations they are
in a position to formulate. Yet comparatively few efforts have been
devoted to the systematic exploitation and improvement of expert judg-

ment—for instance, by consensus techniques—as contrasted with the impatient energies devoted to arriving at suitable laws and theories. (See *56* and *71*.) And on the other side, recognition of the difference between explanation and prediction may help relieve the pressure on theorizers to meet the immediate test of prediction or stand condemned of unscientific speculation. It is surely not too much to say that *some* good work has been done in behavioral science, and that not all of it has been marked by the power to predict. To arrive at some understanding of what is going on is hard enough, without having also to meet the demand that we anticipate what will happen next.

§41. Functions of Explanation

Explanations are often thought to add to our knowledge by contributing only to its growth by extension (§35). The idea is that when something has been explained it is as though we have conquered a certain amount of territory; a new frontier has been established, and, except for mopping-up operations, nothing remains but to continue our steady advance. In an even more popular metaphor, another brick has been laid in the edifice of science, which rises ever higher. Such images imply a finality that explanations do not in fact have; the openness of laws and theories confers a corresponding attribute on the explanations that they make possible. What functions explanations perform cannot be appreciated without a full awareness of how far from finality they are in the actual conduct of inquiry as contrasted with the idealizations of one or another reconstruction. I specify eight ways in which explanations can be open.

OPENNESS IN EXPLANATIONS

1. Explanations are *partial:* only some of the factors determining the phenomenon being explained are taken into account. In the pattern model, the structure is not fully defined; in the deductive model, the set of premises is not quite complete. Even the paradigmatic science of celestial mechanics, when it is applied to particular cases, exhibits this incompleteness—or if not the science, then surely our knowledge of the specific circumstances. The motion of the moon, for example, is subject to some dozens of distinct factors; we may be confident that each of

these can be accounted for by known laws, but the fact is that we cannot say just what all the factors are. In terms of neither the pattern model nor the deductive model can we claim that we actually have a full explanation of the moon's motion. It would be misleading, however, to speak of this feature of explanations (or any other aspect of their openness) as a "shortcoming"—it is of the very nature of knowledge that it is a product of a process of inquiry, or at least of some cognitive activity, and there is no reason to expect any such process to exhaust even the most limited actuality. Yet we can realistically pursue the ideal of making our explanations ever more complete. Only, such efforts must be seen everywhere as a pursuit; what is pernicious is the notion that every science worthy of the name has already arrived at the destination. The trouble with behavioral science is not that it has not arrived, but that so often it seems unwilling to get going.

2. Explanations are *conditional:* they hold true only of a certain range of phenomena, and are applicable only when certain conditions are satisfied. What all these conditions are is not always fully explicit. We arrive at the explanation for certain cases and think of it as applying to all cases "of that kind", but which kind is being referred to is usually specified the other way around: it consists of the cases which can be explained in just that way. When an explanation fails it is always open to us to conclude, not that there is something wrong with the explanation, but that some of the conditions for its application have not been met. If we were always to take advantage of this alternative, of course, we would be precluding the possibility of any empirical test of the explanation. But sometimes it is the alternative to be preferred, and our efforts are better directed to a fuller specification of the conditions of application than to a search for a quite different explanation. The point is that we cannot say beforehand when this is the course that inquiry should take.

3. Explanations are *approximate:* the magnitudes they yield are more or less inexact, the qualities they ascribe are a shade different from what is observed. Hempel (in *41*:101 n) has called attention in this connection to "Duhem's emphatic reminder that Newton's law of gravitation, far from being an inductive generalization of Kepler's laws, is actually incompatible with them, and that the credentials of Newton's theory lie rather in its enabling us to compute the perturbations of the planets, and

thus their deviations from the orbits assigned to them by Kepler". The astronomer's concept of "perturbation" could be given good use everywhere, and especially in behavioral science. Only, the situation is not that things do not go exactly where they should, but that *our* idea of where they "should" go does not exactly correspond to theirs.

4. Explanations are *indeterminate* in their application to particular instances: they are statistical in content if not in explicit form, and may be true generally speaking but not in every single case. We may explain changes in birth rates or in the incidence of suicide by reference to price levels, to anomii, to international tensions, or to traditional culture patterns, but individual human beings have their individual motivations: they do not bring new lives into the world or end their own just for the sake of statistics. It is often held that explanations are indeterminate only just in so far as they are partial, and that if all the factors were taken into account every single case could be subsumed under an appropriate generalization that admits of no exceptions. This view is another form of doctrinal determinism. Restated as a methodological norm, it encourages the search for subclasses of which the individual case to be explained is more nearly representative. But as a metaphysical doctrine it may have a stultifying effect by impugning the worth of statistical hypotheses on no other ground than that they are statistical.

5. Explanations are *inconclusive:* they do not show why what is being explained must be so, but why it was very likely that it would be so. The conclusion of the explanatory inference is established only to some degree. In the case of explanations which adduce statistical laws or theories to explain particular events this quality is quite clear. But explanations which are not statistical on the face of it may also be inductive. Of special importance for behavioral science are purposive explanations, those making reference to motives or functions. We might explain a political act in terms of what was expected to be achieved by it, or a political institution in terms of the interests it serves. But the connection between the act and its motives, the institution and its functions, is not a necessary one. The explanation still has force if the act, given those motives, or the institution, given those functions, is sufficiently frequent or likely.

6. Explanations are *uncertain:* the laws and theories invoked, as well as the data applying to the particular case, are confirmed only to some

degree. The history of science is a history of the successive replacement of one explanation by another. It is possible, I suppose, to say that
the earlier account was not really an explanation but was only thought to
be one. But in that case it would ill become us ever to claim that we can
explain anything, for surely we must expect that our theories will in
turn be replaced by others. What is required of an explanation is that
the propositions adduced be well attested, that they rest on considerable
evidence. Such propositions may eventually be shown to be false, but this
event in the future does not rob them of a scientific use now. "Be not
anxious about tomorrow, for tomorrow will be anxious for itself" is not
bad methodology. For indeed, today's explanation will not be shown
tomorrow to be false; rather, it will be rejected tomorrow because the
weight of evidence we will have by tomorrow is against it. It is proper
to require that what is used to explain be true, but the application of this
criterion is always in terms only of confirmations of some degree or
other.

7. Explanations are *intermediate:* every explanation is in turn subject
to being explained. As I have already pointed out, the circumstance that
what we adduce for an explanation is not self-evident—at least, not so
in a logical sense—does not mean that the explanation is not truly
explanatory. But if this caution is not kept in mind, the danger is that
we either demand of explanations what they cannot give, or else deceive
ourselves into supposing that an explanation is beyond question when all
it has done is answer our questions about what it is explaining. There is
a widespread notion that the hierarchy of explanations must ultimately
ascend to a final comprehensive theory which is itself as ineluctable as a
brute matter of fact—the cast of the dice by which God chose this world
out of all possible worlds. Like all myths of first and last things, this
myth too may give comfort and a sense of closure. But I do not see that
logic stands in need of such an eschatology. As inquiry proceeds, new
problems open before it however definitive its solution of the old ones.
If the time ever comes when explanations do not in turn ask to be explained, it will be only when we are sitting at God's right hand and
sharing in His infinite understanding.

8. Finally, explanations are *limited:* they are appropriate to particular
contexts in which they serve as explanations, not to every possible circumstance of inquiry. Being limited is not the same as being conditional,

spoken of in (2) above. That an explanation is conditional means that it applies *to* certain situations and not to others; that it is limited means that it applies *in* certain situations and not in others. The difference is a question, not of what we can explain by an explanation, but of when that explanation is the relevant one. Being conditional has to do with the restricted circumstances in which it is a sound explanation, being limited with those in which it is a relevant one. Thus, explanations are sometimes of an inappropriate "level": Why does this man experience nausea at the sight of pancakes? Because such and such neurophysiological processes are initiated. To be sure; but what we may be asking is why they are initiated—what do pancakes mean to him, what do they unconsciously symbolize? Every sort of explanation is limited, not just because it is partial or inconclusive or the rest, but because for each explanation there are contexts of inquiry in which questions arise which it does not even begin to answer.

It would be only consistent for me to remark that this list of ways in which explanations can be open is itself an open set; no doubt there are others, and in a more precise formulation not all of them would be quite distinct from one another. Moreover, it may be that not all explanations are open in all these ways at once, or at any rate, that not all of these attributes are equally significant in any given case. The point is that the attainment of acceptable explanations is not the accumulation of eternal and absolute truths; we have not, in attaining them, laid another brick on the edifice, not fitted another piece into the mosaic. What has happened is that we have found something which serves the ends of inquiry at a particular time and place; we have gotten hold of an idea which we can do something with—not to set our minds at rest but to turn their restlessness into productive channels. Explanations do not provide us with something over and above what we can put to some use, and this statement is as true of understanding as it is of prediction. Making due allowances for the prevailing cognitive style at the turn of the century, I think this same statement gives the tenor of Hertz's remark about the explanation or lack of it available in his day for electromagnetic phenomena: "Maxwell's theory is nothing else than Maxwell's equations. That is, the question is not whether these equations are pictural, that is, can be interpreted mechanistically [what was then acceptable as an explanation], but only

whether pictural conclusions can be derived from them which can be
tested by means of gross mechanical experiments" (quoted in *44*:140).

On this basis, explanations can be classified in another way than as
deductive or patterned, providing predictions or understanding. Instead
of asking *how* we explain we might ask *why*, decide what makes ideas
explanatory not on the basis of what they do but on the basis of what we
do with them. Note that this difference is another matter than is involved
in viewing the deductive and pattern models of explanation as different
reconstructions rather than different types of explanation. I am saying,
not only that methodologists can view explanations in different ways,
but also that scientists may be viewing them differently in different circumstances, and be dealing with them, therefore, in correspondingly different ways.

TECHNOLOGICAL FUNCTION

The most familiar and most often discussed function of explanations is
the *technological:* they are used for a better adaptation to the environment,
a more effective adjustment of available means to desired ends. In so
far as explanation makes prediction possible we can control events,
or at least prepare ourselves for what is to come if we are helpless to
prevent it. In so far as explanation provides understanding we can better orient ourselves, choose more wisely among the courses of action
open to us. The technological function, in short, is that conveyed in the
proposition that knowledge is power.

INSTRUMENTAL FUNCTION

We can produce results, however, not just by applying knowledge but
even by merely communicating it. An effect can be produced by helping
others see an explanation, even regardless of whether they have one.
We may call this the *instrumental* function of explanation, though strictly
speaking it is a function of the act of explaining and not of the explanation itself. When someone has been brought to see an explanation he will
in general behave otherwise than he would without an explanation, or
with a different one. A particular explanation, therefore, may be adduced
in a certain context because it is expected to have such an effect. This
expectation is of obvious importance in the practice of politics, psycho-

therapy, salesmanship, education, counseling, administration, and even religion.

Where the instrumental function of explanation is explicitly recognized by methodologists it is likely to be disparaged as unscientific, or at best, as extrascientific. Yet the technological function—that explanations can be *applied* to achieve ends external to the context of inquiry—is regarded as even defining the scientific status of the explanation. The difference is that in order to perform its technological function an explanation must be sound or correct in some measure, while it need not be so for its instrumental function. For the latter it is enough if the persons to whom the explanation is addressed see an explanation, whether or not they really have one. If the instrumental function also depends on some measure of truth for effectiveness, this truth is not a logical necessity. What is called for is plausibility rather than truth, and while usually it is easier to make the truth plausible than any falsehood, this is, alas, by no means always the case.

Yet, when an explanation is about the behavior of those to whom it is addressed, plausibility and truth are more intimately connected, for both what makes the explanation sound and what makes it acceptable to the hearer are embedded in one and the same matrix of personal experience. Some such considerations play an important part in the Marxist idea of class consciousness, as well as in the psychoanalytic concepts of resistance and of insight. The situation is further complicated by the self-fulfilling effect: an explanation may *become* a sound one because it is felt to be plausible by the people whom the explanation is about. I believe that there is important work to be done in examining the conditions under which explanations effectively perform an instrumental function, and the bearings of this effectiveness on their scientific acceptability.

HEURISTIC FUNCTION

Finally, explanations also have a *heuristic* function, stimulating and guiding further inquiry. This function may be analyzed, I suppose, as a special case of the other two: the explanation is being applied to the materials of new problematic situations, and because of the effect on the scientist of his seeing that explanation. "Heuristic" is not to be contrasted with "explanatory": it describes one of the ways in which explanations work. The term, to be sure, is often applied to explanations which are inadequate in one way or another, as though to say that if they are good for nothing else the scientist himself might be able to make some use of them! All explanations, indeed, are more or less inadequate, in the various respects listed earlier; they are all in some degree what Hempel has usefully called "explanation sketches". But to say of an explanation that it is serviceable in the further course of inquiry should be regarded as very far from damning it with faint praise; the best in this kind are but shadows.

It seems to me that for some time behavioral science has been too much concerned with weeding out "pseudo explanations" and not enough concerned with making the most for inquiry of what any explanation is capable of. I do not doubt that there is much obscurantism abroad, and that many runic explanations are preferred to scientific ones. But so far as I can see, this state of affairs is incomparably more characteristic of our society at large, and even of its molders of opinion, than it is of serious students of human behavior, whatever their method or approach. Behavioral scientists might be better advised to elevate the standards of explanation which are used, not by their coworkers of different persuasions, but by those outside the scientific enterprise who give their work—or withhold from it—so much of its human significance.

§42. *Explanation in Behavioral Science*

MEANING AND INTERPRETATION

Behavioral science is occupied with what people do, but the "what" is subject to two very different kinds of specification. We may talk about it as a set of acts—biophysical operations, movements, or events; or we may talk about it as a set of actions—the acts in the perspectives of the actors, expressing certain attitudes and expectations, and thereby having a certain social and psychological significance. In terms of such perspectives we may speak of the meaning of an act, what it signifies to the actor or to those with whom he is interacting; this is what I have called "act meaning" (§4). An action is an act with a certain act meaning, an operation considered in a particular perspective, as voting is the act of marking a ballot when this is performed in the framework of certain political institutions. The question whether perspectives can in turn be described in terms of acts—that is, whether meaning can be given a purely behavioral analysis—is irrelevant to the distinction being drawn; if they can, we can say that an action is an act considered as a component of a certain complex of other acts. Thus a "hit" in baseball is not merely the impact of the bat on the ball, but one that imparts a sufficient speed or distance in a certain direction, and that takes place under the complex of conditions defining a game of baseball. It does not matter whether these conditions can be described in wholly biophysical terms (where the pitcher stands, how far the bases are, and so on); "a hit" has a meaning not involved when the term refers just to the impact.

Actions also are said to have meaning, in quite another sense. Here we are talking about their significance, not for the actors, but for the scientists studying the actions (who may, of course, incidentally include the actors themselves). "Action meaning" is that provided by the perspectives of a particular theory or explanation of the action. In this sense, any event, whether a human action or not, can be said to have a meaning. If it is proper to say that the scientist tries to understand a phenomenon, we can also say that he tries to find what meaning it has. The assignment of meaning of either kind, whether to an act or to an action, is often said to be an "explanation", but the difference is preserved by recognizing that the first is a semantic explanation, the second a scientific explanation. An act is paradigmatically the production of certain speech sounds, and the act meaning is what those sounds signify in the language in which they were uttered. An action then consists in saying those things, not just in uttering those sounds (a parrot can perform the same act, but not the same action): the action meaning is the significance that attaches to saying them, according to whatever explanation we adduce to account for their being said. One sort of explanation elucidates the meaning of certain words, the other throws light on the occurrence of certain events that consist in the use of words having those meanings.

Act meaning and action meaning correspond to two senses of the term "interpretation", a wider and a narrower sense. In the wider sense, an interpretation is the assignment of either an act meaning or an action meaning; in the narrower sense, it is both. An interpretation construes an act as a certain action, then offers an explanation of the action. But these two processes are easily confused with one another. It is often tacitly assumed that as soon as we understand the act, we have thereby arrived at an understanding of the action. The first interpretation is usually easy to come by, especially if we are members of the same culture as the actor and so speak the same "language"—for a wide range of acts and not just the acts of speech. But it is a very different matter to arrive at an understanding of the action, a scientific explanation on the basis of suitable laws or theories of behavior, or of some comprehensive pattern into which the action can be fitted. On the other hand, there are those whose methodological scruples have led them to repudiate act meanings altogether, absorbing them into action meanings, so as to avoid the dangers of confusing the two. This is the position of doctrinaire behaviorists, for example; on this view, explanations which refer to motives or functions are entirely precluded.

It is important to recognize that, although the interpretation of an act provides a "semantic" explanation and the interpretation of an action a "scientific" one, both processes are scientific in the sense of being subject to empirical controls. That it is usually easy to understand an act does not imply that we are not relying on observation and experience, or that we could not possibly be mistaken. For that matter, that the interpretation of an action requires adducing some appropriate general form or pattern does not imply that the adducing is always laboriously self-conscious. It is not that we are proceeding in two different ways but that we are tackling two different sorts of problems, the second incorporating problems of the first kind as constituents. Discovering what certain sounds mean to those who utter and hear them calls for methods which are indistinguishable from those needed to discover an acceptable explanation for the utterance of sounds having those meanings. To be sure, different *techniques* may prove useful in the two cases; for example, questioning the speaker is ordinarily much more useful in arriving at a semantic explanation (that is, an explanation of the speech act) than in arriving at a scientific explanation (that is, an explanation of the action constituted by the saying of those things)—a speaker usually knows what he meant to say far better than he knows what he was up to in saying it.

Because in so much of behavioral science acts are interpreted as actions, and because what interpretation is made depends on the understanding of the interpreter and not just of the actor, the objectivity of the whole undertaking is mistakenly impugned. The point usually arises in connection with the methodology of history. I think it is true, as G. H. Mead argued, that the past must be reconstructed always in terms of the present—our knowledge of the past, that is to say, can be based only on present evidence. In this sense, then, each present has its own past, differing from the pasts of earlier presents not only incrementally but throughout, for our knowledge of the past grows not only by extension but by intension as well; in particular, the same acts may come to be interpreted as different actions. The fixed and unchanging past is a fiction or, better, a construction, like the "true length" of a body, an idealization from the varying magnitudes arrived at in a continuing process of measurement. History, therefore, can have a technological function, enabling us, as Dewey puts it, to deal with the problems of the emerging future, that is, those emerging out of the present in which the history is written; and it can have an instrumental function as well, itself playing a part in the historical process as "ideology" or "utopia". It does not follow, however, that these exhaust its functions, that history has no standing as a repository of fact in the strict scientific sense.

To be sure, the historian does not provide us with a picture of the past, a representation of it "as it really was" apart from any interpretations of his own; but neither does any other scientist with respect to his subject-matter. What a science provides is not an account free of *any* interpretation, but one free of arbitrary or projective interpretations. That the historian must engage in a process of interpretation even to arrive at what are distinctively his data does not mean that his findings are doomed to subjectivity. "When we really get down to the hard facts," it has been said (Becker, in 93:124–125), "what the historian is always dealing with is an affirmation. . . . For all practical purposes it is this affirmation about the event [the interpretation of an act as a certain action] that constitutes for us the historical fact. If so the historical fact is not the past event, but a symbol which enables us to re-create it imaginatively." Well and good; but the literary critic's old distinction between "imagination" and "fancy" might well be given a new application here. Everything hinges on the objective ground for the imaginative re-creation which is offered.

Indeed, the interpretation of an act as constituting a particular action, or of a sequence of acts as constituting a particular historical process or event, has much in common with the interpretation of a work of art. In practice there may be wide divergencies in interpretation, but admitting this is far from saying that anything goes. An interpretation may be based on direct knowledge of the perspectives in which the act was performed, as when the artist himself tells us what he had in mind. It may be based on knowledge of the conventions of action in that society, as when we are familiar with the stylizations in the work of art. It may find support in the coherence of the meanings it assigns, as when a certain interpretation of one stanza of a poem is justified by what appears in other stanzas. It may be preferred to other interpretations because of its comprehensiveness, because it makes sense of so much more of the work of art than alternative interpretations. It may be pressed upon us by a convergence of evidence from a variety of sources, as when folklore, philology, biography, and psychoanalysis all point to the same iconography. And that the same interpretation is made by a variety of interpreters is also a circumstance of some weight in both history and art criticism— intersubjectivity is at least a mark of the objective.

Many other methodological problems concerning explanations in behavioral science stem from the complex interrelations between the two sorts of interpretation—of acts and of actions; it is easy to understand why they are so often confused with one another. In particular, the behavioral scientist often makes use of what might be called the *circle of interpretation:* act meanings are inferred from actions and are then used in the explanation of the actions, or actions are construed from the acts and then used to explain the acts. Thus Collingwood (*21*:214) has said about the historian that "when he knows what happened he already knows why it happened", which has been paraphrased (*51*:186 n) as saying that the historian "is not concerned with 'mere events' (physical movements of people) but with the thoughts expressed in them. These, for the historian, are an essential part of 'what happened', and in discovering them he at one and the same time explains another part of 'what happened', the 'mere events' (physical movements)". Here actions are invoked to explain acts, though observations (evidence) of the acts may have been necessary to learn that these were the actions. Conversely, a psychoanalyst, say, may interpret an act (like compulsive hand washing) as constituting a certain action (the expiation of an unconscious burden of guilt), then justify the interpretation by referring to such acts. The circle of interpretation, however, is not necessarily a vicious one;

as has been said in another connection, everything depends on the diameter of the circle. We move from some acts to certain actions, and thereby explain other acts, of from some actions to certain acts and thereby explain other actions. It is how many of these others are brought in, and how smoothly and naturally, which gives substance to the proferred explanations.

PURPOSE, FUNCTION, AND MOTIVATION

What is characteristic, then, of explanations in behavioral science is that they make use of interpretations in the narrow sense. This is also true, though to a much lesser degree, of biological science; in physical science the distinction between acts and actions has no ground, and the interpretations called for thus have nothing to do with semantic explanation—they are interpretations only in the wide sense. In a word, behavioral science, and to some extent biological science as well, make use of *purposive explanations*. In these explanations, acts are given (or found to have) a meaning, and this meaning then enters as an essential constituent of the explanations offered for the resultant actions. The reconstruction of purposive explanations is not necessarily limited to the pattern model. It is true that the assignment of act meanings puts the acts into a pattern, but how the actions are thereafter construed—that is, how they are interpreted in the context of a scientific explanation, not a semantic one—is an open question. The deductive model can make as good use of premises referring to purposes as the pattern model can of configurations of purposive behavior.

When an act is given a meaning it is interpreted as an action directed toward some end (though it may be an end realized in the action itself—as when an act is interpreted as being playful, for example). All act meaning, as I see it, is purposive, though this statement is by no means necessarily true of all action meaning. (The latter would be the view of certain theologies and metaphysics, for which the course of events is the fulfillment of God's purposes, the self-realization of an Absolute, and the like.) Acts that are not in some sense goal directed are precisely those, it seems to me, that are designated as meaningless. The goals, however, need not be previsioned by the actor; we may distinguish, in Dewey's phrase, between "ends" and "ends-in-view". A purposive explanation, if it makes reference to goals that the actor in some sense thinks of beforehand, may be called a *motivational explanation*, and otherwise a *functional explanation*. Goals unconsciously aimed at are treated sometimes as ends, sometimes as ends-in-view. It is my impression that for psychoanalysis the functional explanations are the more basic, but there is a tendency to formulate them always as though they were motivational: when a person acts to fulfill purposes of which he is unaware, a fictitious agent is introduced (like the "censor") to whom unconscious motives are then ascribed. I believe that the failure to appreciate this transposition of ends is responsible for the naive view of an "unconscious idea" as a contradiction in terms. I would say that the reality of the unconscious consists in the usefulness of motivational explanations of purposive behavior that does not have corresponding ends-in-view.

At any rate, I have no doubt that motivational explanations play an important part in a great deal of behavioral science, as in references to power struggles or the maximization of utility. From a methodological point of view, the objection to motivational explanations is not that they are intrinsically unscientific but that they are so often overextended and misapplied. The purposes at work may call for functional rather than motivational explanations. Functional explanations are appropriate to a great deal of animal behavior, if not to all; the imputation of motives here constitutes an anthropomorphism (which, however, is often only a manner of speaking, and not necessarily objectionable). In human affairs, the wholesale imputation of motives generates the so-called "conspiratorial theory" of society: whatever happens, it is because someone wanted it to happen, planned it that way. There is nothing "pseudo" about such explanations; they are just manifestly false, overlooking the enormous role of unanticipated and even unintended consequences of most actions, to say nothing of natural processes apart from our actions altogether. What sustains these explanations is not evidence but the secondary gain of personification, which makes such explanations so easy to see: they provide a locus for identifications and loyalties, or a target for hostilities. "The Hoover depression" thus constitutes, not merely a distinguishing label, like "the Victorian age", but an implied assignment of responsibility, as in "the Napoleonic wars".

Similar objections can be raised against functional explanations, not as such, but as being too widely applied. Corresponding to the "conspiratorial theory" is what might be called the "utilitarian theory" of society: everything in it serves a purpose. This position is somewhat less objectionable when interpreted historically: what does not now serve a purpose once did. But it seems to me that the universal generalization is maintained in the face of occasional conflicting evidence, and the more frequent absence of confirming evidence, by inventing social needs as required in order to provide a purpose. Institutions are as subject to historical accident and to the constraints of a nonpurposive natural order as are the patterns of personal action. At any rate, I do not see that to explain any item of culture *means* (as claimed by Malinowski, quoted in 53:282) to indicate its functional place within an institution. It may have no such place, and be explained by reference to whatever other circumstances brought it about.

But I wish to reemphasize that there is nothing intrinsically unscientific about functional explanations where evidence is forthcoming that the behavior in question *is* purposive (at the level of actions and not just of acts). Admittedly, when these explanations are applied to social phenomena rather than to individual behavior, they are often formulated in motivational terms, with "society", "culture", "institutions", and the like being spoken of as having motives just as individuals do. But this kind of formulation again may be only a manner of speaking, like the biologist's anthropomorphic locutions. Saying that society erects prisons in order to protect itself from criminals is no more objectionable, methodologically, than saying that a chameleon changes color in order to protect itself from predators. In both cases, the motivational idiom has a functional base, and "protective coloration" is a perfectly good explanatory concept. In the case of the penal system, the functional explanation may be objectionable, not because it is purposive, but because it has not addressed itself to other purposes which may also be at work, like protecting other members of society from the eruption of their own criminal impulses.

Explanations in behavioral science that do not make reference to purposes are sometimes called "structural explanations". But the two types are not necessarily mutually exclusive, to say nothing of not conflicting with one another (117:186). Functionalism need not be taken as a theory either of society (everything in it is purposive) or of behavioral science (only functional explanations are acceptable). It may be viewed as a program of inquiry, a set of methodological prescriptions: to find an explanation for a given pattern of behavior look first to the purposes it might be serving. This approach does not imply, however, that the explanation then arrived at will necessarily be a purposive one. The search for the ends of an action may lead to an identification of the configurations ("structures") with which it is bound up by causal laws. When certain acts are understood as a search for food we may be in a better position to discover what stimuli evoke those responses. Similarly, when certain behavior patterns are interpreted as defense mechanisms it may be easier to discover how they are learned; when we find the functions performed by an institution perhaps we can more easily discover the social forces which maintain it.

I believe that the most common objection to purposive explanations as such amounts to no more than this, that such explanations are not causal, and it is taken for granted that only causal explanations are scientific. It seems to me that there is something pre-Darwinian about this point of view, for what Darwin showed was how the purposiveness of adaptations could be accounted for by the mechanics of survival. It was his replacement of final causes by efficient causes that constituted the most radical departure from the world-view of the theologians. Yet purposive explanations were not really replaced by causal ones but were analyzed in causal terms; it is ironic that even the motivational idiom was retained, in such expressions as "natural selection". In the present century the cybernetic analysis of equilibria and of feedback systems has made possible even a mathematical treatment of purposiveness, so that purposive behavior is explained in terms of telic mechanisms rather than the other way around, as used to be done ("water seeks its own level" and "nature abhors a vacuum").

To my mind, the significance for methodology of these developments is not that purposive explanations are ruled out of science, as the mechanistic followers of Newton and Descartes had maintained against the teleologists, but precisely that the opposition between mechanism and teleology can now be seen to be a spurious one. When we explain some goal-directed behavior by reference to its goal we are not thereby assigning to the future a causal efficacy in the present; the causal agency is the present intention to reach a certain state in the future, and the workings of intentions can be described by reference to feedbacks, including symbolic processes. They "can" be so described, I say; but I am afraid that this is one of those possibilities which is affirmed to hold only "in principle". My point is that the acceptability of purposive explanations does not depend upon our actually being able to reduce them to mechanical terms. Purposes belong to nature and can be used to explain other natural phenomena even when we are not in a position to provide in turn an explanation for the purposes. As Braithwaite says (*9*:334–335), purposive explanations are "no less worthy of credence than ordinary causal explanations. . . . It seems ridiculous to deny the title of explanation to a statement which performs both of the functions characteristic of scientific explanations—of enabling us to appreciate connections and to predict the future."

HISTORICAL EXPLANATION

These various questions arising out of the role of purposes in behavior and of interpretations in behavioral science have recently been brought to a focus in the so-called "problem of historical explanation". I agree with the opinion that "there is no such thing as 'historical' explanation, only the explanation of historical events" (Brodbeck in *41*:254). Yet the distinctive subject-matter may reasonably be expected to call for distinctive treatment.

Of all behavioral scientists the historian is among the most dependent upon the transformation of acts into actions. The sheer chronicle of events gives much less substance to history than might be given by a corresponding record of acts to, say, demography, physical anthropology, or learning theory. And the succession of actions is seen by the historian, not as a bare sequence, but as a configuration made meaningful by purposive or causal connections. The process of putting the raw data into such configurations has been called "colligation" (*134*:59), "explaining an event by tracing its intrinsic relations to other events and locating it in its historical context", which is then said to yield a "significant narrative". I should prefer to say that this "colligation" is an "interpretation" of events rather than their "explanation"—not to deny that it is explanatory, but to emphasize that it is act meanings rather than action meanings which have been provided. A significant narrative is like the translation of a speech from a foreign language into one which we understand; the translation explains why those sounds were uttered—

namely, to say just those things—but it does not itself explain why those things were said.

But the further explanation called for may also be purposive. It is true, as Hempel has pointed out (in *53*:282–283) that the mere listing of prior events will not qualify as an explanation, because a criterion of relevance is needed for their selection. But I do not see that relevance must consist in "causal or probabilistic determination", and that explanation must therefore be nomological. We may explain an action by referring it to its motives or functions even though we are not in a position to formulate a generalization concerning the causes or effects of events of that kind. Yet generalizations do occur in history; there is no good reason, in my opinion, to insist that by definition, just because of their generality, they belong rather to sociology, political science, economics, or some other appropriate nonhistorical discipline. As I pointed out in §11, even the identification of particulars as constituting a continuing individual—a person, group, institution, or event—involves certain generalizations.

And where generalizations do occur in history they function in much the same way as in any other science. "The scientific model of precise correlation," it has been said (*50*:60–61), "is misleading in any attempt to comprehend the role of these generalizations in history, where they function frequently as guides to understanding." To my mind, this guidance is their basic function in all scientific explanations. What *is* true, I think, is that the role of generalizations need not be reconstructed in the deductive model of explanation. The pattern model has an advantage here, not because propositions about purposes cannot be made the premises for deductions, but because it is so much easier to speak of a pattern being more or less discernible than it is to speak of a conclusion being more or less entailed. And historical explanations are notably a matter only of more or less. Even if we knew all the historical laws that apply, we are not likely to know all the initial conditions they require. We cannot brush this circumstance aside by calling historical explanations only "explanation sketches", for all explanations are "sketchy"— that is, open—to some extent and in some respects. It is especially true, as Nagel has pointed out (*102*:301–302), that "explanations of particular happenings in the natural sciences face difficulties essentially comparable to those encountered in historical inquiry".

What must be admitted is that certain histories, and those the ones most conspicuous for the large scope and range of their generalizations, have offered explanations so sketchy as to be either empty or plainly contrary to fact, lacking either in meaning or in truth. Any historical process can be represented as a cycle, for example, or as the resultant of several cycles, if the period is unspecified; dialectical materialism supplies another example of a theory of history which enjoys the dubious advantage of a tautological flexibility. Other theories of history—like those singling out the explanatory potential of bedroom, climate, or geography—have the charm of simplicity and the shortcomings of simple-mindedness. Yet even these simplisms may make scientifically significant contributions: as Marx did in giving economic factors so prominent a role; or as Spengler did in countering the parochialism of identifying history with the development of our own culture, or in emphasizing that a culture is a unitary whole and not a congeries of unrelated institutions and practices.

If there is something distinctive about the methodology of history, I believe it arises from the fact that history is so much closer to the arts than other sciences are. The division between the arts and the sciences is, after all, a matter more of our reconstructions, our categories of analysis, than of the enterprises themselves, and in any case this division is a feature of the cognitive styles characteristic of our culture rather than being wholly traceable to the nature of cognition as such. The great historians do not merely explain events but also allow us to see them (47:367). But so doing is not a matter of encasing a cognitive meaning in an emotive one, sugar-coating a factual pill. It seems to me that Collingwood (in 93:76) is quite right in insisting that the historical imagination is properly "not ornamental but structural", that without imagination "the historian would have no narrative to adorn". Only, I would add that something of the kind is true of all science. For the methodologist to imagine otherwise—that creativity belongs only to the psychology of science and not to its logic, that explanations are discovered and not invented, that understanding events is a matter of classifying rather than interpreting them—would only betray his own lack of historical imagination in tracing the course of science itself.

Chapter X

VALUES

§43   Values in Inquiry
§44   Theory of Value
§45   Behavioral Science and Policy
§46   The Future of Behavioral Science

§43. Values in Inquiry

No doubt other generations than our own have felt themselves to be in the grip of "the crisis of our times"; some of them, indeed, were convinced that the world was quite literally coming to an end. It is possible, however, that no other generation has talked about its crisis so much as we have. That values are changing, that they are in conflict, and that they are altogether precarious is now and has been for some time a part of the general consciousness of the age.

THE CONTENTION ABOUT VALUES

What I think might be distinctively our own is not only the extent of this consciousness but also its depth, the fact that its doubts and anxieties are so radical. The term "value"—"that unfortunate child of misery", as Weber (135:107) has called it—has two sorts of meanings (among many others). It may refer to the standards or principles of worth, what makes something have value, or it may refer to the worthy things themselves, the valuables, as it were (I shall be using the term "value" only in the first sense). Now while valuables have often before been felt to be uncertain, whether in possession or attainment, there has not often been any deep and pervasive doubt as to values, that is, as to whether such things are really valuable, really worth having and pursuing. It is this latter that is now very much in question. There have been various philosophers, like the Greek Sophists and the Cārvākas of India, who challenged the basis of the value judgments characteristic of their cultures; but by and large philosophers have been occupied with examining the specific varieties of value, and the conditions, personal or institutional, under which the values can be achieved. In modern times, however, and most notably in contemporary Anglo-American philosophy, there is an almost exclusive preoccupation with the basis of value judgments rather than with their content. We have still some sense of what is true, honorable, just, pure, lovely, or gracious, and we think of these things; but we do not any more really know what we are saying about things when we ascribe to them these excellences.

This condition of the culture has a direct bearing on the situation of the sciences, and especially of behavioral science, which might be expected to be the one most closely concerned with questions of values. Whether in fact or only in the public mind, science is responsible for the value crisis. The technology which it has made possible has produced the great changes that threaten our valuables, and the ways of thinking which it has engendered undermine the very values themselves. There is, therefore, a widespread attitude towards science (or against it, rather) that with regard to values, the policy must be strictly "Hands off!" Science has done enough harm already, and the scientist should be grateful that he is allowed to go on about his business. In thus protecting values *from* science, this attitude gives up the possibility of supporting values *by* science. By limiting reason we may make room for faith, but we have room enough if we have little faith, and who shall supply our lack? Limiting reason is the policy of achieving the security of the value domain by sacrificing freedom—the freedom, that is, to enrich our lives in whatever ways our knowledge and experience show to be open to us.

There is a contrary attitude, often ambivalently associated with the preceding one, that the scientist *must* occupy himself with values. Here it is precisely the attempt by science to abstract the facts from their value matrix which is thought to be most subversive of values. Thus the psychoanalyst is charged with encouraging libertinism because as a theorist his aim and as a therapist his method is to understand the behavior, not to condemn it. Thus an uproar was produced not long ago when a research agency working on a military contract was found to be engaged in a study of surrender situations, as though the study itself compromised the nobility of our old-guard determination to die but not to surrender. Thus studies of the viability of democratic institutions are viewed as their obituaries. Thus countless expressions of similar attitudes can be adduced in connection with inquiries into a variety of matters where important values are at stake, from economic affairs to sexual ones, and beyond—in both directions.

The hands-off policy may express an unconscious fear of the outcome for our values of subjecting them to scientific scrutiny; repression in society may have functions similar to those of the defense mechanism in the individual psyche. It is possible, too, that scientific "objectivity" is felt to be the sin of hubris: Olympian detachment is the prerogative only of the gods. And perhaps it is tacitly (and unreasonably) assumed that to understand everything is to forgive everything. Whatever the causes producing these attitudes, the effect is that from the standpoint of the public the scientist is damned if he takes values into account and is likewise damned if he doesn't.

What I find ironic in this situation is that the scientist himself so often identifies with his aggressors, condemning himself as a scientist if he is concerned with values and as a citizen if he is not. But the distinctive roles can provide refuge only for a quick-change artist: the blows still smart when we have put on a new hat. I venture to say that most scientists today, in the free world at any rate, embrace the ideal of a value-free science: they might apply the term "science" also to certain normative disciplines, but properly speaking they regard only "positive" (that is, nonnormative) science as truly scientific. If the student of politics, for example, sets forth a conception of good government or of good society, what he has produced is a political doctrine, not a contribution to political science, whatever the considerations he advances to support his conception. The values may be introduced more or less subtly; Aristotle does not sketch an ideal republic, as Plato does, yet values are basic to his analysis of natural and perverted or degenerate forms of polity. A true scientist, so it is supposed, regards everything as "natural", and he asks only for the conditions under which politics takes one direction or another.

The thesis I want to defend is that not all value concerns are unscientific, that indeed some of them are called for by the scientific enterprise itself, and that those which run counter to scientific ideals can be brought under control—even by the sciences most deeply implicated in the value process.

BIAS

Let me use the term *bias* for adherence to values of such a kind or in such a way as to interfere with scientific objectivity, and let me use it without prejudging whether scientific objectivity requires that science be absolutely value-free. Then, by definition, bias is methodologically objectionable, but the question is still open whether values play a part in the scientific enterprise only as biases. I shall want to answer this question in the negative, and to insist further that this wish is not a matter merely of my own bias.

Typical instances of bias are provided by historians of wars, where the standpoints of the victor and the vanquished yield very different accounts, beginning even with the name of the conflict ("the War Between the States"). And it is a commonplace that bias is more or less easily identifiable in many studies of political, social, or economic problems. We may describe bias in general as a kind of inverse of the genetic fallacy: a proposition is accepted or rejected, not on the basis of its origin, but on the basis of its outcome. It is believed or not according to whether our values would be better served if it were true than if it were false. Of course, this anticipated outcome is not adduced as a reason for the belief, but it operates as a cause of the believing. Indeed, the process is often and even characteristically unconscious. There have been many earnest and hard-headed inquirers into the phenomena of parapsychology; there is at least a possibility that some of them are receptive to positive findings, in spite of themselves, as it were, because of the bearings of such findings on unconscious anxieties about death or on guilts about our less "spiritual" impulses. (It is not to be overlooked that such criticisms, made without regard to specific evidence giving them warrant, may themselves reflect bias.) Freud argued that rejection of his views is traceable to the very resistance which plays such an important part in psycho-analytic theory. Clearly, there is a danger that such charges of unconscious bias can impede the establishment of a truth or the refutation of a mere fancy; but the charges may be logically defensible nevertheless in both sorts of cases.

All propositions, to be sure, are judged on the basis of their implications, and not just in terms of what they entail but also in terms of what they make more likely. What constitutes bias is that the will to believe is motivated by interests external to the context of inquiry itself. I find it useful to distinguish between the scientist's motives and his purposes: *motives* concern the relation between the scientific activity and the whole stream of conduct of which it is a part; *purposes* relate the activities of inquiry to the particular scientific problem which they are intended to solve. (This distinction can also be usefully applied in esthetics, especially in connection with the view which confuses artistic expressiveness with the artist's "self-expression".) Thus a scientist's motives may include the love of country, or of money, or of glory; his purposes must be specified in terms of the particularities of the problem in which he is engaged: to show that a given phenomenon is subject to certain laws, or that a given explanation can be extended to a certain other class of cases, or the like. Various purposes may serve any motive, and various motives may be involved in the decision to fulfill a particular purpose. Bias might be defined as the intrusion of motives, which are extra-scientific, on the fulfillment of scientific purposes.

A beautiful if somewhat analogical instance is described by Edward Lasker, who played a game of chess against a grandmaster at an exposition, where the board was many yards square and the pieces were appropriately costumed young ladies. In the course of the game Lasker gradually realized that his opponent was most reluctant to exchange queens, a tactical weakness in the play of the game which was later explained by the circumstance that a captured piece left for the day, while the grandmaster was most anxious to enjoy afterwards the company of the white queen. Interests external to the play of the game interfered with an objective assessment of the position on the board, or at least, with the choice of the move such an assessment would indicate. It may be worth adding that motivations can contribute to the fulfillment of purposes as well as to their defeat, as Ernest Jones has elaborated in just this context in his analysis of the great chess play,er Paul Morphy.

I believe that it is the distinction between motives and purposes which underlies the appeal so often made to the difference between the role of the scientist and the role of the citizen, religionist, father, lover, or whatever. Yet each of these roles may define its own purposes, which are not to be confused with the motives that govern the choice of the role in question. There are right ways and wrong ways to do everything, whatever the reasons we may have for doing it.

Bias, then, is not constituted merely by having motives, that is, by subscribing to values which are somehow involved in the scientific situation. Everything depends on the conduct of the inquiry, on the way in which we arrive at our conclusions. Freedom from bias means having an open mind, not an empty one. At the heart of every bias is a prejudice, that is to say, a prejudgment, a conclusion arrived at prior to the evidence and maintained independently of the evidence. It is true that what serves as evidence is the result of a process of interpretation—facts do *not* speak for themselves; nevertheless, facts must be given a hearing, or the scientific point to the process of interpretation is lost. Describe to someone what appears to be the favorable outcome of an experiment on telepathy; he will say that the proportion of successes or the number of cases was too small to be significant. Ask him to suppose that ten times as many cases were taken, and that the results were ten times as favorable; he will suggest that trickery was involved. Continue with the supposition that this is ruled out by the character and integrity of the subjects as well as the investigators, and he will postulate responses to unconscious cues. And if you say, suppose the conditions of the experiment preclude this effect (the subjects being in widely separated rooms, and so on), he will propound some other possible explanation. But at some point, what he *should* say is, "*If* the inquiry and its results *were* as you hypothetically describe them to be, I would believe in telepathy!" The prejudice is betrayed in the determination to adhere to a certain belief no matter what evidence is brought forward. It is this determination or an approximation to it, and not merely having an interest in one conclusion rather than another, which constitutes bias.

There is no doubt that in the history of science biases of this kind, both more and less blatant, have played a significant role. Identifications with race, class, or nation have made themselves known not just in arguments over priority of discovery but also in decisions as to which theories are acceptable and even which facts are established—nor is this failing limited to such doctrinaires as the Nazis and the Communists. In behavioral science, the scale of radicalism-conservatism may well be "the master scale of biases" (*99*:1038), affecting both the problems chosen for treatment and the conclusions drawn about whether and how they are to be solved. And everywhere in the scientific enterprise power structures develop, whose interests may have as much effect on the course of inquiry, or at least on the assessment of its outcome, as is exerted by comparable forces on the workings of other enterprises. The influence of the Academy may be as objectionable in science as it is in art. Even the culture as a whole has been a massive source of bias, as it no doubt continues to be; and for behavioral science it is especially true, as Boring put it (in *46*:195), that "what may be said of the big *Zeitgeist* may also be said of the little *Zeitgeister* of schools and of the egoist who has no following. They have their inflexible attitudes and beliefs, their loyalties that are prejudices, and their prejudices that are loyalties."

Every scientist is committed to resisting bias wherever he encounters it, and if we see that he is keen to detect the mote in his neighbor's eye, let us remember that he in turn is *our* neighbor, and beware of judging him. Fortunately, science does not demand that bias be eliminated but only that our judgment take it into account. It can be treated as we are accustomed to deal with errors of observation: we insulate ourselves from them where we can, and otherwise try to cancel their effects or at any rate to discount them. Bias is discounted as a matter of course, for example, when we read a "news" story of the size of a political rally or demonstration, or when we find certain film critics useful because we invariably detest what they recommend. And bias can also be canceled out, as was done by the arbitrator adjudicating a dispute, who returned part of the bribe given him by one of the litigants because the other side had given him a smaller sum.

I believe that the profound significance for science of freedom of thought and its expression is this, that only thereby can we hope to cancel bias. The power structures in science can be relied on to serve the general welfare of the scientific community only if they are subject to some system, however, informal, of checks and balances, so that what is rejected by one journal or professional association may find acceptance in another. Perhaps even more important is what Derek Price has called the "invisible university" of our time, constituted by the personal exchange of ideas among highly mobile scientists. That free competition in the marketplace of ideas will invariably yield up the truth may be as much a myth as the more general belief that such a process is the source of every social good. The conflict between freedom and control is an existential dilemma for science, whatever it may be for society at large. Yet for science, at any rate, it seems to me that reason requires that we push always for freedom, freedom even for the thought which we enlightened ones so clearly see to be mistaken.

The question may now be considered whether values play any part in the scientific enterprise in ways which do not necessarily constitute bias. I believe that they do, and in a number of different ways.

VALUES AS SUBJECT-MATTER

To start with, values occur as subject-matter for scientific investigation. In this capacity they do not in the least make for bias, because what is being inquired into is their existence, not their validity (135:39). We ask what values are held by various persons and groups, under what conditions and with what effect, and plainly, no answer that we give in itself commits us to sharing or rejecting those values. To be sure, our answer may be a biased one; but if so, the bias is due to *our* values and not to the values of those whom we have been investigating, even if they coincide. It may be hard to recognize that other people have values different from our own, but for that matter it may be just as hard to recognize that other people have beliefs different from ours. To be sure also, if we find that the values we are studying have certain conditions or consequences we may thereby be induced to change some values of our own, so that the prospect of such a change may subtly affect our findings; but again, this influence may apply equally with respect to subject-matters which are not themselves valuational.

The fundamental point is that a proposition affirming something about values is different from a valuation—unless what is being affirmed is precisely the *value* of those values, that is, their validity or worth. Let me call such affirmations *value judgments*; they constitute a special class of judgments about values, namely, those for which making the judgment expresses the judger's own values. Plainly, not every statement which we make about someone's values says something about our own; the statement may be a "factual" one, as it is called, even if it is about values. The recurrent difficulty here is that it is not always easy to see just what a statement does say in this respect, and even the man making it may be unclear in his own mind. The language of behavioral science is often marked by *normative ambiguity*, allowing for interpretation both as reporting a value and as making a valuation. This ambiguity is obviously present in statements about what is "normal" or "natural", but it may also be present in such less obvious cases as "lawful" or "rational". What is worse, normative ambiguity is only temporarily removed, at best, by changing notations. As Myrdal has warned (*99*: 1063–1064), "In the degree that the new terms would actually cover the facts we discussed in the old familiar terms—the facts which we want to discuss, because we are interested in them—they would soon become equally value-loaded in a society permeated by the same ideals and interests". Talk about "deviant" behavior, for example, has by now about as much normative ambiguity as the old-fashioned talk about "abnormal" behavior.

There are certain propositions about values that unequivocally appear to be making valuations—they seem unambiguously normative—yet are actually factual in content. Nagel (*103*: 492–493) calls them "characterizing value judgments", affirming that "a given characteristic is in some degree present (or absent) in a given instance", and contrasts them with "appraising value judgments", which conclude that "some envisaged or actual state of affairs is worthy of approval or disapproval". Thus, we can say that someone is a "good Nazi" without necessarily meaning thereby that being a Nazi is in any way good; we are saying only that certain characteristics are present in that instance without committing ourselves as to whether they are worthy of approval. That this distinction is not an absolute one will be argued in discussing the ethics of the profession, below. But it can usefully be made relative to any given context. Although appraisals may entail certain characteristics, we can characterize without appraising, Nagel insists; at any rate, we can surely characterize without then and there making appraisals of just those things being characterized. We can judge that something conforms to a certain standard without making *that* standard our own, even though the judgment may presuppose our own standards of what conformity is.

VALUES IN THE ETHICS OF THE PROFESSION

Values occur in a second way in science without making for bias, as constituting the ethics of the profession; here, indeed, they work to eradicate bias, or at least to minimize it and to mitigate its effects. That certain professional pursuits have moral prerequisites is beyond question; I am saying, in the broadest sense of the term "moral", the same of scientific pursuits. In our society it is usually taken for granted that moral prerequisites will be satisfied by those entering politics, medicine, or the church, and that such prerequisites are absent or irrelevant for the army, business, and the law. Science, like the philosophy from which it sprang, has an equivocal status. The love of wisdom or truth is a virtue, yet the first sin was eating of the fruit of the tree of knowledge, and the myth of Faust—that those who seek knowledge sell their souls to the Devil—is thought by many, especially today, to convey a dismal reality.

Yet the expression "a good scientist", as used by scientists themselves, seems to me rather more like "a good man" than like "a good Nazi": it embodies a valuation, conveying an appraisal rather than merely a characterization. Being a scientist in itself commits a man to the values embodied in being a good one. We might say that science is a calling and not an occupation only, or at any rate, that it cannot flourish if it is always an occupation only. And the difference between these two sorts of pursuit lies in this, that we choose an occupation while a calling chooses us; we are impelled to the calling from within, which is to say that we are committed to its values. To be sure, all purposive behavior has its own goals and therefore its own values. But in the case of an occupation the values enter only into the purpose (in the narrow sense introduced earlier), and not also into the motives. The values are operative only in the limited context of the purposive behavior, but the purpose which the behavior is to fulfill may have no intrinsic importance, calling for no emotional investments and not reaching beyond the peripheral regions of the personality.

But the passion for truth is just that—a passion: and the thirst for knowledge may be as insistent and provide as deep satisfactions as do needs less specifically human. To follow his calling, even to do his work, a scientist must have what Aristotle called the "intellectual virtues"; and he must not only have them, but also regard them as virtues, that is, seek and cherish them. In a word, they must be his values.

Thus, the scientific habit of mind is one dominated by the reality principle, by the determination to live in the world as it is and not as we might fantasy it. For the scientist, ignorance is never bliss. A robust sense of reality, in William James's phrase, is above all a willingness to face life with open eyes, whatever may confront our sight. The scientist is humble before the facts, submitting his will to their decision, and accepting their judgment whatever it might be. This humility of his is counterpoised by integrity and honesty, by the courage of his convictions, and—if I may paraphrase—by firmness in the truth as God gives him to see the truth, and not as it is given him by tradition, by the Academy, or by the powers that be. And there is a certain distinctive scientific temper, marked by judiciousness and caution, care and conscientiousness. How far all this view is from the model—or rather, the myth—of science as the work of a disembodied, unfeeling intellect! Surely these attributes of the scientist are all virtues, in the scientist's judgment, as well as in our own; and surely the possession of these virtues is a value to which the scientist has wholeheartedly committed himself.

It is true that what I have described is only an "ideal type", something to which actual scientists only approximate in some degree. But it is nevertheless also an ideal, something to which they aspire. For a man to have a certain value it is not required that he have attained what is in that respect valuable—even the sinner may acknowledge the claims of righteousness. It is also true, as Weber (*135*:110) reminds us, that "the belief in the value of scientific truth is the product of certain cultures and is not a product of man's original nature". How and why the scientific mentality arose when it did is an important question. I think myself that a religious attitude—a sense of awe and wonder, and a spirit of dedication—may have played a more positive role than is often recognized. Were there a Scientist's Oath it might well quote from Job: "As long as my breath is in me and the spirit of God is in my nostrils, my lips will not speak falsehood and my tongue will not utter deceit." But whether or not science is in the fullest sense a calling, it has a professional ethics which it seems to me methodology cannot completely ignore.

There is also a *metaprofessional ethics* (not to be confused with the "metaethics" which philosophers today profess), a set of values concerning, not the conduct of inquiry, but the contexts in which it is carried out. The metaprofessional values consist of the commitments to create and maintain conditions under which science can exist—for instance, freedom of inquiry, of thought, and of its expression. Such values are particularly important to the behavioral scientist, for it is he who suffers most from restrictions on those freedoms. If metaprofessional ethics is a matter of self-interest, at any rate the self as scientist is the self being served. But there is no need to be victimized here by our own idealizations; scientists are as subject to human failings as the rest of us are. (Academic freedom, for instance, is not always matched by academic responsibility, and scientists may be more concerned with the priority of discovery than with its significance.) Yet these are admittedly failings. In short, that a scientist has values does not of itself imply that he is therefore biased; it may mean just the contrary.

VALUES IN THE SELECTION OF PROBLEMS

Values enter into science, in the third place, as a basis for the selection of problems, the order in which they are dealt with, and the resources expended on their solution. Weber (*135*:21) seems to contrast "the social sciences" with "the empirical disciplines" in that the problems of the former "are selected by the value-relevance of the phenomena treated". But so may be the problems of any kind of subject-matter. The contrast, if any, is just that behavioral science deals with matters where the values involved are likely to be more conspicuous, and perhaps more widely shared, or more directly affecting many people. Whatever problems a scientist selects, he selects for a reason, and these reasons can be expected to relate to his values, or to the values of those who in one way or another influence his choice.

This obvious point is often obscured, I think, by a too facile distinction between so-called "pure" and "applied" science, as though values are involved only in the latter. In fact, much of what is called "applied" science can be seen as such only in a subsequent reconstruction: a theory is developed in the course of dealing with a problem of so-called "application", it is abstracted from such contexts, then afterwards referred back to them as "applied science". A great deal of science, in other words, is "applied" long before it is "pure". The fact that a scientist has reasons for his choice of problems other than a thirst for knowledge or a love of truth scarcely implies that his inquiry will be biased thereby.

That so much of the research carried on today is subsidized by government and industry does not in itself create new dangers to scientific objectivity: research has always had to be paid for by someone or other The real dangers, its seems to me, lie in the pressures for too quick a return on investments, and perhaps even more in the scarcity of risk capital, the reluctance to depart too far from what the Academy judges to be sound and promising. Artists have long had their patrons and have not for just that reason created bad art. It may even be doubted whether better art might have been produced if they had created only for other artists, or for critics: bohemia is not the sole habitat of genius and integrity. Values make for bias, not when they dictate problems, but when they prejudge solutions.

VALUES AND MEANINGS

Values also play a part in science, and especially in behavioral science, as determinants of the *meanings* which are seen in the events with which it deals. But here the confusion between act meaning and action meaning (§42) is especially dangerous.

Weber, for example, has argued (*135*: 80) that behavioral science cannot even have a subject-matter except as marked out by certain values: "Knowledge of cultural events is inconceivable except on a basis of the significance which the concrete constellations of reality have for us in certain individual concrete situations. In which sense and in which situations this is the case . . . is decided according to the value-ideas in the light of which we view 'culture' in each individual case." Interpretation he then defines (*135*: 143) as the consideration of the "various possible relationships of the object to values". Very well; but the question is, whose values? Cultural events must have a significance, or they are only biophysical occurrences, but in this respect it is not, as he says, the significance which they have for us which matters. It is the significance for the actor (and those interacting with him) which makes an act a determinate action.

Thus, in speaking of mental illness the psychologist is no more dependent on his own values than the pathologist is in speaking of organic illness. It is true that what is a symptom of illness in one culture may not be a symptom of the same condition in another; but it is the culture of the subject which counts here, not the scientist's culture. And the subject's culture counts, not because its values define health and illness, but because they determine the *meaning* of the behavior in question. It is not that what is psychopathic in one culture may not be so in another, but rather that a different "what" is occurring in the two cases. And how "*we* view 'culture' in each individual case" has nothing to do with it. The problem posed by this example is complicated by the normative ambiguity of the terms "health" and "illness", so that a diagnosis may be viewed either as a characterizing judgment or as an appraisal. My point is that before either sort of judgment is made the acts in question must be interpreted, and that for this interpretation our values are not decisive.

With respect to action meaning, however, the situation is quite different. Here it is a matter of the sorts of conceptualizations we will apply, the formulations we will give to the problem, the hypotheses we will entertain, and the theories we will invoke. In all these we are making choices, and our values inescapably play a part. Here it is significance for us which is involved, though this involvement does not make our interpretation pejoratively "subjective" (§44).

[margin note: "Action meaning"]

There is an extensive literature examining the influence on science of various interests and institutions. These range from the most general metaphysical concerns, whose effect is discussed, for instance, by Philipp Frank, E. A. Burtt, F. S. C. Northrop, and others, to the most specific sexual interests studied by Freud and his followers. And in between are a number of other interests (R. S. Cohen in *46*:210): religious, as traced by Weber, Tawney, and Robert Merton; social and technological, as examined in the work of Veblen, Lewis Mumford, and countless others; Marxist economic determinants; political interests and institutions, from Nietzsche's will to power to the studies of Karl Popper and M. Polanyi; and even esthetic concerns, whose implications for science have been pointed to by Bergson, L. L. Whyte, and Herbert Read. To be sure, such factors have often, and perhaps usually, made for bias. Yet they have also another part to play: they do not necessarily predetermine what inquiry will disclose, but give shape and substance to the interpretation of its results.

What I have in mind might be illustrated by the role of key metaphors in various periods of science, the sorts of models which dominate thinking. The eighteenth century was much given to clockwork conceptions, from theology to economics; the nineteenth century, to organismic ideas, from the theory of the state to the application of principles of growth and decay in philology; and the twentieth century, to formulations in terms of the workings of a computer, appearing throughout behavioral science. (These three sorts of models might be said to correspond respectively to the basic categories of matter, energy, and information.) The point is that in most of their application these ways of formulating both problems and solutions are to some degree metaphoric, conceptualizing their subject-matters as though they were something other than what they actually are. But our own metaphors always tend to present themselves to us as literal truths. They are the ways of speaking which make sense to us, not just as being meaningful but as being sensible, significant, to the point. They are basic to semantic explanation and thereby enter into scientific explanation. If there is bias here it consists chiefly in the failure to recognize that other ways of putting things might prove equally effective in carrying inquiry forward. But that we must choose one way or another, and thus give our values a role in the scientific enterprise, surely does not in itself mean that we are methodologically damned.

VALUES AND FACTS

But the judgment whether a particular choice is an effective one is itself in some degree a matter of our values. Whether a particular way of conceptualizing problems yields solutions for them is a question of fact, but values enter into the determination of what constitutes a *fact*. Here is the central issue in the question whether science ought to be, or even can be, value-free. I am not referring to the effect of values on the willingness to embark on an inquiry into a question of fact. Here, indeed, we are likely to encounter bias, as in the refusal of Galileo's colleagues to look through his telescope, or in the difference between British and American attitudes today toward psychic research or investigations of telepathy (or, for that matter, in my own felt need to disclaim any belief in such phenomena whenever I mention them). What is at stake here is the role of values, not in our decisions where to look but in our conclusions as to what we have seen.

Nature might better be spoken of as an obedient child than as a protective mother: she speaks only when spoken to, is often seen but seldom heard. Data come to us only in answer to questions, and it is we who decide not only whether to ask but also how the question is to be put. Every question is a little like the wife-beating one—it has its own presuppositions. It must be formulated in a language with a determinate vocabulary and structure, the contemporary equivalent of Kant's forms and categories of the knowing mind; and it follows upon determinate assumptions and hypotheses, on which the answer is to bear. How we put the question reflects our values on the one hand, and on the other hand helps determine the answer we get. If, as Kant said, the mind is the lawgiver to nature, it also has a share in facts, for these are not independent of the laws in terms of which we interpret and acknowledge their factuality. Data are the product of a process of interpretation, and though there is some sense in which the materials for this process are "given" it is only the product which has a scientific status and function. In a word, data have meaning, and this word "meaning", like its cognates "significance" and "import", includes a reference to values. "The empirical data," says Weber (*135*:111), "are always related to those evaluative ideas which alone make them worth knowing and the significance of the empirical data is derived from these evaluative ideas."

There are behavioral scientists who, in their anxieties about bias, hope to exclude values by eschewing theories altogether, in the spirit (but not in the meaning!) of Newton's "I invent no hypotheses!" They restrict themselves to what they regard as "just describing what objectively happens". But this restriction expresses "the dogma of immaculate perception" all over again (§15). What is thus being attempted simply cannot be done, or if it is done, the outcome is of no scientific significance. There is an interesting parallel here to the position of the esthetes at the turn of the century, who viewed art as a matter of pure form or decoration, at the cost of making of it an idle song for an idle hour, with no significance for anyone but themselves. What is even more basic is that, even if carried out, this program does not succeed in eradicating bias. As Myrdal (*99*:1041) points out, "Biases in social science cannot be erased simply by 'keeping to the facts' and by refined methods of statistical treatment of the data. Facts, and the handling of data, sometimes show themselves even more pervious to tendencies towards bias than does 'pure thought'."

How values enter into the decision as to what the facts are in a given case was discussed in §29; we cannot arrive at such decisions without regard to the payoffs associated with the various sorts of estimates and errors. "Epistemic utility", as such payoffs have been called (Hempel in *41*:153), is, after all, a value, even though of a particular sort; I do not see that its measure can be declared a priori to be independent of other sorts of value. I agree with Frank (*46*:viii) that the validation of theories "can not be separated neatly from the values which the scientist accepts". As I see it, characterizing judgments always presuppose appraisals: we are confronted always with the decision whether, given certain findings, it is worthwhile characterizing something in a certain way, and this worth is not in turn only characterized. There is a reconstruction according to which the ascription of a certain probability on the basis of given evidence is a tautology, so that the only decision to be reached is whether to act on that probability in a given case. But in these terms it is only this decision which embodies an empirical belief, so that even on this reconstruction values enter into the determination of fact.

Nagel has argued (in *90*:193) that "there is no factual evidence to show that the 'content and form' of statements, or the standards of validity employed, are logically determined by the social perspective of an inquirer. The facts commonly cited establish no more than some kind of causal dependence between these items." This argument is sound if "logical determination" has the sense of entailment; indeed, no factual evidence can possibly be given for an entailment. But this is not to say that what is "no more than some kind of causal dependence" can have no methodological import. To ignore some of the evidence, for example, is illogical: even though ignoring it does not *entail* that the conclusions arrived at will be false or even improbable, the ignoring may well cause us to arrive at false conclusions. The more basic point, perhaps, is that even though values are not *sufficient* to establish facts it does not follow that they are therefore not *necessary*. The ultimate empiricism on which science rests consists in this, that thinking something is so does not make it so, and this negation applies even more forcibly, if possible, to wishing it were so. The predicted eclipse occurs whether we like it or not, and would have occurred whether it had been predicted or not. But values enter both into making the prediction and into the conceptualization of what "it" is being predicted.

OBJECTIVITY AND VALUES

I believe that the insistence on science as value-free stems from the very proper determination to free science from any imputation of a subjective relativism, of the kind that may well be involved in certain conceptions of the sociology of knowledge and of "class science". But whether conceding that values have an inescapable part to play in the scientific enterprise has this consequence depends on the theory of value which is brought to bear. The objectivity of science demands its being value-free only if values are necessarily and irreducibly subjective. I agree with the proponents of value-free science in this basic respect, that *either* values (as appraisals) must be rigorously excluded from science, or *else* they must themselves be given an objective ground. It is this second alternative which seems to me methodologically sounder. For I do not see how values *can* be excluded. With Myrdal (*99*:1043), I believe that "the attempt to eradicate biases by trying to keep out the valuations themselves is a hopeless and misdirected venture. . . . There is no other device for excluding biases in social sciences [or any other] than to face the valuations and to introduce them as explicitly stated, specific, and sufficiently concretized value premises." And, I would add, to provide an objective basis for them. The problem for methodology is not *whether* values are involved in inquiry, but *which*, and above all, how they are to be empirically grounded.

§44. Theory of Value

GROUNDS

What philosophers call a "theory" of value is not, strictly speaking, a theory in the scientific sense, but a set of guide lines for the analysis of the meaning and ground of value judgments. By the *ground* of a value judgment (or of the corresponding value), I mean not causes but reasons: the justification for making that judgment or having that value. Offering the ground does not necessarily produce acceptance of the value—it is like having an explanation as distinguished from seeing one. Every value has its *basis*, what causes it to be taken as a value; but whether any values have grounds, and if so, what they are, is very much in dispute. The difference between basis and ground corresponds to that between belief and knowledge: one may have beliefs whether or not he has evidence for them. Moreover, just as a belief may be true even without evidence for it, a value may be *genuine* even though we do not know its ground. Of course, when we say that it is genuine, we imply the existence of a ground, just as when we say that a belief is true we imply that we have reasons for saying so—that is, that there is evidence for the belief (the implication, to be sure, is from our saying that the belief is true, and not from the proposition itself which is believed in). The question is, then, whether any values are more genuine than any other, and if they are, what makes them so.

Two major sorts of answers to this question have been given in contemporary philosophy: the corresponding positions are known as *emotivism* and *cognitivism*. For the emotivist, a value has no ground distinct from its basis, though urging that something *is* a ground may itself help constitute the basis. All values are equally genuine, so that the predicate is empty; but again, the *use* of such a predicate may help give basis to one value rather than another. (Outside the contexts of philosophical inquiry, therefore, an emotivist would not *say* that all values are equally genuine.) The attribution of genuineness is a device for persuasion, and a perfectly legitimate one, legitimacy itself being a value like those receiving approval in the original attribution. To say that a value is genuine is to express that the speaker has that value and to induce the hearers to share it. For the cognitivist, on the other hand, ground and basis are indeed distinct. To say (or to imply) that a value is genuine is to make a factual claim about it, which is to be supported by evidence; if the evidence is forthcoming the value judgment is grounded. Just which sorts of facts enter into the claim depends on the particular version of cognitivism (I shall sketch one such version in a moment). In any case, a value judgment has cognitive content, and this generalization applies as much to appraisals as to characterizations. The mode of expression of the judgment may make it awkward to say of it that it is "true" or "false", but this awkwardness is a matter of grammatical form and not of logical content.

In my opinion, both positions have important contributions to make to methodology, and more is to be gained by treating them as supplementing one another than by pushing either to the exclusion of the other. This treatment requires that they be so construed that they are not strict contradictories. I believe that they can be, and that the two views differ more in what they call "value judgments" than in what they say about one and the same thing, as I shall make explicit shortly. Thus emotivism usefully emphasizes the difference between objective and biased allegations of fact, as well as between factual statements which embody data for problems of value and proposed solutions for those problems (like the difference between a proposition of political science and a judgment in a particular political doctrine). Emotivism sensitizes us to normative ambiguities, and heightens awareness of the possibility that purported grounds express only a concealed basis, as amplified in Pareto's distinction between "derivations" and "residues", or in Freud's analysis of "rationalizations". On the other hand, cognitivism usefully directs attention to important differences: the difference between a value judgment which issues from a process of deliberation and the expression of a mere whim or caprice; the difference between a choice that is grounded in a careful evaluation of the conditions and consequences for given values of a range of alternative courses of action and a choice that is based only on habit, tradition, or compulsion, whether psychic or social. Cognitivism keeps alive our distrust of the insidious doctrine that whatever is, is right, reminding us that whatever majorities or preponderant forces support a given policy it may still be a mistaken one.

The conception of values which seems to me by far the most appropriate to behavioral science is some form of *naturalism*, as it is called. As used in this connection, "naturalism" refers to the view that the ground of values is something in human experience and of a piece with everything else we experience—as contrasted with supernatural grounds like a divine commandment, or with nonnatural grounds like a unique quality of "goodness" apprehended by a distinctive "moral intuition". Specifically, the ground of values consists, with suitable and important qualifications, in the satisfaction of human wants, needs, desires, interests, and the like. With C. I. Lewis, we may speak of *intrinsic value* as "experienced goodness", the sense of satisfaction or fulfillment, the direct (that is, unmediated) experience of gratification. Judgments of value then say something, in effect, about the intrinsic values empirically associated with what is being judged. Intrinsic values play a role in the grounding of value judgments comparable to that played by perceptual qualities in the validation of other propositions about matters of fact: sooner or later such propositions come down to what we may expect to perceive under appropriate conditions. Notice that in both cases we may be mistaken, not only in our predictions, but even in the judgment that we are then and there having the direct experience in question. The liquid in the test tube may not be yellow, as we think, and what we feel may not be gratification, as we consciously suppose. Errors of observation are possible in both sorts of cases. We need not develop a theory of value on the basis of value experiences which are taken to be beyond question, any more than we need to develop a theory of knowledge on the basis of incorrigible "sense data"—though both positions, it must be said, have their ardent supporters.

CONTEXTS

It follows at once that every value judgment is *contextual*: it must specify, at least tacitly, for whom and under what conditions there would be intrinsic value. In the concrete, a value judgment is an utterance, made by a particular person in particular circumstances. Its meaning derives from its use in the problematic situation which called it forth. That it is grounded by reference to the facts of the case, while judgments of fact in turn presuppose values (§43), does not generate a vicious circle. What is problematic in one situation need not be so in another. A particular value judgment made in a certain context is grounded in facts established with the help of values which are not problematic in that same context. Value judgments can be generalized over a wide range of contexts, but they cannot be abstracted altogether from the concreta in terms of which both the value problem and its solution must be formulated. To ask, for example, whether the end justifies the means is like asking whether the commodity is worth its price; the answer can only be, "It all depends!"

Three sorts of contexts can usefully be distinguished. *Personal contexts* make relevant only the intrinsic value experienced then and there by the person expressing the valuation. What he says has no reference beyond the context of his saying it, save that which is involved in the possibility of an error of observation (such an error might consist in his being unaware of the true state of his feelings). The only prediction implied is that subsequent evidence will confirm that his experiences at the time of the utterance were indeed those conveyed by the utterance. In a personal context, what is being voiced is a *value expression* rather than a "judgment" strictly speaking. It is part of the act of valuation rather than the reported outcome of an *e*valuation. If we can speak of the expression as being "true" at all, this "truth" can have only the sense of self-awareness and sincerity. Emotivism seems to me to be concerned chiefly with value expressions; for these, questions of ground simply do not arise. "This is how I feel about it, and that's an end of the matter."

Now the context to which a value judgment refers (explicitly or otherwise) may be quite distinct from that of the judgment itself. The judgment may be predicting that under certain conditions, not necessarily those prevailing in the circumstances of the prediction, certain people, not necessarily the speaker, will find intrinsic value. We may speak of these contexts *in* the judgment rather than *of* it as *standard contexts*, and distinguish the utterances referring to them as *value statements*, rather than as "expressions" or as "judgments" proper. Value statements are thus propositions about matters of fact in a quite straightforward way, once it is made clear just which context is being taken as standard. Whether a film is a "good" one, for example, is an unequivocally factual question if it concerns success at the box office; similarly for statements about "middle-class values" (in a nonpejorative sense), and in general, for characterizing judgments, so-called. It is to be noted that the judger himself may be constitutive of a standard context; his statement may be reporting or predicting what he himself has found or will find to his liking. Such a statement is as capable of being true or false as any other. Often, too, the expression in a personal context, our own or another's, may provide us with a ground for statements about some other, standard, context, as when a critic uses his own reactions to predict an audience response.

We can also meaningfully speak of *ideal contexts*. They are those which allow for the widest possible range of predictions about intrinsic values, stating what can be expected on the whole, and in the long run. Here we have *value judgments* in the strict sense. The judgment that something *is* good contrasts with the statement that it *seems* good (to me or to some other specified persons) in very much the same way that the proposition that something *is* yellow contrasts with the proposition that it *seems* yellow. The reality is not set over against appearances as such but only against any arbitrary appearance. We do not select as standard a context which is appropriate to some special purpose but one which will be serviceable whatever our purposes may be. If the colored object is to be viewed under certain artificial lighting, we say only that it will look yellow under those conditions (which corresponds to a value statement), not that it *is* yellow (which corresponds to a value judgment). A value judgment is still contextual, for human needs and interests are inescapably involved, but the possible contexts of application of the judgment are not limited by the judgment itself, as is the case with value statements. It is value judgments with which cognitivism seems to me to be chiefly concerned, for such judgments, like value statements, are perfectly capable of being true or false, though it is admittedly most difficult to say which in a given case. But while the statements only affirm how something seems under certain conditions chosen as standard, the judgments affirm how it is—which is to say, how it would seem under ideal conditions.

OBJECTIVE RELATIVISM

On this view, then, values are relative but nevertheless objective— hence the label *objective relativism* for this position. It is only value expressions which have a subjective reference; value statements, and especially value judgments, affirm something whose truth does not depend on the state of mind which evoked the affirmation. The proposition that one man's meat is another man's poison does not in the least impugn the objective validity of biochemistry but on the contrary presupposes it. Values are themselves facts, about actual or potential human satisfactions. When A states that *x* is a value for B, or judges *x* to be really valuable, the value of *x* is relative to B, or to others like him in comparable situations, but it is not relative to A. A value judgment, like any other, is always made by someone, and can always be countered with "So *you* say!" But what it judges is that something is the case whether anyone says so or not. There is thus a systematic distinction to be drawn between what we like and what is worthy of being liked, between taste and judgment, the desired and the desirable, or in Dewey's favorite terms, between prizing and appraising, valuation and *e*valuation, what is satisfying then and there and what proves itself to be truly satisfactory. The second member of each pair is constructed from the first, or takes it as a point of departure. Values are thus in this very special and limited sense "reducible" to human desires, but they pertain, in judgment, to the whole (and open) set of desires that we may have under varying circumstances, and above all, to the wholly objective conditions and consequences of their satisfaction.

What is responsible for much of the confusion as to the objectivity of value judgments is that they have a normative use, unlike the functions performed, at least in as obvious a way, by most other propositions about matters of fact. This use is then misconstrued as constituting a distinctive noncognitive content, an interpretation reinforced by the imperative and exclamatory modes in which value judgments are often formulated. But even a pure imperative may have a cognitive content: the cry for help is surely to be understood as telling us, among other things, that someone is in difficulty or danger, and this telling can be as true or false as in a flat declarative. To be sure, this "derived cognitive meaning", as I have called it, belongs, not to the words themselves, but to their being said in a certain situation. Value expressions, and perhaps even some value statements and judgments, have the kind of reflexiveness that characterizes sentences containing words like "I" and "this": their meaning depends in part on who says them and when. But when they are properly understood, their truth is not constituted just by their being said.

MEANS AND ENDS

What has been said is usually conceded by reformulating the statements as concerning the relations of means to ends. Values may be distinguished as *instrumental* or *inherent* according to whether they are prized in themselves or because they are believed to lead to something else which we prize. (It is the attainment of something of inherent value which has intrinsic value, though the expectations aroused by a mere instrumentality may also become intrinsically enjoyable, as the lover will delight even in a token from his beloved, and the miser gloat over his gold.) Many imperatives embody a cognitive value judgment only in the sense that they imply that something is of instrumental value with respect to a presupposed inherent value. These have been known, since Kant, as *hypothetical imperatives:* "If you want y, do x!" What might be called the "extended cognitive meaning" of such an imperative (as contrasted with the direct cognitive meaning of a simple declarative) consists simply in this, that *x* will in fact lead to *y* (in accord with tacit conditions of minimizing certain costs, and so on). But value judgments proper, so it is argued, must be expressed as *categorical imperatives,* in which there is no "if" but only a "Thou shalt!" and "Thou shalt not!" Hypothetical imperatives, it is admitted, embody beliefs, concerning the means appropriate to given ends; but categorical imperatives are held to embody only attitudes, to which truth and falsehood cannot be applied.

The argument is that pure imperatives cannot be grounded in factual statements; a value premise must somehow be smuggled in to provide the ends for which something can then be factually judged a suitable means. The position I am taking amounts to this, that such premises are always there, and are rather smuggled *out* by the reconstructed logic which isolates values from facts. Categorical imperatives are not in fact unconditional, but may be tacitly referred to conditions of human aspiration and fulfillment so general as to serve as presuppositions of value judgment, comparable to the presuppositions about reality and reason underlying factual judgments in the narrow sense. A categorical imperative differs from a hypothetical one, not in lacking an antecedent, but in presupposing one: instead of reading, "*If* you want *y*, do *x*!" it reads, "*Since* you want *y*, do *x*!", the condition being suppressed in the second case much more often than in the first precisely because of its general applicability. My cry for help not only implies, in an appropriate sense, that I need help, but also that you would do well to assist me, that it is to your interest as well as mine. The most categorical of imperatives, in the words of the Deuteronomist, find their ground in presupposed ends: "I have set before you life and death, blessing and curse; therefore choose life!"

The basic error in the fact-value dualism lies in the supposition that sooner or later every value judgment must come to rest upon an absolute end, one which is valued unconditionally, without ifs, ands, or buts. Factual considerations relate only to such conditions, and when these have been let go, we are left afloat in a sea of subjectivity. That absolute values are groundless does indeed imply that rationality precludes them; but the conclusion that they underlie all value judgments, which therefore cannot be objective, only begs the question. It is to be noted that the question is not whether there are intrinsic values but whether some of them can meaningfully be distinguished as not genuine. The question being so put, I confess that it is hard for me to understand any doubts about the answer; surely, we can simultaneously concede the delights of the opium eater and maintain that they aren't worth what they entail. Man is the measure, but nothing less than the whole man and all that he is capable of will serve. It is precisely here where judgment comes into play.

Dewey has elaborated this position in terms of what has come to be known as the *means-end continuum*. The distinction between instrumental and inherent values is functional and contextual. All ends are means to further ends; a value is inherent only relative to something else serving as an instrumentality, but in itself it leads us on to further ends. In an apt metaphor this ongoing change has been called "the mountain-range effect": we climb a peak only to find other peaks beyond us; no matter when we leave off climbing, other peaks remain beyond. We cannot postpone the experience of intrinsic value to the time when we stand on the last peak, for there is no last peak; the joy must be experienced in the journey, not in the destination. A final end can be defined only as an abstraction; in the concrete, there is always something more to be done, even if it is only at last to learn how to enjoy what has been achieved. There is much logical insight as well as irony in Nietzsche's aphorism that men do not strive for happiness, only Englishmen.

Moreover, ends are appraised in terms of the means they call for, as well as providing a basis for the appraisal of means. We make our choices on the basis of costs, as well as on the basis of the satisfactions inherent in what we might buy. To say so is another and perhaps more convincing way of pointing out that ends are also appraised as means, for the costs represent other ends to which those being considered will lead. Weber (*135*:26) has said that "strictly and exclusively empirical analysis can provide a solution only where it is a question of a means adequate to the realization of an absolutely unambiguously given end." But this exclusion overlooks the fundamentally contextual character of all judgment; in every context there is something which is unproblematic, but this is not to say that there is anything which is "absolutely unambiguously given". There is always a price to be paid; actions have their conditions and consequences, and these inescapably reach beyond whatever end we might have in view as an end. The whole set of values is in-

volved in the appraisal of any one of them, much as the whole of our
knowledge is at stake in the test of any particular hypothesis. Relevance,
whether of facts or of values, cannot be prejudged but is ascertained in
the course of inquiry. One of the most common mistakes in the application of behavioral science to policy is the supposition that ends can be
isolated and used for the appraisal of means without themselves being
subject to appraisal by the other ends with which they are implicated—
the mistake involved in the standard of "efficiency" too narrowly conceived.

THE ROLE OF VALUES

In short, allowing *a* role to values is not what makes for bias; what
makes for bias, rather, is allowing them only a role that insulates them
from the test of experience; they are prejudicial when they are prejudged. "The soundness of the principle that moral condemnation and
approbation should be excluded from the operations of obtaining and
weighing material data and from the operations by which conceptions for
dealing with the data are instituted," Dewey (*28*:496) has explained,
"is often converted into the notion that all evaluations should be excluded. This conversion is, however, effected only through the intermediary of a thoroughly fallacious notion; the notion, namely, that the moral
blames and approvals in question *are* evaluative and that they exhaust the
field of evaluation. For they are not evaluative in any logical sense of
evaluation. They are not even judgments in the logical sense of judgment. For they rest upon some preconception of ends that should or
ought to be attained. This preconception excludes ends (consequences)
from the field of inquiry and reduces inquiry at its very best to the trun-
cated and distorted business of finding out means for realizing objectives
already settled upon."

The position that ends are to be excluded from inquiry, so that our
own ends need not be examined, is often rationalized by the argument
that they are unproblematic because they are universally shared—that is,
shared by all "decent, right-thinking people". The defense mechanism of
projection then easily passes over into the political mechanisms of enforced conformity: the imposition of our own values on others and the
repression of differences. In our own eyes, of course, we are imposing

nothing, but only helping others to realize what they themselves want, and to achieve it. The segregationist, for instance, may be convinced that the "right-thinking" Negro really wants to be segregated, and that the problem has been created by "outside agitators". As Myrdal (*99*:1029) has observed, "The temptation will be strong to deny the very existence of a valuation conflict. This will sometimes bring in its wake grossly distorted notions about social reality. There is a sort of social ignorance which is most adequately explained as an attempt to avoid the twinges of conscience."

The irony is that the formulation of a value problem as a disagreement "only" about means already raises all the issues involved in the problem. For the principle of the means-end continuum is precisely that means determine their ends as well as being determined by them. Many roads leading to the same destination is a poor model for the pursuit of values: inherent values do not have an existence over and above their instrumentalities but are constituted by them. In human life, what happens meanwhile is everything.

What has been said is not meant to deny in the least that there are real difficulties in the empirical validation of value judgments. The problem remains, for example, of dealing with interpersonal values, of actually tracing the communities of interest which can be used to resolve conflicts of interest among the members of a group, or among whole groups and nations. And there is the problem, too, of the comparability of various values, even where they are all valued by the same person. For to speak of a "system" of values is usually no more than a courtesy; its unity is not antecedently given but is something to be achieved. There is always a question of the consistency of our values among themselves, of their compatibility in given situations, and of their coherence or mutual support. Where several values must be taken into account jointly—and where can we do otherwise?—appraisal by the method of configuration rather than the method of summation (§24) seems inescapable, but its ground is still obscure. The position that values are not in their very nature impervious to scientific treatment faces serious difficulties here and elsewhere, but not, to my mind, fatal objections. At any rate, it is beyond dispute, I venture to say, that values call for incomparably more inquiry, both into general questions and into specific value problems, than has yet been undertaken.

§*45. Behavioral Science and Policy*

ANTISCIENTIFIC ASPECTS OF POLICY

Whether the behavioral scientist should concern himself at all with matters of policy, personal or social, is a question on which no consensus has been reached in the scientific community. On the one hand, many behavioral scientists are very much occupied with the problems that arise *in* human behavior (and not only in the attempt to describe or explain behavior), and are also professionally engaged with questions of what is to be done by people in quandaries, in contexts ranging from marital relations to foreign affairs. On the other hand, there are those who regard such concerns as lying quite outside the scientific enterprise itself, and perhaps even as antithetical to that enterprise. Science, as they conceive it, is the search for truth, not usefulness. Whether the truth is useful is of no professional interest to the scientist, but only whether it is indeed true; how it is put to use is no business of his. If it is expected that the outcome of an inquiry can be put to use, the scientist's efforts will be bought and paid for; but to engage in inquiry so as to achieve a utilitarian end is nothing other than a prostitution of the scientific intelligence.

This second point of view strikes me as singularly lacking in perspective, especially on the history of science itself. Even the eighteenth-century tradition of science as an occupation for gentlemen of leisure manifested a striking concern with the practical interests of war, commerce, industry, and agriculture, and even the purest of the sciences owe a not inconsiderable debt to such interests. The fact is that the distinction between "pure" and "applied" science, whatever its logical ground, is not of much help in understanding the actual growth of knowledge. "Every practical problem is really a problem in research," Campbell (*13*:182) has pointed out, "leading to the advancement of pure learning as well as to material efficiency; indeed, almost all the problems by the solution of which science has actually advanced have been suggested, more or less directly, by the familiar experiences of everyday life." The irony is that the behavioral scientist, in his aspiration eventually to achieve the scientific standing of physics, is so often more royalist than the king; the first two laws of thermodynamics, for example, were formulated long after the scientific data were available, "and they arose because of the social stimulation of steam power engineering" (R. S. Cohen in *46*:203). In its resolve to remain "pure", as in so many other respects, behavioral science is imitating physics, not as it is, but as particular reconstructions have represented it to be.

I do not mean to be detracting in the least from the importance of basic research. What I am saying is that the opposite of "basic" is "derived", or some such adjective, rather than "practical". Basic research may be even more practical than inquiries directed to less fundamental questions, and not necessarily only in the long run either. An inquiry which is specifically directed to the solution of some practical problem is not for that reason alone to be excluded from the category of basic research. (Consider the fundamental questions which would arise in the attempt to devise a time machine, to synthesize life—or to prevent wars.) The disadvantages of the practical problem, from a scientific point of view, are that the limited context of the problem is likely to involve special conditions from which it may not be easy to abstract, and that purely empirical techniques may succeed in solving the problem without correspondingly adding to our understanding of how and why they are successful. On the other hand, relating the inquiry to practice has the advantages of providing anchorage for our abstractions, and data and tests for our hypotheses. For behavioral science these advantages are especially great, counteracting the tendency to empty verbalization characteristic of some sociologies, for example, or the self-contained formalism of certain economic theories. The practical problem may bias an investigation, if this is carried out only to provide justification for a policy prejudged to be the best. But the determination to exclude from an investigation the data and hypotheses pertaining to practical conditions and consequences may be just as much an expression of bias. "Science becomes no better protected against biases by the entirely negative device of refusing to arrange its results for practical and political utilization" (*99*:1041).

EXTRASCIENTIFIC ASPECTS OF POLICY

A position more plausible than the view that a concern with matters of policy is *anti*scientific is that it is at any rate *extra*scientific. This is the conception of science as a *neutral instrument*, which can be used equally

for good or for ill. Science provides only means, for ends which are to be
determined outside the scientific enterprise. Here the tactic of role playing is invoked. The scientist, it is conceded, is as much concerned as anyone else with the determination of ends, but not *as* scientist, only as citizen or in some other social or personal role. But the lines drawn become
ever finer and ever more remote from what is actually done in the performance of any of these roles, in so far as the behavior is rational and
realistic. For the decisions actually taken undeniably call for considera-
ion of the facts of the case and for inferences as to what might be expected from alternative courses of action. If there are ends to which scientific findings are wholly irrelevant, they have a way of receding to an
"ultimate" analysis rather than playing a part in the decisions on what
to do next; and it is the sequence of such decisions which determines
what actually gets done, even ultimately. Only absolute ends preclude
inquiry, but they belong only to final action; and no man, whatever his
role, is called upon to make the Last Judgment.

The distinction between an instrument and its use is well founded.
What makes situations problematic is the range of possible uses of the
instruments at our disposal: where there is only one thing that can be
done there is nothing to think about. But the question is whether science
is limited to posing these problems of action and has nothing to do with
solving them, creating instruments but providing no instrumentalities by
which to decide on their use. We can say it is thus limited only if science
is identified with the product of inquiry and not with the process as well.
The product is always capable of a variety of uses, but this versatility
does not imply that the appraisal of these uses therefore lies outside the
process. The new product may in turn pose problems of use, calling for
still further inquiry—the mountain-range effect again (§44)—but this
kind of endlessness does not put ends beyond science nor make science
neutral. What a political scientist learns about the workings of legislative
bodies can be used in various ways—to block certain legislation or to
secure its passage. Yet if he extends his inquiry to include an appraisal of
specific Congressional reforms, surely he has not thereby abandoned the
role of scientist, even if it makes him a more informed and thoughtful
citizen, just as the citizen has not abandoned his role by engaging in
reflection on the political issues put before him.

Would that more thought were taken, by both citizen and policy maker! "The evils in current social judgments of ends and policies," Dewey (28:503) has unceasingly emphasized, "spring from the fact that the values employed are not determined in and by the process of inquiry." True, the results of this process are being given more and more attention. To commission scientific studies has become standard operating procedure in industry, government, and the armed services; whole new disciplines have sprung up, from market research to operations research. But the roles which are distinguished in the theory of the neutral instrument are confounded in the practice of decision making. Scientific findings are set aside when they conflict with preconceived ideas, or with policies predetermined by internal power struggles, and this exclusion is rationalized as wisdom by the formula that decisions, after all, must be made by men of action. On the other hand, the expert consultant often makes *virtual decisions*, presupposing certain policies in his very formulation of the problem or in the tacit assumptions underlying his solution, and this intrusion is rationalized as nonexistent by the formula that as a scientist, he is only providing the basis for a decision which others, after all, must make. Thus the policy maker wills ends without scientific assessment of their conditions and consequences, while the scientist exercises power without corresponding responsibility, refusing indeed, "as a scientist", to assume responsibility. Too often, the behavioral scientist especially has so defined his role as to put himself in the posture of a physician saying to his patient, "*You*'re the doctor!"

UNSCIENTIFIC ASPECTS OF POLICY

There is a third line of argument for the divorce of science from policy. This defends the position that policy guidance is *un*scientific, whether or not it is anti- or extrascientific. It is unscientific because we almost never know enough, or with enough certitude, to provide a scientifically valid basis for adopting one policy rather than another. To my mind, this point of view is very understandable, and I have much sympathy with it. What we actually know with any confidence about human behavior is pitifully little compared with the magnitude and complexity of the problems confronting us. That more research is needed is undeniable, and must be proclaimed over and over again to counter the pretensions of the bigot, dogmatist, and doctrinaire within the scientific enterprise as well as outside it. I have no quarrel with the premise of this argument, but I cannot follow it to its conclusion.

For first of all, the premise proves too much: more research will always be needed, at least research into the particularities of specific concrete situations. Even with as complete and perfect a system to guide it as Newton's mechanics, engineering is not a merely mechanical application of already sufficient knowledge, but calls continuously for further inquiry; nor is its research limited to securing additional data. Approximate and probabilistic solutions to its problems are the rule rather than the exception. The term "social engineering" has the abhorrent connotation that men are to be treated only as materials and means for the attainment of social ends; purged of this connotation, the term may refer to the attempt to treat social problems on the basis of theoretical knowledge as well as merely empirical know-how. For this treatment it is not required that we know everything, but only that we know something relevant. A scientific approach does not suddenly come into being at the magical moment when we know "enough"; such moments never arrive. To await them constitutes what I have called the "ordinal fallacy": first this, then that—first I will achieve power, then use it for the public good; first I will master my medium, then use it to say something significant; first I will pursue wealth, then use it in the pursuit of happiness. And as in politics, art, and morality, so here—first I will acquire the knowledge, then use it as a basis for sound policy. But whether it be due to a human failing or to the human condition, we must do as we aspire from the very beginning, or else resign ourselves to not doing at all.

What is certainly clear is that the decisions to be taken cannot wait. It is hard enough to find time even for the inquiries which we are already in a position to carry on, to say nothing of finding time to wait beyond any foreseeable future for a well-founded and comprehensive behavioral science. We are playing lightning chess—with this difference, that if we stop to analyze all the variations the move will be made for us, and with supreme indifference to its outcome. But we need not therefore play altogether unthinkingly. The point is that by using such knowledge as we have or can acquire, whatever its shortcomings, we can do better than by setting it aside altogether. What makes policy formation scientific, in a real sense rather than in a purely honorific one, is procedural rather than substantive, as in the case of any other belief: it is not the content which is decisive, but the procedure by which the content is arrived at. There is an interesting parallel here to the abdication of responsibility by contemporary philosophy, an abdication which is sometimes motivated, I am sorry to say, by a cowardice masquerading as humility. Modern philosophy has become so anxious to abandon the old pretensions to wisdom that it has also abandoned the pursuit of wisdom, thereby leaving that pursuit to journalism, psychiatry, and nuclear physics. The behavioral scientist would do well to remember that when science is divorced from policy, the result is not only that science is "set free" but also that policy is thereby thrown on its own resources— which is to say that it is left to be determined by tradition, prejudice, and the preponderance of power.

I am far from arguing that behavioral science should become a hand-maiden to policy, as in an earlier day it was thought that science should be subservient to theology. Science inevitably suffers when its freedom is lost to the church, the army, the state, or whatever. I end as I began, with loyalty to the principle of the autonomy of inquiry. But a concern with the interests of policy need not express subservience to them, and indeed demands independent thought. The "manipulative standpoint", as Lasswell calls it, is distinguishable from the "contemplative stand-point", but the two standpoints are not therefore antithetical to one another. There is much point, indeed, in Lasswell's designation of the various branches of behavioral science as "policy sciences", to mark their orientation toward bringing their results to bear on the needs of policy formation. For it is this orientation which gives the results their significance—not just for society, but often for science as well.

PLANNING

The application of behavioral science to policy is most self-conscious, deliberate, and explicit by way of planning, which may be defined as the enterprise of facilitating decisions and making them more realistic and rational. Decisions are facilitated as choices are made more clear-cut, and alternatives are more concretely and specifically demarcated. Decisions become more realistic as the values they involve are confronted with facts, and ideals are translated into concrete objectives. They become more rational as values are confronted with other values, and as what Reichenbach called "entailed decisions" are taken into account. Thus a plan is a configuration of goals, presented as consistent with each other and as grounded in the facts of the case, and specified in terms of an action sequence expected to lead to their attainment. Planning has particularly the function of jointly determining ends and means. Without this reciprocal determination, action is directed to limited objectives having no significance beyond themselves, while aspiration drifts into fantasy, without purchase on the real world.

But planning has its limits—science cannot do everything for policy. Much of our action, even with regard to important matters, is necessarily unplanned. The urgency of a decision may preclude a well-designed and carefully executed study. Yet if too many decisions confront us with such urgency, this may itself mark a failure elsewhere in the planning process: we can prepare at leisure for contingencies which may never arise, but which are sudden and urgent when they do arise—as the military appreciates so well. Again, action may be unplanned because the problems it faces are too complex and its data too subtle and elusive—in the given state of knowledge—for anything but the unanalyzed judgment of experience. Yet even such choices as that of a career or of a marriage partner can even now profit from the counseling for which behavioral science is providing methods and materials. A particularly important difficulty is that decisions are often not isolable as such, so that there is no well-marked phase in the process of decision making where planning can intervene. Administration, for example, is not merely the execution of policy but also includes helping to form it, as the judicial function is continuous with the legislative: the judge participates in making the law in the course of interpreting it. Yet virtual decisions can be made ever more explicit, and as their grounds are set out they may be subjected to inquiry. Personnel policies and the legal defense of insanity are examples of areas of virtual decision with which behavioral science has fruitfully concerned itself, to help make the decisions more explicit and well-grounded.

Planning is further limited by the occurrence of the unexpected: choices made by others; unanticipated consequences of our own actions; and acts of God—random or accidental factors. The bearings of behavioral science on policy are much better modeled by the relation of the pregame strategy to the actual play of the game than by the relation of a computer program to the computations carrying it out. The policy sciences need not be conceived as aspiring to program social action, but only to make it more informed, realistic, and rational—in a word, more effective. That unanticipated events will occur must itself be anticipated and taken into account in our plans—as is done with insurance, for example. Events of this kind—the expectedly unexpected—are sufficiently important to deserve a name; I propose the word *agathonic:* it is probable, Agathon says (as quoted somewhere in Aristotle), that the improbable will happen. Chance events become agathonic by being subsumed under statistical law, and thereby being brought within the purview of rational decision making—for instance, by the adoption of what the theory of games calls "mixed strategies".

Planning is also limited by the realm of the uncontrollable, which surrounds on all sides the little area of our own free choice. No man has power over the wind, says the Preacher. Behavioral science may be as useful to policy in pointing to the constraints which must be accepted and recognized as in opening up new possibilities. And planning is also subject to intrinsic limitations imposed by the ends pursued, which may be such as to preclude forethought and deliberation. We cannot organize "spontaneous demonstrations", nor force men to be free. Yet there is an important species of indirect planning, to which behavioral science may make significant contributions—planning for ways to help others plan for themselves, or to arrive at rational though unplanned decisions. So far as the logic of the situation is concerned, nondirective therapy may be as scientific as any other. And to provide a decision maker with a clear-cut alternative beyond which the scientist cannot go in the given case may be a greater service than to provide a poorly grounded recommendation for one alternative or the other.

SCIENTISM

In all I have been saying, I have been anxious to ward off the danger of scientism, the pernicious exaggeration of both the status and function of science in relation to our values. The *Philosophes* of the eighteenth century and the positivists of the nineteenth proclaimed, in the spirit of "Love conquers all", that science will achieve everything. In the present century scientism especially manifests itself in the confusion of scientific method with particular scientific techniques, whose use becomes both necessary and sufficient for scientific standing. Policy must be formulated with the help of charts and graphs, equations and computers. To acknowledge imponderables as the locus of important values comes to be seen as unscientific and even obscurantist. It is not only the law of the instrument which is at work here, but also a belief in the magic of symbols, and perhaps even a trace of the infantile delusion of omnipotence. A more mature perspective recognizes how little we know, and how little we can do with what we do know. The progress of behavioral science does not make good judgment expendable but spares it for the more important tasks than those on which it is now dissipated. What is so difficult is to insist, as I have tried hard to do, *both* on the promise of science for values and on the desperate need for—why mince words?—wisdom.

§46. *The Future of Behavioral Science*

Many behavioral scientists, I am afraid, look to methodology as a source of salvation: their expectation is that if only they are willing and obedient, though their sins are like scarlet they shall be as white as snow. Methodology is not turned to only as and when specific methodological difficulties arise in the course of particular inquiries; it is made all-encompassing, a faith in which the tormented inquirer can hope to be reborn to a new life. If there are such illusions, it has been my purpose to be disillusioning. In these matters, the performance of the ritual leaves everything unchanged, and methodological precepts are likely to be as ineffective as moral exhortations usually are. There are indeed techniques to be mastered, and their resources and limitations are to be thoroughly explored. But these techniques are specific to their subject-matters, or to distinctive problems, and the norms governing their use derive from the contexts of their application, not from general principles of methodology. There are behavioral scientists who, in their desperate search for scientific status, give the impression that they don't much care what they do if only they do it right: substance gives way to form. And here a vicious circle is engendered; when the outcome is seen to be empty, this is taken as pointing all the more to the need for a better methodology. The work of the behavioral scientist might well become methodologically sounder if only he did not try so hard to be so scientific!

In any case, whatever normative force methodology has derives from scientific practice itself. A study of the history of science, in a variety of disciplines and problematic situations, is likely to be far more rewarding for the actual conduct of inquiry than a preoccupation with an abstract logic of science. Methodology cannot dictate to the working scientist but can only help him to understand how other inquiries have been effectively conducted. In particular, it seems to me to be very far from helpful to demand of the scientist conformity to our own favored reconstructed logic. I do not deny that there are on the fringes of every discipline certain systems of ideas which are the mark of quite undisciplined minds, and behavioral science is especially, though not exclusively, cursed with such lunacies. But it is one thing to lay down the law to the outright criminal and quite another thing to establish a police state. I am pleading for the right of the honest citizen to go on about his business even if we do not quite approve of his way of life.

The very label "*behavioral* science" has restrictive connotations from which I hope I have freed myself. It suggests that only the study of acts is scientifically admissible, and that to deal with actions, which require interpretation, is already to go beyond the data. The label "behavioral *science*" also connotes an insistence on the use of certain techniques, involving either brass instruments or advanced mathematics, preferably both; and a determination to *get* somewhere, to make the study of man scientific at last, which in philosophy Morton White has called the "hup, two, three" school. All these connotations belong to scientism, not to science, and I would be sorry indeed to be accessory to it. I have used the label "behavioral science", in spite of its scientistic flavor, to emphasize the continuity, in spirit and method, with physical and biological science, and because terms like "social science" might be thought to exclude psychology, while the term "human sciences" seems to rule out relevant animal behavior, like learning, and to take in far more of human biology than would interest, say, the physical anthropologist. But of course, the chief reason for using the label is that it is well on the way to becoming the established usage; and it is not words which need to be changed.

I have tried throughout to emphasize the great range of cognitive styles and interests which make up the scientific enterprise, and the methodological freedom to pursue any of them, even those which are of lesser importance to a given reconstructed logic of science. There are scientists who work chiefly in libraries or in clinics as well as in laboratories; there are generalists and specialists, synthesizers and analysts; system builders and perfecters of instruments; theoreticians and experimentalists; those probing for breakthroughs and those engaged in mopping-up operations. It is a matter not of justice but of plain fact that science excludes none of them; ἀnd certainly none is to be excluded by the philosophical bystander in the name of methodology. I would even go so far as to insist that the domain of science shades off into that of the humanities (quite apart from the humanistic values in science itself). Many histories, many autobiographies like those of Lincoln Steffens and Henry Adams, many biographies like Erik Eriksen's of Luther, and countless other studies are both literary and scientific in treatment, and these are two perspectives on one and the same substance, not a scientific content presented in a literary form. Behavioral science may even have as much in common with literary criticism as with literature: it sets out to understand and appreciate human conduct, to throw light on it and reveal its hidden meanings; the ways in which the critic achieves his ends may be shared by behavioral science. Methodology, in short, offers the scientist only a nondirective therapy: it is intended to help him live in his own style, not to mold him in the image of the therapist.

What I have tried to emphasize is a catholicity of outlook, which has no need for the tactics of defensive incorporation and exclusion. There is a wide range not only of styles, but also of interests, problems, and approaches. That a behavioral science is divided into schools is not necessarily a mark of scientific immaturity; the adolescent tries on various personalities as he might a garment, but even the mature personality is all the richer for its multiplicity—if only it is not a congress of warring selves. There is as much danger in the distinction between disciplines as in the division of schools. A school will at any rate apply its own methods to the whole problem, but a discipline fragments problems to accord with an antecedently given division of labor. That the danger of such fragmentation is widely appreciated is marked by the proliferation in our time of interdisciplinary projects. But what is needed is to unite the disciplines in one mind and not just under one budget. A new generation of behavioral scientists has sprung up in whom this need is beginning to be realized, and I believe that the future is theirs. They are not, like the polymaths of an earlier age, generalists in a number of distinct fields, but men who can bring to special problems specific materials and techniques deriving from whatever disciplines bear on such problems, even from those disciplines lying wholly outside the conventional departments of behavioral science —like engineering, neurology, and public administration.

There is room in behavioral science—indeed, there is need—for a variety of theories and models, scales of measurement and conceptual frames. Nor is the need limited to those which have been given the most exact formulations. I have argued for a tolerance of ambiguity, a recognition of the openness characteristic of fruitful ideas. "The hits in science," Conant has said (22:134), "are usually made with a crooked ball." It is not just serendipity which is involved here, the fortuitous discovery; it is that retrospectively scientists are so often seen as succeeding better than they had a right to—according to our own more rigorous methodological principles. If the wicked seem to flourish, it is not always God's fault, but perhaps a failing in our own moral perceptions; they may not be so wicked after all.

Yet I would not wish to condone a moral slackness, as it were. Mathematical advances seem to me to hold out great promise for behavioral science, especially in making possible exact treatment of matters so long thought to be "intrinsically" incapable of it. I have no sympathy with principled, purposeful vagueness, even where it is not a cover for loose thinking. The argument that what we say about human behavior must be vague so as to mirror the richness of our subject-matter mistakes the nature of both description and explanation, as though these are to picture the reality, the first as it appears and the second as it is underneath the appearance. I have taken instead an instrumentalist approach, asking always for the function in inquiry of scientific structures. Accordingly, I have viewed science as a process, not just as a product. The question for the scientist is not how to get there, but how to get on; an ultimate destination envisioned in one or another philosophy of science is replaced by the goal of carrying inquiry forward. It is from this viewpoint that openness is important: to enlarge the perspectives of those who, as Joseph Tussman once put it, always know the score but never the game being played.

Even values, it seems to me, have their function in inquiry, if they are explicit and empirically grounded. But it is at just this point that behavioral science faces the most marked hostility. There are many by whom behavioral science is hated and feared as making possible the manipulation of man, adding to the rule of force the new dimensions of brainwashing and engineered consent. I think it is true that knowledge is power, and that power over the mind may confront us with greater problems and dangers even than the power over the atom. I cannot agree that "nothing in the social sciences increases the capacity to manipulate an individual against his will" (*82*: 30). But the knowledge which confronts us with dangers by the same token presents us with opportunities. It may be that we will learn enough, or perhaps that we already know enough, to destroy ourselves; but if we turn our backs on knowledge, forgo the opportunity to ward off the danger, we are as if dead already. There is no guarantee that the true and the good go always hand in hand, but it is man's estate to reach out to both.

REFERENCES

1. Abel, T.: "The Operation Called 'Verstehen' ", *American Journal of Sociology* 54 (1948–49) 211–218.
2. Ackoff, R. L.: *The Design of Social Research*, Chicago, 1953.
3. Alexander, F., and H. Ross, (eds.): *Twenty Years of Psychoanalysis*, N.Y., 1953.
4. Arrow, K. J.: *Social Choice and Individual Values*, N.Y., 1951.
5. Ayer, A. J.: *Language, Truth, and Logic*, London, 1946.
6. Beckner, M.: *The Biological Way of Thought*, N.Y., 1959.
7. Bergmann, G.: *Philosophy of Science*, Madison, 1957.
8. —— and K. W. Spence: "The Logic of Psychophysical Measurement", *Psychological Review* 51 (1944).
9. Braithwaite, R. B.: *Scientific Explanation*, Cambridge (Eng.), 1956.
10. Bridgman, P. W.: *The Logic of Modern Physics*, N.Y., 1928.
11. Burtt, E. A.: *Metaphysical Foundations of Modern Physical Science*, N.Y., 1951.
12. Campbell, N.: *Measurement and Calculation*, N.Y., 1928.
13. ——: *What is Science?*, N.Y., 1952.
14. Carnap, R.: *The Unity of Science*, London, 1934.
15. ——: "Testability and Meaning", *Philosophy of Science* 3 (1936) 419–471 and 4 (1937) 1–40.
16. ——: *Logical Foundations of Probability*, Chicago, 1950.
17. Cartwright, D., and F. Harary: *Theory of Direct Graphs*, forthcoming.
18. Chernoff, H., and L. E. Moses: *Elementary Decision Theory*, N.Y., 1959.
19. Churchman, C. W.: *Theory of Experimental Inference*, N.Y., 1948.
20. Colby, K. M.: *An Introduction to Psychoanalytic Research*, N.Y., 1960.

411

21. Collingwood, R. C.: *The Idea of History*, Oxford, 1946.
22. Conant, J. B.: *Modern Science and Modern Man*, Garden City (N.Y.), 1953.
23. Coombs, C. H.: "A Theory of Psychological Scaling", *University of Michigan Engineering Research Bulletin*, No. 34, 1952.
24. ——: *Theory of Data*, forthcoming.
25. Copi, I. M.: *Introduction to Logic*, N.Y., 1954.
26. Craig, W.: "Replacement of Auxiliary Expressions", *Philosophical Review* 65 (1956) 38–55.
27. Danto, A., and S. Morgenbesser (eds.): *Philosophy of Science*, N.Y., 1960.
28. Dewey, J.: *Logic, the Theory of Inquiry*, N.Y., 1939.
29. ——: "Theory of Valuation", *International Encyclopedia of Unified Science*, Vol. II, Chicago, 1939.
30. Duhem, P.: *The Aim and Structure of Physical Theory*, Princeton, 1954.
31. Durkheim, E.: *The Rules of Sociological Method*, Glencoe (Ill.), 1950.
32. Eddington, A. S.: *The Nature of the Physical World*, Cambridge (Eng.) 1928.
33. Edel, A.: "Some Relations of Philosophy and Anthropology", *American Anthropologist* 55 (1953) 649–660.
34. Edwards, A. L.: *Statistical Methods for the Behavioral Sciences*, N.Y., 1954.
35. Einstein, A.: *Essays in Science*, N.Y., 1934.
36. Ellis, A.: "Principles of Scientific Psychoanalysis", *Genetic Psychology Monographs* 41 (1950) 147–212.
37. Feigl, H., and W. Sellars (eds.): *Readings in Philosophical Analysis*, N.Y., 1949.
38. —— and M. Brodbeck (eds.): *Readings in the Philosophy of Science*, N.Y., 1953.
39. —— and M. Scriven (eds.): "The Foundations of Science and the Concepts of Psychology and Psychoanalysis", *Minnesota Studies in the Philosophy of Science*, Vol. I, Minneapolis, 1956.
40. ——, ——, and G. Maxwell (eds.): "Concepts, Theories, and the Mind-Body Problem", *Minnesota Studies in the Philosophy of Science*, Vol. II, Minneapolis, 1958.
41. —— and G. Maxwell (eds.): "Scientific Explanation, Space, and Time", *Minnesota Studies in the Philosophy of Science*, Vol. III, Minneapolis, 1962.
42. —— and ——: *Current Issues in the Philosophy of Science*, N.Y., 1961.
42A. Festinger, Leon, and Daniel Katz: *Research Methods in the Behavioral Sciences*, N.Y., 1953.
43. Fisher, R. A.: *The Design of Experiments*, N.Y., 1953.
44. Frank, P.: *Modern Science and Its Philosophy*, Cambridge (Mass.) 1949.
45. ——: *Philosophy of Science*, Englewood Cliffs (N.J.), 1957.
46. —— (ed.): *The Validation of Scientific Theories*, N.Y., 1961.

47. Frankel, C.: "Philosophy and History", *Political Science Quarterly* 72 (1957) 350–369.

48. Frenkel-Brunswik, E.: "Psychoanalysis and the Unity of Science", *Proceedings of the American Academy of Arts and Sciences* 80 (1954) 271–350.

49. Freudenthal, H. (ed.): *The Concept and the Role of the Model in Mathematics and the Natural and Social Sciences*, Dordrecht (Holland), 1961.

50. Gardiner, P.: *The Nature of Historical Explanation*, Oxford, 1952.

51. Gibson, Q.: *The Logic of Social Enquiry*, London, 1960.

52. Goodman, N.: *Fact, Fiction, and Forecast*, Cambridge (Mass.), 1955.

53. Gross, L. (ed.): *Symposium on Sociological Theory*, Evanston (Ill.), 1959.

54. Hanson, N. R.: *Patterns of Discovery*, Cambridge (Eng.), 1958.

55. Hartmann, H., E. Kris, and R. M. Loewenstein: "The Function of Theory in Psychoanalysis", in Loewenstein, R. M. (ed.), *Drives, Affects, Behavior*, N.Y., 1953.

56. Helmer, O., and N. Rescher: "On the Epistemology of the Inexact Sciences", *The Rand Corporation*, Santa Monica (Calif.), R-353, 1960.

57. Hempel, C. G.: "Problems and Changes in the Empiricist Criterion of Meaning", *Revue Internationale de Philosophie* 40 (1950) 41–63.

58. ———: "Fundamentals of Concept Formation in Empirical Science", *International Encyclopedia of Unified Science*, Vol. II, Chicago, 1952.

59. ——— and P. Oppenheim: "The Logic of Explanation", *Philosophy of Science* 15 (1948) 135–175.

60. Hilgard, E. R., and others: *Psychoanalysis as Science*, Stanford, 1952.

61. Hook, S. (ed.): *Psychoanalysis, Scientific Method, and Philosophy*, N.Y., 1959.

62. Hutten, E. H.: *The Origins of Science*, London, 1962.

63. Jahoda, M. and others: *Research Methods in Social Relations*, N.Y., 1954.

64. Jevons, W. S.: *The Principles of Science*, London, 1892.

65. Kantor, J. R.: *The Logic of Modern Science*, Bloomington, 1953.

66. Kaplan, A.: "Definition and Specification of Meaning", *Journal of Philosophy* 43 (1946).

67. ———: "What Good is 'Truth'?" *Journal of Philosophy and Phenomenological Research* 15 (1954) 151–170.

68. ———: "Psychiatric Research from a Philosophic Point of View", *Psychiatric Research Reports* 6 (1956) 199–211.

69. ———: *American Ethics and Public Policy*, N.Y., 1963.

70. ———: "Logical Empiricism and Value Judgments", in *125* below.

71. ———, A. L. Skogstad, and M. A. Girshick: "The Prediction of Social and Technological Events", *Public Opinion Quarterly* 14 (1950) 93–110.

72. ——— and H. F. Schott: "A Calculus for Empirical Classes", *Methodos* 2 (1951) 165–190.

73. —— and H. D. Lasswell: *Power and Society*, New Haven, 1963.

74. Kaufmann, F.: *Methodology in the Social Sciences*, London, 1944.

75. Kemeny, J. G.: *A Philosopher Looks at Science*, N.Y., 1959.

76. —— and J. L. Snell: *Mathematical Models in the Social Sciences*, Boston, 1962.

77. Kyberg, H. E.: *Probability and the Logic of Rational Belief*, Middletown (Conn.), 1961.

78. —— and E. Nagel (eds.): *Induction: Some Current Issues*, Middletown (Conn.), 1963.

79. Lazarsfeld, P. (ed.): *Mathematical Thinking in the Social Sciences*, Glencoe (Ill.), 1954.

80. —— and M. Rosenberg (eds.): *The Language of Social Research*, Glencoe (Ill.), 1955.

81. Lenzen, V. F.: "Procedures of Empirical Science", *International Encyclopedia of Unified Science*, Vol. I, Chicago, 1938.

82. Lerner, D. (ed.): *The Human Meaning of the Social Sciences*, N.Y., 1960.

83. —— and H. D. Lasswell (eds.): *The Policy Sciences*, Palo Alto, 1951.

84. Lewin, K.: *Field Theory in Social Science*, N.Y., 1951.

85. Lewis, C. I.: *Mind and the World Order*, N.Y., 1956.

86. ——: *Analysis of Knowledge and Valuation*, La Salle (Ill.), 1946.

87. Lindsay, R. B., and H. Margenau: *Foundations of Physics*, N.Y., 1949.

88. Luce, R. D., and H. Raiffa: *Games and Decisions*, N.Y., 1957.

89. MacCorquodale, K., and P. E. Meehl: "Hypothetical Constructs and Intervening Variables", *Psychological Review* 55 (1948) 95–107.

90. Madden, E. H. (ed.): *The Structure of Scientific Thought*, Boston, 1960.

91. Marx, M. H. (ed.): *Psychological Theory*, N.Y., 1955.

92. Merton, R., and P. Lazarsfeld (eds.): *Continuities in Social Research*, Glencoe (Ill.), 1950.

93. Meyerhoff, H. (ed.): *The Philosophy of History in Our Time*, Garden City (N.Y.), 1959.

94. Mill, J. S.: *A System of Logic*, London, 1936.

95. von Mises, R.: *Probability, Statistics, and Truth*, N.Y., 1939.

96. Morris, C. W.: *Signs, Language, and Behavior*, N.Y., 1946.

97. Mosteller, F., and others: "Principles of Sampling", *Journal of the American Statistical Association* 49 (1954) 13–35.

98. Mount, G. E.: "Principles of Measurement", *Psychological Reports Monograph Supplement* 2 (1956) 13–28.

99. Myrdal, G.: "Methodological Note on Facts and Valuations in Social Science," in his *An American Dilemma*, N.Y., 1944, 1027–1064.

100. ——: *Value in Social Theory*, N.Y., 1958.

101. Nagel, E.: "Principles of the Theory of Probability", *International Encyclopedia of Unified Science*, Vol. I, Chicago, 1939.

102. ——: "Determinism in History", *Journal of Philosophy and Phenomenological Research* 20 (1960) 291–317.
103. ——: *The Structure of Science*, N.Y., 1961.
104. —— and C. G. Hempel: "Concepts and Theory in the Social Sciences", in *Language, Science, and Human Rights*, American Philosophical Association, Philadelphia, 1952.
105. von Neumann, J., and O. Morgenstern: *Theory of Games and Economic Behavior*, Princeton, 1944.
106. Pearson, K.: *The Grammar of Science*, London, 1943.
107. Peirce, C. S.: *Collected Papers*, Vols. II and V, Cambridge (Mass.), 1934.
108. Poincaré, H.: *The Foundations of Science*, N.Y., 1913.
109. Polya, G.: *How to Solve It*, Princeton, 1948.
110. ——: *Mathematics and Plausible Reasoning*, Princeton, 1954.
111. Popper, K.: *The Logic of Scientific Discovery*, N.Y., 1959.
112. ——: *Conjectures and Refutations*, N.Y., 1962.
113. Price, D.: *Science since Babylon*, New Haven, 1961.
114. *Psychological Review:* "Symposium on Operationism", 52 (1945) 241–294.
115. Quine, W. V.: *From a Logical Point of View*, Cambridge (Mass.), 1953.
116. ——: *Word and Object*, N.Y., 1960.
117. Radcliffe-Brown, A. R.: *Structure and Function in Primitive Society*, London, 1952.
118. Rapoport, A.: *Operational Philosophy*, N.Y., 1953.
119. Reichenbach, H.: *Experience and Prediction*, Chicago, 1938.
120. ——: *Theory of Probability*, Berkeley, 1949.
121. Ritchie, A. D.: *Scientific Method*, Paterson (N.J.), 1960.
122. Rose, A. M.: *Theory and Method in the Social Sciences*, Minneapolis, 1954.
123. Ryle, G.: *The Concept of Mind*, London, 1949.
124. Savage, L. J.: *The Foundations of Statistics*, N.Y., 1954.
125. Schilpp, P. A. (ed.): *The Philosophy of Rudolph Carnap*, forthcoming.
126. Schlick, M.: *Philosophy of Nature*, N.Y., 1949.
127. Schutz, W. C.: "Some Implications of the Logical Calculus for Empirical Classes for Social Science Methodology", *Psychometrika* 24 (1959) 69–87.
128. Simon, H.: *Models of Man*, N.Y., 1957.
129. Skinner, B. F.: *Science and Human Behavior*, N.Y., 1953.
130. Spence, K. W.: "The Methods and Postulates of 'Behaviorism' ", *Psychological Review* 55 (1948) 67–78.
131. Stevenson, C. L.: *Ethics and Language*, New Haven, 1945.
132. Tomkins, S., and S. Messick: *Computer Simulation of Personality*, N.Y., 1963.
133. Toulmin, S. E.: *Philosophy of Science*, London, 1953.
134. Walsh, W. H.: *Introduction to the Philosophy of History*, London, 1951.

135. Weber, M.: *The Methodology of the Social Sciences*, Glencoe (Ill.), 1949.
136. Wertheimer, M.: *Productive Thinking*, N.Y., 1945.
137. Weyl, H.: *Philosophy of Mathematics and Natural Science*, Princeton, 1949.
138. Whitehead, A. N.: *Science and the Modern World*, N.Y., 1948.
139. Whorf, B. L.: *Language, Thought, and Reality*, N.Y., 1956.
140. Wiener, P. P. (ed.): *Readings in the Philosophy of Science*, N.Y., 1953.
141. Wittgenstein, L.: *Tractatus Logico-Philosophicus*, London, 1947.

INDEX OF NAMES

417

INDEX OF SUBJECTS

grounds of, 387–388
inherent, 393–396
instrumental, 393–396
intrinsic, 389–390
judgments, 377–378, 391
and meanings, 370–371, 382–384
and objectivity, 387
and problem selection, 381–382
role of, 396–397
statements, 391
as subject matter, 377–378

theory of, 387–397
  validity of, 377–378
Variance, 238–239
Verifiability theory of meaning, 36–39
Verification, 37–39
Verstehen, 33, 142–143, 163
Vertical indication, 73–76

Wholes, 81

Yield, of experiment, 157–158